ORAH
The Deathless Dancer

THIRD THUNDER, BOOK I

The Fall of Etan, Volume 1
By MSI

ORAH, THE DEATHLESS DANCER

THE FALL OF ETAN, VOLUME I
THIRD THUNDER, BOOK I

by
MSI

Printed and bound in the United States of America.
First Printing
SFA Publications
130 Biodome Drive
Waynesville, NC 28786

ISBN #0-931783-09-7
Library of Congress Catalog Card Number 97-65521

ORAH, THE DEATHLESS DANCER

by MSI

Dedicated to all the manifestations of Almira
throughout space and time

Vitam impendre vero
-- Juvenal

TABLE OF CONTENTS

LIST OF ILLUSTRATIONS

INTRODUCTION

Ancient visionary experience, because of the long passage of time and the changing world, has lost its usefulness to humanity. The ancient visionary structures have become fragmented, have lost their holistic nature — and therefore their practicality has decayed. Ancient visions made sense at the time of their creation, for they were representative of Truth in their spatial and temporal environment. But times have changed and the visions have not.

Therefore, although much beauty can still be appreciated in the old stories, the life has flowed out of them, leaving empty shells where before were the living mechanics of contact with the Divine. Revitalization of the human condition comes from re-creation from the Source, not from re-translation of the past.

The physical, human mind — a structure of earth — needs a modern vision of its highest purpose. With all the fragmentation in today's world, it is imperative to have a clean, undistorted vision of the Source. To uplift the quality of human thought to its true, glorified Reality is, in part, an annihilation of any understanding of the human as weak, sinful, decayed or limited.

The path of communication with the higher Self must be revitalized from the root. This path is not created out of Idealism — it is created out of the blood and guts of human life-experience. This explains why the ancient myths were often violent. But it is not necessary to focus long on the problem, on the decay — there has been enough of that already. What *is* necessary is to acknowledge the reality of negativity, then focus on re-creation. The period of acknowledgment can be brief compared with the time devoted to reconstruction.

The human being is a divine machine that needs to be re-centered. This does not happen through a process of "shoulds" and "should nots"; it happens from the introduction of new experience of the One. In terms of visionary experience, re-centering occurs through the process of identifying the different internal characters, discarding those who do not serve the growth process, strengthening those who do, destroying that which is useless, creating that which is useful.

We are filled with myriad sub-personalities: to understand and integrate all our internal characters, it is necessary to have a comprehensive vision of the highest nature of our God-Self. The path to perfection, then, is to recognize the perfect parts of our inner being. We are all filled with misplaced and misunderstood gods and goddesses. We need to reconstitute the rainbow bridge from the Cosmic Mind of the Divine to the minds of the human.

The gods and goddesses form a model of the inner life which (when working properly) shows us how to deal with the different aspects of ourselves. They are models of how to resolve the conflicts between the various sub-personalities and how to manifest a higher, truly holistic personality. All the tales of the gods describe the nature of the inner life for the purpose of gaining perfection. What makes one imperfect? The false concepts, beliefs and judgments — it is precisely these that the tales of the gods and goddesses seek to heal and remove. Humans are part and parcel of the Divine — we are those stray sheep who are being led homeward to perfection by the breath of the wind, by the scent of Mother Earth, by every story of the nature and existence of the gods and the goddesses.

The THUNDER series is written as mythic stories because these are the highest form of expression of visionary experience. Myth is a process of growth into joy in which every step is one of joy. It is a map to understand our existence, a treasure map of our great hidden inner resources. Myth fulfills the longing of the right brain for emotional experience as thoroughly and completely as the logical form and analysis of the structure of Creation fulfills the left brain.

The visions described in the three volumes of THIRD THUNDER occurred while I was studying with the Ishayas in their monastery. During this time I was instructed by Durga in the Third Sphere Ascension techniques of the Ishayas. During this instruction, I began to recognize clearly that the significance of human life is not to be found in the external world but in the internal. I had thought that Sharon was lost to me forever; I learned in the Third Sphere that such thinking was a projection of my erroneous and painfully limited beliefs — nothing more. The internal is the Real; the external is the dream.

I had understood this before intellectually, but the power of the experiences recorded in these three texts convinced me on the basis of my own expanding awareness that the external is the domain of illusion; the internal is the domain of the Real.

Modern humans have by and large reversed the dominance of these two. It is common to believe that the external is the only reality and the internal is subject to illusions and cannot be trusted. The Reality is quite other. In the language of *A Course in Miracles:* "Your holiness reverses all the laws of the world. It is beyond every restriction of time, space, distance and limits of any kind." This was proven to me in the Himalayas. The three volumes of THIRD THUNDER describe the expanding appreciation of Reality of a soul rising to full Unity Consciousness.

— *MSI*
dedicated on Maha Sivaratri, 1997

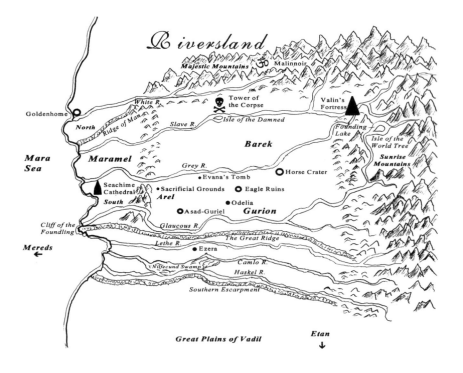

Riversland

Majestic Mountains   Malinnoir

Goldenhome

White R.

North

Ridge of Man

Slave R.

Tower of
the Corpse

Isle of the Damned

Valin's
Fortress

Founding
Lake

*Mara
Sea*

Maramel

Barek

*Isle of the
World Tree*

*Sunrise
Mountains*

Grey R.

Horse Crater

• Evana's Tomb

Seachime
Cathedral

• Sacrificial Grounds

Eagle Ruins

South

Arel

• Odelia

Gurion

◆ Asad-Guriel

*Cliff of the
Foundling*

Glaucous R.

Lethe R.

The Great Ridge

Mereds

←

• Ezera

Nilfecund Swamp

Camlo R.

Haskel R.

Southern Escarpment

Great Plains of Vadil

Etan
↓

PART I

GURION,
THE CLAW OF
THE HAWK

1.
A Dancer of Etan

Orah stood alone on the high cliff as the winds of dawn whirled his golden hair behind him in soft rhythms of glory. As was customary among the Lords of Etan, he was wearing a sleeveless argent robe; on his feet were molded wooden sandals laced halfway to the knee.

The Etan Lord was strong: even standing relaxed, his powerful body flowed in innocent rhythm, expanding and contracting in divine harmony from nothing more than the throbbing of his pulse.

The Etan Lord was beautiful: if the unknown land below held observers, they might easily mistake him for a god. Vestige of his pre-dawn climb, his slightly azure skin glistened, accenting his perfect features in the same way as the morning dew dances over a flawless copen hyacinth.

The Etan Lord was sad: again today, expanding his awareness to the north had revealed nothing new.

At last Orah sighed, gave up trying to wrest impossible solutions from the virgin land below and strode swiftly down the scree and shale, thinking, *Two months northward without a sign. How much further will Althea's request propel me?* But even as he asked, he knew the answer was in the question: to fulfil a desire of his sister, the Healer of Etan, he would travel to the end of their world.

"Seven rivers," she had told him soon after the birth of the new year. "Find me this lost land of seven rivers, Orah. There lies a treasure so precious no price can do it justice, a secret warded by a power so heinous the future of Etan itself is held in the balance."

"What force of this world could challenge our father Swayam?" he had laughed back at her words in utter disbelief.

But Althea had only repeated, "Find me this land of seven rivers, brother. For there the fate of the Etanai will be determined for all time."

And so, understanding nothing, Orah had that day left his father Swayam and mother Shatarupa, his wife Chavva and his many brothers and sisters and walked northward from Etan across the ice and then the vast barren plains.

~ ~ ~

Seven rivers. The one below running westward to the sea I shall count and name. For this much I know: none has passed this way before.

Orah was saddened by this long and so far pointless journey over the desolate plains, but his sadness was tempered by gratitude that he was at last coming down from Vadil's continental plateau. Perhaps these lowlands might hold something more interesting than rough heath and small scurrying rodents. Nothing of the world outside of their paradise Etan seemed worth even a moment's passing glance. *Treasure? Danger? What was she talking about? As Swayam always told us, I have confirmed in these two months: save for Etan, Martanda is dead.*

~ ~ ~

The river passed near the base of the cliff. It was broad, languid, yellow, green, oddly warm for early spring. " '*Haskel,*' I name you, first river," Orah said as he waded into the water. "For truly, I am in need of wisdom."

Fording the river proved easy — a short, effortless swim. Here the Etan saw the first animate life in the lowlands — small, silver-gray fish, primitively scaled and armored.

The jungle on the far shore was dense; Orah followed the narrow beach eastward until he discovered a small tributary heading due north. Here he discovered that the water of Haskel had stained his robe a light ocher. A sudden wave of dismay flowed through him, followed by mindless fear. Pushing his heart away from the unfamiliar emotions, he reasoned that the two months of solitude had started affecting him.

Orah did not at once recognize how the malefic power of the land was responsible for altering his mood. But marking his return to calmness, he discovered he no longer felt alone! He felt two others closely watching him, studying his progress. One, with a deep hope and fathomless love imperfectly cloaking a profound despair; the other, with emotions never before encountered and therefore not understood: contempt, hatred, a dark, brooding malice.

Orah searched the jungle but found no source for the feelings of these two. Was his mind creating them from loneliness? Fantasizing to compensate for his long solitude?

~ ~ ~

After leading Orah northward through the jungle for an hour, the small stream bent westward. The Etan continued along it for awhile as its banks steepened and its current accelerated, but soon its path ended in a small pool and spring.

Should he turn again northward here or retrace his steps to the bend? The jungle looked equally impassable everywhere. But when he knelt to fill his pouch from the pool (When might he find such clear water again?), Orah saw an odd little rock shaped exactly like a hand, pointing directly northward. He pulled the moss and lichens from it but could not learn if it were carved or natural.

How can I question its origin? he asked himself, surprising himself again by the possibility of doubt. No one else has come here since father Swayam and mother Shatarupa planted Etan. Of this much I am certain.

Grateful for the sign, Orah shrugged off the mystery. Muttering, "North, always north," he adjusted his few belongings in his shoulder pouch, then clambered up the hill and into the jungle.

~ ~ ~

The trees seemed tightly woven from the stream, but they grew closer and thicker until the passage was virtually impenetrable toward the true north. Whenever there were openings, even crawling holes, they led westward. He fought his way until twilight; a more or less dry and open place in the multiplying swamp was too inviting to ignore.

He did not trust the plants enough to taste them — he had seen nothing since the plains that he knew. And the fundamentally disquieting feeling of the land was increasing; Orah felt anything growing in such an emotionally distorted space would have a questionable effect on his mind. But the Etan had carefully portioned his waybread through his two months' journey, fasting often rather than partaking of it. As he felt the life from her work restoring his mind and spirit, he was thankful again that his sister

Orah saw an odd little rock shaped exactly like a hand

Althea was an incomparable master of the subtle powers of life, of the earthbreath.

Orah lay back on the moss, contented with life, dreamily identifying his newly discovered constellations, Archer, Bull, Ram, Lion... "Lion!" He leapt to his feet, gaping at the firmament. "The eye! Where is the eye?" The brightest star of the group was missing.

The Etan waited impatiently for the cloud to pass as he quieted his heart, but no vapor covered the heavens: the eye of the Lion was simply, irrevocably gone. An eclipse! It must be eclipsed, he thought, but knew it was impossible. Searching the sky feverishly, he found nothing else amiss.

Orah stared until the Lion was hidden by the trees, but could wrest no further meaning from the suddenly imperfect order of Narain's Garden.

The remaining few hours of night were not restful. But at dawn, Orah quieted the inner conflict, telling himself there was always a logical explanation for everything.

The jungle had remained utterly still during the night. Apparently neither diurnal nor nocturnal animals existed below the plains. "A land of questionable plants and no beasts!" he cried, already learning much of contempt. "Hah! That is too generous. *'Nilfecund Swamp'* I name you, first river's land: you are riotous with deadly malodorous plants, devoid of animate life."

~ ~ ~

The Etan came to a second river by noon of the third day following. A few noxious insects had made their appearance, still no mammals. He had therefore confirmed his mistrust of the plants and moved warily, almost as if fearing they might attack him for crossing their demesne.

Dry land was a memory; he had constantly waded and swum for the past two days. The first warning he was finally through the Nilfecund Swamp came when he pushed through two interlaced trees and was pulled by a gentle current.

The new river was a lighter green than Haskel, but not as wide. Golden light filtered through the trees to sparkle and dance on its water; dappled fish leapt for the iridescent lacewings and enormous variegated butterflies flitting everywhere over its surface.

"*'Camlo.'* This is your name, river; you are lovely," he murmured as he swam across. He felt the vibrant life of the many small creatures of the new shore; he knew the plants here would not harm him.

He washed his robe, but it was permanently altered: erratic gray and amber blotches competed chaotically with dull umber stains, the unpleasant memories of the foul waters and poisonous secretions of the hanging plants and grasping vines of Nilfecund. Orah lacked the skill to cleanse it.

The trees grew less closely together on this shore, as if they had abandoned the primitive struggle of the far side, or had once even felt the touch of a civilized hand. Yes, this land could be the remnant of a garden! badly deteriorated, but intelligently planted and maintained in the not-too-distant past. Finding what might have long ago been an orchard, he filled his nostrils greedily with the blossoms' sweet scent, wondering the improbable, *How?* almost as much as the impossible, *Who?*

Fewer and larger grew the trees as the ground rose and became rockier: willow and cottonwood gave way gradually to spruce and maple, then hemlock and cedar. The Etan saw a bare hill to the northwest and decided to climb above the forest and finish recovering from the swamp in the warm afternoon sun.

~ ~ ~

The hill was strange — smooth, spherical, a polished dome of fused ebony metal. He examined it carefully but could discover no reason for its existence. "Yehokhanan-Ishtar could perhaps explain it," he said, thinking fondly of his brother, the Architect of Etan.

The hill responded to his emotion, coloring the metal slightly lighter. His surprise one of delight, he played with different feelings: friendliness, love, happiness. With each impulse, the hill brightened; by the end of an hour, it was a brilliant scarlet.

Orah laughed and, abandoning all caution, danced a movement of unrestricted joy on the sentient hill, wedding his graceful talent to the flowing color beneath his flying feet. Faster and faster he leaped and spun; the metal returned his perceptions in graceful moving patterns, dancing lightning in harmony with his soaring spirit.

But as his expression rose closer and closer to the supreme catharsis of universal ecstasy, a doubt erupted in his mind, *Who created this hill?* At once the metal changed to an angry carmine, spotted by a rapidly returning ebony. Orah at once started down, thinking with fear, *It could be a beacon...*

Perhaps the Etan might truly have gone on then; the fate of the Lion Lords of Gurion would have been vastly different. But as he was about to step into the forest, a message from Althea flew to him, bearing the form of a golden dove. The bird landed gracefully on his hand, folded her aureate wings with the deftness of a master, then sang in Althea's voice, *"Pass the night on my thought-hill Ezera, brother; your dreams will be of truth, they will direct you well into the unknown north."*

The bird ruffled her feathers, cooed once softly, then disintegrated with a gentle cascading of sound and light — like a thousand tiny golden bells dulcetly ringing, then collapsing into rainbow prisms. Ezera responded with a flash of purest silver and then with a kaleidoscopic display centered around the dual themes of aureate and argent. Its gradually slowing rhythms lasted well past sunset.

When the hill at last ended its changes in a gentle saffron, the Etan found a depression near the summit and lay down to watch the stars appear. A low haze had hung over the swamp every night after the first; he had not yet confirmed the strange damage to the heavens. But now the sky was crystal clear, there could be no doubt: the Lion's eye was as gone as if it had never been. With this discovery, he heard distinctly what he had subtly felt since descending from the continental plateau: a distant, persistent sobbing and an answering, dark laughter of hideous malice, of conscious desecration, of purest hate. Hearing these perversely related voices was at once a challenge and an abomination far beyond the range of previous experience. Orah stared toward the missing star and let the sounds carry him, sure his imagination must be creating such odd violations of the silence.

As Orah drifted to sleep, the keening of sorrow and the echoing scorn gradually transformed to become the background music in a large hall filled with strangers, men and women with black and white and yellow and red skin, men and women not of Etan.

Orah had never before known anyone other than his immediate family: they were the only inhabitants of their city Etan; as far as anyone knew, the only people on Martanda. And this was his first journey, the first of any Etan toward the north.

His father Swayam had not forbidden his odd desire, but the absence of approval was still a heavy burden. But Althea had constantly nourished the sapling of his intention, until it had grown to become a mighty oak of unwavering desire.

Dancing was no longer Orah's great passion in his dream. Now his life's duty was simply to hold a torch. At first he felt it a unique honor, but then saw that everyone in the hall held similar torches or gems alive with radiant fire.

They are all expressions of the One, he thought; the walls vanished as the Oblation Bearers floated away in every direction. No one moved with effort, yet all retreated from him alone. With a flash of intuition, he realized they all shared the experience. *Like the suns of the expanding universe,* he thought, wondering how to become a star.

With the question, his dream changed: he was back in Etan with his family. But now he alone held a torch. Perhaps because of it, the old familiar understandings no longer applied to him, no longer bound him to their implicit demands. It was not that he loved Chavva or the others any less, but now his mind appreciated a more complete truth. Althea alone empathized fully; the others considered him with a peculiar admixture of amusement and curiosity, but did not, could not, understand. "How can it matter? All limited pain leads to universal good," said Yehokhanan-Ishtar. And Bhishaj, Althea's husband, said, "It is beautiful, but what of your dancing? Is not Father's gift enough?"

The answer was on Orah's lips, "Dancing is my all!" but his dream changed again: now he was once more fording the river he had named Haskel. He crossed as before, but the sculpted stone hand on the tributary was now living but ulcerous flesh, grotesquely beckoning him northward. The Nilfecund Swamp was rife with quicksand and poisonous serpents; the Camlo River no longer deserved its name — it was moiling with crocodiles and small deadly water snakes. Ezera was the decaying skull of a dead giant, Orah a small black ant picking at the rotting flesh.

The dove Althea sent to him was pursued by a blood-red hawk, screaming in his father's voice, *"The desire to possess opens the gateway to hell!"*

Althea's message also changed, *"Run Orah! Flee northward! Etan dissolves!"* The dove disintegrated with a shriek of agony into a flood of gray and sanguine teardrops.

A dark emptiness, a nothingness, was pushing into Orah's mind, struggling to gain form. It swallowed Etan, then the world, then devoured entire suns from its insatiable need. Orah tried to run from its terrible hunger but found it surrounding him everywhere. It choked him, attacked his soul, inexorably forced his spirit to mimic its vile nothingness.

Orah awoke with heart palpitating. But he was thinking calmly, *A satellite in a synchronous orbit could block a star's light. But why would it not reflect the sun?* He sat up. At first the hill seemed covered by pustules, cankerworms and carbuncles, but then, as he rubbed his eyes, he remembered where he was and saw the Red Moon Rohini rising through the quiet beauty of the starlit night. Orah laughed, remembering dancing under Martanda's seven moons with Chavva. Ezera responded by transmuting into a crystal sphere of lambent sparkles and reflections.

The depression in the rock which at first had felt perfectly molded to his body now seemed two sizes too small. He reversed his position so that his head was toward the south, then let his mind explore the heavens. He sent a triple fiber of earthbreath toward the Lion's eye, but something blocked his power so he could learn nothing.

The effort led him gently back to sleep; his energy trine carried him in dream to a silver castle hidden in the mountains of the distant north. This vision transformed into a beautiful woman, golden haired with a pale sky-blue hue to her skin, yet unfamiliar, not of his family.

"I am Leor," she said in a gentle, wise voice. "I have waited for you throughout time." In spite of (or perhaps, because of) the lovely melody of her voice, the distant hopeless sobbing and scorning laughter returned.

"Who are you?" Orah asked, trying to ignore the increasing cacophony of despair and contempt.

"Your youngest sister," she answered, her sweet tone not masking the fact that she also heard.

"I could not have failed to see your birth." It was the habit of the Etanai to attend every nativity.

The laughter had become so obtrusive he feared Leor might not understand him. But she replied, "You did not fail, yet did not know me. Althea carried me here. I am the hidden and forgotten fourth child. To him that can discover and release me I shall reveal all knowledge. Behold!"

Leor raised her hand in a commanding gesture; the wailing and the dark laughter at once stilled. Then she expanded toward him, around him, became more and more refulgent until sunlight seemed like shade. Orah was alone in the light, became the light, lost everything of himself other than the infinite, unchanging, perfectly still yet vibrantly alive light.

~ ~ ~

Etan's farsighted Healer saw her brother's dreams reflect in her thought-hill Ezera, gaining much of hope and grief in the experience: she alone of her kindred knew of the ill decaying the firmament.

But the further unexpected and unfortunate fact was that the Lady Althea of Etan was not alone in viewing Ezera's answers to Orah's first dance in Riversland. And far away, a saprophagous mocking laugh fed itself on purest malevolence, fed itself and grew stronger.

2.
Jessie

Orah awoke with the sun, vividly remembering the birth of his three youngest sisters. Gauri the Fair had come first, then Rohini the Scarlet, then Kali the Dark, named for three of Martanda's moons. Shatarupa fell asleep with the last: childbirth had become almost routine by now, after so very many. Thus she missed the tearing loss of her fertility that accompanied the fourth, her only stillborn.

Althea had run from the birthing room with the dead fetus, cloaking it with iridescent power. But she said she failed! It was impossible she would lie! There could be no reason for keeping such a secret from the Etanai! And yet... and yet, something in the deepest recess of Orah's heart said that not only was it possible but, unlikely as it might seem, here was a truth that questioned the whole of his life in Etan. For if the Healer Althea could do such a thing, no premise structuring his mind could be held sacred.

To save himself from such devastating thoughts, he dismissed the problem as insoluble. Instead, he sent a double impulse of love and joy home, flying toward the south as a mated pair of perfect swans.

Ezera did not respond to his emotions: it was now static in a soft burnt orange. As Orah walked down the north slope, he wondered how long his dance and dreams might affect it. When would the hill return to ebony?

~ ~ ~

By late afternoon of the fourth day following, Orah stood on the bank of a third river, looking across at a cliff certainly twice as high as the southern escarpment across the Haskel. As it seemed no easier to the east or west, he decided to cross just here: at least there was a thin copse before its granite impossibility reared toward heaven.

The river was a light turquoise, narrower than Haskel or Camlo, but not particularly swift. He drank some of the water as he swam across, feeling its gay power. *"The Sweetwater!"* he laughed, surprised by the flavor. But that was a misnomer: the Lord of Etan was betrayed. "Amnesia" would have named it far better: by the time he reached the far shore, Orah had forgotten everything but his name.

~ ~ ~

Orah looked curiously through his provisions, but could understand little of their purpose.

The herbs were incomprehensible, he set them aside. The six small loaves smelled interesting — he ate one hungrily then dropped the others. The watercask seemed pointless; so did the extra sandals. A small silver sphere held his attention for a moment but soon joined the little pile, as did a parchment map he had drawn. This last seemed more important than the others: the pencilled names evoked different feelings, particularly a warmth from "Etan" and a deep longing toward the question mark in the blank north. Nevertheless he put it down as he examined his last possession, an intricately carved silver box. He worked at it for some time but could discover neither how to open it nor how to decipher its strange etchings. But when he set it with the others, a feminine voice echoed through his mind, *"No, Lord of Etan! Keep Valin's Curse always; it alone is an irreplaceable tool in Riversland."* He fingered the box for a few more minutes, seeking the secret of its catch, searching for its meaning. Failing, he replaced it in the secure fold over his shoulder that served as his pack.

The bread had left his throat dry; he knelt to drink from the river but then felt (for no known reason) that he should not. Glancing up, he saw a bright scarlet fruit hanging overhead, unlikely memory of abundant autumn; in a moment he was up the bank and tree. But as he reached for it, someone cried, "Touch it not!"

"Why not?" he asked the pretty young girl of six or seven sitting above him in the tree. "I am thirsty." Her flashing gray-blue eyes filled him with new and unexpected emotions: a strong yearning, love, desire to protect, yet an unreasoning fear.

"Because, brother, you would find it poison." She smiled at him with incomprehensible force and shook her head so fast that she started to giggle.

"Am I your brother?" He withdrew his hand from the false apple and looked at her curiously. "I don't remember you."

"Do you remember anything?" she cried. Unable to hold back her exuberance any more, she climbed quickly up the tree, laughing as explosively as if the sheer joy of life were impossible to contain.

He examined his mind and realized that he did not. But this caused him no anxiety, for he remembered no need for memory. "I am Orah from Etan. This much I know. Who are you?"

"You may call me Jessie," she called with giddy mirth from the highest branches.

"Jessie? That is a funny name. What does it mean?" He considered climbing after her, but decided the tree's old half rotten branches and the considerable drop to the river were two very good reasons to stay where he was.

"'I am,' Dancer-brother. Do you know what Orah means?" She stopped giggling for a moment to steady her aim, then launched herself to the nearest tree. But as soon as she was secure, her joyful laughter began again.

"Dancer! Yes, that is it! Or... part of it," he said as an unlooked for relief mingled peculiarly with his increasing confusion. "Why are you in this poisonous grove?"

"Waiting for you, of course, to remind you where you are going!" That was so funny that her chortling broke into uproarious whoops for a full minute before she could continue. Even then, she had to stop for breath every few words. "A pity you drank from the River Lethe! You might have found me even here. But now you must work rather harder. Sad too you threw your belongings away: each might have helped you, especially 'Ishtar's Recorder.'"

"They're just there —"

"Are they?"

He looked down with sudden terror. She was right! Was that a squirrel running away with the last of his possessions, the silver sphere? Or was his mind, suddenly made aware of its emptiness, inventing meaning from the impossible?

"Strange, isn't it, how it can be so very hard to remember where you put things?" She laughed a final symphony, then vanished with a small pop.

He stared dumbly towards where she had been. A moment later she called from higher up the bank, "Over here, silly! How slow your mind is today! Catch me if you can!" Then she scrambled up the gravel.

~ ~ ~

The Etan hurried after her. But no matter how swiftly he climbed, he never came any closer. As the day ended in a massive cumulus bank racing inland from the west, the slope became steeper and steeper, until it became as the sheerest of cliffs. The failing light demanded careful study for ever more precarious hand and footholds. For Orah, that is. Jessie was always ahead, laughing and chattering, leaping from ledge to precipice to ledge as if she were made of essence of mountain goat.

By midnight the clouds had buried the moons and stars under sable cerements; Orah continued on by feel alone. More ominous by far was the encroaching tiredness threatening to buckle his legs at any critical moment. Yet his guide was forever ahead, laughing cheerily, taunting him boisterously for every pause or tentative advance. As his grim intensity degenerated rapidly into a febrile desperation, he had no choice but to go on, slowly, cautiously, praying that the top must surely be near.

He lost first the left then the right sandal; his hands and feet were severely bruised, the skin torn in many places. A torrential rain drenched him, within another hour it turned to ice sleet, then snow. The winds whipped him, threatening to pull him from his ambiguous holds and throw him to his ruin. He would gladly have stopped anywhere, but no place on the cliff was wide enough for more than a moment.

There was not even faint light to guide him; his hands were so numb they could no longer grip well. Clinging to the cliff with his left hand, he slipped his right under his robe, but his cold flesh did little to reverse its imminent paralysis. Worse still, he was no longer certain his legs could be trusted to hold him: his feet felt as if they were lifeless, frozen. He knew he must have already damaged himself severely, but with a mental shrug, he thought, *I'll deal with that in the morning.* So much at least the Lethe could never steal from him.

He could feel no further outcroppings or crevices anywhere. He thawed first one hand and then the other under his arms, but could make nothing of the arrant wall. He broke the ice from his face and eyes, wincing to feel the bite of the hyperborean air on his raw skin, but could see nothing. How much longer before the end?

Jessie was far away; her laughter was like the last memory of warmth, often obscured by the howling wind, faint when the rare pauses came. "Jessie! Help! Help me! I can't keep up!" he cried, then nearly fell from surprise when he heard her voice next to his ear.

"You say you are a dancer, Etan! Dance! The way will open before you! No not there! That's not stable. No, higher to the left; yes, that's it! Now the right foot; no, higher — yes! Feel the life of the rock, its rhythm, its melody! Dance with the earthbreath, brother!"

~ ~ ~

Within another hour, he had lost all sensation below both knees, could only feel his hands by the pressure on his elbows. Why was she doing this? It was brutal, incomprehensible, mad.

How could Jessie see in this raven nightmare? He might as well be blind. Maybe he was! He pressed his fingers to his eyes; there was not the slightest response.

Panic enervated him. His right foot slipped and hung in space, but he lacked the strength or courage to pull it back. Tears welled up and turned to ice behind his frozen eyelids.

Jessie's voice was still next to him, pleading, cursing, changing from anger to fear to anger again. "What kind of an Etan are you! To think I thought of you as my brother! Where is your sense of the earthbreath? Are you so asleep the rock is inanimate? Feel the power in the stone! Do not fail me now! Live the earthbreath, Orah! Dance, brother, dance!"

"Help me," he sobbed, but could not force himself to move, either to restore his dangling limb or even release his holds and fall. He felt frozen to the stone, a ruined fly on the winter window of life. Perhaps if he could relax, the numbness and darkness would take him, he would fall and be free. *Less,* he thought slowly, as if his mind itself were freezing. *Freedom lies in emptiness.* But Jessie's insistent nagging would not let him be, demanded rather some sort of preternatural response. Yet the force of her passion was not enough to impel him to such an effort.

"I can't do it Jessie," he whispered. "Let me fall and be free. Please. I can't go on. I can't."

At once she was all around him, slapping his face, punching his ribs, pinching his legs and arms, even tickling him. But it was too late: he could barely feel her, let alone react. All that remained of his life was focused on his grip. And yet he was unable to break it, either to move onward or fall to a preferable oblivion.

Shouting, crying, Jessie struck him again and again with the full force of her child's body but could elicit nothing. "Orah," she sobbed, "Beloved Dancer of Etan. I can not help you! Please, my ancient heart, please if ever you have loved me, try once more. If not for me, then for... for *Chavva.*"

His wife's name resonated briefly through him, giving Jessie a spark of renewed hope. She redoubled her attacks on his face and arms, struggling to break his somnolence, screaming, *"Althea! Bhishaj! Swayam! Shatarupa! 'Vanya! Malinda, Mirabeth, Mirabel! Lemuel-tamara! Yehokhanan-Ishtar! Krishanu! Uchai-sravasa!"* She ended shrieking and pounding his face. And with the mention of each of the Lords of Etan, a little more life flowed through his tortured flesh, a little more of the unyielding spirit inherent in the rock vibrated deep in his marrow. And then a single shaft from Gauri pierced through the blizzard, for a moment he could see! His deepest spirit-urge responded to the Fair Moon's light, cracking the Lethe's power. One thing more he remembered! *All becoming is my being,* he thought, channeling the rhythms of life present in all of creation through his body. The earthbreath of the cliff raced through him, forcing his protesting limbs to move, to dance! Slowly, slowly, he re-began his crawl up the algid stone.

It was over almost at once. He reached upward for a hold, his hand closed on empty space. He half fell over the last lip of the precipice and lay panting his exhaustion to the snow.

Jessie was sitting there, waiting for him. Cradling his head in her lap she warmed him with her tears, then tried a tentative little chuckle.

"Jessie, I —" he whispered through his torn lips, but she brushed away his words with her hand.

"Shhh! Lie quietly, conserve. Feel the powers of life renewing you. Soon comes our shared love, the sun." She held his hands in hers, breathed on their shredded and frozen flesh, kissed them and his eyes. "You *are* the Dancer," she smiled, then kept silence in honor of the dawn.

The storm's violence broke with the first light, as if its fury had been a creature of the night. Already the spring day promised fair.

Something in Orah forbade him to look back down the cliff. In the early birth of color, his eyes instead quested northward over the unknown.

Jessie began speaking in a slow, mournful, shuddering threnody which transformed gradually into a paean of joy, conversely contrasting with the sense of her words, "Behold Riversland, brother. First is the land of Gurion, for there are lions. North of that, across the Gray River, is Barek of the evil Asurs. Beyond the Coastal Range, to the west and northwest, lies the Seamen's land of Maramel, today suffering under ruinous assault from Barek. Far to the north lies my home in the Majestic Mountains. I am chained by a formless and formed power that strives forever to destroy me. It has so far failed, but has succeeded in hiding me from my family and all people everywhere. Thus have I not returned to you sooner. Anyone attempting to break my prison will strive with Terror and Death to free me. And if none succeeds by the spring equinox of the fourth year hence, it will be too late: my immortal blood will be irrevocably corrupted by the Asur Emperor Valin; he will live forever in my stead."

She paused as if she expected him to comment, but all he could think to say was, "How can you be imprisoned there and free here?" It was puzzling, but the world below was beautiful and felt wonderfully normal after the terror of the night; the question was from a fraction of his spirit.

In the furthest north he could see the peaks of what must be extraordinarily high mountains. A sudden sparkle off one of them caught his eye — what caused that? Meanwhile Jessie sighed as if he had asked the wrong question or missed all the essential parts of her knowledge. "Life is rather simpler than Swayam has taught you, yes, even simpler than Althea has led you to believe."

"The Healer! I remember her! My sister! She bade me search to the north for — why? I don't know. But *who* are you?" He sat up and looked at the young girl strangely, as if for the first time.

"The Fourth Child, your youngest sister. I looked like this when I left the Security under Ezera and crossed the Lethe. My thought-word here has retained this shape, waiting for you. I am rather older now." She sprang up and began a little dance as she started to laugh again. But now her joy seemed less spontaneous, her laughter less exuberant. Was it tainted with fear?

"But how? And *why?*" The need for meaning was returning, making his confusion more immediate.

"Oh, who can talk sense to an adult!" she cried with a stamp of her foot. "Let's go find some breakfast." She ran northward down the gentle slope.

Orah pushed himself up, then looked hard at his hands and feet. "The picture of health," he murmured. Shaking his head in a vain attempt to clear it, he followed Jessie northward into Riversland.

~ ~ ~

"I will go no farther with you until you tell me how you can be both here *and* there." As the day had aged, Jessie had continued in her insistence that they hurry northward, but had refused to explain anything more. Orah had persistently matched her sprint, but his need for information was growing too large to deny.

He stopped walking and grabbed for her. But his hands clasped empty space where she should have been; she ran ahead with her perennial laugh almost transmuted to a sob.

"There is no time!" she called back to him. "If you fail to cross the River Glaucous by sunset, you may never regain your memory."

"I will not continue with you until you explain yourself! All day have I asked, all day have you denied me. I will go no further." He sat as firmly as if he wished to imitate a stone.

"Please, Orah! It is not far. You're so close, so close! Come with me northward; I will guide you, tell you what you wish to hear. Please, brother?"

But he answered only, "Why have you become so transparent?"

She ran back to him, wringing her hands, starting to cry. "Run with me! You big fool! Dance with me! I will lead you through Riversland! Every step you take, I shall prepare for you! Come with me! Please?" Her voice was vibrant with fear, but Orah's stubbornness continued unbroken. He crossed his arms over his chest, shook his head firmly, refused to move or any more speak.

She slapped him once, but still he sat unmoving. Sobbing, she turned away, moaning, "Confound it, curse your stupidity, why will you not come!"

His arms unfolded with lightning-like speed. But Jessie was again quicker. Leaping away from him, she ran once more toward the river, crying, "It is over! My time fails! Follow me north!"

The Etan Lord felt before he saw the beast bounding for her. He jumped up and raced after her then, but it was too late. She did not scream, but saved her breath for her final command, "North, always north! Brother, save the stars!" Then was she caught beneath the lion.

Orah had never run so quickly, but space tunneled as time distorted around him: Jessie was destroyed and devoured, the lion leisurely strolled away, the sun set and rose and set again, months and seasons and years passed before he completed the final few strides. The few yellowed and broken bones scattered about were all that was left of the little girl.

~ ~ ~

The Etan Lord knelt in the dust as the day ended and the stars appeared; unhindered, his tears ran down his cheeks and mingled with the soil of Riversland.

~ ~ ~

Orah had remembered loneliness.

3.
Death of a Dove

The three raven-haired, hazel-eyed and carmine-skinned hunters crossed the river Glaucous at dawn, seeking antelope. They wore leather leggings and vests; on their feet were buckskin moccasins. Each bore a bow, quiver, short sword, dagger, and a painted shield. Two of the shields depicted rampant lions, one crossed by a sword, the other with a superimposed tree. The third had a lightning bolt and a crooked shepherd's staff as foreground to a white dove.

Adrian, who bore the Sword and Lion shield, had formed the hunt: he had sensed the antelope would return early this year. As his brother Aland and young cousin Cahlil paddled, he stood with his arms crossed in the center of their canoe, feeling the powers of the wind. Therefore he recognized the strangeness in the air a moment before his brother.

Aland of the Tree and Lion shield would have preferred an older hand on the bow paddle, but usually deferred to his elder brother's wishes. Adrian was not only a dour warrior; he had the just reputation of being the best hunter in Gurion. And, to be complete in the telling, Aland never risked his brother's equally well-famed anger without good cause. If Adrian had agreed with his Uncle Ered and Aunt Hannah about Cahlil's readiness to hunt, Aland was not about to interfere. Yet even so, some vague foreboding warned him the danger for his young cousin was far more than logic dictated: he could not keep the lump from his throat and the moisture from his eyes whenever he looked at him. Telling himself, "Too young, too young," he bent his back into his paddle. Cahlil looked over his shoulder with a surprise mingled with a large measure of awe, then redoubled his efforts.

Aland noticed his brother's hand move toward his sword hilt at the same moment he also discovered the queerness in the air. Yet

while Adrian greeted it with doubt, Aland felt a wave of warmth toward the strange-familiar, exotic, spice-like aroma ahead. *Like Evana!* he thought joyfully. *She also came unheralded from the south. Perhaps atonement may yet be purchased for her death.*
Adrian's thought was similar, but the currents of his life left him with "vengeance" as the ruling emotion. Although he had never permitted himself the luxury of believing in her, he could not deny she had almost brought peace to their dismembered land. He hated with a virulent passion the Redhawk Arelai who had murdered her. Adrian nodded back to Aland as the canoe accelerated: plunging boldly into the unknown he always believed the wisest course.

~ ~ ~

The long journey over the wide Glaucous ended with a soft hiss as the canoe skimmed through the reeds. Adrian cautioned silence with a simple wave of his hand, then waited until the craft was well hidden to whisper, "You smelled it?"

Aland nodded, but Cahlil, trying to keep his excitement under a firm hand and yet sound twice his age, said, "'Lope already?" The conflicting demands on his voice caused him to slip clumsily from his baritone into a not much earlier tenor.

"Not the false deer," whispered Aland gently as Adrian, grimacing at the noise, started off in disgust. "A stranger. Not of Gurion."

"A Maralord seaman?" cried Cahlil with loud excitement.

"No. Quietly, Cahlil. Not an Asur either, so you needn't mimic a frightened rabbit. An Outlander. Not of Riversland. Come." He hurried after his brother, already far ahead.

~ ~ ~

The three ran as quietly as only the hunters of Gurion can: a wild creature twenty paces off would have heard only the soft rustling of leaves in the vernal breeze. *In this at least, the boy proves well,* thought Aland as they circled behind the stranger.

The Outlander was kneeling, staring at the ground before him. If he were aware of the Gurions, he did not show it.

The Outlander was kneeling, staring at the ground before him.

"You are right!" whispered Cahlil. "His skin is not ebony, bronze, carmine, saffron! Nor even yellow nor white! Cerulean! He looks like, like —"

"Like Evana," finished Aland. Standing abruptly, he cried, "Welcome, Azure Lord!" at the same instant that Adrian with drawn bow shouted from the other side of the stranger, "Hold, Outlander!"

Orah reacted with unthinking instinct to the dual stimulus: he leaped up and charged Adrian. The Gurion's arrow strangely missed its mark *(How could he fire at him?* thought Aland in amazement); the Etan's speed allowed him no second chance. One swift flying kick, Adrian was down.

Aland felt his brother was not seriously harmed and kept Cahlil from a similar tactical error. They dropped their weapons, keeping only their shields, then walked slowly to the Outlander. He was kneeling beside Adrian, gently massaging his chest. Aland felt an odd little hum in his brain, but did not have sufficient understanding of such skill to know that his speech center was being read and known.

"I am Aland of the Lions, Azure Lord," he said with the low bow common to Gurion. "This boy is my cousin Cahlil of the Doves. And this who dared attack you is Adrian, Eldest of the Lions."

Orah paused from working on Adrian as he finished integrating the language. But when his mind returned fully to an outward flow, he stood up with surprise and demanded of Cahlil in Gurion's tongue, "Why are you transparent?"

The boy had been gathering the courage to say something bold like, "If you have hurt him..." or hopeful like, "Is he going to be all right?" But the Outlander's size and question threw him into a quandary that came out, "I — you — I am not!" He looked himself over quickly to be sure, then added the only other words he could think of, "You sure are big." Orah was at least a head again above Aland, himself uncommonly tall for a Gurion.

"No, you look like Jessie before the lion." The Outlander's voice was curiously flat, as if he were unused to speech.

Aland, spying a glimmering of meaning, asked, "Jessie?"

"A young girl, about half this one's age, my sister. She told me to continue northward by sunset, but that was a while ago: two or three days, I think. Though time here sometimes moves differently." He paused, staring at the ground where he had been kneeling. Then a barrier seemed to vanish inside and he added, "Excuse me. I am Orah of Etan."

"Etan!" cried the Gurions together. *So he is of Evana's kin,* thought Aland. "Then you have come to aid us?" The universe seemed to smile once more for him alone.

But Orah said, "How could you name this one, *'Eldest?'* When I touch his breastbone, I know his bones and flesh: scarcely thirty-five years have passed since he entered this world! Where are your parents?" This Riversland was most confusing.

"We are no longer a happy or blessed people, Lord of Etan. Many of our people have been slain in intertribal warfare. He *is* Eldest of the Lions: there remain but a handful of us alive."

"Is that why he is so afflicted? Even his sleep is not gentle. His mouth seems permanently scowled. And so many scars. Why does he not heal properly?" He did not add that Aland looked like a dreamer whose visions had been violently twisted into nightmares, a gentle lover whose heart had been poisoned by too much grief for one being to absorb. Mystical hazel eyes that should have bubbled with laughter and joy were shrouded with pain and sadness. It wounded Orah's spirit just to look at him.

Aland, not knowing how to answer, instead glanced where the Etan kept returning his gaze. There was nothing there except a few old bones. At one time part of a deer?

Suddenly Adrian leaped up, grabbed the Outlander from behind, and held a knife to his throat. "Move," he panted, "it will be your last."

"No!" cried Aland. "He meant no harm. You challenged him, he reacted. Let him go!"

"No harm! He nearly murdered me! If I do not kill him, he will try again." Waking up a bit more, Adrian was already feeling mistaken, but saw no easy way to rectify the moment.

"I will not. Release me," said Orah in a tone that demanded obedience, though the dagger nicked his skin as his throat moved.

"Very well," answered Adrian, waking up still more. "But if you strike me again, I will end you." He pushed the Outlander away and sheathed the knife.

"You behave like an Asur, brother," said Aland with rare contempt. "Even the Redhawks are not so discourteous."

"I owe nothing to the azure race." The Lion Elder sat down abruptly again — standing was too painful.

Aland saw the guilt and knew then the cause. His anger melting into pity, he thought, *So. You loved her too.* Looking at him with compassion, he added, "I believe the Lord of Etan drank from the Lethe." The slight incongruities had indicated the probable cause.

"Yes! Jessie told me the same! Is there a cure?"

Aland looked helplessly at Adrian. But his brother laughed abrasively, "An un-memoried Azure Outlander! Even child Evana was of more use." A little tentatively, he pushed himself up again and started back toward the river.

"We are finished hunting?" asked Cahlil, trying without much success not to sound hurt.

Adrian laughed again, this time without the chafing quality. "Come, little cousin. Any 'lope are safe from us today. Those two may hunt them if they like. Me, I think I'll see if your mother remembered her famous liniment."

~ ~ ~

Adrian squatted moodily in the middle of the canoe during the return over the Glaucous, hugging his knees to ease the pain in his chest, maintaining a harsh silence. Orah knelt near Cahlil in the bow, thoughtfully chewing the dried fish and fruit he had been given, occasionally glancing northward with an odd mixture of longing and dread. Aland and Cahlil paddled at a leisurely pace, respecting the others' silence. But near the middle of the river, Cahlil could contain himself no more and, twisting his head around and up to look at the Outlander, said, "Are you truly of Evana's kin?"

The Etan looked at him curiously, wondering again why he was transparent, and said, "Who is she?"

"An Azure Lady," the boy answered with a veneration so intense Orah almost felt pushed backward. "She was the greatest, most beautiful woman I've ever known."

Aland continued in an oddly diaphanous tone, as if the memory came from a different world, "She was Cahlil's age when she came to Gurion. She was with us seven years."

Orah, looking still at the boy, asked, "What became of her?"

Cahlil could not abide his gaze and turned back to the prow as he answered with anger and horror, "Last fall! Redhawks! They betrayed and murdered her, even as she journeyed to help them."

As Adrian scowled at the river's green-blue water, Aland added with deep melancholy, "There will be war again." Orah turned toward him now, his azure eyes at once childlike and older than the mountains. Aland felt himself falling into their silent depths as he continued, "The Shield Conference has been called — in forty days the tribes of Gurion will gather to pledge their stand against the traitor Arelai. An offensive will be mounted early this summer, probably immediately after the solstice celebration." He did not know what effect his words would have, but was surprised to see a glint of water on the Outlander's cheek.

"Treachery," Orah murmured. "Murder. War." Each word was like an indictment against Gurion. "Such violent concepts, so strange, so painful. This, then, is Riversland. It might be better not to remember." He let silence underscore his words as he trailed his hand through the warm water. Finally he said, in a tone that might have marked his final judgment, "Your shields are different."

Adrian glowered through his scarred visage and remained stonily silent. Aland meanwhile searched for a complete yet concise response. But Cahlil swallowed twice and, stroking hard to mark each phrase, said boldly, "Purity and Truth. These are my naming oaths. The Lightning on my shield represents the Truth that cuts asunder all lies; the Staff the Purity that compels right action. It is said an Oathmaster of the Vow of Truth can say anything and have it happen. By my sister Chali's advice, I marry Purity to Truth so that I will speak only wisdom." He paused as if reviewing the whole of his short life, then finished, "And the Dove, of course, represents my tribal vow of Peace."

"Noble oaths," commented Aland with a warmth that colored his cousin's cheeks, "among the best in Gurion... The Lion on my shield represents my tribal oath of Contentment, said to be the doorway to supreme happiness. The Tree I have engraved on it is not only in memory of my mother's mother — she was born of the Tribe of the Tree — but to represent my high oath. For my life is dedicated to the Grandfather and his power flowing through all creatures and creations. The Tree is his icon in Gurion."

The Etan felt lighter in heart from these words, but the happiness was tempered with a deep abstract sorrow, intensified by Adrian's adamant silence.

Yet the Lion Elder did speak finally, just before they reached the shore, *"Truth will not long endure lest Evil be destroyed.'* Thus spoke the last of the Oathmasters' disciples to reach us across Barek, in the days before the Eagle and Horse tribes were destroyed by the Asurs' black art. That is my belief and pledge to the age. And behind the Sword I retain the tribal emblem — the rampant Lion — only to mark what we have lost."

Evil. Orah was shocked by the many rank corners and dark defiles Adrian had intoned in the word. The Etan shook his head violently, then stood to step ashore.

Eight arrows sped by him, deflected by the earthbreath he had absorbed from the land. But the ninth had been drenched with lore and power; the archer was familiar with the potencies dwelling in fire, wind and earth.

For a timeless instant, the Outlander looked dumbly at the shaft deep in his chest. Then he toppled into the water.

Aland leaped over one side of the canoe as Adrian dragged Cahlil over the other and into the forest. By the time the second flight of arrows reached for them, they were armed and returning the attack.

"Go, get Ered and Hannah," the Lion Elder rasped to Cahlil.

"I wish to fight! They have murdered the Azure Lord!" The boy was terrified, angry, confused. The emotions writhed in him, pulling him in incompatible directions.

"Don't remind me of blessings," Adrian scowled, cuffing Cahlil's ear. "Go, get us some *help!"* Then he began circling the Redhawks without another thought of the boy.

He moved like a living shadow from tree to tree for a quarter hour but came no nearer anyone. Suddenly the sound of battle to the west told him Aland had been more fortunate. Two death screams followed each other rapidly, then came the unmistakable sound of swords striking shields. "Always the lucky one," he grimaced as he sprinted toward the skirmish. One more abruptly terminated scream violated the forest, then came a more terrifying silence.

He discovered the three bodies in a small clearing. Aland's arrows were in two, one was missing his head. His brother's shield, cleft down the middle of its tree, lay near the corpses. *A good warrior,* thought Adrian as he leapt over the bodies and ran into the forest. *Perhaps when I bring him back he will respect the new Vow of the Sword more than the ten musty Staff Oaths...*

He soon saw the Arelai running westward, carrying a body that could only be his brother's. Loosing an arrow, Adrian caught the last of the enemy squarely between the shoulders. The Redhawk threw up his hands with a cry of surprise and fell. The others did not slacken their pace but raced on as if they were close to accomplishing their purpose and even moments were too precious to lose.

"The solstice sacrifice!" cried Adrian with sudden understanding, as images of the Arelai rites flashed through his mind. The Redhawks claimed they sacrificed only animals, but the old tales spoke of human blood... The Lion Elder ran after them with renewed anger. But before he had gone twenty more paces, he heard a scream that froze his heart as he discovered he had made the one unforgivable error of a leader. For it came from the River Glaucous, and was unmistakably Cahlil's voice.

For an agonized moment, he hesitated; then, throwing one final look of vowed vengeance after his brother's captors, he leapt toward the southeast with a snarl of bestial rage. Again came a scream, a scream of death — not Cahlil! Then Cahlil's cry again, and again!

The Lion Elder swore heavy oaths as he raced through the forest toward his cousin. Never had he run more swiftly, but something deep in his heart told him he was wasting his time.

~ ~ ~

Fog. Dull, aching, dark. A sanguine bolt of pain tore through his chest where something had been and then abruptly wasn't. His voice gasped in agony as if it were his own heart being thus torn out. Another's voice, half in surprise, half in condemnation, swore — "He lives! Lives! If I had not seen this miracle with my own eyes..." And then all sensation faded again into fog for a long, long time.

~ ~ ~

A gentle rain awoke him to predawn gray. He stretched hungrily and tried to remember where he was. Opening an eye experimentally, he saw two older warriors sleeping beyond the embers of a dying fire. Their shields were unfamiliar to him —one depicted nothing but a dove, the other a dove, scroll and crooked shepherd's staff before a lion. A silver and wooden staff leaned against the second shield. The staff was engraved with an emerald serpent; its eyes were rubies.

A confused pile of bodies lay nearer the river — six or seven corpses with carmine-painted faces, arms and legs, and scarlet feathers in their hair. *Redhawks,* he thought grimly, then noticed a third warrior a little way off, leaning wearily against a tree, standing guard. The warrior's robe covered his features and his shield was slung over his far shoulder, but certainly no other but Adrian could stand so: even exhaustion could not mask his tightly controlled anger. Aland was nowhere, but Cahlil's Lightning, Staff and Dove shield was propped against a new mound of earth near the head of the sleeping warriors.

Odd he should leave it there, thought Orah. Then he stretched again, breaking something constricting his chest, and sat up.

Adrian was at his side in one swift run. "By the Ten Shield Oaths — !" he began, but then turned pale as he saw the Outlander's flesh where the bandage had been. With a cry of rage and horror he drew his sword and backed toward the fire.

Terror, thought the Etan. *In a human. I did not remember this possible.*

"What is it?" shouted the other two as they hurried to them. The man was carrying the Dove shield, the woman the Dove, Scroll, Staff and Lion. Did the Gurions never allow themselves to be separated from their shields? They unconsciously lifted them as soon as Adrian's shout woke them. Were their shields for defense? Were their lives so filled with fear? Or was the symbolic expression of their life-vows the most important element of their personalities? Orah noticed the woman had also taken the time to pick up her staff. Were the Gurions used to few possessions, but were the few they owned as much a part of them as their clothing?

As these thoughts flashed through the Etan's mind, Adrian was barking, "The Outlander! You saw me pull that shaft! You saw his wound, Aunt Hannah, as did you, Ered — look at his chest! Look at it! An Asur! He must be demon born!"

"An Asur with the azure skin of Evana? That is more than I can believe." Ered had reached a time in life when he would like mostly to sit by the fire and laugh about the good times. But life was too hard, the pleasant memories too few, and now (if he but relaxed into it for a moment) this recent loss would overwhelm a final time his prayed-for peace. The deep lines in his face that could have been born of gentle wisdom seemed to have been molded by a hellish agony of existence. As Orah looked at him, he sensed the markings of a demonic, mocking laughter he could almost hear, almost remember behind the scenes of this new world, a cold and utterly hateful authority that found its hollow joy only from others' pain.

Hannah also seemed in the final stage of being crushed by that hideous strength. Her reddish eyes and generally sallow appearance stood out like dried bones on a once fertile plain that should have been the blissful playground for careless grandchildren. How many times had she nurtured hope only to see it blighted?

Yet once more she mustered her spirit from the hidden recesses of her heart and supported her husband, "I cannot think so either, nephew. Look at his face! Surely you see nothing can be hidden there. Other explanations must exist." She turned the serpent staff slowly between her time-worn hands; a feeling of peace radiated from it, calming Adrian sufficiently for him to sheathe his blade.

"How?" he asked harshly, then kept silence, trusting his piercing eyes to unveil the Outlander's secret.

But the Etan was only confused, "What is the problem? Do I not seem well?"

"There!" cried Adrian, pointing at his chest. "You had an Arelan arrow! There! Almost in — nay, *in* your heart! Yet now you appear never touched! Asur work, I say!"

"Innocent health has never been their skill, nephew," said Hannah, twirling her staff a little faster. "Let the Lord of Etan explain."

"I do not understand. I live. I am well. Is that not right?" As the Gurions could think of no answer other than awe, silent faith and violent disbelief, he continued, "Where is Aland? And Cahlil?"

As Ered and Hannah exchanged a brief but intense glance of despair, the Lion Elder spat viciously and replied, "Cahlil lies forever there." His left hand jerked in the direction of the mound of earth.

Orah stared at the blood-stained bandage on Adrian's arm, preferring to experience something besides the disfiguring pain of the others. *Will that become another scar?* he thought as Adrian continued with ire, "He stayed to help you, rather than obey me. Kept you from drowning. If you can die that way either, Outlander! And my brother is captive. I was pursuing them but heard Cahlil's scream and thought he might be saved. I saw my cousin murdered — saw him murdered! — yet you, Outlander, impossible as it is, *you* still live."

Orah had no choice: he could not run from both the despair and the bitterness. Choosing that which seemed the less terrible of the two, he allowed Adrian's spirit to flow through him. A life of frustration, of pain, of rage, a life of waking nightmares and restless nights of violent dreams, a life cursed with impotent anguish in which every hope for a better world was inexorably violated, distorted beyond all recognition, then inevitably crushed, such a life had spawned this outraged heart. How many of his Gurions had the Lion Elder seen violently slain?

The Etan was buffeted by the terrible stress of Adrian's damaged life, but returned his gaze steadily and asked, "Why do they want Aland?" Understanding in Riversland was a terrible weight.

Adrian spat again but could not find the strength to answer: the Outlander's compassion overwhelmed his animosity with a seething miasma of sorrow, hope, despair. What was the value of more words?

But Ered, grateful for any temporary respite from his own agony, replied, "They practice burial sacrifice, Azure Lord, an abomination they learned from the Asurs. On the day of the summer solstice. Apparently they desire a royal victim."

"My path lies toward the north," said Orah, which simple assertion caused Adrian to hiss snake-like as his hand impulsively moved again to his sword. *Strange they hate the north. Do they not know that dark precedes the light?* The Etan started over, "I must journey northward, but I will not permit my new non-uterine friend to be buried alive. I will pursue them."

"They have a full sixteen hours," said Ered. "We will alert our people. An invasion will be mounted quickly."

"What is quickly!" cried Adrian with contempt. "The solstice will be passed and Aland a tragic song before the United Tribes muster. I at least am going after him this dawn — I have waited only for the light to read the tracks. But *you* need not come, Outlander. That dozen would not have attacked were a large war party not nearby. You are weaponless."

"My hands and feet are whole; the earth of Riversland is alive. I am content and will seek to aid Aland. With you, if you wish; separately, if not." He removed the last of the bandage and inspected his robe. The tear was small; a few twists of the fabric concealed it. The brown stain of his blood was another matter; he decided to leave that for now as tribute to Cahlil's peculiar present state. He took the proffered fruit and cheese from Hannah with gratitude and added them to his carrying pouch, discovering with an odd mixture of joy and despair that the mysterious silver box was unharmed.

Adrian eyed these preparations with a disdaining silence, pacing impatiently back and forth beyond the coals. But the sight of the engraved box moved him no less than the Etan: he felt the unlimited might it concealed — an authority so vast Riversland could be instantly transformed if Orah but remembered or even studied it.

Inadvertently damning his own future, the Lion suppressed the feeling and said only, "Your feet, Outlander. You should protect them." He gave Orah a pair of Arelai moccasins, embroidered with serpents. Orah accepted them, giving his imitation of the bow Aland had shown him in return.

On the basis of such a truce, they disappeared into the forest, Adrian shouting back to Ered and Hannah, "Send the warriors west at once. Fail me not in this, else the last of the Lions pass untimely from Gurion."

Hannah cried, "Doubt not! We will not fail you."

Ered stared after them, chanting the old song softly,
"Azure skin, filled with fire, filled with ice
Do you bear the Secret of Life or the Curse of Death?
Riversland will die to be reborn
Or will descend to hell until the end of time
On the day the Dancer of Despair
Begins the northern march.
Azure skin, filled with fire, filled with ice
Do you bear the Secret of Life or the Curse of Death?"

Hannah touched his arm gently; he started as violently as if he had awakened from a dream. "It's time, then?" he mouthed, dully, distantly.

"Yes, life-mate, Cahlil waits to complete his crossing. Let us finish his task without burdening ourselves with Staff Lore beyond our potential to aid or alter." She took his hands and pulled him toward the grave.

"I apologize, it is of course your song. I was thinking of our daughter Chali. I pray only that she fares well in Maramel!" This was proving easier than the ordained acts.

"Yes," she replied, supporting his spirit as well as his body. For the moment, she too willingly turned to the dream. Why had life become so senseless, so cruel? What value her life now with all but one of her children slain? She had been betrayed; they had all been betrayed. Only the thought of her last living child, safe in Maramel in the Seamen's capital, provided even the most meager measure of solace, the faintest ray of hope through this dismal fog of gloom. "Yes, Chali must have mastered her first five vows by now, begun on the second circle. I believe Oathmasters still walk in Maramel, never mind what Aland says! Chali will be a boon to the United Tribes — a lorewarden to rival Amina himself before she is half his age." Then she could pretend hope no more. She knelt with him beside their ruined son and let the grief bear her where it willed.

They wept for an hour, honoring his short life by remembering its joy. Then Ered, summoning courage from tradition only, took Cahlil's knife into his left hand. But he began to shake so violently he could not continue: the sight of where he had found the blade would not leave his mind — Cahlil's final act had been to bury it in the abdomen of one of his slayers. Custom had lost the battle to despair: he could not go on, not again. "Hannah," he breathed, "Help me! Help me. I can't. I can't! Too many times. Too many times."

She again mustered some hidden power, took the knife in trembling hands and deeply cut his right forearm, just below the other five parallel scars. "The last son!" she cried as his blood flowed over Cahlil's shield.

Clenching his teeth, Ered shouted through the pain,

"Brihas! Jamad!
Bear him past the seven moons!
Let no evil cross his path
Nor his purpose waver!
Guide him to the sacred sun!"

When the shield's dove was wholly sanguine, he fell forward over the grave, groaning, "Four sons, two daughters! Life's hope ashes, dark the moons! Ah, my heart! Why do you yet beat that I witness this perverse desecration? Better far to have been slain a young man. I am lost! Heirless! Lost! Dust is my soul! Forever shall I rot in hell! Sacred Grandfather, master of my heart, I have died to Martanda. Claim my breath now! Show me mercy, carry me home, I pray!"

4.
The Wounded Lion

"There remain three routes they could follow from Asad-Guriel to Arel," said Adrian heavily. "We cannot know which they choose until tomorrow. We must wait another night. But tomorrow —I swear it! — tomorrow we shall be upon them."

They had gained slowly but continually on the Arelai for the past week as the forest of oak, hickory and walnut transmuted gradually to pine. There had as yet been no definite sign of Aland; Adrian had cycled like a moon between hope and despair. The five still living of the Redhawks who had attacked them had been soon joined by two score others; Adrian had not even the beginnings of a plan. But it had never been a part of his character to doubt; he assumed whatever resources he needed would be made available at the appropriate moment. To this extent at least the Lion Lords of Gurion had retained through the centuries the profound genius and otherworldly skills of Ahaman, First Lion King.

Orah had followed the Lion Elder without pause, complaint or apparent tiredness. At first, he had asked questions about Gurion, but Adrian had consistently rebuffed him. But by now, the Lion learned to respect the Outlander's unfailing strength. If it had been a happier age, he would have cultured his friendship, from reverence for physical prowess if for no other reason.

After their sparse meal this final evening, the Etan tried once more to increase his knowledge of Gurion. Adrian ignored him again, keeping a terse silence. But as the moon Rohini's light mingled with Gauri's through the heavily scented pine boughs, the Lion Elder's heart opened to the Outlander. He had seen nothing in him to imply treachery. It could not be counted as Orah's fault they had been ambushed. Adrian had been the leader, any ill to his men had been his responsibility, his alone. Aland was right, Adrian was judging the Outlander unfairly.

"Once there were sixteen tribes of the carmine people in Gurion," he began without preamble, just as the Etan was drifting to sleep.

Orah sat up at once, correctly reading the repressed pain and rage in the Lion's voice without understanding it. Adrian and the others seemed to walk a taut, thin rope built of fierce emotion and wild danger that permitted not a moment of laxity lest torment or death result. The Etan felt life should not be so but, remembering no alternative, was forced to accept Riversland on its own terms. And yet, in spite of all he had already experienced, a significant (and perhaps larger) part of him refused to think pain was a necessary reality of life. Thus was he divided within himself. All that felt true and good was contained in the earthbreath, the living powers of the land catalyzed by his climb with Jessie, expressed in his natural, spontaneous and profound love for her and the Lion Lords. Opposing that mightily was the Gurions' deep sorrow and an underlying, not fully visible force, antithesis of wholesome life: a sinister, destructive authority that forever sought to weaken, maim, destroy.

"There are sixteen no longer, then?"

Adrian responded to his eagerness with a tightly controlled desperation. He nodded brusquely and answered darkly, "Two of the tribes were annihilated in my grandfather's grandfather's time by the Asurs' black art. They were burned by a fire so terrible I have never been able to imagine it, not even in my foulest nightmares. The Eagle and Horse Tribes were peaceful peoples; all were gathered at their winter festival when the dual attacks came. None escaped: they perished in an instant in two similar yet different infernos. For life can again survive in the Eagle Ruins, but the Horse Crater still poisons all who venture near it.

"The Asurs destroyed the spirit of our race in a single day. We died to Martanda during those fiery demonic blasts; now we live in mindless fear. Few of us even dare cross the Forbidding in the Coastal Range to travel westward to Maramel; no one is bold enough to attempt the far north. Thus the lore of the Mountain Lord Oathmasters has not increased in Gurion; we know nothing of the truths beyond the ten preliminary oaths, only what little we can glean from the Seamen of Maramel. But they are strange and follow different rhythms from the Shield Tribes. Our mutual intercourse has grown less and less with the passing of the years: my cousin Chali, Cahlil's sister, is the only one of our generation studying in Maramel. Of those most recently returned, some say the Maralords have abandoned the Way of the Vows altogether, either from complete success or complete failure. But Aland believes they have developed other knowledge that captures their imagination more than the Oath Powers: a mastery over the elements similar to that once held by the Eagle and Horse Tribes, similar even to that of the Asurs; this perverse diablerie they prefer to the study and development of the Ten Perfections enlivened by our vows."

"What do you believe, Lion Elder? Why have the Asurs not attacked again?" The statement of opinion was a signpost to the territory of Adrian; the Etan did not overlook the rare possibility of a tour.

But the Gurion snapped closed again as if he were a door held shut with a powerful spring. The inconsistencies engraved on his heart were too painful for even compassionate observation. "Who knows? Who has time to believe? Some say the Seamen warred with the Asurs, others that their slaves rebelled in a brief but bloody debacle. Amina holds that the Oathmasters rallied when they learned of the Asur's infamy, rallied and broke the siege of their mountain kingdom Malinnoir.

"But others say that Asur agents crossed the Gray and perverted the Redhawks, hired them or coerced them to share in their evil. Truly, Outlander, why should they bother with us at all? With the power of such conflagrations under their command, why strike Gurion again?" Adrian paused as he drank the bitter impotence of his life. What could be more crippling to a noble spirit than the belief that one's life was meaningless in the central drama of the age? When he began again, the new depths of agony he revealed caused Orah to wonder anew why he was curious to understand him.

"I had seven brothers, Outlander. All have died in the Tribal Wars save the youngest, Aland. Cahlil was my last male cousin. The two tribes bordering Arel of the Redhawks have been utterly ruined. The Doves, the tribe devoted to the Oath of Peace, non-violence to all creatures, have paid the heaviest price but one. For we who dared to honor the Lion, the Vow of Contentment, have been destroyed, reduced to the smallest handful. Yet once we were the rulers of Gurion; our will was law. This has been the gift to us of Brihas and the other Oathmasters! If we had not followed them —" He stopped the words so violently they caught in his throat. Something about this Outlander kept pressing him into areas he had long ago abandoned and attempted to forget.

Once more he forced the return to the familiar path, "Thus the Eagles, Horses, Doves and Lions are all but extinct; twelve tribes remain entire or nearly so — the seven who dwell in the central lands, the four of the eastern highlands and, to the west, the traitor Arelai, the Redhawk Nation."

Orah was not well understanding Gurion: his appreciation of life and emotion was still linear; evil was not a particularly lively or subtle concept. But he could read the lines of being in the Lion Elder more and more clearly and continued probing the repressed areas, "Why do they persecute you?"

"Their vow was Non-grasping," choked Adrian, as if that explained everything, and as if the words were formed from bitterweed. He paused for a long, painful moment before adding as an almost unconscious afterthought, "My shield bears a second image, even though I am Elder of the Lions. I stand alone against our time-honored tradition by adding a second figure to an Elder's shield: before the rampant lion, I have painted the Sword of Non-stealing that I may slay the blood-stained hawk of their broken troth... Though in days less foul," he ended with a barely audible mutter, "and still among one tribe of the Sunrise Mountains, the Kaystarbha gem or seven stars were the symbols of my Naming Vow."

The Etan hesitated to press further, but intuited one more breach of his taciturn ally's fortifications and attacked again, "Much confuses me in Gurion, my friend. Is the Redhawks' land not large enough? Do they lack food, shelter?"

"Pah! A hundred times their number could live in Arel uncrowded; it is one of the most beautiful lands in Riversland: their Coastal Range, the border with Maramel, rivals even the Tribe of the Tree's Founding Lake region in the Sunrise Mountains. Their land is abundant, fertile; they have food in plenty..." His voice trailed off in vague malice. But once more his mouth turned briefly upward in a bitter, mirthless grin as he added, "Their treachery began before the Tenth Vow, the Oath of Devotion to the Creator, was fully explained to Gurion by the Tribe of the Tree. In this I almost envy them, for that vow cripples the Shield Tribes more than the Oath of Peace; yes, even more than the other nine vows taken together. Yet Aland says the Grandfather's power is our only true hope... No, Etan, I am a simple hunter by desire and a warrior by necessity; I cannot oppose the Shield Council. It is too far for my gaze." He fell silent a final time, brooding dark musings.

"Yet, your brother walks the Grandfather's Path of the Tree," whispered Orah, not knowing if Adrian heard him or not.

The Etan Lord spent the rest of the night huddling his knees, trying to understand and remember.

~ ~ ~

Just before dawn, he saw a golden dove flying high from the south in a weaving pattern, apparently searching for a place to land. She discovered him at the same instant and flew swiftly toward him. Suddenly a blood-red hawk fell from nowhere and tore into her. Orah bent the power of the earth upward, weakening the predator enough for the dove to break free. Fluttering desperately on damaged wings, she struggled to reach him.

At the final moment before she would have alighted on his hand, a bolt of nothingness struck from the north; the dove vanished. A single golden feather drifted slowly downward onto the Etan's outstretched palm.

"What is it!" shrieked Adrian, violently awakening to the sight of the Outlander standing over him: Orah's face was a ghastly scene of brutality, death, murder. *He could not look worse had he fought Asurs all night!* the Lion Elder thought, staring up at him with terror.

"The stars," the Etan half-choked, then moaned a little louder, "the stars, Lion Elder, the stars! I saw it! I saw it happen last night! Have you not looked to the heavens, hunter?"

Adrian rarely sought the mystery or solace of the night sky: his life was rife with too much agony to dream of other worlds.

Orah felt his ignorance and explained, "A pattern is forming, Lion Lord. An emptiness, a nullity is strangling Martanda — stars vanish without a trace! Three last night! The Lion is all but gone! The Crab is attacked! The Polar Triad —"

He spoke with forthright conviction, but Adrian gaped at him, "Stars, Outlander? *Stars?* This cannot be: they cannot be touched. Oathmaster Jamad taught us that they are the suns of different worlds, impossibly distant."

"Nevertheless! They are swallowed by that ruinous despair. In actuality, or only for our Martanda, it bodes little difference for us. This I knew before my memory failed. The strength of the Enemy waxes awesome; I must hurry northward."

"Aland —" Adrian grappled with the inchoate ice in his heart with desperate hands — he had not realized until now how much his hope had grown intertwined with the Azure Lord.

"Yes. The younger Lion." The Etan stared a moment longer upward, as if the gray light of dawn presented no barrier to his analysis of the corruption ruining the firmament. Then he shuddered as deeply as if it were the essence of his soul being thus attacked and abruptly ran after the Redhawks. A somewhat perplexed Lion Elder hurried to bring up the hindmost.

~ ~ ~

By mid-morning, they were running down a broad ancient way roughly paved with flagstone, bordered by ruined buildings, granite columns no longer supporting anything, fallen aqueducts, marble statues canted at improbable angles.

"We near the last capital of Gurion, Asad-Guriel," explained Adrian. "Here my forefathers ruled for more than two thousand years. Long before the Oathmasters began wresting the secrets of power from the earth, long before the saffron Asurs left their caves to develop their perverse society, here prospered a civilization the like of which Martanda has never known... nor is likely to again. In this great city the commerce of a vast empire that spanned Riversland and the Mered continents to the west thrived and brought affluence to the world."

"The rise of the Asurs destroyed it?" Orah was impressed by the change in his friend — the weight of pain had lifted, had been replaced by a mantle of tradition and authority. Here the Lion Elder became a Lord indeed — the very last of an ancient and proud race.

"The Asurs? Pah! Those barbarians would not have lasted a day before Ahaman and the first Lion Kings, if the old tales are sung correctly. No, not the Asurs, Valin spawn though they may be. A force rose against Gurion from the heavens, some say; others from deep within the world's core. The first Lions pursued knowledge in every direction: some sought Vanas, Lord Father of Trees, in Shamir and Sarojin to the east, and may have activated a long-forgotten curse; in the far west, in the crystal land of Tilvia, some sought the Kaystarbha gem and may have released a ruinous corruption. Or perhaps Aland is right, perhaps the Creator simply reached the limits of patience with an arrogant race and acted to right the balance.

"Whatever the cause, the face of the land changed in an instant — the oceans were torn from their beds, ruining our fleets and cities; the land rose up, building the Coastal Range where once our richest farmlands lay; the Glaucous fled to the south so that Asad-Guriel became land-locked and slowly died; the heart of Riversland, the Laughing River, turned black with silt and mud from the pollution of the Founding Lake. We call that river Gray today, for it has not yet regained its beauty — after more than three thousand years, it remains a defiled course. Aland says the Sealords speak of a day when the Gray will be purified, and then the Age of Darkness will end. But such wisdom is not within my ken; I did not study in Maramel as he did."

The broad way they were running along ended abruptly in a vast amphitheater. Orah gave a loud cry of joy, "This is far enough! This will do!"

"What!" exclaimed Adrian, pulled back from a different time. "What? They are still an hour ahead, running hard, but two days from their homeland, where doubtless many await them! We must race —"

"No, I tell you! We are near enough. Keep on if you like, but I must dance! My flesh must taste this amphitheater!" He ripped off the Arelai moccasins and began walking slowly around, feeling the historical usages of power in Asad-Guriel's Royal Theater.

Adrian stared at him in disbelief. He opened his mouth to protest, but his jaw remained hanging, forgotten, as he watched the Lord of Etan dance.

He had not known anyone could move like that — such frenzied yet deliberate grace, such profoundly spaced swellings of majestic form, such hypnotic rhythms of physical mastery — the Lion Elder felt hesitantly transported to a super-conscious state in which fundamental Ideas strove for mastery of space and time, of life and death, of becoming and being.

This much of Orah's second dance in Riversland was seen. And perhaps because it was the Elder of the Lions who witnessed until his consciousness was overwhelmed by the raw struggles it strove to comprehend, or perhaps because of the ancient lineage founded by the First Lion King Ahaman on the broad shoulders of Compassion and Wisdom that the Lion Elder represented in the very heart of Gurion's one-time world empire, or perhaps because Adrian was the most unusual and gifted of the Lions in many generations of men, today there was not the least response from the powers of desecration: no wail of agony impugned the Etan's triumph; no sardonic laughter challenged his absolute victory.

~ ~ ~

Adrian had no idea how it happened, could never after understand it: he awoke with a large yawn and long stretch to a new day. When had he felt so fresh, so clean? He lay quietly, listening to the singing birds of Asad-Guriel, dreaming of his innocent childhood, seven full decades after the Asur attacks on the Eagle and Horse Tribes, before the First Redhawk War. Life had been so simple then, there was so much to be seen and enjoyed. Then had begun the terror of the perennial treachery: before he was six, he had learned to live with unseasonable death. One by one he had seen his family slain until none of them remained save his youngest brother.

Aland! With a rush he remembered and leaped to his feet, his brave heart pounding at his chest as if he had just awakened from a pleasant dream to a nightmare.

The Outlander was nowhere to be seen. With a curse, the Lion raced after the Redhawks. But he had not gone fifty strides when he saw two men running eastward toward him. The first was certainly the Etan, and behind him could only be — "Aland!"

He embraced his brother as though he were returned from the grave. Then he was too preoccupied with joy to hear the explanation; most of it had to be repeated twice, parts thrice.

" — All asleep! I woke an hour ago and realized the Grandfather's skein of fate had ordained my reprieve. And do you know! All the animals were also sleeping — even an entire pride, fast asleep over a fresh kill! Lions lying senseless around decaying flesh! Never seen anything like it! Just when I was sure I must be dreaming, along strolls this Azure Lord, humming a little tune as if it were a Festival Day and there wasn't an Arelan within three days' march! Now *that* scared me! I was sure I'd died, for I had seen that arrow slay him. But he only laughed with joy and proved I was alive. And now I believe beyond question that Evana has sent us a successor."

"No, Lion Lord; I am sorry, but it is not my task to save Gurion. Jessie insisted I hurry north, somehow to halt the desecration of the heavens." A light smile of innocent mirth still lingered on the Etan's lips: this act of his new life had been most pleasant.

"Will you not at least journey with us to the Shield Conference?" asked Adrian as amiably as he could feign, hoping thus to conceal his duplicity.

He was successful, for Aland warmly seconded him, "Yes! The Eagle Ruins are to the northeast, a fortnight from here, as good a route as any northward without entering Arel and a bad reception."

Orah seemed to weigh half-formulated maps and timetables in his mind before answering, "Any path that takes me from the true north I must suspect... Yet I would be assured of your safe return to your people. Therefore will I accompany you to the Eagle Ruins, Lion Lords, praying those who framed my purpose may approve of it."

"Let us hurry then," said Adrian with great relief: his half-formulated scheme needed time to mature. "I don't suppose we can expect the traitors to sleep all day."

5.
Odelia

For ten days they journeyed towards the northeast, sometimes running, but generally moving much more slowly than the Etan liked. Neither of the brothers were well: Aland was bruised internally and was hard put to keep up; Adrian's arm was not properly healing. The Lion Elder attributed this to the strange wind blowing from Maramel: normally the air from the ocean was a gentle zephyr, replete with health and life; now the harsh wind was filled with putrid death. Far over the horizon to the northwest were brilliant patterns of warring light every night; Orah could not look toward Maramel without feeling Evil itself walked there unfettered. He could not tear his gaze from the nightly display of diabolic violence: even the steadily progressing decay of the firmament did not so move him.

"You should dance there," said Aland in early morning of their eleventh day together. The Outlander's painful observation of the northwest had become extremely oppressive to the Lion Lord.

"Yes," agreed Adrian fervently. "Could you dance again? Like that?" The question had been long coming, had sought such an opening for days. Perhaps the Fourth Redhawk War would be far shorter than the others... *If* the Lion Elder could learn to direct this God-given tool.

But the tool was unfortunately subject to broader demands and different realities and replied, "Like that? Again? I think not. . . No, I *know* not. A different place, a different time, a different power, all will produce a different dance. Even active resistance would change the result. No, place not your hopes on me to end your insane internecine war."

Adrian blushed to find his deepest thoughts so easily read; when the Etan continued with his own doubt, "Lion Elder, why do your people follow such rigid vows?" he turned his head in shame and hurried ahead, feigning preoccupation with the flora. It was not altogether implausible: the forest had ended the day before; they were walking through a lovely meadowland of gently rolling hills. The small yellow, white, crimson and orange flowers of spring had not yet given way to the tall grasses of summer; they robed the gentle undulations of the land with fragrant life.

They followed him swiftly, Aland speaking in his brother's stead. If he were conscious of Adrian's discomfort, he kept it rigidly private. In times of war or peace, there could not have been a more loyal or conscientious subordinate. Nevertheless, he had begun to wonder where the loyalties of fraternity and devotion divided; he had been regularly praying such a test would never come.

"Do they not pledge oaths in Etan?" Aland asked with surprise. The Ten Shield Vows were as much a basis of normal existence as breathing. Except for the strange Maralords, he had assumed any civilization would naturally honor them.

"I think not," Orah answered, leaving the unspoken, "from what I remember of my family, oaths would be superfluous," to be inferred by both brothers.

"In Gurion, men require such guidance. We need a polar constellation to remember the true north. When Brihas, First Mountain Oathmaster, came to Gurion, he found the sad remnant of a once proud civilization reduced to barbarism by endless civil wars. See that hill to the east?"

"Odelia? You told me the Tribe of the Crooked Staff have a village there?"

"Just so. They live there with their herds at the base of Odelia, near the Eagle Highway.

"The last Civil War of the ancient world ended on Odelia: the United Tribes of the West retreated at great cost up the hill before the Eastern Alliance, aided by the newly emerging Asurs. Gwynne, last Lion Queen, raised up her voice in supplication to the powers of life that the doom might be changed. And she was answered! That very night Kanaan-dora, the evening star, sent her eldest son Brihas from the north, bearing the human form of an Oathmaster. He raised up his Lightning Staff the next dawn; Gwynne's army charged down Odelia; the forces of the traitor Hagan were swallowed to the man.

"In gratitude for his service, Gwynne dedicated her people to the Path of the Oaths. Brihas planted the World Tree Vanas at the Founding Lake, then taught the tribes the First Great Oath, Non-violence. Century after century, until the establishment of the Asur's Forbidding on the Gray River, Staff Lord Oathmasters came to us from the north. In time, ten Oathmasters, each the embodiment of the virtue and power of an oath, entered Gurion. After the completion of our instruction in the ten oaths, Brihas promised us Gurion would be freed from evil: he said the Oathmasters would teach us six practices of Ascension that would bring perfection to our land and people.

"But the Ten have been known for many ages of men; no more Oathmasters have crossed Barek of the Asurs, nor have any come via Maramel. Some say the Asurs' siege succeeded and the Mountain Civilization was destroyed; others, that the Oathmasters long foresaw the Redhawk treachery and concluded we were unworthy of the Six Higher Teachings. And a few complain that the price Gwynne paid was too high, for Brihas abolished the rule of the Lions and established the Way of the Shields, with all tribes equal behind their Elders."

"One such am I," said Adrian caustically, his wrath overshadowing his earlier shame. "Aland and I are the only living purebred descendants of Gwynne, Last Queen. Much folly would have been averted if the tribes had held to their traditional pledge."

"Perhaps, brother, but much beauty and good has come from the practice of the Oaths, as you well know —"

A distant shout interrupted his logic, "Adrian! And Aland!" A young woman galloped toward them on a mare. Her features and clothing were similar to the men's, except that she wore a sable cloak, clasped by a large emerald; her shield bore the single image of a white stallion on a raven field. She seemed little more than a child, but something about her was wise with an early maturity.

"Nediva!" the Lion Lords cried together. Aland explained, "The last of the Horse Tribe. Thus she places her vow on darkness."

"My Myrhna told me you were almost here," she laughed as she leaped down to embrace the brothers. "I *knew* you would rescue Aland! You are the best warrior in the whole of Riversland."

She laughed as she leaped down to embrace the brothers.

Nediva gave the low bow of Gurion to the Outlander and added, "So they spoke truly — a kinsman of Evana! This bodes supremely well."

"Ered and Hannah — ?" asked Aland.

"Yes, a week ago. I am grieved for you and them. Cahlil was so young."

"Grieve for everyone, Horse Lord," commented Adrian. "Riversland is a poorer home since he passes untimely."

"Truly. Ah, I am honored, Azure Lord, to meet a brother of Evana?" she tried again: the Outlander had not taken his eyes off Myrhna.

"Is this a horse, then, Adrian?" Orah asked, hearing neither attempt. "Never have I envisioned such beauty, such grace."

"Myrhna is more than just a horse, my Lord," answered Nediva, slightly perplexed. "Even if her kind were common in this age, she would be unique. Would you care to ride her?"

"Ride? Such a being? *Ride?* No, I think not. But I would race with her — if you would like?" he asked, looking at the mare for approval. Then he threw back his head and laughed; Myrhna neighed and pranced; together they ran toward the northwest, frolicking, dancing. To canter, to lope, to run, this was Myrhna's love; the Etan matched her pace for pace, league for league, ecstatically sharing in the majestic bending and coalescing of the earthbreath that made her what she was.

They played for hours, scribing a large circle that took them to the very outskirts of Odelia, then, one of them tired at last, back by mid-afternoon to the others following the linear route. Another warrior had joined the Gurions: Eliora, an older woman bearing a shield embossed with the single image of a shepherd's staff.

Orah was impressed by the unconscious kindness and happiness of her face and manner. *At last! Here is one who has known only unaffected love!* he thought joyously. But the exhilaration of his day with Myrhna was coloring his vision: he was for the moment incapable of seeing the undercurrents of agony that had sculpted her. Eliora had been as lovely as Nediva when younger; now she wore her chiseled courage as perennial beacon to the people who named her Elder, a firmness of resolve that never bent for a moment even to fatigue. It was only the conscious repression of her agony that made her appear the embodied expression of that which is wholly positive.

As they walked together toward Odelia, Eliora talked quietly of life in the Crooked Staff Tribe. In those few hours, the Outlander learned more of the wholesome beauty of Gurion in peace than he had in his three weeks with the Lions.

~ ~ ~

His experience of Odelia brought her words to life. The village was a lovely town of pastel stone homes. Carefree children played tag and seek-and-find around their feet as if having an Azure Lord among them were the most ordinary thing in the world, and yet the ordinary itself was marvelous. Gentle nursing mothers waved to them as they passed their windows; the old and infirm gave them good greeting.

Orah had not seen a more harmonious or replete expression of the earthbreath in Riversland. The doubts attempting to grow in his heart he uprooted as the vilest of weeds, returning instead to the innocent attitude of patient observation.

~ ~ ~

Eliora's cottage consisted of three small rooms. In the center of the largest was a round oak table; several straw mattresses were against the walls. The Staff Elder was apparently no stranger to guests.

Following a hot and large meal, deeply appreciated after the weeks of sparse fare, Eliora explained that she and Nediva alone of the warriors had waited to greet the Lion Lords should they successfully return: the others had left Odelia to journey to the Shield Conference, scheduled to begin in seven days.

"Seven days!" cried Adrian with something akin to a sneer. "Is that how the Council responds to 'urgent'?"

"Don't be harsh with us, Lion Elder," said Nediva. "It is six weeks until the Solstice: if you had failed, we would have had that long to try again. And the forces of Gurion gather slowly, as you well know."

"And, to be wholly honest," continued Eliora, "the United Tribes do not believe the fate of the Doves and Lions will be theirs: you know there has never been an attack on a village of a different tribe. Amina argued for as much time as possible to convince the Elders of the need."

"Who else counseled thus?"

"The Lightning Elder Jyot."

"Of course," said Adrian with a tone none of them understood or liked.

Eliora clapped her hands to banish fey moods and requested a tale, explaining it was the custom of Odelia to repay hospitality with knowledge or entertainment.

As the others searched their memories, Nediva said, "Let me be first! The Horse Tribe remembers the longest; I would so honor the Azure Lord." She stood slowly, clutching her sable velvet cape tightly around her as she centered her mind on her heart. Staring over their heads at Eliora's one painting — the first Lion King Ahaman, wearing the iridescent gem Kaystarbha and garlanded by the Serpent King Sesha — she smiled slightly and began in her sweet voice, "Orah, blessed Lord of Etan, my tale we of the Tribe of the Horse know to be older than Gurion itself.

"Long before the days of Ahaman, First Lion King, the horses of the land were more numerous than the people. From the time of early childhood, every boy and girl was matched with a mount, by mutual love and appreciation.

"Yet some of the independent spirits did not share the love of humankind, and lived wild and free as the 'lopes of the southlands still do. A few of these were masters of the lore of earth and wind, wise beyond those of the modern world.

"The noblest of these was Hnohnymn, a mighty stallion as black as a stormy night in Mastra, when the moons are not seen for a full week. He lived where Maramel now lies, for when he stood on the high promontories there and gazed over the Mara Sea he melded the breath of ocean with that of earth and sky and felt like a god. In those times of transcendental dominion, he read the winds of the west as easily as his kin the life of Riversland. Thus he alone of the horses knew of the exotic lands lying far across the sea.

"Hnohnymn longed for the far shore, but not enough to forsake Riversland. Thus he stood divided for many seasons, held in a peculiar balance of forces that compelled yet chained his power.

"It so happened that a kin-strife in a far corner of the Mereds went poorly for the elder brother, Dalmara. He was the rightful heir to the throne, but had traveled far and studied in foreign lands for many years, during which time his father sickened and his younger brother grew accustomed to power.

"Dalmara sailed swiftly home when the messengers of death reached him; but when he prepared to ascend the throne, his brother Adumbura cast him into prison. Those loyal to tradition in the land, particularly the elder generation who had been true to the aged king, gathered an army and defeated Adumbura in seven campaigns, finally laying siege to his capital.

"Adumbura knew that if he killed Dalmara, the loyalists would slay him in return. So he falsely filled his brother's ears with the fate of the loyalist army. Then he permitted Dalmara to escape to the harbor; there, before the agents of both armies, he made it seem his brother was forsaking them all again for the sea life.

"Dalmara's crewmen were without exception traitors. They sailed farther to sea than any ever had; then, revealing at last the truth of the war, they threw the prince to the sharks.

"But the Sea-god Varun was gracious, or else Dalmara was more than he himself knew, for the seven dagger wounds did not kill him; not one shark answered the blood spoor. The salt water cauterized his wounds as he floated semi-consciously wherever the currents willed.

"For three days he lay thus exposed, yet still he lived. I know of no example of human will and divine grace more extraordinary than this.

"After he had danced with King Death for more than seventy-two hours, Hnohnymn came racing to him over the waves, as effortlessly as lesser horses over the dry plains. The stallion had felt the evil in the air and acted from love alone. I don't know, perhaps it was his influence that had kept Death at bay.

"If there had been any light of awareness left in the prince, he would surely have avowed he had died: in those days, even ordinary horses were unknown in the Mereds. But he did not know of his savior: the last of his life-essence had chained his brutalized arms to the cedar log the breath of the sea brought him.

"Hnohnymn dove beneath the sable water and bore Dalmara back to Riversland.

"The prince was long in the mending: the stallion brought him the best of Riversland's fruits and berries of manifest earthbreath that long summer, but the soul of the man was badly seared by the treachery and would not heal.

"Hnohnymn searched further and further for the precious healing plants to cure his odd biped friend, but his offerings had less and less effect. By autumn the body was well, but the prince sat staring dully out to sea, as if mimicking the stance the stallion had so often assumed before learning of compassion.

"At last, in desperation, Hnohnymn concluded that if health for the man lay anywhere, it would be at the Founding Lake: there the eldest of the horses journeyed for their final seasons. He nuzzled Dalmara repeatedly; the prince at last lethargically mounted him. The stallion galloped eastward.

"Hnohnymn raced as though the prince's life were at stake — which, in truth, it probably was: a spirit can be broken permanently, this I know. If Dalmara dwelt too long in the vale of death, would not his body inevitably follow?

"At the Founding Lake, Hnohnymn took the human to the oldest mare of his kindred. She regarded Dalmara with nearly blind eyes, then nudged him into the water. A flicker of life re-surged in the prince, so that Hnohnymn rejoiced. But the mare told him the human would never be made whole until he returned home and settled with his brother.

"Dalmara revived in spirit as soon as the stallion began the long journey over the Mara Sea.

"He was revered as a god in his homeland, partly because of his return from the dead, partly because of the magnificent beast that bore him: Adumbura's armies fled in terror and would not fight.

"But Dalmara had changed: no longer was he the reckless explorer of his youth. Even though his despair had largely eclipsed his inner light, he had fallen in love with Riversland, with Hnohnymn and his kin, with all he had known of the new world.

"Dalmara returned to Riversland, leading seventeen ships filled with those devoted to him, leaving a repentant Adumbura to rule his longed-for kingdom.

"Thus was Maramel founded, Azure Lord, by one who, as you, came from another world." Nediva lowered her eyes from the painting and gazed at him shyly, her expression speaking volumes. But Orah knew not how to answer her — he loved what he had

Dalmara revived in spirit as soon as the stallion began
the long journey over the Mara Sea

known of Gurion and feared for its people, but Jessie's command drove him northward; he did not know that he should or even had the right to interfere.

"That is a very moving tale, most beautifully spoken," he said at last, repeating the acclamations of the others. "I regret I have no memories to share with you."

"Tell us of Jessie, Lord of Etan!" said Aland. "That is surely worth hearing."

"I — Jessie... I suppose I — yes! I can do that." Orah spoke of her miraculous appearance, of her spontaneous joy, of her knowledge and skill as she led him up the Great Ridge, of his impotent anguish as he watched her destroyed.

When he finished, Eliora murmured, "You are more to Riversland than I believed." Even Adrian shared the general awe; but unlike the others, he filed the knowledge under, *Instructions in Proper Use of the Weapon from Etan.*

~ ~ ~

As they left to begin their journey the next morning, a large old man wearing a dirty gray robe was squatting beside the gate in the stone wall that surrounded the cottage, holding a handful of gray wooden stalks, humming an odd little tune to himself. The Gurions avoided looking at him; Aland whispered to Orah, "An Oathbreaker! Don't talk to him."

The Etan was surprised to find such condemnation in his companions and whispered back, "Which oath did he break?"

"Who knows? Avoid him as if he were death! The words of such a one are unfailingly evil."

"Can words be evil? Or do the listener's thoughts not make them so?" Orah could not understand how such a harmless looking beggar could be so abhorred. Eliora passed him without a glance, as did Nediva, then the Lion Lords. It almost seemed they subtly desired him to speak: their aversion was like a half-known, half-denied measure of respect — twisted yet genuine. The Oathbreaker possessed a certain animal magnetism, a peculiar distortion of the earthbreath that made him at once more complex and yet somehow more childlike than the others of Gurion.

The Oathbreaker returned his stare with unwinking raven eyes; when the Etan was next to him, he cried raucously, "Beware!"

"Of what?" Orah answered quietly.

"Of yourself, Blue One. And beware, Gurion! the Northern March of ancient song has begun. Beware, Outlander, I say! Your ignorance sows death where you could create life! Despair, where you should bring hope! You bear the Secret of Life, yet those Gurions who cross your path shall one by one be slain until you alone remain. And why? Because of all of Riversland, you alone can see, yet will not act! You alone know, yet choose to forget! Beware, Odelia! Fair crooked staff village, doomed are you lest this one awaken today!"

"Enough soothsaying," cried Adrian, drawing his sword. "Begone, fallen one!"

"I fear you not, Lion Elder! Beware this Outlander! Beware, I say! If you and your brother continue the March past the Eagle City, the prides of Gurion will seek another master but find none!"

"Orah. Adrian. Will you not come? The Conference awaits us." Eliora's calm authority contrasted sharply with the Oathbreaker's feral intensity: she pulled them from him as effortlessly as a seamstress a thread from a damaged cloth.

~ ~ ~

Soon they were laughing and singing old tales as they passed northward onto the Eagle Highway. Except for Orah, who was deeply troubled by the Oathbreaker's words and brooded alone several paces behind the others. He caught up to them in midmorning and asked, "The Oathbreaker said I choose to forget. What meaning is there in this?"

"Who can understand such a one?" laughed Adrian with grating scorn, but the Staff Elder answered in her gentle, wise voice,

"Everyone always builds his own causeway, Lord of Etan. If you have mapped a hard journey for yourself, there can be no doubt you felt it necessary at its inception."

"What of outside intervention?" asked Aland, bewildered and dismayed by Eliora's words. "Or accident? Surely he did not choose to drink of the Lethe."

"It could not have been an accident, not that," said Nediva softly. "No one so steeped in the powers of the earth could have been so beguiled. No, it was conscious choice. Or treachery."

"If the Oathbreaker spoke the truth, I chose. But why? And how could I choose now? What alternatives are there?" For some reason, the hidden box began to feel warm against his shoulder. Why had he not even yet taken the time to examine it?

"That can you only answer for yourself, young man. But we do know that you can use the power of life we in Gurion name the earthbreath — Jessie reawakened that skill in you."

"Yes. And?"

"Then I say that hidden in the mysteries of the earthbreath lies the lore to cure your loss, as well as the prophesied powers of hope and despair you bring to Gurion."

~ ~ ~

The Eagle Highway was broad and true. In places, a gray artificial stone still showed between the spreading brush. Aland told the Outlander that the Eagles had made self-powered chariots which ran at high speed over their branching networks of stone highways. Orah asked why anyone should care to ride when he could walk and feel the lifeblood of the earth pulsing through his feet. Aland answered few (if any) felt that enough to use it well. The surprise of this kept Orah marveling to himself for several hours, innocently enjoying the earthbreath of Gurion flowing upward through his body.

But in late afternoon, he turned back toward Odelia and screamed, "No! My Father! NO!"

"What? What is it?" The others shouted, but the Etan was already racing back the way they had all day leisurely walked.

Nediva on Myrhna caught up with him and shouted, "Orah, what is it? What's the matter?" But she regretted she asked when she saw his face: never had she imagined such disfiguring horror.

Even so, his two words terrified her more than his appearance could ever do. "Odelia," he panted, though not from the exertion of a run Myrhna was hard put to match, "Redhawks." Then he said no more, but concentrated solely on achieving the ultimate of speed and endurance. It was a strong statement for the trueness of Myrhna's lineage that she kept pace with the Azure Lord's display of manifest power: together they pounded down the Eagle Highway and reached the first outlying cottages by sunset.

~ ~ ~

The violence in the air that the Etan had felt was well past its zenith now: the wrenching screams of agonized terror and death were stilled; the abominations of desecration that had pierced his receptivity like infernal arrows of doom were ceased, or nearly so. Yet on he ran as though the fate of Odelia was still held delicately in the balance.

A small boy ran out of a copse so abruptly that the Etan almost collided with him and Myrhna reared in surprise, nearly throwing Nediva. The child looked as if he had witnessed hell itself; with a nasty shock of recognition, Orah recognized this as one who had played around his feet the day before.

The boy had lost his voice to fear (which was certainly all that had saved him), but he tried desperately to pull them into the wood.

They did not want to forsake the final sprint into the village, but neither could they ignore the urgency of the child's desire. They plunged after him through the trees and found his mother, sighing just then her last breath as the blood frothed from her mouth. A single carmine-feathered arrow was deep in her breast.

"I must go on!" cried Orah. "But the baby lives! You must cut her out!"

"What? Wait! I have not such knowledge! Wait!" But the Outlander was gone, racing toward the center of the sacrilege. Nediva gaped after him for half a heartbeat, then leaped from Myrhna's panting and heaving back, thinking, *How can she yet stand after such a run?* The Horse Lord kept the mare's unfailing devotion in her heart as she gripped her dagger tightly in both hands to keep it from uselessly shaking. She swore afterward that skill entered her from the Azure Lord, for she made an incision an expert would have envied as the boy screamed at last in utter desolation and infinite fear to see his mother's body so abused. Then the drowning fetus was free, but inanimate and very blue. Nediva sucked the blood and mucus from its nostrils and mouth, then breathed gently once, twice, thrice into the miniature body, fervently praying to the Powers of Life.

~ ~ ~

Adrian out-paced Aland by a hundred strides when they returned to Odelia. Everywhere the mutilated dead were lying at improbable angles, their final agony grotesque in the mingled light of five moons. The Redhawks' practice was to take the useful women, but slay and desecrate all others, excepting none. Adrian's eyes misted with a sanguine rage as he looked around, seeing a score of other similar villages he had known in health and ruin.

They found the Outlander sitting as if deranged in the Center Circle, the meeting place and core of life of a village. He was staring around incoherently, in no way understanding the carnage his eyes were showing him, saying over and over with deep mourning, "Laughing children. Loving mothers. Laughing children..." He looked up and through them and, raising one trembling cerulean arm, broke his dirge with, "They were not like this, this morning. What happened to them?" It was at once an accusation and an admission of fathomless guilt.

Aland found he could not get an answer past the boulder in his throat, but Adrian said, "It is known as death, Outlander. War and death." He did not know if he had been heard or understood. Nor did he anymore care, but went instead to begin the search for survivors, expecting none. In that, he was hardly disappointed.

6.

The Shield Conference

The ruins of the Eagle City were on the summit of a lonely butte, so high and steep it took the warriors a full day to climb its serpentine approach.

The city was once renowned for its gardens and flowering trees; but after its destruction, not so much as a blade of grass had as yet braved the fused ground: everything of the city, all the animals, people and buildings, had been congealed into an amorphic plasma by a deflagration so intense that stone itself had melted and boiled.

Even so, the fate of the Eagle Capital had been more gracious than that of its fairest neighbor: nothing remained of the Horse City but a gaping crater surrounded by lifeless slag. A Shield Conference had been held there once, one of the first after the dual holocausts. But all who attended died horribly of a disease that deformed them or caused their hair to fall out or their skin to develop many ulcerous sores, a disease that gifted them incessant nausea or massive recurrent headaches before slowly and painfully killing them all. After nearly a hundred years, the whole of the traditional land of the Horse Tribe, once Gurion's loveliest garden, was still accursed.

~ ~ ~

Ten thousand warriors gathered in the melded remnant of the Eagle Council Hall. They were but a handful in the colossal open air theater — thirteen times their number once sat without crowding there.

Sixteen shields were set in a semi-circle facing the gathering of Gurion's strength, yet six were unrepresented: no one sat behind the Serpent, the Cow, the Tree, the Mountain, the Scroll and, of course, the Hawk. Orah was surprised to see Nediva behind the

Horse — she was so very young to be named Elder; no one had told him her status.

Of the sixteen, only Adrian's shield bore a second image. This much freedom the United Tribes permitted their one-time liege lords.

The Etan could read much of Gurion's illness on the faces around him. As a rule, the warriors were angry or fearful, but most of the Elders shared the weight he had seen disfiguring Adrian — too much violent death and war to comprehend. Nediva and one or two of the others clung passionately to hope. But it seemed as friable as a castle of sand. And raging violently around it was a dark surging sea of desolation and despair.

Orah sat at one end of the semicircle, next to the six unrepresented shields. At the far end, behind the shield painted with an imperial eagle, sat the wiry, white-haired Amina, eldest of the Council. His full-length robe consisted entirely of eagle feathers; forty-five narrow golden chains hung from his neck, one for each year he had presided over this Council. When younger, Amina had been considered the wisest in Gurion, for he was master of much of the science of his lost tribe. The last decade had begun to erode his mind and body; his hands as he gestured to express his thoughts danced to their own rhythms, oddly discordant with the vibrant strength of his voice.

Behind him stood three of his sons. Their eyes were like their father's, gray; but their attire was the same as most of the Gurions: buckskins, shields, daggers, swords, bows and quivers. Half a dozen eagle feathers hung from their dark hair; their expressions as they stared across the semicircle at the Etan were ice-cold, steel-indifferent, metal-hard. Their devotion to the Eagle Tribe's fundamental vow of Austerity reflected well in their similar yet subtly unique demeanor.

Next to the Eagles sat Adrian, scowling at the ground through Amina's long ceremonial introduction, wandering distantly through his mind. He had long known how he intended to move the Council today; the fact that some of the Elders would oppose him if they understood his full intent was adding to his habitual burden of distress and despair, making them at once more awkward and far heavier.

Next to Adrian's Lion shield was a bright red shield bearing the image of a golden flame. Behind the shield sat Tejan, Elder of the Fire Tribe, those who follow the Vow of Truth. From his neck hung a single, large crystal; he unconsciously held it and thoughtlessly turned it whenever he felt troubled.

Tejan was middle-aged, sturdily built, skilled at his appointed tasks, woefully short-sighted. His appreciation of reality was as abrupt as the brutal edges of his crystal: life to the Fire Elder was all black and white, never gray. Evana had been personification of his vision of the good; the Redhawks were the expressed essence of evil.

Tejan stared moodily across the semi-circle, trying to decide on which side of the scale this Outlander belonged. The Etan was Evana's brother, that was good; but Adrian had talked to the Fire Elder at length that morning, expressing his fears; Tejan realized he did not trust this Etan at all. The crystal hanging from the Fire Elder's neck was keeping his hand quite busy today.

Behind Tejan stood his wife Kanya. She was lovely in face and body, younger than her husband by nearly three decades. She had been Evana's closest friend in Gurion; the sight of her brother was at once a deep unassuageable pain in her still open wound and a thinly veiled promise for redemption. Staring unabashedly at the Outlander, she tightly held the crystal hanging from her own neck, blinked fast to keep back the tears, and remembered Evana's beautiful laughter, serene smile, innocent love.

Next to the Fire Elder Tejan was Nediva. The murder of Odelia was still a raging fire in her breast; its scenes of grisly death had violated her sleep with vivid nightmares for the past week. Her waking was not much better: her dread of the coming war was uniting with the dark memory of her immediate past to produce unending visions of terror. Nediva still believed life should be joy, but the intensity of the assault on her spirit was steadily and continually increasing. Orah was her one anchor now; the hopes she had attached to him comprised her final lifeline to stability — and raging around him ever more irreversibly were the hurricane seas of despair.

Next to Nediva was the Moon Elder Chand, sitting hunched behind a shield engraved with the crescent moon in mother-ofpearl. His face was phlegmatic, his emerald eyes fearful. He also did not wear buckskin: his white robe was made of cotton; on his corpulent fingers were jeweled rings; his necklaces were of filigree; a tiara of alabaster crowned his head. All the other Elders looked like warriors; Chand alone was overweight: his muscles were hidden behind rolls of fat. The Moon People were merchants; they were responsible for commerce between the tribes. Before Arel had learned of treachery, the Moon Tribe had been the wealthiest in Gurion. But the past thirty years had translated into great suffering for them; they more than any others of this dismembered land voted always for peace, holding any price acceptable if it meant their commerce could resume. Chand was terrified even by the thought of another war. His eyes scurried furtively everywhere over the assembled thousands, seeking in every one relief, pausing on no one, discovering solace nowhere.

Behind Chand stood two aides, similarly dressed in white. They also seemed much more interested in the weight of gold than in the tone of steel; the ornate swords hanging from their embroidered belts were elegant anachronisms, purposeless ornaments.

Next to the Moon Lord sat Eliora, grim, tired and impatient. She drummed her fingers on the rim of her Crooked Staff Shield as she waited for Amina's long introduction to wind down. Of what use words today? The demands of the hour were clear enough. The destruction of Odelia had heightened the diverse elements of Eliora's face: the lines of care seemed years deeper, yet the resolve was greater, as if she now believed she was the final bulwark of her people. In that, she may have been very nearly correct: the Crooked Staff people were now the closest tribe to the Redhawks' Arel.

Next to the Crooked Staff shield was a shield set with seven precious stones; behind it was the representative of the five eastern tribes: the Starlord Ahanatar. He was not an Elder, was actually quite young, not much older than Nediva, about Kanya's age. He was powerfully muscled, blond with azure eyes and taller than the other Gurions, not much shorter than Orah.

The Etan paid only light attention to Amina's ceremonial proceedings, but when Ahanatar was introduced and spoke in reply, Orah listened more closely: "Greetings, Tribes of the West!" he began in a richly melodious voice with just a trace of an accent.

"I am Ahanatar, Gemstone and Starlord of the Star and Jewel Tribe. I represent the five tribes of the highlands. With me journeyed here one hundred and eight of our bravest men and women. Our Elders dared not send more: those who marched the three times before did not return; the wolves and catamounts multiply again."

"Beasts," Adrian muttered, scowling. "While we watch our people butchered."

Ahanatar turned quickly to face him but evidenced no rancor in his reply, "A four-legged enemy can slay as well as one with two, Elder of the Lions.

"But you must also remember that we guard the mountain passes as we have since the time of Ahaman himself, so that the Mlecchas never again enter Riversland. And surely you know that from the highest mountains around the Founding Lake, Valin's Fortress itself can be seen." A shudder passed through him at the word, "Valin"; Orah had a brief vision of a darkness so deep and impenetrable that hope and meaning could not exist even in memory.

As if to apologize for the violence the mention of the Asur Emperor caused, Ahanatar continued hurriedly, "Of the one hundred and eight, eighteen come from the Cattle Tribe, dour-handed bearers of iron spears; thirty-three from the Tribe of the Mountain, archers unrivaled in the whole of Gurion; sixteen from the Scroll Wardens, masters of the wisdom of the second circle of Oaths; and the remaining forty-one from my Gemstone People, swordmasters and loremasters of the first wheel of five. Thus two powers from the second circle of Vows and two from the first are here to join with you against the Oathbreaker traitors."

Beside Ahanatar was Jyot, Elder of the Lightning Tribe. He wore a black robe, embroidered with lightning bolts on his chest and both sleeves. His face was angular, gaunt, harsh; his usual expression was one of disdain. He turned once only to stare at Orah when the Etan first entered the Council Hall — the look was most certainly not one of welcome and may have imperfectly disguised a dark rage. Behind Jyot stood half a dozen aides, also attired in black, but without the embroidered lightning. Unlike the other Gurions, these alone did not carry shields: the Lightning Tribe considered their knowledge of electro-magnetism the only worthwhile knowledge in Gurion; they believed the other tribes to be little more than barbarians. Nor did they carry bows; they trusted rather to their swords and obsidian-hilted daggers to resolve all large and small disputes.

Next to Jyot sat the Sun Elder Elid. He was a cousin of the Fire Lord Tejan but was in every way a stronger man. His eyes were dark, fathomless; his face as scarred as Adrian's but harsher, more grim. His two sons stood behind him; each seemed a perfect copy of their father.

Last before the unrepresented shields was Hannah, looking small and alone behind Ered's Dove Shield. She sat here in his stead because he had not yet begun to recover from the loss of Cahlil: he was lying now in their tent, running his hand over the old and new wounds on his arm, fasting as he waited for death to claim him.

Hannah was hardly more stable: she was like a reflected image of the Four-oath Oathmaster the Doves had known and loved, a hollow, vapid memory that the smallest breeze would scatter into wisps of tainted cloud. Her body was present at the Shield Conference, but her mind remained with her husband in their tent. And her heart was nowhere — crushed, broken, denied, discarded.

~ ~ ~

After a long hour of ceremony, Aland suddenly came forward and stood next to the Etan. The Lion Lord intuited a strong and growing malevolence in some of the assembly; he desired to protect his friend. *Why here?* Aland wondered, doubting his intuition. But he whispered to Orah, "Before the Lions were destroyed, thrice as many would have answered the summons. Now Gurion lives in fear. But the Arelai are not invincible! We would have won the last war but for treachery. They know this and sued for peace these past seven years."

Amina ended his prepared speech abruptly when Aland came forward. Frowning slightly, he said, "The Lions give us direction still, warriors of the shields. An age passes; let none hinder the new. Traditions change with the needs of humankind. Of what use rhetoric today?

"We bid you welcome, Lord of Etan. For the successful return of the young Lion Lords, the deepest gratitude of the whole of Gurion is yours. These are the last purebred of their line, the last scions of Ahaman and the Lion Kings of Gurion who ruled the whole of Martanda long before the Oathmasters taught us equality before our Ten Sacred Vows, the last remnant of a noble tribe now decimated by the treachery of the Arelai, the last —"

"Even your brevity is excessive, Amina," Eliora interrupted with dry humor. "It is enough. Even we poor shepherds have learned the value of terseness in this age. He knows Aland and Adrian well enough already. Let us rather ask the young Azure Lord why he ventures among us, then seek his counsel."

"You wish to replace our beloved Evana, Outlander?" asked the Sun Elder Elid, turning to stare at Orah. His eyes seemed even darker than usual; his tone was not one of welcome.

"He does not so seek," said the Lion Elder in a decidedly coarse voice. Then he continued as if disparaging Orah, "He wishes to cross over Gurion, heading *north.*"

Aland gaped at him; Kanya yelped as if she had been stung; all the others gasped in astonishment; many of the warriors cried, "No! Stop him! Is he mad?"

Only the Lightning Elder Jyot seemed amused by Adrian's words. He leaned back and whispered to an aide who quickly ran off. Exchanging quick glances with the timid Moon Lord Chand, Jyot said in a loud stage whisper, "A fool then. Or, to be gracious, mad. None can pass the Forbidding on the Gray River." Chand smiled weakly back at him but seemed too startled by Adrian's words to reply.

Amina let the assembly babble for a few moments, then stood and cried in a voice so loud it belied his aged body, "Silence! You grind the nobility of Gurion into the dust! Are we become Asurs?"

"Perhaps he has not been told of that road to death," Eliora answered Jyot calmly in the sudden silence.

And Hannah from behind Ered's Dove Shield agreed in a tight voice, "Yes, he has only just come from the south, where Cahlil..." Her voice trailed off as she clutched her staff with painfully twisted fingers.

Her "Cahlil" hung in the air for several long moments. Then Adrian coughed once in sympathy and renewed his offensive, speaking quietly now, as if he were tolling the Outlander's doom from the Seachime Cathedral in Maramel, "This Etan Orah drank of the Lethe."

Jyot laughed with undisguised scorn and cried, "An amnesiac desires to journey north and we waste the Conference's time discussing it?" Chand gave a little supporting laugh that ended as abruptly as if he were being strangled. His rabbit eyes hopped everywhere, seeking everywhere a companion, failing everywhere to find any to share his oppressive burdens.

Aland noticed Orah staring at the Moon Elder and whispered, "Bears too much, never at peace. I marvel the Tribe of Seven Moons suffers his authority." But the Etan was contrasting Chand's laugh with another he had suddenly remembered and gave the Lion Lord no sign he had heard.

Eliora answered Jyot again, "Lack of memory does not inevitably alter character, Lightning Elder. Nor necessarily diminish power. We must consider more wisely." She looked curiously at the Lion Elder, puzzled. Why was he doing this?

The Fire Lord Tejan said, "For nearly thirty years have we warred with the 'Hawks. Two of our Tribes have been destroyed. For a while we hoped the Azure Lady of Etan might save us; but her murder and now the slaughter of Odelia proves we can not hope for outside help and can tarry no longer, lest one by one our families be ravaged. We can spare no one to aid this man and should spend no time on futile arguments. We must attack the traitors at once."

"Let us give respect to justice," said Eliora tersely. "The Shield Tribes always succor those who seek aid, do we not?"

"This is a difficult age," said Chand in a rather high voice. His eyes, for a moment calm, soon began racing again. "It is too much to ask us to trust any." He paused a long moment before adding, almost as if it were an afterthought, "Not of our race."

Orah answered them, "I do not request your aid. I promised my sister Jessie I would travel northward. This I will do."

Tejan's wife Kanya cried out again when the Etan said, "Jessie"; her husband looked up at her with a fond mixture of love, wonder and an almost paternal sternness. "Ev — Evana told me," she stammered, blushing scarlet, then added with a rush of conviction as she remembered her lost friend, "Evana told me she called herself Jessie when she was young."

"Yes," said Hannah, echoing just a little more of her once vibrant life. "That I remember as well. But did she not also say it was a 'Lost Name?' And what can that possibly have to do with this Outlander's desires?"

"I — I don't know. But when the Azure Lord mentioned her, of a sudden I recalled Evana as a young girl and —"

"Enough, woman," admonished her husband. "This is an adult's tale, not some child's fantasy."

"You know I am not a child," she muttered, but then returned with loneliness to her painful silence of lost dreams and fractured memories.

"You must forgive us, Azure Lord," said Eliora with deep compassion. "This is not a courageous age; we are no longer a bold people. Once we would have held festivities for a fortnight in honor of a traveler from a far land. Yet today we cannot even agree to let you pass our borders."

Orah looked at her warmly and began to answer there was nothing to forgive, but Jyot interrupted him, "Why should we aid you?" A hint of a sneer touched the corners of his mouth.

"Again I say I do not seek your assistance, Lord of the Lightning Tribe," answered the Etan impassively. "I wish only to pass through your Gurion."

"Even for that, the Law states the Council of Elders must decide," declared Amina. "Is there more you can tell us so we may judge fairly?"

"The final command Jessie gave me I must hold to be binding. First, because she considered her last breath its worthy vehicle; second, because she apparently believes I can achieve it; third, because I have now learned something of the horror she implied. Odelia should never have ended so; but I fear that which now occurs in Maramel encompasses abominations that make the death of a village in Gurion — even a village as lovely as was Odelia! — seem almost humane. For these reasons as well as for love of her memory, I must continue on."

"But why northward if you fear for Maramel? What were her exact words?" Elid leaned forward into his Sun Shield eagerly, tightening his knuckles to white on its rim. He half desired, half dreaded the possible response.

Orah sat silently, weighing alternatives. Something in him rebelled against a direct answer — he felt it would somehow strengthen the antithesis of the earthbreath he was feeling more and more strongly as subtle undercurrent of everything in Gurion. But why should that be so? There was no obvious reason to deny the Sun Elder's request. As he looked around at the ten Elders and the warrior ten thousand patiently and impatiently waiting, he almost heard again the two supranatural voices of despair and hatred struggling against the profound health and holistic beauty that was the birthright of any nation, but especially of a land such as Gurion, high civilization in mortal decay. Accompanying this memory-feeling, he discovered with amazement there was something else here, something more immediate and sinister than the transcendental background forces, a local evil on the verge of raging forth into complete manifestation: rather than a constant but impersonal underlying corruption, an immensely powerful pivotal force of chaos, present in this assembly!

The Etan ached to dance, to let his feet discover the powers of the Eagle City, for he knew that beneath the surface of tortured stone and metal lay a long history of resplendent truth he could direct through his body to reveal the local evil. He knew it was not the death of the city he felt, for as terrible as that had been, it was quick and essentially clean. No, this was more like what Adrian had told him of the Horse Crater: a festering ulcer that could never be cleansed simply or end untainted.

Orah searched the faces of the Conference uneasily, but argued down his intuitive feelings. He was, after all, new not only to Gurion but to himself; surely he must simply be externalizing his horror at the death of Odelia. None of these people had shown him the slightest reason to doubt them. Could the Redhawk treachery be marked on their account?

"Sun Lord Elid, my sister Jessie said to me as she died, *'North. Always north. Brother, save the stars.'*"

Many of the Lords and warriors scowled deeply at that tardy response. No one was unaware of the slowly vanishing constellations, but that was a terror so vague and remote, few had spent long hours contemplating what such portents might mean. A few of the oldest singers had revived some tales of the First Lion King Ahaman, for it was said he originally fell to Gurion from the sky. Further, he had prophesied from his deathbed, "We near a crucial moment in the history of the universe. The Enemy of Being has again taken on physical form; the day approaches when he will make war across Martanda. In time, Narain's Garden itself will be challenged, for the life of the stars will be absorbed by his desire. Despair not in that season, for a single error could release him from this prison and set him free once more to roam the heavens. It is the burden of Martanda alone to save the rest of the Grandfather's Creation from such a blasphemy."

Elid remembered these words now as he studied the Outlander, seeking further for confirmation or denial. "Are you a god, then, that you can affect the empyrean realm?"

Orah smiled at him and said unconsciously, surprising himself by his words, "With the knowledge, any human can touch the stars."

Confusion was the primary response of the conference to this. But the Sun Lord laughed, banishing the remainder of his doubt, and replied with good humor, "So! Even without memory, you remain a profound philosopher. Well, this we cannot debate — we cannot judge that which we do not understand. Amina! I call the vote."

"Be it so, Elid," the Eagle answered gravely, then began the ancient ordering, "Lion Elder?"

"I owe the Outlander my brother's life," said Adrian slowly. "And I — I have spent more days with him than any of you." He looked squarely at his brother for a moment, but could not abide his gaze. *Curse it,* he thought, *we need this tool! Whatever the cost.* "Yet I... I do not wholly trust him. I counsel that we keep him close by us until we are sure of him." *May Oathmaster Satya forgive me,* he thought as he stared at his hands.

"What!" cried Aland in disbelief. "What? Would you question the sun, brother? We do not know to what purpose —"

"Exactly. We do not *know.* I am sorry, Outlander, my vote is cast." He sought forgiveness in the Etan's eyes, but found there only an inscrutable depth that may or may not have concealed compassion. Or forgiveness. Or was that only a projection of his own desire?

"Don't demean your soul further until all the Elders have spoken," scowled Aland, then maintained a tight-lipped silence, although he longed to take Adrian aside and remind him of honor with his sword.

"Fire Lord?"

Tejan turned the crystal hanging from his neck for a moment, watching the sunlight fracture into its component colors, then answered, "I see no good reason to allow him passage. Perhaps he could teach us that sleep dance he used against the Arelai. I vote he stay." Kanya underscored his vote with a cry of horror — she had not believed what she was hearing until he finished. Now she looked at him as though for the first time and clutched her own crystal as if she more than half wished to tear it from her breast.

"You *cannot* do this!" cried the Starlord Ahanatar, jumping to his feet, clutching his sword's hilt, his royal azure eyes flashing fierce rage, his voice no longer calm or sweet, "Do you wish to be like the traitors, Lowlanders, force unwilling servitude?"

"Do not judge the Council, Emissary," replied Amina with a wry smile. "At least not until all the votes are cast. May we continue?" Ahanatar stood a moment more, his mouth still moving, but now silently. Seeing no alternative, he sat again behind his shield, far from content. "Thank you, Starlord. We respect your opinion, though perhaps your presentation could learn somewhat of refinement. Horse Elder?"

Nediva stood in a simple fluid motion that unconsciously mimicked consummate artistry. Orah had not noticed before how stunningly beautiful she was — she made Kanya, quite lovely in her own right, seem like a moon in the presence of the sun. All eyes were easily lost in her. The Etan wondered with a ruby melancholy if she were typical of the vanished tribe.

"Elders, Emissary, warriors, Azure Lord, look at me. You see I am young; I am not here as an elected representative, nor from age nor wisdom, but rather simply because there is none other of my race yet alive: most of you know that my parents and cousins were killed in the siege of Asad-Guriel, defending the Lions. So have I not put myself forward to comment until requested by tradition.

"My Lords, I am young. And my youth does not understand how any one of you can question him! In honor of Evana, if for no other reason, I vote that the Azure Lord shall have free passage wheresoever he wills, with whatever aid he will accept from a people such as ours."

"That could make a matter for some further debate," said Amina, "if the Council permits his freedom. But never disparage innocence, Nediva. Only a fool mistakes that for ignorance. Chand?"

The Moon Lord glanced quickly, fearfully round the circle, but found solace only in Jyot's steady gaze. Then he said, barely audibly, "Stay."

Ahanatar jerked, with difficulty restraining himself from a second ireful speech; Aland flourished his cape in a way that reflected the sunlight from the gems on his sword hilt; Amina hurried on, "Ah, Eliora? Staff Elder?"

She stood, stretching her short stature to its full length, and said, "I have seen nothing evil in this man. He returned life to an unborn baby of Odelia and a Lion prince, and would have saved my village had he been able. I say he be allowed to do as he wills." Her gray eyes flickered beauty for a moment, lovely hope glimmering briefly beneath dark dread.

"Now, Emissary of the East? I assume you favor free passage?"

Ahanatar stood, slowly this time, tightly controlling his wrath. "I cast the five votes of the East for freedom for the Lord from Etan."

"You have only one, child," said Jyot, now not even making the pretense of covering his twisted mouth. "Or are you more of a man than you seem?"

Amina grimaced at the corrupt humor and the ridiculing laughter it caused among some of the warriors. *Are we truly thus?* he thought, then said as gently as he could, "You have but one vote, Ahanatar."

"But I represent five tribes! They will not rejoice in this!"

"Nevertheless, it is the Law. The Elders will remember: one Lord, one vote. Lightning Elder?"

Ahanatar opened his mouth to protest again, but Jyot was already rising to speak. The Starlord remained standing for a few moments, feeling out of place and time. *How much more so the Lord from Etan must feel,* he thought, then sat again, remembering Evana when she visited the Eastern Tribes' Shield Conference at the Founding Lake. "This is the Age of Decision," she had said in her profoundly moving ethereal voice. "Let none live in doubt, for that will bring certain destruction to Riversland. We have been gifted a precious boon of choice: we can unite to face the mounting tide of evil, or we can remain separate and be destroyed like barbarians or wild animals. This is the burden that distinguishes our age from all others. If we fail now, there will be no future chance: Martanda will be doomed to a fate of thralldom difficult even to imagine. For I tell you truly, your Arelai traitors to the west are the least of the enemies Gurion faces."

~ ~ ~

Jyot stood to begin a long discourse on the folly of trusting the Outlander. But when he looked at the Etan to confirm his prejudice, a nebulous area deep inside he had long ago spurned and thought well-mastered resonated so violently, his face contorted into an almost bestial snarl of rage. *Evana,* the neglected heart cried with terror, *what have I done?*

Infuriated at himself for his resurgent weakness, fearful lest his treachery show through his habitual mask of disdain, he half choked, "I insist he stay." He sat hurriedly, cursing his voice for its penury.

"Insist!" cried Elid with a vehemence that surprised everyone. "Majority rules among the Shield Tribes, Mara's son. I am next, Amina? Very well. I vote for passage, and would further help this man if he asks us or not." The Sun Lord was not a gentle man, but was firm in his conceptions of justice and was fond of such clear choices. The Council was dividing perfectly between those he understood and always respected and those he sometimes questioned. Except for Adrian. That dissonance confused him; he suspected the Lion Elder was holding more than he was revealing, of intention if not of knowledge.

"Four to four," murmured Amina. "The tie is yours to sever, Hannah. How do you speak?"

The whole of the Conference leaned forward to hear her. She regarded them through her pall of impenetrable misery; but nothing at all passed from her lips. Finally the Eagle asked again, "Hannah? You sit here in the stead of Ered, by his command. You have assumed his mantle and must exercise his prerogative. We require your vote."

She stared at him a while longer, but saw only her husband, sitting in their tent, running his hand over the old and new wounds on his arm. At last the pressure of the assembly broke the equilibrium and she cried her lamentation, "Ah, Brihas! What? What am I to say? My last baby would still live, but my brother's son would remain captive. How can I judge? I cannot! Satya, Brihas, Jamad, Santosh! No! I cannot weigh this man. I cast the Dove to the dust." She tipped the shield forward in the traditional gesture of abstention.

Only one dared break the awful ensuing silence. "So," said Jyot, having rededicated himself to his private oaths. "So. The decision is yours, Eldest. Shall we break the Conference while you decide?"

If the Lightning Lord had hoped to catalyze Amina into consonant action, he misjudged his words. The Eagle flared in anger, "I need no hours for an honorable decision, bearer of the Lightning Shield! The memory of the Azure Lady would be defamed if we did not respect her kin, though the darkness of that direction and his blocked mind bode deep evil.

"I vote for justice, for a more decent age which we have lost yet which may, by the grace of the Ten Oathmasters and the Powers they eternally represent, the sixteen shields and the sun, moons, stars, and our Martanda itself, an age we pray will come again, I say the Outlander may come and go in Gurion as he likes."

"What madness this!" cried Tejan, leaping up in fury. "Evana's tomb is but freshly made; our only hope we send away! How can we be so foolish!"

"We cannot hold where the heart is not freely given, Fire Lord," answered Eliora with fervent compassion. She too wished the Etan would remain in Gurion, but from free will only. That many more would die if he forsook them, she did not doubt. That some might be saved by his odd course she did not believe, but hoped fervently it might be so. "If the Azure Lord chooses to pass from us, we must accept his will, praying the end he thus creates will bless us all."

Jyot scowled and began to reply, but Amina touched the eagle on his shield and declared loudly, "I am Eldest! I am Amina! I am son of Chatur, the son of Yajus! I today pledge the Shield Tribes of Gurion to the aid of the Azure Lord. Let no one hinder his way, lest they arouse the Elders' wrath. There are perhaps greater evils in this world than our own Tribal Wars. For this reason, I further decree that one from each tribe may accompany you, Orah, to aid and guard you. I would that I could send more, but in such a fearful time I cannot condone a larger potential loss of life."

"Seven would be better for speed and caution," said Aland cheerfully, thinking the relevance of the Shield Conference suitably ended. "If so many can be found. I at least would go with you. Perhaps a Lion in Gurion will still count for many."

"If you go, I must follow," groaned Adrian, "though to be fully honest at the last, I hoped the Outlander could be to us as the diamond staff of light was to Brihas."

Almost none of his apology was heard, because many were crying, "No! Folly!" The Eagle was gesticulating wildly for silence, uncovering energies many thought long withered, shouting, "No! It cannot be wise! Both must not go! You are the last Lions, neither has an heir! If you both fall!"

"Such is certainly not my intention," Adrian replied sourly when the uproar stilled. "Perhaps we will discover that the mountains still harbor Oathmasters. There must be more to this life than the ten simple rules we have learned." But then he remembered the fell words of the Oathbreaker at Odelia and a gelid wind sliced through his heart. Out of the corners of his eyes he thought he saw a blood-red rain; a strange breeze brought the howling of jackals far to the west. With a muttered curse, he thrust the presages aside and ended, "Certainly I cannot allow my little brother this entire adventure."

"I would also accompany this living image of my lost guide," declared Nediva, interrupting Amina before he could continue his protest. "I pledge my lore, shield and person to the Azure Lord's service." Never had she seen a more logical act.

"And I will come!" exclaimed Ahanatar with joy. "The desecration of the heavens should not be considered lightly by the tribes of the East, especially by the Starlords and Gemstones. Further, Lords and warriors! Now am I free to reveal what Zuriel, Elder of the Tree Tribe, sent to you in place of an army. You know that distillation of truth, subtle intuition and prophecy are the skills of the Tree Lords: they look into the waters of the Founding Lake and meditate in the living groves of the World Tree Vanas to read the flow of the seasons and discover the ways of the world. Zuriel's message was senseless to me at the time, as Evana's murder had made its meaning impossible; but he nevertheless bade me repeat it to you after the Council proved True.

"Be not angry with my Lord! This is a hard age; many years of ruinous warfare can sicken a people to their core, can turn them into that which they hate. Zuriel made me swear a binding oath I would not reveal his message until you demonstrated honor and compassion. I have seen much that I question, much that frightens and saddens me. Yet I deem that the spirit of Gurion lives and is essentially sound. The body is wounded. But the soul struggles to follow the Way of Oathbinding.

"My Lords, warriors, Azure Lord, these are the words of Zuriel, Elder of the Tribe of the World Tree." Ahanatar paused to shut away the Gurions' variegated emotions and focus on his mentor's wisdom. When he began again, it was in a slow, rhythmical voice which sounded older, more deeply experienced. "'There is an ancient song, sung first by Ahaman himself:

> *Azure skin, filled with fire, filled with ice*
> *Do you bear the Secret of Life or the Curse of Death?*
> *Riversland will die to be reborn*
> *Or will descend to hell until the End of Time*
> *On the day the Dancer of Despair*
> *Begins the northern march.*

> *Azure skin, filled with fire, filled with ice*
> *Do you bear the Secret of Life or the Curse of Death?*
> *Let all be forewarned*
> *For in prophecy lies hope:*
> *A race divided will not endure*
> *A sundered Riversland will be lost*
> *On the day the Dancer of Despair*
> *Begins the northern march.*

> *Azure skin, filled with fire, filled with ice*
> *Do you bear the Secret of Life or the Curse of Death?*
> *Gather your good seeds while time allows*
> *Nurture love while it lasts*
> *For death ensues betrayal's wrongs*

And treachery wears countless faces
On the day the Dancer of Despair
Begins the northern march.

Azure skin, filled with fire, filled with ice
Do you bear the Secret of Life or the Curse of Death?
All oaths will be sundered
All paths lost but one
For he who wears the azure skin,
Made of fire, made of ice
Carries the Great Asur's Curse
Yet knows nothing of himself.
Raise your voices, howl or pray
It will make no difference
On the day the Dancer of Despair
Begins the northern march.

"'People of the lowlands! I who tend the World Tree have analyzed the flow of time and say unto you through my sister's son Ahanatar, *Beware! Spurn all that is base, lest that which is worse than death plague Gurion from eternity to eternity. Today the instant of choice is freely given us! Suffer not the Azure Outlander to pass unguarded through Riversland.*" Ahanatar sat abruptly, his face sourly contorted.

"That is all of the message?" asked Amina as Jyot murmured, "I can see two senses in this."

The Starlord looked at them both quizzically but added only, "All that is appropriate." He tried but could not force out the last warning, *"Yet be doubly sure of those who follow him, for one alone of Gurion will with him reach Malinnoir, the Mountain Valley of the Oathmasters."* No, it was too intimately opposed to his own desire. *Zuriel! I pray my omission not lead to evil!*

"I too will accompany you!" cried Kanya abruptly. Ahanatar's message had catalyzed her spirit — nothing in her young life now seemed more important than aiding the Lord from Etan.

Tejan roared, "No! This I forbid!"

But she laughed gaily and replied, "I am of age. I choose the bow, husband, as did my mother. Before the whole of the Conference, I pledge myself to the Etan. You cannot deny me!"

"She speaks the truth, Fire Lord," said Jyot, letting his palpable amusement rend his habitual frown into a strange combination of grimace, sneer, and smile. "If your lovely wife so chooses, she may go. It is the Law."

Tejan's rage flashed death in his eyes, but he could not dishonor his tribe, and so argued no further.

"One more will make seven," said Aland, very pleased. He knew Kanya's skill with the sword and bow and deemed her perfect in most ways. Adrian scowled deeply but kept silence.

"Then I will be your seventh," said Tejan heavily. "But by the Sacred Oaths, this is a foul weight. I forebode I will not merge my crystal's power with the opal throne in the Fire City again."

7. Evana's Tomb

"What troubles you, my friend?" As the companions had journeyed toward the northwest for the past fortnight, Aland had become increasingly concerned by the Outlander's brooding silence. Whenever the Lion Lord looked at him, he saw what seemed a deep sorrow, incompatible with the Etan's inner spirit. What was so afflicting him?

By his choice, the Outlander had walked alone each day. But today his step was erratic, as if the forces struggling inside him were reaching a climax. Nediva read him well and suggested Aland speak with him. So that she could also listen, she rode just before them; Tejan and Kanya were not much behind. Adrian and Ahanatar were far ahead, scouting the flanks. Elid and Jyot, who for divergent reasons were accompanying them as far as Evana's Tomb, were the rearguard this morning.

The nine of them were directly north of the army: the Shield Conference had ordered the Gurions west to attack the Arelai on the solstice. Their one hope was that breaking the tradition of celebration might serve them well in their desperation: the Redhawk warriors numbered more than three times those who had mustered for Gurion and were generally far more experienced. Evana had hoped to convince them their strength made any further warfare unnecessary. But she had apparently not read the twisted depths of their spirit and had been betrayed.

Aland tried to invest his question with his full measure of compassion, love and wisdom, but the Etan turned his tormented eyes away and said only, "Why are the Asurs so bound to destruction?" *A dancer must have freedom of choice,* he thought again. It had become an all-but automatic rejoinder to the complex and frustrating demands of the new world. His speech of truth at the Conference, his revealing of all of Jessie, had unexpectedly opened him, made him vulnerable. He could feel the passionate needs of every Gurion, particularly those of the Lords and Elders, as a persistent and powerful pressure — as clear to his intuitive vision as his worldly eyes saw the sun filtering through the spring green leaves of tamarind and oak. He could not ignore the explicit and implicit expectations everyone had for him, but neither could he respond: he would not abandon his northward quest and cooperate with their desires, for that would translate into warfare with the errant tribe. He had no illusions about his ability: he knew he had been lucky with Aland's rescue; he could never hope to replicate such a peculiar combination of events and places. And he had no desire to kill. He had seen enough of the strange coldness of death to last him throughout Eternity; he would not participate in that. Yet he could not simply forget the plight of these people he had grown to love and abandon them for his journey.

So it was that his path bent still from the true north. He did not fear the Gray River's Forbidding, the wall of pure energy the Gurions said killed instantly: a deep intuition told him it would not mortally wound him. But so long as he was accompanied by others, he had to respect their limitations; they believed without question that to cross the Gray meant certain death.

Ahanatar had said passage around the river to the east was impossible because of Valin's Fortress. Therefore they had set out to the west and north, to pass through the Seamen's Forbidding in the Coastal Range, then journey northward through Maramel. Aland had visited the Sea Kingdom once before, taking Ered and Hannah's daughter Chali to study with the Maralords at the Seachime Cathedral. He said he well remembered the secret door through the Seamen's Forbidding.

And there was Maramel itself that pulled the Etan strongly westward. Whenever his attention was drawn there, such pulsations of horror struck him that it was hard to continue to think with any degree of calmness. Whatever were the diabolic forces that warred there, he knew he must not avoid that hellish inferno. Perhaps he could do nothing; perhaps this same stasis would paralyze him there. But he could no more ignore the cries of tortured humanity in Maramel than he could have stopped his race back to Odelia — the essence that made him a dancer was the same substance being perverted and murdered there.

The immediate difficulty with their route, of course, was that it crossed the northern tip of Arel, homeland to the Redhawks. Thus even geography seemed to conspire to involve him. But the consolation was that Evana's Tomb lay directly before them; that thought alone brought him what little peace he had from his sympathetic agonies for the dark enigmas and corrupt palls of Riversland.

Aland studied him the more curiously and answered, "Truly, we know not why the Asurs are so hateful. Legend speaks of a time after the fall of the Empire of Gurion and before the Binding of Oaths when there was free trade between the carmine and saffron races across the Gray. But then Valin assumed the Asur throne and joined with Hagan and the Eastern Tribes in the war against Gwynne, Last Lion Queen. And when the First Oathmaster Brihas came and defeated Hagan, he refused to share his teachings with the saffron Asurs, saying they were unworthy of the Ten Perfections because of their incapability of experiencing the One.

"It was a difficult and dangerous passage for the Mountain Lords, but age after age teachers were sent to us. For almost seven hundred years they strengthened us with increasing complexity of Oathlore.

"But two thousand years ago, there came a darkness from the east, a kind of foul-smelling fog that hung over the whole of Gurion for a full generation, spoiling our lands and hearts. When it dissipated at last, the Forbidding had come over the Gray, so that none could pass it from the south except the Asurs who know its secret. They too had changed: they withdrew from market intercourse, became increasingly sinister in their dealings with the rest of Riversland. Their siege of the Mountain Oathmasters' homeland — Malinnoir — began soon after.

"Eventually the deathless Valin rose again as Emperor of the Asurs; the Eagle and Horse Cities perished by Asur magic; the Arelai turned to treachery."

"Two shields had no representatives at the Conference: the Hawk and the Serpent." Aland's answer had served only to intensify the conflict. Couldn't they see the impossibility of their silent demands? The Etan threw out his words as if they were his last hope. To be unkindly brusque was better far than a quiet acquiescence, for that would mean victory to the logic of Gurion, to the reality of Evil, to the existence of Death, and therefore to the lessening or even defeat of the wholly positive power of the One. If he were to lose the ability to channel the earthbreath through his body, to dance!

Orah buried the thought with rage and swore that he would not only understand but succeed in answering all his heart demanded. No more must die! Somehow, somewhere, there must be an alternative. He would, he must! analyze and re-analyze until he discovered it.

Tears crept into Aland's eyes. Was his friend in such pain? "The Sixteenth Shield does not denote an hereditary tribe — rather, a few from all of Gurion take the Snake Vow of lifelong continence. Those who bear the Green and Gold Serpent are among the most revered and feared of Gurion. Some hold that oath to be the first to be mastered; some, the last; some say it is not proper for the Shield Tribes at all: they say the Oathmasters passed it to us only to hint at the full range of virtues they practice. For it is commonly said that the Mountain Lords take the Ten Oaths that are the totality of our aspiration as but a child's beginning for a knowledge so nearly incomprehensible and a power so vast that none in Gurion — even after so many centuries! — none in Riversland is suited for."

This brought a pain of further possibilities in the garb of glimmering hope — if it were true that there were those with vastly greater knowledge! Perhaps they could help him regain himself and solve these intractable problems. *And* they were supposed to be in the north...

The Etan slowed his pace to walk beside Kanya and ask her of Evana. Perhaps there at least solace for his torn heart if not further knowledge could be found.

Aland was hurt only by Orah's agony. He caught up with Nediva, now walking beside Myrhna: the forest had grown too dense for easy riding.

"What troubles him? Does he so miss Jessie still?" Aland was unquestionably her favorite: in a happier age, they might have shared a cottage by now. She grasped his hand and squeezed it.

"I am sure he must. Yet that which devours his peace seems more like fear." Who could see more clearly than the Horse Elder?

"For us then. We seek to aid him, instead cause him further grief. My Lady Matri would be disappointed with us. Still, I know not how to help him, save by striving to perfect our Vows... Come, let us change with Adrian and Ahanatar." She ran forward, the Lion Lord close behind. Myrhna paused a moment, eyeing a small meadow not far off the trail. Deciding that to run with Nediva would be more fun than the tall succulent grass, she cantered after them, gently whinnying her sweet freedom.

~ ~ ~

Before Kanya could answer the Etan, her husband said, the vehemence in his tone as much from anguish as anger, "Why re-open old wounds, Outlander? My wife was like a sister to her."

She touched Tejan's arm gently and shook her head. "No, life-mate. I honor her memory by sharing it. Perhaps her brother's compassion will serve to lessen our sorrow.

"Azure Lord, she was less a sister than a mother, although I was slightly older. My mother Trilla and father Asand died in an Arelan raid shortly after my birth; I was raised by an elderly relation among the Sun People, those who worship Truthfulness of thought, speech and act as the Supreme Oath. Thus was the sundering from my parents ultimately productive of good, for Evana was found on the banks of the Glaucous by my adopted tribe; she spent most of her time in Gurion with us.

"She never seemed other than the complete embodiment of our Vow, indeed, of all the Ten Oaths. I bear the White Shield as witness to my commitment to strive for both the circles of five — this is my inadequate dedication to her perfection. I do not know if Martanda will ever again be graced by her like; certainly our generation has been blessed beyond measure to meet one of her stature. And yet she told me she was naught but the handmaiden of him who would one day come! Ah, I did not believe her! If the Mother of Creation ever came to our troubled land, she would be no other than Evana." Her fullness of emotion constricted her throat, she added only, "My impoverished words fail to do her the slightest justice." Then she stopped speaking altogether, her heart's pain silencing her.

Tejan looked at her with a compassionate and frustrated curiosity, then added his own perceptions, revealing a portion of that which had marked him, "Evana brought peace to our riven land, or so we all thought. Treachery alone unmade her! Her one fault was innocence — trust where none was due." He struck his shield and cried, "Brihas! That I should have been so blind."

"Do not blame yourself, cousin," said Elid, coming up with Jyot to change the rearguard with them. "No one could have fought more bravely for her than you did." In spite of the inconsistencies he could not overlook in the Fire Lord, still Elid knew him to be a valiant man — he had stood beside him throughout the last war and had never known him to falter in danger.

The Sun Lord explained to the Outlander, "Tejan, Jyot, Adrian's father Arva and I were the four Elders charged with her safe journey that fearful day. Arva and five score of our finest warriors were killed in the ambush. The Fire and Lightning Lords were both sorely wounded. Her tomb stands now on that accursed ground."

"Yes, we fought nobly," agreed Jyot with a wild undercurrent of passion, "and Tejan most nobly of all, until that arrow creased his brow. Then I alone was left to defend her from the onslaught, but also fell at last before them. By the time Elid had fought the rearguard to us, I was down and she had been murdered by the serpentine-carved blade known as a kris."

"A dagger? Not an arrow or sword?"

"No. Treachery in the end by a trusted warrior. I myself slew him before I fell, though I exposed myself to do so and was struck from behind. How he cried for mercy! But my dark rage could not be appeased until his heart was split."

"Also from the back," murmured Tejan so that none but Kanya and the Outlander heard.

Orah did not know what the strange lines of force that swirled in Jyot meant, but he did recognize something in them that reminded him of a certain preternatural diabolic laughter. He shuddered and returned to his solitary march.

Jyot stared with deep longing after him for a suspended moment. Then, gruffly saying to Tejan, "No, I'll go alone," he resumed the rearguard.

~ ~ ~

At noon, they arrived at the tomb. Built in a small pleasant dell, it was a large earthen hemisphere with a single entryway, guarded by ten sentries, one for each Oath that Evana was revered as having embodied. There were three shifts each day; many that had loved her well had competed for the thirty positions.

The Etan looked at the sentries and learned the meaning of horror.

"What is it?" cried Aland, seeing the agony twist Orah's face as the tension writhed through his body.

"He — they — all these ten! Ah, no! Again? Aland! They are transparent! Transparent! No! Swayam! What comes?"

"What does he mean?" shouted Adrian. "Why is he so upset?" He had not known the Outlander could be so affected. Tools were not supposed to have emotions.

Aland tried to bend what he knew of the earthbreath to Orah's aid. But seeing that his manipulations of the One's energy had no effect, he answered his brother with a shiver, "When first he saw Cahlil, he said the same."

"Then let us be swift!" exclaimed Elid. "Evil portents bode supreme caution."

Ketura, eldest of the sentries, gave them good welcome. The Etan overcame his prophetic vision sufficiently to be surprised at the Tree engraved on his shield — members of that tribe left the Founding Lake but rarely, only under the gravest of vows. But he said only, "Show me the crypt! We can spare no time for the elegance of formality." He had seen what might be a flicker of transparency in all of his companions and was even more distraught.

"Here she met her doom," said Ketura, leading them into the tomb. They were followed closely by Aland and Adrian, then Tejan and Elid, then Kanya and Nediva with Ahanatar. Jyot had not yet rejoined them.

The coffin was sculpted in Evana's image. Ketura told the Outlander, "This was formed from a single living branch of the World Tree by my people; Ahanatar here placed the Star Jewels; the Sun and Lightning Tribes breathed life into her image. It is well made, don't you think?" But Orah was not listening: as he beheld it, the image melted into life. As he knelt before her and touched her hand, a brilliant amber light pulsed through his body.

Evana smiled with the self-possessed gaiety that had been her most pronounced life-mark and said, "Brother, one stage is nearly passed. But before you quit Gurion, you must learn to offer what aid you can, whenever you can — thus only will there be hope."

"Would you have me kill? I do not think I could do that. How else can I help them? Is there no longer need in the north?"

"Orah, beloved Dancer, you must reach me in my prison before spring of the fourth year hence is come, lest Valin's dominion grow even beyond the Etanai's power. You must rescue me! Together we can turn Martanda against him."

"Should I not instead return to Etan? Surely Swayam could chain him."

"No, none of the Etanai would respond. Not even Father. You have forgotten. Your amnesia is not evil, it is the basis of your value to Riversland — this is why I permitted your loss. You see with new eyes, as if you had not lived so long knowing only the One. You alone can learn enough of the Betrayer to discover the lost secret of his destruction. But you have not yet experienced enough and do not yet understand the subtleties of warring with him.

"You could not make Father and the others see the need until you know it fully; they would answer now that all limited pain must result in universal good. So do I prepare the way for your knowledge, brother, praying you will forgive me and yet trust it must be so if we are to succeed. For if those who Live cannot be made to defend the world, what hope will our poor children have?"

"I must accept your counsel, Jessie: you have lived many years in Gurion, and remember Etan. Only tell me what power holds you, so I may think how to dance to free you."

"I can tell you only that the firmament will disappear forever if you do not succeed, Orah; Etan will fall or remain as an ineffectual island in a world of sunless misery. And the peoples of Martanda will be slaves and playthings to Valin, who will live forever in my stead.

"But return now to yourself: the traitor has alerted your present enemy, all your loved ones are in danger. *Betray not their trust!*" She vanished from before him.

~ ~ ~

His companions had only seen him fall forward onto her image. As they gathered around him, earnestly feeling for pulse and breath, a sudden shock of battle erupted outside. One of the sentries stumbled through the entry, two carmine arrows inelegantly protruding through his chest, coughing, "We are dead!" He was, at least: with a final paroxysm of blood-froth vomiting he died at Nediva's feet.

"Surrender, fools!" cried an eerily familiar voice. "Give us the Azure Lord for our Solstice Celebration and we may condescend to let you live out your days in servitude to Arel."

"Looks like about ten score," said Elid from the vestibule. "Nearly two companies. Odd that they know of the Outlander. Now I wonder —"

"The only question is whether or not we can fight through them," snapped Tejan harshly. Elid was forever abstracting at the most preposterous times.

"There is a better solution," said Ketura. "Over here! There is another exit, known only to the sentries, in case the need ever arose to protect Evana from sacrilege — here. Thus." He touched the ground, a wide hatch fell open. Aland and Ahanatar at once carried the unconscious Etan down the stone stairs; then came Kanya.

But Nediva protested, "No! Myrhna is outside!"

"She will find you later! Hurry!" cried Ketura, pulling her toward the tunnel; she had no choice but to follow the others.

Tejan and Adrian also hesitated, wishing to turn and fight but torn by their duty to the Azure Lord. But Elid, still in the entryway, cried, "They are here!" and, finishing his preparations, struck a spark. At once that whole end of the tomb burst into flame.

Ketura ran back to protect Evana's sepulcher, crying, "No! Stop this! The Tree! The Remains!"

While the Fire and Lion Lords stared in confusion, the one saying, *"I* never taught him that," and the other, "Where *is* he? In that?" Ketura threw himself over the coffin. The flames immediately roared into the wood and over him, as if he were the necessary offering to begin Evana's final rites in Gurion. Tejan and Adrian stood motionless for three more heartbeats; then as one they gathered their minds and raced down the stairs and into the tunnel.

8. The Lair of the Serpent

The companions could not rouse the Outlander until late in the afternoon; when they succeeded at last, he came out of his trance wildly, crying, "No! What pain, what cruelty this?"

Aland clasped his hands and gazed up into his azure eyes. But what he saw brought him no solace, for the death of Martanda burned there like Asur fire. He loosed his grip and stared vacantly at the ground, but Adrian could not be dissuaded by a mere glance and demanded, "Say it, Outlander! What do you see?"

"Do not ask me! Even Swayam could not bear this! I command you not to ask again." The Lion Elder found he couldn't persist against the Etan's vehemence any more than his brother had against his eyes and also fell silent.

But Ahanatar recognized the new thread and pulled it, "Twice today you have mentioned that name, Azure Lord. Who or what is this Swayam?"

"My father," Orah began, grateful for the change of subject, "the High Lord of Etan —"

He stopped with a sudden light of surprise that gladdened them all. With the loss of Elid, destruction of Evana's Tomb, disappearance of Jyot and the Outlander's somnolence, there had been precious little to ease their hearts that day. But now they eagerly closed around him, asking, "Your father? You remember your family? Etan?"

"Etan? No. Or dimly — golden glory concealed within the thickest of fogs. But the hoary Swayam — yes! He opposed my sister Althea when she told me to journey northward. He, she — I don't understand this! They are so compassionate in memory, so good, so powerful, yet Evana said they would not help you, and... "

"*Evana* said?" Tejan was the first to put the impossible incongruity into speech.

"Yes! I saw her — alive — at the tomb. She is Jessie as I hoped. She I seek in the far north. But she said first I must aid you lest my quest to unbind her fail. She sent me back, saying you were in danger. But ah, Father! Cruel is fate! I have come too late!"

"How is that, Azure Lord?" said Jyot, rising from the bushes to greet them as if he had been sitting comfortably there for half the afternoon.

As they cried happily to see him, he explained he had deemed the attack too large to oppose and had run this way, foreseeing most of them would escape.

"It is strange," said Orah, staring at the Lightning Lord after he finished his tale, "but I do not think they know of evil in Etan. I think Swayam has never even conceived of its existence. He could remake Riversland, rebuild or destroy, with one gesture of his hand. But he cannot know the need, else he would act."

Jyot could not bear his gaze. Staring at his hands and rubbing them as if he were trying to cleanse them, he mumbled, "We should hurry —"

But Tejan demanded with harsh sternness, "First tell us, Lord of Etan, why you behold us so strangely."

Orah did not know the art of mendacity and could think of no more diversions. He looked around at them in panic, his incipient control under violent attack from the awful truth, then said in a choked voice, "All of you — all of you! You, Jyot. You, noble Aland... You, lionhearted Adrian... You, loving Nediva... You, strong Tejan... You, wise Ahanatar... You, true Kanya. . . You are all, all! transparent." He knelt before them and wept bitterly as they looked at each other in confusion.

By dusk, the Etan had adjusted to their fate sufficiently to want to gain as much knowledge as possible while he still could. Aland and Ahanatar were walking close by him on either side; Adrian was far ahead, Jyot the rearguard. Tejan, Kanya and Nediva were in a tight group nearby, debating how to call Myrhna without alerting the Arelai of their presence.

"Why is there a Forbidding between Gurion and Maramel?" Orah asked. "The Seamen are not like the Asurs; why do they protect themselves from you?"

"Not from us, Azure Lord," answered Aland. "From Barek. The Maralords' science has always been comparable to the Asurs': as soon as the Forbidding was on the Gray, they duplicated the mechanism. Yet they did not desire to sever themselves wholly from Gurion, and so passed the knowledge of its gateway — in the greatest secrecy — to a few of the Elders of the Shield Tribes. Ered and Hannah possess it; because I escorted Chali to Maramel, so do I; but we are among the last."

"Can you explain it to me?" Orah was not sure why he asked: he feared the Seamen's Forbidding no more than the Asurs'. But an arcane intuition moved in him.

The Lion Lord answered hurriedly, not wanting to think about the Etan's reason for desiring this information. When he finished, Orah asked, "Tell me of the north. Where would an important prisoner be kept?"

"There are three obvious possibilities. In the far north, on the Isle of the Damned in the Slave River, stands one of the ultimate horrors of our world: the Tower of the Corpse, so named not only because it resembles a skull, but because not one in history has escaped alive from it.

"In the most secluded valley of the Majestic Mountains lies Malinnoir, the Retreat of the Oathmasters. I mention it since it is inaccessible except through the air. If the Mountain Lords have fallen before Valin, there could be no more secure keep."

"There are no overland routes?" asked Ahanatar with something rather other than a scholar's curiosity. His omission of the whole of Zuriel's prophecy was slowly but inevitably corroding his spirit. The mention of the Staff Lords' valley clouded the warm memory of his discipleship with a deep shame for not speaking the entirety of his master's message. If anything unfortunate happened to these people, would the blame not be his?

"I have heard the Oathmasters possess the secret of travel through the air," Aland began, then stopped as he noted the Starlord's discomfort. With a shrug, he chose to ignore it: they all had more than enough ill to bear without searching each other's hearts too deeply. Almost as a harbinger of the next few hours, the warring lights of Maramel's doom sprang up again in the far west. Orah looked that way with deep melancholy; Aland hurried to continue, locking them away from their potential salvation, "Adrian thinks they, like the Maralords, have large balloons which they fill with gas. Perhaps. I personally believe they have discovered more sophisticated means, more advanced than those of technology."

"Third?" asked Orah, refusing to explore the infinite potentialities of hope and fear Aland's words revealed.

"Third is Valin's Fortress itself, where the Majestic and Sunrise Mountains meet, astride the Gray and Slave Rivers. It is said that the byproducts of the Asurs' evil art are what permanently stain the rivers' waters."

"I pray our quest not end in that vile place," shuddered Ahanatar. "It is impossible to enter uninvited by any route: Forbiddings surround it on every side, above, even below. Just the sight of that keep is enough to poison the blood. I beheld it once when I climbed the Sunrise Mountains seeking moonstones. My sleep was torn by nightmares for two full years because of that one careless glance." *Are omission and commission equal sins?* he asked himself fervently, but knew no answer.

"Why has Valin not attacked the Founding Lake?" Consciously ignoring his friends' translucence was helpful. With a quieter mind, the Etan could almost feel the seed of an idea sprouting.

"Perhaps the power of the World Tree deters him," said Ahanatar, also grateful for the diversion. "The Tribe of the Tree is dearest to the Grandfather of any, I dare say, for they hold to the One the most closely. Perhaps Valin waits until his hold on Riversland is perfect. Or perhaps this is strictly vanity — what power of ours could slow him for a day? Yet I feel the Founding Lake shall not be attacked until much nearer the end, for —"

Adrian's loping return from his scouting position swallowed Ahanatar's reason. The Lion Elder hissed, "Redhawks! At least two score!" He considered his companions carefully, weighing their skill.

"We are too few, Lion Lord," said Tejan, reading his thought.

Adrian began to protest but abruptly stopped as he stared back the way they had come. At the far side of the dell a file of Arelai was running toward them at full speed. Gathering his mind, he roared, "Like it or not, we have to! Look there!" *If Jyot is still alive, he is a traitor.*

"Perhaps I could talk to them," said Orah, "reason with them, learn why they are so hateful." *Swayam! Is there no averting their fate?*

"No!" cried a new voice. A handsome woman stood suddenly from her concealment in a thick scrub of buckbrush and wild rose. She was dressed in a rough cloth that could have been woven cedar bark. Her long dark hair was tied carelessly in a topknot; she bore an oddly carved staff in one hand; but her most distinctive mark was the very alive timber rattlesnake gliding in spirals over her arm.

"A Serpent!" cried Adrian with an odd mixture of disdain and awe.

But Aland laughed with relief, "Bhuja! Thank Narain!" He approached her as if he intended to embrace her.

"Not now, Tree-lover! Quickly! Come! We can evade those easily — follow me! Brother Suka will mislead them when I steal their prey. Hurry!" She disappeared back into the brush. Aland followed her at once, the Etan and the Starlord Ahanatar immediately after. Tejan followed Kanya and Nediva through the scrub, leaving Adrian for the last. Muttering curses, he sprang after them just as a red-barbed arrow hissed by his ear.

The ground fell away quickly from the pathway. They ran swiftly after her until the last light of day was gone, then stumbled on through the darkness for nearly an hour until coming at last to a very large and rusty iron pipe.

"Inside!" Bhuja ordered, "I will alter your track then return. Quickly."

But Adrian cried, "No! We would be trapped in there." Something was wrong: was someone other than Jyot missing? He could not easily discover in the murky gloaming. The pipe seemed the worst of all theories in a dismal philosophy — to hide like a snake rather than be free in the open air contradicted every instinct by which he had survived for three and a half decades.

"No, don't fear! It is open at both ends. And a friend awaits you. Go now, quickly! I must efface your marks."

"What friend —" began Adrian, but a gentle whinny caused Nediva to push past him, crying gladly,

"Myrhna! Myrhna!" She embraced the mare tearfully as the others followed her into the pipe. Bhuja vanished into the forest with a rustle like the sighing of autumn leaves.

~ ~ ~

A handsome woman stood suddenly

The pipe was musty but dry; the water it once carried had long made other paths to the sea.

Orah asked Aland with surprise why anyone would have so poorly treated water; the Lion Lord explained that the Eagle Highway must have passed overhead, skirting the hills of Arel, almost touching the Gray River before climbing into the Coastal Range.

"So the Gray is nearby?" the Etan inquired with a peculiar intonation. Adrian gasped and tried to see him through the darkness.

His brother's response was a jolt to Aland — he had been talking unconsciously, relating facts as though reading a map. Shaking his head, thinking now only of his friend, he felt his way to the far end of the pipe to take up the guard.

Kanya gave a low cry: a small band of Redhawks ran overhead. They moved as silently as any of Gurion, but they could not stop the ground from resonating the pipe. Nediva held Myrhna's muzzle tight to her breast, fearing the mare might betray them.

The Arelai took an inordinately long time to cross the culvert; when the vibrations finally ceased, Adrian let his breath out with a long sigh. He had not been aware he was holding it. Again he felt someone was gone, now more strongly than before. He walked the length of the pipe, touching Tejan, Kanya, Nediva, Ahanatar, Aland. Where was the Outlander? "Orah?" he whispered hoarsely. Fear began to devour him now.

He tried again more loudly, "Outlander?" but the Etan was gone.

~ ~ ~

Adrian cursed and ran back toward the entrance. Too late he discovered Bhuja's error — a spear tore into his right shoulder, just below the clavicle, throwing him back into the darkness. As his awareness exploded in sanguine agony, he heard the sword battle raging at both ends of the pipe like a maelstrom of doom, marked with the savage lightning screams of death.

The defender at the far end fell with a hideous cry; a brilliant violet fire nearby burst outward. Hard hands ripped the spear from his breast, pressed cloth over it, then pushed and pulled him to his feet. "Come!" cried a voice that might have been Ahanatar's. "The Fire Lord has cleared the way; can you move? Good."

The fog in his vision blurred the fires outside the pipe's mouth; but Adrian could still see well enough to learn it was the Arelai who were burning.

An arrow struck Kanya in the back; she fell with a cry of surprise that ended in blood as her lungs filled with her life. Her eyes rolled violently; she shook once and was still. Tejan knelt by her, smothering her in his arms. Nediva pulled at him, crying, "No! Too late! She is gone! Flee!"

"Flee yourselves!" he sobbed, "Brihas! How could this happen? Her only sin was innocent love! Flee, fools! This forest is dead!" As he pulled her onto his breast, he loosed his crystal's full power. Flames enveloped him and began expanding in a fierce frenzy of wild passion.

They could not bear the heat and were forced to retreat. On the far side, a band of Arelai were caught and fell screaming into the conflagration. Suddenly an answering wave of fire roared toward Tejan's creation.

"No!" cried Nediva, "A lorewarden is with them!" They watched in horror as the two forces warred for supremacy, thrusting larger and larger areas of the forest into an inferno of death.

"How can he survive that!" cried Ahanatar.

Adrian answered around his blurring pain, "Why do you think he wants to? Behold!" The entire side of the hill burst into flame; both of the smaller fires were dwarfed by Tejan's death act, a supernal holocaust hot enough to melt iron.

Hot enough to melt iron... Iron... The pipe! "Aland! Where is Aland?"

Silence alone answered him; the Lion Elder knew then whose death cry he had heard. And now for the first time in years his anguish brought the hot tears from his grim eyes. He stumbled blindly on as Ahanatar struggled to help him. The crude bandage was long gone; the blood gushed freely down his chest and arm. Adrian was too numb with grief and pain to ask further.

The Starlord alone was not wounded. How could he help the others far? Nediva's thigh was sorely slashed; her hastily contrived tourniquet was dripping at a disturbing rate. It was unbelievable Adrian was still moving at all; only the repeated pulses of the earthbreath from Nediva kept him clinging to a febrile awareness.

Soon the Lion Elder could no more walk. Sighing, "Aland, oh, Aland," he lapsed into a semi-conscious torpor from which he could not be roused.

"I cannot help him any more," said Nediva bleakly. "And I must look to my leg or I will not be able to continue." She knelt and merged her mind with her flesh for a few moments. "I need more time. But the bleeding stops. Now —" She looked up abruptly, trying to deny her ears, then cried, "No! Ahanatar! They're coming! I hear them!"

The Starlord did not answer, but lifted Adrian and lunged onward. She hurried after him, ignoring the screaming pain in her thigh. Not knowing how she could possibly continue on, she nevertheless matched his pace. *The memory of Aland deserves no less,* she thought savagely. Yet no matter how quickly they moved, the sounds of pursuit drew closer, closer — the Arelai that had escaped Tejan's fire-storm were closing with unerring skill toward them.

Ahanatar ran onward, praying, *Zuriel, help us! Brihas, help us! Ah, Zuriel!*

As the Starlord tasted the bitterness of defeat, knowing they could no more go on — *Will they honor surrender?* he thought, then harshly laughed at himself for it — a sharp whisper to his right brought him to an abrupt halt. Half in terror, half in belief, he heard again, "Here, Gemstone, here!" He had to decide quickly, quickly — the Redhawks were but moments behind! He had to move, to act!

With a shudder born of the marriage of hope and fear, Ahanatar carried Adrian and dragged Nediva toward the voice.

Behind a wall of thick vines opened a small cavern, lit by a faint phosphor light. An ageless cripple, clad mostly in living snakes, greeted them and identified himself as Bhuja's brother, Suka.

"Bhuja?" whispered Ahanatar as he laid Adrian on one of the two moss beds.

"Dead." He answered without inflection, as if he were either immune or inured to pain. "She tried to lead the 'Hawks off your track, but their captain is a 'warden and penetrated her."

"Was. Tejan fought him and died. To save us." Nediva was more drained than she believed she could be and still live. She threw herself on the second bed as she added, "Are we secure here?" Her tone said she hardly cared if they were or not. As she began to move her mind fully into her wound, she barely heard Suka's reply.

"More so. More time have we had to weave our illusions here. In broad daylight, a commoner could stand ten paces from this cave and not know it."

~ ~ ~

The Lion Elder swam dully to consciousness as Suka cleansed his wound. He heard him say, "Not to the death, thank Brihas! Not to the death."

Then Adrian remembered Aland and turned his face to the gray stone of the cave wall, letting the pain and darkness engulf him again, more than half wishing the spear had lodged in his other breast. As he sank once more into that lonely sea, the Oathbreaker's fate-speaking at Odelia, "The prides of Gurion will seek another master but find none..." and Amina's warning, "Both should not go... If you both fall..." repeated through his mind like the two sides of an engraved coin falling into a well, reflecting the failing light again and again as it sank forever into oblivion; like the receding echoes of despair tolling from a lost and foundering ship; like a steadily withdrawing tide of hope and love; like a dirge of ultimate desolation...

9. The Passing of Dominion

Adrian awoke to a gray and confined world, and tried to discover where he was. The small stone cavern seemed too sparse to sustain residents; he could not recall how he had come there. But when he sat up on the crude moss bed, the deep throbbing pain on his right side reminded him he was wounded again; in a rush he remembered the night and wept bitterly for his youngest brother's end. His self-blame was still consuming him an hour later when Suka returned, bearing herbs.

The Serpent was upset to see Adrian upright and insisted that he lie down, saying that his chest had not begun to mend. But Adrian ignored him, instead began seeking his clothes.

"Nediva and Ahanatar?" He had rediscovered purpose.

"They left at dawn to seek the Etan Lord — she has nearly mastered her Vow and healed overnight. They said you should follow them down the Eagle Highway when you are recovered. But your cure is not yet effected; you must lie down!"

"I cannot rest! My brother's death cries for vengeance." The need for action steeled his will. He stood rather unsteadily and pulled his buckskin vest over his bandaged chest and arm.

"A man's time comes when it comes. The Azure Lord tried to buy him more life and failed." Seeing no response in his truant patient, he altered his reasoning, "Can you fight the entire Redhawk nation with just one arm? I tell you, you should wait." But Suka's aim was poor: living as a recluse for so many years had weakened his interpersonal skill. Rather than being calmed, the Lion Elder was further impelled to rash action. It was all the Serpent could do to restrain him long enough to re-bandage his wound.

At last he could no longer delay him and said as farewell, "If I cannot dissuade you, at least let me offer you this." From his left hand, he took a silver and verdigris ring, fashioned in the form of a coiled serpent. "It contains venom from the emerald moccasin," he said, slowly turning it between his fingers. "If you touch it here — so — the smallest scratch from this fang; death is certain."

Adrian checked his eager rage long enough to say warmly, "Thank you. Your tribe is a blessing to Gurion. I shall wear your talisman with great honor." Then he was gone, following his destiny in the only way he understood.

Suka, staring sadly after the last living Lion, let his slow exhalation absolve his frustration. Then he returned to his meditation on the One. Weaving his mind throughout the waves of change, the Serpent did what he could to improve the tendencies of Riversland.

~ ~ ~

Adrian hurried as swiftly as his aching chest permitted along the overgrown highway, seeking signs of one and two but discovering marks of many. Tejan's death pyre must have claimed scores, but not less than a hundred had passed that way today. He could only assume that Ahanatar and Nediva were before him and behind the Arelai, and that the Outlander was before them all, racing westward toward Maramel, believing all his companions slain. *Or soon to be slain,* he thought grimly. *Who has the right to demand the fulfillment of visions reflect a strict time continuum?*

He topped a small rise and was charmed in spite of his mordancy by the sudden sight of the Gray. But in another half an instant, he threw himself off the roadway in despair: in a little glen not two thousand paces away were what must have been the whole of the enemy in northeastern Arel — an entire legion, apparently still at their campsite.

Adrian had torn his wound open again, his chest pulsed with a crimson agony that threatened expansion with each heartbeat. But he was accustomed to pain; it was not unbearable.

He could hardly believe he had not been seen. Slithering into the undergrowth, he lay as quietly as would a fawn.

But there were no sounds of pursuit; no sign they were aware of him. What could they be doing? He crept slowly up the ridge.

The high ground narrowed to form a promontory: it fell quickly down to the Gray on one side and to the highway on the other.

He crawled on slowly, until he was near the highest point. He researched his escape route toward the river carefully, fearing his curiosity might betray him.

When he was confident about his retreat, he slid forward far enough to see the Arelai. All five thousand were sitting in a semicircle, watching something — no, someone — intently. With a sudden groan of recognition, Adrian recognized the Outlander at their center.

It was too far to see what Orah was doing; but Adrian felt sure he was bargaining with them. "The fool," he breathed, "thus Evana failed." It took all his strength of will not to jump up and scream his rage at the enemy below.

At the last possible instant, some sixth sense enabled him to roll swiftly over and kick himself upright.

Jyot's sword deeply slashed into the earth where Adrian's neck had just been. The blade nicked the Lion's skin, but the wrenching effort that saved him caused the greater ill, for his chest wound was deeply re-opened and agonized in bitter fire.

"I know you!" Adrian screamed, for the moment forgetting that he and the Lightning Lord were not the only warriors within days of marches. "Betrayer!" he shouted as if his soul were bursting forth from the sudden indemnifying recognition. Yet if his straining face was out of control, his left arm was not: he drew his sword and savagely struck at the leering traitor.

"Betrayer?" taunted Jyot, effortlessly parrying. "When did I ever betray nobility? Or myself? Only fools and slaves have been destroyed by me." His sword flashed as quickly as the name of his tribe; Adrian's defenses grew erratically weaker.

"Is that your definition of honor, Jyot?" he panted, wildly seeking alternatives — the slope to the river now seemed mad, a delusion born of his wound, yet what other choice was there? With a single convulsive motion, he leaped to the very lip of the cliff.

Jyot did not follow him; he knew his allies were racing up toward them. Discretion seemed wise, perhaps the more so because his prey was wounded. *Wild animals at bay are often the more ferocious,* he thought, but said, "Why not be sensible? The Outlander is in our hands. He will offer his life that the wars may end; naturally, we will accept — at least until after the Burial Celebration."

"What is the price for treachery? Dominion over the eastern tribes?" Why did the cliff seem so much steeper now? What could he do?

"Fool! There will be no tribes left when they are done. If I can preserve the Lightning People, I will have justified my life." He watched Adrian curiously, as if the degenerating agony of the Lion Elder was a fascinating biological process, similar to the dissection of a living insect. He dropped to one knee to study him more closely.

Adrian snarled his rage and backed along the cliff. The throbbing in his chest was like elemental convulsions of being, deeply affecting his senses. His perception of distance was failing; a bitter incarnadine fog alternated with dizzy sensations of height. How could the river be so very far away? How close were the Redhawks? "You are mad! Can you palliate death? They use you! Your tribe may be the last, but they will be devoured as well! The Arelai are insatiable."

The Lion pretended to turn toward the river, then spun and bounded down at Jyot with a roar. The Lightning Lord's blade caught his right arm, deeply damaging it; Adrian screamed, but then laughed insanely as he saw that his aim had been true — Jyot was staring dully at the small scratch across his forearm from Suka's ring. "Adrian... Evana... I... I — Brihas. . ." He fell onto his face and rolled down the ridge.

"Brihas shall never rise again for you, traitor," said Adrian, holding his arm together. The crimson pain seared through him like the holocaust of World's End, blinding him ever more finally with every labored breath.

Another half minute he waited, savoring his victory, then leaped over the cliff the same instant half a dozen Arelai reached the crest of the ridge.

The ledge below met him more slowly than he calculated it should; his ankle twisted sharply as he threw himself onto his side to avoid the edge.

He lurched to his feet, then almost fell as his ankle bent under him. Screaming as he forced his tortured body to move, he hobbled along the ledge toward a copse covering what hope he still possessed — a small ravine.

He felt before he saw the Redhawks on the cliff above. One scarlet barbed shaft whipped past him; then he was among the trees.

He scrambled and fell down the cleft, knowing his only chance lay in the questionable sanctuary of the Gray. He caught glimpses of it as the arroyo wound down the cliff, but could not force his ruined body to move any faster. He intuited when they entered the canyon above, knew full well they would easily catch him before he could reach the bank. Feverishly he sought another alternative.

But his conclusion was false, or else his final struggle pushed his maimed flesh to superhuman speed: he reached the river well in advance of the enemy.

The Lion Elder feared the ancient tales as much as any who had lived three and a half decades under their spell naturally would; but the immediate threat at his back plunged him headlong into the moiling flood.

Now was his mind lost. The soundness of its being, the connection with the One that gives all life its stability, was shrouded by a force that knew nothing of health save in its absence.

The body that had been the most prized tool of the last of the Lions struggled across the river and crawled up the steep bank of the far shore.

The Arelai watched with amazement. Was the Forbidding protecting Barek no longer functioning? But when he who had been Adrian reached the top of the bank, their doubts vanished, for the body was suddenly outlined by an amber and saffron hissing and crackling that held it paralyzed in the air for a long moment, shouting its final word (which may or may not have been, "Brihas!") as it was consumed.

Only when the ashes had fallen to the earth of Barek were the Redhawks satisfied that their duty to Arel was accomplished. Exchanging grim smiles, they returned to the climb.

~ ~ ~

In Asad-Guriel, an ancient throne carved in the image of a lion crumbled into dust, releasing the power of sovereignty wrested by Ahaman from the prides of Gurion, the regal power used and abused by his descendants almost beyond number, the ancient fundamental root of royalty finally abandoned and largely forgotten when Brihas created the Order of the Shields.

The authority held its form for a few seconds, as if in memory of many honorable generations. Then a gelid wind from the north dissipated it like the last thought of summer in January, like the last breath of the dying, like the last smoke from a scattered fire.

Yet another age of man had ended, an age to be remembered ever after only imperfectly in song and lore.

~ ~ ~

By the Seven Words of the Ancient One, may our song be true and full of light; may our hearts reflect the All and the One without distortion or loss of meaning.

— Brihas

Last of the Lions

10. Conception

Ahanatar had awoken first that morning. The memory of the night washed over him like the terrifying flood of a nightmare. Shuddering, he sat up and looked around the cavern. Suka was still gone — did he spend the entire night misleading the enemy?

Ahanatar inspected Adrian's bandage and found it expertly done. Then he knelt by Nediva and flowed his spirit into her trance of health. She was more advanced than he had thought: her wound was nearly healed. For an hour, as their minds flowed together through the macrocosm, he knelt with his head bowed, touching her feet.

With a languid suspiration, her eyes fluttered open; she smiled in purest innocence and perfect wholeness. Ahanatar for the first time saw the Lowlands as they were in the springtime of Gurion. But then anamnesis smote her, a killing frost that shriveled her heart as she remembered the depth of her permanent loss.

"Aland." Her one word expressed as much feeling as her untarnished spirit could bear — lost treasures of unrealized happiness, perfect jewels of love forever denied.

"Yes. He is lost." Ahanatar was still floating through the Ascendant One, but the changes in Nediva were hammering at him like physical blows.

"And Myrhna." She turned her face from him and wept bitterly.

He could practically hear the shutters slamming closed on the windows of her soul.

A little while longer she entertained her sorrows, adding them to her crystal storeroom of precious memory: diaphanous chalice-moments of transcendental beauty, bittersweet adamantine crowns of supernal agony, the sundered threads of lost dreams and shattered hopes woven into the filigree warp and woof of if-and-when. Finally she stood, straightened her hair and said purposefully, "Come, Gemstone. We must seek our Orah."

~ ~ ~

"You loved him well?" They had walked together for two hours before Ahanatar felt sufficiently dispassionate to test her.

"He was a brother to me. Perhaps one day he would have been more. Which other could equal him? Never was he embittered by the gall of our hard times. Empathic harmony was his distinguishing quality. And to end so..." She ended with a bottomless shiver, "No, Starlord, I cannot relish such talk. Speak of something more joyous — out of Riversland all together, if you have the knowledge. Look! There! Is that not his mark?"

"Most certainly. The hawthorn still rejoices at his touch — the Azure Lord passed here during the night.

"I cannot travel far in my speech: I know other continents only indirectly. But the Uplands are perhaps dissimilar enough for your need. Let me tell you of Zuriel, my mentor. Save for Evana, he is the most perfected person I have known. In troth, I hold him to be one of the Seven, journeying among mankind to aid us in Oath-mastery." He spoke fervently, expressing a belief he had never before voiced.

Nediva looked at him with a strange intensity of passion, "If only I could believe that..." She paused for an inward moment, then smiled and continued, "Yes, tell me of him. How came you to him? I have heard it is rare for the Tribe of the Tree to accept one not of their own as a student."

"It is a scarce boon. Brihas commanded that in any generation one only not of their house could receive their knowledge. The First Oathmaster spent his final years at the Founding Lake, as you know... No? I am surprised that knowledge has passed from the Lowlands."

"It may not have. For many years I have devoted myself wholly to my Vow and have had small ear for any teachings not of my own school. I do know that our first Oathmaster, Matri, visited the Founding Lake as her final act in Gurion."

"The simple truth is that all the ten Oathmasters did so, my Lady... Cautiously! Here the enemy crossed the Azure Lord's path — within the hour."

"Yes. So you imply the full knowledge of the Ten Vows is held by the Tribe of the Tree, not just Shraddha's teachings?"

"Exactly. Among them alone was full knowledge of the Ten given. Zuriel is the last of a line descended directly from Brihas. Every subsequent Oathmaster has, before he entered the Lake for the last time, placed his hands on his most developed student, passing on the priceless gift of prescience as well as the twenty-seven lesser perfections. Thus I hold Zuriel to be the direct embodiment of all the Oathmasters, in perfect descent of consciousness; therefore he is a full expression of one of the Seven. It is even said that he wrestled with Valin as a young man and survived to return to his people. I can hardly believe how fortunate I am to have lived with him for so many years."

"How were you chosen?" Ahanatar's words were proving a useful anodyne. She felt the pain being slowly masked.

"I was marked before my birth by Zuriel's master, Aranel. He told my mother her firstborn was elected to be the Tree Tribe's one Outsider for this generation. When I was seven, she sent me to Zuriel. Were it not for Evana, how could I have left him? And until I met Orah, there was good cause to question my intuitive belief that I should come; but now I have no doubts —"

"Hold! Just ahead! Feel it?" Her eyes alternated rapidly between bright hope and gray fear.

"Silence in the forest. He is there! But — surrounded by Redhawks! Let us climb here; perhaps our eyes will explain this mystery."

Together they walked up the same ridge as would Adrian an hour later, then looked down on the peculiar sight of the Etan confronting the Arelai legion.

"Ah, no!" whispered Nediva with a deep indigo agony. "He hopes to deal honorably with the Arelai. But it can never be so. By the Ten! They have been fouled by Asur blood! I —"

Whirling around, Ahanatar whipped out his sword and brandished it toward the brush.

Elid came from the forest, transmuting their amazement to a stunned silence with a simple wave of his hand. He led them back down the ridge, far enough to speak without danger of being heard.

The Sun Lord explained, "The eye of the hurricane is calm. My fires do not touch me. I have followed you since my way was clear. Tell me of the others."

"The Outlander is as you have seen," answered Ahanatar heavily. "Brihas alone knows his mind."

"That much I fathom," said Nediva. "He falls into the trap that snared Evana, trusting where no trust is due."

"Perhaps his purpose is different," said Elid thoughtfully, "or perhaps he has greater skill than his sister, even though he is without memory. The test of that awaits now the solstice, it seems... The Lions? And my cousin?"

"Aland was slain protecting us. Kanya fell shortly after. Tejan sacrificed himself that we might live. The 'Hawks captain was a lorewarden — the Fire Lord fought madly with him, blinded by his grief for Kanya's loss, and destroyed him." Elid covered his eyes as Ahanatar continued, "Adrian was wounded in the breast, just here, at the same moment that Aland was slain. He rests now under the care of the Serpent Suka, 'warden of all living things."

The Sun Lord forced himself to self-mastery and replied, "This at least is good; I have heard of Suka's skill. Any news of Jyot?"

"The news of Jyot is here," the Lightning Lord said with a sour smile as he came toward them through the scrub.

Ahanatar and Nediva clutched their sword hilts but, finding no clear reason for their distrust, argued down their feelings. Elid greeted him warmly as they exchanged histories, then said, "It is good that we are four: now everything needful can be done. I will journey southward to the army to deliver news of Gurion's bereavement and offer counsel. But someone should pace these 'Hawks in the unlikely chance their intention is different than we believe. Nediva and Ahanatar?"

"Never would I do else, while he lives," declared the Starlord. Nediva echoed him passionately, almost pyretically.

Elid glanced at her quizzically, more than half intuiting her desire, then continued, "And Jyot, could you seek Adrian and help him homeward?"

"I doubt that he will be happy to abandon this quest. But I will make the attempt to send him home," he answered.

Nediva, remembering a serpent she had once slain, unconsciously hissed; Ahanatar, thinking with deep melancholy of all the raiment of the heavens that no longer shared its light with Martanda, sighed deeply. Far away, a lion roared once; a tense silence settled over the forest.

But Elid missed (from absorption in his personal grief) or ignored (from years of shared responsibility) these portents. Concluding his assignments were correct, he said, "It is well; let us begin," and strode away southward. Now he could be alone to let the dark agony flow through him.

Jyot with a private smile clarified the direction from Ahanatar and headed toward the east.

"Come," said Nediva, attributing her discomfort to the loss of Aland, "let us witness the Outlander until we can follow. No, that ridge is not only higher but better protected, is it not?"

~ ~ ~

Thus it was that the Star and Horse Lords alone of Orah's companions witnessed Adrian's end. They heard the conflict, but did not know who was involved until he entered the river. As they watched in mute horror, the life of Gurion's last Lion consummated like the death of a meteor.

Through his clenched teeth, Ahanatar repeated until it became a dirge, "They will pay for this. They will pay." Now had he learned full well the debility of the western tribes.

But Nediva was far too damaged to speak: she held her knees as she rocked back and forth, crying her grief to the stained soil of Riversland.

~ ~ ~

That night was clear and cold. They stared at the damaged heavens from their secluded hollow, discussing whether they should risk a small fire. Finally they decided not, embracing for warmth instead. Nediva was at first surprised, but then responded with spirit to Ahanatar's tentative advances. Neither had experienced physical love before, but it proved no difficult task. Nevertheless, their sharing was ambivalent. The Horse Lord was highly separated in herself; in her grief, she joined with him from repudiation and doubt rather than affirmation. And the Gemstone was unconsciously seeking to check the steadily advancing decay of his spirit. Was life truly so much more evil than he had believed? Was the loss of his companions his fault alone? Had he betrayed them all by not speaking Zuriel's warning?

~ ~ ~

At dawn they set forth again, flanking the Arelai to the south. As they cleared a small rise, both deeply preoccupied with the memory of the previous night, two red feathered arrows raced toward them. One sped by Nediva like a harbinger of doom, but the other ended its flight securely in Ahanatar's midriff.

The Horse Lord screamed and knelt by him, cradling his head in her lap. "Nediva," he coughed as a trickle of blood ran from the corner of his mouth, "I — flee — army — Orah..." Then he fainted.

She began to merge her spirit into him, but rough hands dragged her away from him. Kicking, sobbing, she screamed, "No! Let me go! He's *dying!"*

Her half dozen captors laughed harshly as one said caustically, "They normally do with our shafts in their guts."

Another, leaning over the Starlord with drawn blade, said, "Finish him, sir?"

The first nodded, ignoring Nediva's cries, but at the last instant he recanted, "No, hold! That cannot be a Lowlander. Explain, woman."

"He — he is Ahanatar, a Lord of the Star and Gemstones," she sobbed, her mind racing. "Zuriel — Zuriel, Lord of the World Tree Vanas, sends him as ambassador to Arel."

"You speak truly?"

"Examine his shield, his sword! They will not belie me."

"Blast it! The witch is right. Narim, Banyrn, run to the legion for a litter. Nagym, Mantor, resume the flank. Confound it, Hern! *Let her go!"* He bent to his work but then looked back up at her and said, "If you lie, woman, I will personally bury you at the solstice."

Ignoring him, she knelt again beside Ahanatar. "You have astringent?"

The captain did not seem particularly evil, but was peculiarly intent and doubtless a powerful warrior. The thought of fighting them flitted through her mind, but she quickly abandoned it as impossible with the Gemstone so.

"Our travel mead will cauterize," he answered, then began the operation. "Hern, break that. No! There. Good. Now, turn him. Yes, out the back, good. Now, help me, pull! Again! Good.

"Blast it, look at the shaft. Must have sliced him about as badly as it could. A pity our 'warden fell. Heal him by noon. Hern, the mead. There. Again. Now the cloth. Good. There. Tighter. Right. Bind it. Good, Hern. That's it. Now we'll rest him 'til the litter comes."

"He must not be moved!"

"Woman! No one of Arel, and I mean not even those on their deathbeds, no one ever misses the Solstice Celebration. We take him when the litter comes. Understood?"

She bit her lip to cut short her protests, but thought, *How can I aid him if I have to keep moving? But I will try.* And she let her mind flow into his ruined body, giving, pouring life into life, sharing freely everything of her soul that he might yet live.

11. The Solstice Dances

Orah did not abandon his companions until the last vestige of opacity had vanished in all of them. As the grief of their inevitable loss flowed through him, he slipped out of the pipe past Aland and wandered off westward through the woods. Was he thus fated to lose everyone he loved? How much of this was artificially constructed by Jessie-Evana, how much was destiny? Could nothing be done to alter these dreams before they degenerated into nightmares?

About the time Suka aided Ahanatar, the Etan could walk no more: pain of loss and pain of ignorance permeated him like the last anguished hope of one with terminal disease. His soul ashes, he sat unmoving through that long night, his head buried deep in his palms.

But an hour before dawn, a small woodland creature, a chipmunk, scampered early from her burrow near Orah's feet. The Etan's senses were opened: he heard the songbirds hymning their joy in life and by Swayam! he *knew* Gurion might yet survive. He did not know if he had the ability to succeed, but if he could! Then perhaps payment at least would be had for his friends' loss.

Orah walked as invisibly as a shadow into the Arelai camp and sat facing the dawn. A flash of intuition burst through him from the volcanic rock beneath his feet; he remembered the Sun Dance of One Step. Cathedraling his hands, he gazed toward the east.

The first to awaken stared for a full thirty seconds before his alarm woke the others. Within moments, the Arelai seemed so many ants the Etan had disturbed with a rock.

They clustered around him with swords, spears, drawn arrows; but no one spoke to him until their angry and very surprised colonel came and demanded, "Who, what are you?" The Outlander made no reply: he was sitting with half-opened eyelids, staring at the sun.

He might have been a statue: he was not breathing, there was no pulse.

"A corpse! Who set this here? Move it! Full report in five minutes." And the colonel stalked back to his staff meeting. But one, then two, then half a dozen could not so much as lift the Etan's hand. The second time the colonel came that morning, his mood was no better. But Orah remained as immovable as if he were a steel statue with foundation five leagues below ground. The warriors ate their morning meal, sitting around quietly, staring at him. The guards drifted in after their shifts and joined them; none replaced them. A few suggested they rebegin their march, but the colonel ignored them to continue gazing at the Outlander.

The entire morning drifted past in this way. The Arelai periodically subjected the Etan to various experiments, but more often they simply stared at him with wonder, watching spell-bound as his eyes followed the sun to its zenith.

Just as Adrian crawled up the ridge, the sun had climbed so high that Orah would have had to turn his head to continue to dance with it.

"I have discovered a family with sixteen children," he began abruptly in melodious and perfect Arelai-san, native tongue of the Redhawk nation.

Absolute silence covered the camp like fog while the Arelai pondered their surprise that a living statue could speak. Too long had they lived without wonder; little now indeed possessed the power to move them. This the Etan intuited sadly as he continued, "All the sixteen were precious in their own right; each matured uniquely and beautifully. Two died from a foreign disease; one, the strongest, was so twisted by the same illness that he violently murdered his eldest brother and fairest sister. What punishment, men and women of Arel, should a just father and compassionate mother impose on this diseased child?"

The colonel stared at him blankly and said, "Ah, Azure Outlander, we have heard of you and wish to, ah, *honor* you at our Solstice Celebration. Will you come with us?"

"Another family was wealthy," continued Orah as if hearing nothing. "But their relatives through no fault of their own were so indigent they could barely sustain their lives. Yet were they pious and humble and did not beg from their affluent cousins, who could have raised their estate easily without self-harm, yet refused to do so. Which family, bearer of the sanguine hawk, do the powers of life favor?"

"It appears we have captured a philosopher. Wherein lies the question? The reality you describe shouts the answer — the wealthy family is the more favored. Now please answer me — will you freely accompany us for the glory of Arel's great god Hcolom?"

"A third tale I tell you, bold Arelai." Orah was growing discouraged: one or two only had evidenced even the slightest response. Still he felt he should again try: certainly their common humanity deserved no less. And how else could he comprehend the extent of their disease?

"A man came to a new world. Some greeted him with love, some with suspicion, some with greed, some with anger. Some even tried to kill him. What accounting should that man give to those who sent him? Should he speak of the good and just, or of the evil? Travel carefully here, for there is quicksand and lurking death."

Exasperated, the colonel turned to his captains and said, "What can we say? Will he come or not?" Before any could answer, Adrian's shout tore through the air; the camp broke into activity as if they were awakened from a dream. A score grabbed their weapons and raced up the ridge.

Sighing, Orah stood and said, "Shall we go? The solstice approaches."

The colonel blinked at him once, twice, then gave the orders to break camp.

~ ~ ~

The legion reached the Sacrificial Grounds one day in advance of the solstice. The Etan had not spoken again to the Arelai during their journey together: he accepted their food and directions, but always walked before them. Any chance observer would certainly have been of the opinion that he led them into the heart of Arel.

He spoke now only to ask which of the pavilions was to be his. The phalanx which had guarded him since he joined them directed him to a small gray-blue tent that bordered the burial grounds. With one look at that scene of horror, Orah's will crystallized into its final form: never had he seen a more complete corruption of the earthbreath. No more did he have even faint doubt as to his intention.

Yet once that afternoon, he did waver briefly. He was sitting quietly, conserving, planning the direction he would attempt to move the forces of life on the morrow, when he heard children gaily laughing. Remembering the careless innocence of Odelia, a smile tickled his heart as he opened his entryway. But what awaited him there transmuted his blood to ice, for nearly two dozen children were watching with glee as three of them held a kitten to a tree and nailed its paws to the trunk.

He seized the nearest Arelan guard by the shoulders, lifted him fully off the ground, shook him as if he were a leaf and demanded, "Why? Why don't you stop this?"

"Stop, stop what?" the warrior chattered through his teeth. "That? But they are learning the way of life. It makes my heart glad to see them enjoying themselves."

Orah dropped him to the ground, adding this as the latest of many logs to the raging fire in his breast, molding it into the Dance of Wrath he ached to manifest yet refused to begin. Hoarding every impulse of his energy lest it fail to achieve its fullest result, the Lord from Etan awaited the proper instant.

Holding back his anger, he ordered the guard calmly, "Remove that kitten from the tree or I will break your neck. And then send me someone with deep knowledge of Arel. My understanding of your people is incomplete."

~ ~ ~

An older man, dressed in the tight-fitting grays common among the rulers of Arel, came to him that evening and introduced himself as a lorewarden of Hcolom, Yarin by name. He seemed intelligent and certainly possessed an ability to wield the earthbreath, but in ways far removed from the Etan's.

"Your knowledge is great of Arel?" Something about Yarin's appearance was making him most uncomfortable. What was it?

"I am one of the Syner of Sixteen, rulers of the land."

"I want to know why you persecute Gurion." That was it — the lorewarden looked only at his mouth, never at his eyes.

"We do not. We have perfected our vow — we do not grasp; we have no desire for their lands, wealth, or wives."

"Yet decade after decade you make war." Where lay logic in Riversland?

"Listen, Outlander. We have perfected the Oath of Non-grasping. We therefore possess knowledge of the past and future and of distant places. Thus have we seen Riversland; thus have we known the world. Barek teems with powers none may resist. Our lives are tolerated merely. As long as we are non-offensive and perhaps amusing, we are spared. Arel alone saves Gurion from destruction! The fire that consumed the Eagles and the Anti-life that devoured the Horses are but two of the Asurs' numberless weapons. We have discovered this in our Syner! We have seen! We know! Maramel this day dies because it dared oppose Barek. Even the firmament, Outlander! Even the stars fall before the immortal emperor Valin! How could we hope to answer such force? So we make war to entertain the north. Some die, but the largest part of Gurion lives! Can you not see this as good?"

"I do not accept that there are no alternatives." Orah could almost understand how children of such a philosophy would torment helpless beasts and how their parents would murder innocent villages. "Despair wears many guises, Yarin. I believe you have been lied to or perceive somehow wrongly. If you opposed Barek, you would be aided."

"How? The Seamen are devoured because they dared resist the Asurs. And the Mountain Staff Lords are either defeated or so crippled by their mysticism they have become wholly ineffectual. The foreign continents have been subservient for too long, first to Gurion, then to Maramel, now to Barek, to help us, even if they had the knowledge or skill, which I doubt. What other powers are there?"

"Etan," began Orah, but he wondered as he spoke if it were a real thought. He believed that his brothers and sisters really did know nothing of the rest of Martanda; but it was inconceivable that Swayam could be wholly unaware of the condition of their adopted world. Or was it? For how many centuries or even millennia had the Father looked inward, enjoying his self-created paradise, wholly absorbed and forgetful of any other knowing? Orah did not remember. He was beginning to wonder if he even wished to remember.

Yarin laughed, a harsh cachinnation that might have been born from — or attempted to mask — despair, and replied, "I know nothing of your hidden city. Your Evana said much the same; but our Syner subjected the fate of your homeland to our Vision of Knowing and found its future effect on Martanda as nil as its past. Either it will be destroyed or pass in some other way. But it will never help us. Etan *will* fall."

"Is there then no choice in your fateful viewing?" How much was truth, how much Valin-inspired illusion?

"There remain but two paths, Outlander. In one, the Asur Emperor assumes control of Martanda and rules with a firm hand. Those who aid him survive; the majority live comfortably. Some, in fact, live very well indeed. Who would not have chosen a better ruler? But we have no alternative. For the other path — aid to you, Azure Lord — leads in one direction only: to the certain destruction of Martanda."

~ ~ ~

A full minute passed before Orah gathered his shocked mind together for another attempt, "Even if what you say represents truth, Yarin, still I would question if honorable death is not preferable to slavery." It was not a particularly cunning answer. How could he perceive reality in this lorewarden? That his Syner had read possible futures Orah did not doubt, but he was certain its long treachery had colored its vision. How could Swayam remain inactive and create no better solutions? It was inconceivable. If only he were shown the forces at work in Martanda, he would not hesitate. Unless... unless there was something in the persistent gaps in Orah's memory that made that future impossible.

The Etan killed the thought with anger and ordered Yarin to leave him, brusquely denying the offer of Arelai entertainment.

~ ~ ~

Orah stood in his entryway and stared at the heavens. Nearly a quarter of the constellations were damaged in one way or another. Some were wholly missing; others had but one or two of their weaker suns remaining. Half of Martanda's sister planets had also vanished. *How? How can this be possible? Where does their light go?* he thought, questing upward with his senses, seeking knowledge of Valin's machinations, offering hope and love to the diminished sky. He felt the answer must be as obvious as life itself, but the firmament made no reply he could understand.

Yet just before the first gray of dawn began to cloak her remaining children, a different thought was revealed. The Etan had been waiting for Kali, Martanda's darkest and smallest moon, to rise. She had always been his favorite; he made it his habit to bow mentally before her whenever she was visible. But today she was preceded over the horizon by Kanaan-dora.

Orah stared in wonder and joy, for the planet had been invisible for a fortnight. "Not absolute!" he cried aloud as the tears played down his cheeks. "Valin's hold is not perfected! Kanaan-dora has escaped! What supernal power has worked to free her? Ah, by Swayam's Seven, Evana spoke truly. There *is* hope!"

~ ~ ~

The Arelai came for him at dawn. Nine ranks of spear and swordsmen lined the route from his tent to the sacrificial bethel; they were fully armed, ready to thwart any wayward tendencies in their chosen offering. But the Lord of Etan walked through them with a brisk step and cheerful heart, anticipating the sunrise and the fulfillment of his intention.

Yarin and seven other lorewardens were already at work, weaving their peculiar distortions of power over the pit, generating a multi-colored array dominated by red and black. Eight women dressed in flowing raven-colored robes and bearing full wicker baskets of earth stood with them; behind were at least five score ranks similarly laden. Beyond these, stretching for several leagues, were the whole of the Arelai, silently waiting.

The pit was deep, laboriously carved from volcanic rock in the form of a perfect cube. The Etan was directed to descend a steep stairway, lined with black igneous stone. As soon as his foot touched the first step, the lorewardens began a new chant; at once a huge and misshapen verdigris demon with sanguine eyes and vicious dripping fangs appeared over their arching beams of light. "A Rakshasa," murmured Orah, not surprised, yet abstractly wondering how he knew of the being's kind.

As he started down and the Arelai chanted, "Hcolom, hai! Hcolom, hai!" the Rakshasa waxed stronger and larger. The Etan stood quietly at the base of the pit while the Syner hymned their god, heralding the rising sun. When the first sunlight touched the ground at his feet, the Arelai women began to throw their baskets of earth upon him.

Raising his arms, he breathed in the sun's power, then allowed his feet to absorb the blasphemous agony the rocks had endured for centuries. As he did so, he began to move, to dance, to return a hundredfold his sympathetic passion. Within moments, the dust from his syncopation was spiraling amber upward into the morning air.

One of the lorewardens broke his hymn to cry, "Look! The Outlander fights Hcolom!" More fiercely chanted the Syner as Orah's serpentine wreathing dust manifested a golden lion. The Rakshasa leaped on his congealed earthbreath and wrestled with it. More and more quickly the Arelai emptied their baskets; faster and faster whirled the Azure Lord; higher and ever higher twisted his vortex of dust.

At last he judged it high enough; slowing his spin he summoned the far winds of Martanda. From the Mara Sea to the west came Strength and Health, mighty tempests; from the frozen north roared Bitter and Courageous, winter's long arms; from the south he drew in Spring's Balm and Summer's Pestilence; from the east blasted Death and Youth. The Wind Lords of Martanda tore into his mushrooming tower, sending it as hurricane throughout Arel.

~ ~ ~

The Azure Lord of Etan sat and wept as he saw the result of his labor. Around him everywhere, all the Arelai — every man, every woman, every child, even every beast — were writhing helplessly on the ground, clutching their eyes, screaming.

~ ~ ~

A thump behind him followed by a vile cursing informed him one of the lorewardens had fallen into the pit.

It was Yarin. The Etan smiled bitterly and said, "You see. There *are* alternatives, Yarin."

"You, you *blasphemer!* If I could see through this burning dust I'd have Hcolom swallow you —"

"There is no more dust, Arelan: the sky is clear. And Hcolom is dead, rent by Gurion itself. Thus has your evil returned to you. All of you — everyone of the Arelai, from your lowest domesticated beast to your highest Lord, excepting only your slaves — all have reaped the reward of your treachery. The sense ruled by the sun, that of sight, has been stripped from you, from all of you. Unalterable will this doom be until you march with the United Tribes of Gurion against Barek.

"For this I tell you truly! Your Vision of Knowing has been betrayed by Valin. The present you perceive may be real, but the future is not determined, not while my breath nor that of the least of my people endures. For of Etan, this much have I remembered: my father's name means 'The Lord of Fate' — the power of changing time was bequeathed him by his birth."

"How long?" moaned Yarin, rubbing his eyes as if he wished to erase them."How long until we can see again?"

"Four years. Rather, by the spring equinox of the fourth year. This much time may pass before the call comes. If it comes at all. But you must inform the other tribes that they may prepare. For you spoke truly that you were the lesser evil."

"They will not listen. I am a lorewarden of Arel, member of the Syner. We have made war on them for more than thirty years. They will slaughter us in our helplessness."

"You know them not if you think a people led by Amina and Eliora could harm you now. No, they will listen. Tell them first of Adrian — tell them how your insatiable desire murdered the last scion of your one-time liege lords. Then repeat my words. They will believe you; they will prepare for my summons."

~ ~ ~

The Lord of Etan turned from Yarin and climbed out of the pit; everywhere the Arelai were lamenting and wailing. But he had eyes only for his bitter memories of those who had aided him and died for their trouble, inculpable children whose only error had been to try to help him — him! Amnesiac reflection of Etan's glory, who should have been able to save them. *Cahlil! Odelia! Elid! Ahanatar! Nediva! Tejan! Kanya! Aland! Adrian, ah, Adrian! Why has your love thus torn me?*

The Azure Lord walked in desolation out of the Sacrificial Grounds, heading toward the Coastal Range and Maramel, hoping to discover in the Sea Kingdom the elusive means to restore his heart.

~ ~ ~

He had not gone far when he felt someone following him. He flirted with the idea of concealing himself, but abandoned it as opposed to Evana's desire. Instead, he climbed a little rounded knoll that from similarity almost triggered a memory of the hill Ezera, then stood in plain view, staring westward toward the ruin of the Sea Kingdom.

The Etan did not have to wait long: the two pursuing him ran quickly up to him. He turned to see what final challenges Gurion would bring to him; it took the space of three breaths for his mind to believe what his senses told him: "Ahanatar! Nediva!"

He threw his arms around them and crushed them to him as the Starlord laughed, "The Eldest told us to guard you. And guard you we shall, no matter how often you try to escape us, until we die." His voice ran through Orah like music from a different world.

"My — my *friends!* I thought you all — you were faded! Transparent! You should be dead!"

"Almost we were," laughed Nediva in the lovely descant he had thought lost for all time. "I have felt such pain that I almost preferred death. My beloved Myrhna saved me from my end in that foul pipe, for she thrust her breast forward to catch the spear marked for me. She freely gave her blood that I might live. And I learned from her sacrifice and shared my diaphanous breath with Ahanatar to return him from his doom. But is our tale not weak compared with yours? What did you do to the Redhawks? Never have I beheld such a pathetic people."

"Little. I showed them themselves; they could not bear such truth and blinded themselves," Orah began, but then his face distorted to hideous death as the full weight of the awful truth he had just learned washed through him. As the agony writhed in him, he cried, "No! You were transparent but survived! No! Aland! Adrian! What have I done! Of course there can be no certainties in this world! I could have, should have saved you! No!" His voice became a scream of horror as Nediva and Ahanatar looked on, dismayed and terrified, unwilling witnesses to his despair.

For this dance, the Etan did not stand in a place made powerful by other humans, nor did he draw power from Nature, from the earth or the heavens. Instead, Orah created from within himself in a rhythmical, almost mechanical outpouring of his raging soul. The

Azure Lord stamped his pattern with violence into the passive soil, forward, backward, forward, while his arms folded and unfolded as if he were a Valin machine gone mad, tearing its heart out into the afternoon.

Nediva threw her hands over her eyes and screamed; faster and more furiously came the Etan's cadence. Ahanatar held her tightly and tried to calm her, though he felt he must flee himself lest surely he go mad; the Outlander's dance increased in speed and savagery of passion. How could the Starlord bear more and live? Yet the hypnotic frenzy increased, smashing through him, distorting and rending his spirit until he collapsed at last, following Nediva into dark oblivion.

The ambient air could endure little more than had Ahanatar. Wild lightning erupted around the tortured Etan; from nowhere a massive thundercloud exploded overhead in a violent cataclysm of dark rain and howling wind.

Still the power increased, spiraling upward toward a maelstrom of destruction as the Azure Lord danced and danced to ease the breaking of his heart; yet still the pain of loss and agony of despair grew faster and could not be abated or appeased.

The last light of the dying sun shafted a single ray under his lightning storm. There was a lone white bird, a dove, nearly spent, yet struggling still northward toward him through the violated air.

With a shudder that sounded as if it were torn from the very bowels of Riversland, Orah stopped in mid-step, arms outstretched towards the clouds, every tortured muscle crying for release. His will was divided against itself, but his body could not endure the pressure and forced passage: the Azure Lord screamed, a scream that would have permanently maddened any human still conscious within his Circle of Power, a scream that could have been the summation of all the pain in Gurion since humans first walked there and were betrayed, a scream that tore the clouds from the sky and rent the earth in violent quakes as far as the Founding Lake, a scream that reached even to distant Etan and troubled his brethren in their golden halls — *Swayam for the first time wondered if his daughter might be right that the Enemy had not truly perished, wondered too if the Seven he had left to protect the world were properly performing their function* — a scream that began deeper than the vibrations of mountains and rose shrieking in intensity and pitch throughout and far beyond the auditory range, a scream that said simply, "ALTHEA!"

His final convulsion of grief threw him to his knees as he whispered, "Sister. Oh, beloved sister, Healer of Etan. Why?"

~ ~ ~

No human could have lived had they witnessed the whole of Orah's passion, but 'Ishtar wrote and passed to us that all the prides of the Southlands gathered to view the Etan Lord's final dance in Gurion. And their silver tears fell like rain for the passing of the Lion Lords of Gurion...

End of Part One:
GURION, THE CLAW OF THE HAWK

PART II

MARAMEL, THE LIMITS OF TECHNOLOGY

12. The Seamen's Forbidding

"I really don't see how this wall can be passed," said Nediva crossly. For the past seven days, she and Ahanatar and Orah had followed Maramel's Forbidding, seeking the passage Aland had described. They had found every landmark he had mentioned, but where the Eagle Highway passed through the energy field, the double-blinded doorway "fifty-seven paces to the north" was simply not there.

They had searched far north and south through the mountains, but returned each time to the summit of the pass. Now they were sitting on the ground where the doorway should have been. Ahanatar was facing the obstinate Forbidding; Nediva and the Outlander were opposite him, looking back over Arel.

"I still say they closed it because of the war," said the Starlord, wondering why she was so short-tempered lately. It seemed she couldn't speak without sharpness.

"Perhaps they no longer rule Maramel," said Orah with intuitive certainty, regretting his words almost before they passed his lips. They had failure enough without adding such a dismal thought. Still, hope now must be considered almost irrational folly: the lights that had warred over the Sea Kingdom had been absent since the solstice, an ominous normality more disturbing than the brilliant warfare of the preceding months. Did this caliginous silence mean he was too late to aid the Maralords? Was his chain of failure and inadequate success doomed to continue indefinitely?

His brooding silences had been long and deep since the Gurions rejoined him — he almost seemed a different man from the innocent amnesiac they had first known and loved. How permanently had the passing of the Lions changed him?

"Perhaps from the other side it could be opened," said Ahanatar, trying to disguise the unhappy changes in his friends with the only positive material at hand. He knew before he finished that the result was other than desired. Yet he continued, "If you were to pass through the Forbidding, surely you could divine its secret."

Orah turned eyes on him that would have held accusation had such an emotion been part of his nature. Was it truly come to this? He had avoided raising the idea himself, preferring to exhaust all other possibilities rather than risk the loss of his friends. For if the gate proved secure to them, he would have no choice but to leave them and continue on alone. He could spare no more time, had probably already waited far too long. "Can there be no alternatives to this cursed fate?" He did not know if he said that or just thought it.

"Can you truly pass that without harm?" shuddered Nediva, glancing over her shoulder at the iridescent wall, higher than the clouds, longer than Maramel. Why did humanity require such perversions? She sighed and turned back to gaze at Ahanatar with a peculiar mixture of love and repulsion, seeking solace if not an answer.

The Starlord looked at them both, perplexed, and began to comment that he had not the slightest doubt that Orah could succeed from the inside. But he choked on the first word as he stared past them toward the Forbidding. A circular opening was dilating exactly where Aland said the doorway should be!

Nediva jumped up, exclaiming, "Matri! You heard my prayer!" Orah was already ahead of her, racing toward the sea. But he stopped within ten strides of the wall, more astonished than had been Ahanatar: a youth of sixteen with skin the color of the midnight sky and dressed in the flamboyant scarlets and electric blues of Maramel ran screaming in fear or pain through the shimmering portal. Close behind him was a sphere of variegated silver metal, riding the air and flashing brilliant rays at a dozen floating featureless black cubes that responded in kind.

Nediva gagged from the smell of ozone and smoke. But she saw that the Maraboy was savagely burned over his entire body and ran to him, merging her mind toward his, leaving the others to deal with the war machines.

Though he had never seen the gorlems of Barek, Ahanatar had studied them with Zuriel and knew some of their secret commands. "Gorlemai! Barek-Valina Gorlemai! Chaim adir gozal kasim! Kasim!

A youth of sixteen ran screaming in fear
or pain through the shimmering portal

Amarid marhir gozal amarid, amarid!" This Orah understood to mean, "Valin's gorlems of Barek, noble birds of life, divide! Be non-rebellious; withdraw, perfect birds; be docile and obedient." The dozen sable cubes floated half a league above them and stopped firing.

The silver sphere raced to hover over the wounded Maraboy, lying unconscious in Nediva's arms, and bathed him with a gentle crimson light. Within moments, his wounds closed and healed; he slept.

Nediva looked up, bewildered. "I had only begun to touch him, when the energy from this creature of steel entered his spirit and cleansed him. What manner of being is this?"

Orah was also staring at it curiously, wondering how the earthbreath had been so strangely modified to create such a personage of metal.

"I am Kumbha of Maramel," intoned the silver sphere in a richly melodious contralto. It was speaking in Maratongue, which the Gurions understood with difficulty and the Etan perfectly.

"What are you?" questioned Orah as Nediva asked,

"How did you cure him?"

"I am Kumbha of Maramel. I protect this one."

Ahanatar tried his luck, "Have the gorlems violated the whole of the Sea Kingdom?"

"The Seachime Cathedral yet resists. And, we believe, Goldenhome. But our transmissions are blocked and we know not. The rest of Maramel is death."

"Who is this?" the Gemstone asked, indicating the Maraboy.

"Hamar."

"Son of Haman?" asked Nediva with surprise. "Why does he enter Gurion?"

"The same. He brings Haman's request for aid."

"Who is Haman?" asked Orah.

"The master," answered the sphere.

Nediva explained, "He is the hereditary ruler of Maramel south of the Gray, cousin of the High Maraking Marasad who rules at Goldenhome. Hamar is his eldest son. Can the Maralord's need be so urgent they would send such a one to ask of Gurion?"

"My Lady, it is," began Hamar, rising stiffly. But then he saw the Outlander and cried, "Ravi spoke truly! Our Redeemer comes!" He threw himself at the Etan's feet and kissed them after the fashion of the Maralords.

Orah looked down at him awkwardly, wondering what his response should be, wondering also if the prince's words truly implied that Evana-Jessie had passed through Maramel. If so, where was she now?

Hamar genuflected a moment more, then said, "Already her words bear fruit! You have saved my Protector and turned Valin's evil."

"No. The Starlord ordered the gorlems."

"Who is the Starlord? Your servant?"

"No, an equal, befriending me to his own disadvantage," Orah began.

But the Gurion interrupted him, "I am Ahanatar of the Star and Gemstones. I gained this knowledge of the gorlems from Zuriel of the World Tree."

"Much value I place on these knowings, Starlord. There are double blessings today. And this is?"

"Nediva, Horse Elder of Gurion, Maralord. Speak to us of your quest. What has befallen your people?"

"If you journey with me, your own eyes will reveal the truth more perfectly than my words. Simply put, the Asurs' science surpasses ours. They penetrated our shields and fell upon us, unprepared and unsuspecting." He paused as shadows of death played over his young face. Then he continued quietly, speaking thoughts close to his heart, "To our present shame, we have rested content with our technology while they continued to advance. We have for generations been inclined toward the artistic: we are sculptors of wood, bronze and marble and painters in oil. But the Asurs created violent tools of death and invaded us in force at the beginning of spring. Our Protectors fought bravely, but have been vastly outnumbered since the first. Those who survived have retreated to the Seachime Cathedral.

"Father sees no hope, but I believed Ravi and risked the passage. We set out seven days ago, five score Protectors and eight men in the Pride of the Sea, our finest dirigible. We were set upon by the gorlems almost as soon as we passed the Cathedral's shields. One by one I have seen my friends slain as our Protectors were destroyed. This one is the last to accompany me, last as she was the first; if it were not for your timely aid, her fate was certain. As was mine! You have earned my life's fidelity."

The Maraprince seemed on the verge of falling again before the Outlander, but Orah said swiftly, "Ah, let us not tarry — in a week's time, the forces of the enemy will have further concentrated. We should hurry."

"Well said!" cried Hamar. "Follow me!" He jumped up and ran toward the portal. The Protector Kumbha raced past him to precede them into Maramel. Ahanatar and Nediva followed at once, but the Etan halted before passing the Forbidding for a last look over Gurion. With a dispirited sigh for the losses and gains that made his passage there so ambivalent, he turned and stepped into the Sea Kingdom.

"Hold, Outlander!" cried a not unfamiliar voice from behind. Orah whirled with the word, "Adrian—?" half passing his lips. And for one sweet moment of hope, his eyes allowed his heart its perception. But then the running figure drew closer and the illusion born of sorrow was shattered.

"The Oathbreaker!" Orah hissed, the memory of Odelia's death raging in him once again. "Indeed, I shall hold! You owe me much."

"I owe you naught, Azure Lord. But I would accompany you into Maramel." The Oathbreaker still wore his soiled gray robe, but now he also carried a shiny staff that might be of a particularly knotty lignum vitae; on his back was an improbably large pack, filled to overflowing.

Orah was angry, yet not enough to miss the fact that after the Oathbreaker's uphill sprint, he was not even breathing hard. There was a depth here the Etan did not understand, a range of life (and death) larger than those universally accepted by the others of Gurion. With a sudden intuition that made his skin crawl under the pocket that contained his silver box, he recognized the old man as one of the missing keys to Riversland.

"Perhaps 'owe' is too strong a word, Oathbreaker. But I want to know why you did not speak plainly of Odelia when we could have saved it."

"I plainly told the Lion Elder his destiny; he chose to ignore me. And I did plainly say the village would perish if you did not act; yet you chose to stroll away with your short-lived companions. Fate is fate. Why bemoan it?" He looked past the Outlander at the Protector Kumbha following the others back into Gurion and snorted his contempt. "So the Maralords have grown so desperate as to copy the Asurs' perversions. Perhaps you are too late already."

"How dare this uncouth person criticize the Protectors?" cried Hamar with undisguised disdain. "Tell him of yourself," he ordered the sphere.

"We serve the Sea People. In life and health we do the manual labor to preserve their time for the arts. In war and disease we protect. Such is our meaning and law."

"Of what use such if the Vows are mastered?" asked the Oathbreaker, not expecting or receiving an answer from the Maraprince or the silver sphere.

"How can you speak of perfection in the Vows if you are an Oathbreaker?" asked Ahanatar with a strange mixture of curiosity, contempt, attraction, hatred.

"Who has not broken the Oaths," said Nediva as if she were reciting from a text. Then she added, "He may be one of the few truly honest men in Gurion." Something in this old man was much more vital than she had seen before. How could she have missed the authority concealed in those sable eyes? To be so deluded by the external was unworthy of her aspirations.

"Daughter, I humble myself before you. Few have so honored me in many years." He gave her a truly elegant half bow, not quite low enough for him to lose control of his pack.

"At least tell us your name," said the Starlord, insisting on knowledge of companions. He had sworn a mighty oath in Arel never again to be beguiled by the likes of Jyot.

"You may call me Abrihas," the Oathbreaker answered with an odd cackle, "for of all of them, I certainly broke Brihas' Oath the first."

"No," said the Etan, "there is more water in the well than you claim. Speak to me again, Soothsayer, if you would accompany us. Tell us what awaits us in Maramel."

Abrihas stared at him awhile, as if evaluating him, then said humbly, "Very well, Outlander." Kneeling on the ground, he drew out fifty wooden sticks from his pack. He put them on the ground, took one and set it aside, divided the rest, counted them, placed some aside, reunited the rest, divided them again.

"What is he doing?" whispered Ahanatar.

"It is an ancient oracle," Nediva whispered back. "It was common among the Eagles, but fell out of favor a century or more before their destruction. Odd the Oathbreaker knows it! It makes me wonder the more about him."

Abrihas finished his eighteenth swift division of the stalks, tied the fifty back together and replaced them in his pack as he exclaimed, "Thus! Part of Maramel at least shall live because you enter there, Outlander, at least until the fate of Martanda is determined. But the cost may be bewailed by some, for the price for your aid is exceedingly high. Greater, perhaps, than the tribute you exacted from Gurion."

Orah, ignoring most of that, asked, "And Etan?"

"By the Seven, I cannot undo your sisters' mapping! Most of your family will survive regardless." He looked away from the Azure Lord, unwilling or unable to endure his gaze.

"Tell me then who I am."

"You are unyielding!" Abrihas laughed with good humor. "How can I speak of such a thing? The Grandfather's Breath, I suppose; or a Dream of Narain. The Deathless Dancer of Etan, certainly; and a Lord Son of the Progenitor Swayam. The Seeker of the Fourth Child — that's good. The Original Man. The Bane and Boon of Martanda, of course. And of Valin, perhaps. Outlander. He who is Lost and Forever Found. The Dancer of Despair. He who Loses all that is Precious yet Preserves all that can be Preserved. Twin Lord of the Sixth Wheel. The Bearer of the Secret of Life.

"Lord of Etan, I would accompany you into Maramel!"

"For what reason?" asked Ahanatar as the Azure Lord contemplated these titles, particularly the last. What was in the silver box?

"I seek the Mountain Kingdom." Enough revealing for the present. The need in Maramel was more than any trial he had faced, yet he feared there was almost nothing he could do. At any rate, another persona was needed now. "I can be of good use. I am strong; I surmise your supplies from Arel are almost gone. I have enough here to feed five for a week or more. I will do no harm and may prove a powerful ally."

Ahanatar began to protest again as Hamar exclaimed, "How could such as you hope to pass through our ruined land!"

But the Etan interrupted them both, "I do not understand your sayings, Abrihas. Nor do I seek your company, although perchance I should. You may accompany us as you will. Now I think we had best hurry — I have come too late too often already in this tale of Riversland. Ahanatar, can you hold the gorlems?"

"I believe so," he answered, scowling still at the Oathbreaker, "unless an Asur with greater knowledge gives a higher command. After the Arelai, these seem like so many toys."

"If that is meant for humor, Gurion, you have much to learn," said Hamar grimly. "My desecrated land and murdered people cry in my breast unceasingly for vengeance."

"It may be we are not so very different after all, Maraprince. I apologize for my hasty words. The unknown seems less vivid than the experienced past. Forgive me."

"Accepted. And now let us hasten. Perhaps with your knowledge, we can return to the Cathedral while yet it stands." Hamar again led the foreigners into the Sea Kingdom.

After Abrihas passed the portal, Kumbha re-closed the Forbidding with a snap and crackle like lightning that caused Nediva to shudder at the memory of Adrian's death. *"Such knowings lead inevitably to destruction,"* she quoted Matri.

"'Unless wisdom is like the inner life of the seed,'" concluded Abrihas; she looked at him with doubt.

13. The Oathbreaker

The Coastal Range in Maramel was more verdant and lush than its eastern slopes in Arel. The pines were soon replaced by fir, cedar and hemlock; the ground cover became more dense. Hamar explained that the prevailing westerly winds precipitated more on the ocean-side slopes, leaving the Arel mountainsides semi-arid.

Orah ceased contemplating Abrihas' sayings with a firm shake of his head and asked, "Who is that Ravi you mentioned?"

Hamar was so startled that he stopped walking to stare at him. "I don't understand. You claim not to know your sister? Are you testing me?"

Ahanatar explained, "He does not know his people, Maraprince. He drank of the river we name the Lethe."

"That is the most grievous news I can even imagine!" replied Hamar, looking for the moment like a terrified child.

"It complicates," said Nediva, "but does not diminish his power. With one dance, he cured what the tribes of Gurion could not — the cancer of Arel. If Maramel can be aided, the Etan Lord will succeed."

"I would hear this tale of the Redhawks! A brighter world to the southeast can never be considered aught but auspicious."

The Star and Horse Lords told Hamar of Orah's dances in Gurion. As they finished, the path they were following rounded a small bend; a vista opened below them that moved all their hearts — verdant and cerulean, the coastal plain spread before them, running away from the mountains in smaller and smaller steps. Far to the west rose a single, mighty, radiant silver spire, surrounded around its center by heavy black lightning clouds.

"The Cathedral!" cried Nediva and Ahanatar. But Abrihas and Hamar gnashed their teeth in rage and fear, for the clouds around the ten league spire were composed entirely of Valin's gorlems, amassing for the final attack.

"The body of the Pride of the Sea is within a day's journey!" shouted Hamar, running ahead.

"Hold!" cried the Oathbreaker. "Look there!" A horde of gorlems was racing toward them, resembling nothing so much as a swarm of hornets. Slightly behind and above them was a much larger sable cube, apparently directing or coordinating the others.

"I should have reasoned thus! Your domesticated gorlems nevertheless transmitted to the enemy! And an Asur is with them! Ahanatar! Can you mold them?"

The answer was manifest before the Starlord could speak — the gorlems he had turned at the Forbidding fired at Kumbha in one intense carmine wave. The Protector fell to the ground like a rock, smoking, ruined. Hamar knelt by her, his tears flowing unchecked. Kumbha had been assigned to him at birth.

Abrihas leaned on his staff and stared at the advancing war machines, seeming to be either in a daze or concentrating. Then his knees buckled beneath him as if they had turned to water. He sat heavily, muttering something under his breath.

Ahanatar was meanwhile trying every word of Barek-san he knew — without the slightest effect. Orah also struggled to respond to them, but was also wholly failing. He could not understand where the One was hiding in them. The Protector Kumbha had been hard to understand, yet had at least been a modification or extension of principles he knew. But the gorlems were not, were absolutely sinister in their absence of any of the known powers of life, of the earthbreath.

Nediva stared with frightened and divided eyes at the men. And then, as sometimes happens when life changes rapidly, a precognitive intuition explained fully what it was inside that had been irritating her recently. She glanced at the Azure Lord in despair and found he was taking the time from his analysis of the enemy's war machines to look back at her with complete understanding. *How long has he known?* she thought as her emotions swirled uncontrollably through embarrassment, happiness, pride, sorrow, fear.

One of the gorlems floated down toward them and said in a harsh and guttural mechanical Maratongue, "I spare you only because you are not all of Maramel. How came you here?"

"Who are you?" asked Ahanatar in a halting Barek-san.

"The conqueror need not answer slaves. If you wish to live out the hour, I suggest you bow before my authority. And answer swiftly."

The main body of the gorlems would be over them in moments. Abrihas began a low moaning and, hunching up his knees, began rocking back and forth as if he were addled. But he looked sharply and steadily out of the corner of his eye at the Outlander.

The Starlord exhausted his command vocabulary for the third time and stopped speaking, leaving their only response Abrihas' sorrowful but nonsensical keening.

Orah focused his mind deeper and deeper into the essence that was the gorlems, seeking understanding. But continually he failed: at the center of their being where their spirit should have been, a gently shimmering veil of the earthbreath cloaking the One, there was only a dark no-thing, an Emptiness that absorbed every impulse he passed into it. Where was their meaning? How could they exist at all, let alone be created? Never in rock, tree or water had he seen such a vacuity. It was not similar to the transparency he had witnessed in Gurion, harbinger of death, but rather an external expression of absolute nihility. His soul shuddered to experience such a ghastly blasphemy, shuddered and withdrew into itself, chilled to its deepest core by such a hideous deformity.

And then the gorlems were all around them. The Asur's craft stayed high off, maintaining a discreet distance.

"Bhishaj," said Abrihas clearly in the middle of his meaningless lamentation, staring still at the Outlander.

The incongruity of the name of a Lord of Etan from the Oathbreaker fundamentally shook Orah's spirit. He looked back at Abrihas with confusion and then suddenly amazement, for the intuitive vision he had been using on the gorlems he at that moment turned onto the Oathbreaker. Abrihas was built of the same Emptiness as the war machines! But in the Oathbreaker the nothingness alternated with a normal pulsation of the earthbreath to create a spiral of force that passed through him, extending beyond vision upward. Orah stared at him in wonder as the Asur spoke again through the gorlem, "I grow impatient. Who are you and how came you through the shield wall into our Annexed Lands?"

The Etan turned his attention on the Asur, but it was immediately repelled by a force that was similar to the Emptiness of the gorlems, but active and far stronger — a violent repudiation of all that was good and healthy and alive, of the One itself. He felt physically assaulted. Once again he attempted to touch the Asur's being with his awareness; once more he was repulsed by a terrifying force of anti-life that made him almost nauseous. He sat heavily on the ground beside the Oathbreaker and said flatly, "Even Bhishaj could not cure *that.*"

"Perhaps not, Lord of Etan," replied Abrihas with a sincerity of expression that resonated Etan in Orah, "but he would surely try. As would Althea."

Orah stared at him again, trying to understand how the Oathbreaker knew him so intimately. But how could he? How could he possibly know of the Etanai?

Abrihas returned his stare for a few more seconds, then shrugged and said, "Ahanatar, what was it Zuriel said when he fought Valin?"

"That's it!" cried the Starlord, then shouted, "Gorlemai! Marid, marid! Nihilo mared! Valin mared! MARAD!"

"No!" screamed the Asur, but too late — the gorlems fell to the ground in flaming ruin like so many meteors. The Asur's craft spun on its axis and raced back westward.

"Ahanatar!" cried Abrihas, "Stop him! He will return with thousands!"

"I cannot! I have not the knowledge!"

"Curse it," said the Oathbreaker. Standing fluidly, he struck his staff to the ground. An effulgent flame shafted from it to the Asur's craft. Its shields vaporized; it exploded, a shrieking mass of protesting metal.

Abrihas, perceiving the danger to his plans from untimely revelation, wound a thin fiber of Emptiness into each of his companions' minds then exclaimed, "Good work, Gemstone!"

"So much for the moment," agreed Ahanatar, puzzled by the last few events. *Where had the Asur gone?*

"They will doubtless send more gorlems, reprogrammed and en masse, very soon," said the Oathbreaker calmly. "I suggest we move out of plain sight. Hamar, is there another route?"

"I won't leave Kumbha!"

"Don't be a fool! That thing is scrap metal! The fate of your land is here. Leave it!"

"I cannot! She can be repaired at the Cathedral! I did not know how much I cherish her." He was still kneeling by the fallen sphere, holding an extended manipulator with both hands.

Nediva came to him and gently stroked his hair. "Maralord, we need your guidance to reach the Seachime Cathedral and aid your people. You must help us; you know we have little time. If we are successful, you can return here and reclaim Kumbha. But if we fail, no one will ever try to heal her. The only certainty is that we must hurry."

He looked up through his blurred eyes into and beyond her auburn beauty. Finally he gave a curt nod and said, "Gurion teaches Maramel today. Follow me!" He jumped up and ran down the path.

Abrihas was after him at once, barely in front of Nediva. Ahanatar, somewhat heady from his triumph, followed them quickly. But the Outlander sat awhile, staring at the bent grass where the Oathbreaker had been sitting, thinking, *How can Emptiness exist?*

~ ~ ~

Hamar led them swiftly down a devious series of mountain trails, reaching a ruined village by sunset. The central structure was a single spire, surrounded by many once-comfortable homes of argent metal and clear glass, all destroyed. Countless melted Protectors were fallen everywhere. But the most devastating sight were the skeletons of all sizes, picked clean by the wild animals, scattered all over. The Asurs had spared none.

Hamar stood before the spire and said, "Hear me, Seachimes!" He waited a moment, then tried again, "Goldenhome! Answer!" Sighing, he explained, "Not just for worship. The spires gave us vision and hearing throughout Maramel. They were one of our finest inventions. Any villager could speak to the Cathedral or Goldenhome from here."

Orah pushed aside his feelings of impotent wrath and said grimly, "Why did Ravi permit this desecration?"

"She tried to warn us. But we would not listen: we trusted our time-honored wall. For two thousand years we have contained the

Asurs' ruinous aspirations. But our shields were proven ineffectual at the last, even as she prophesied.

"Ravi came from the south seven years ago, speaking her fears and foretelling your journey. Almost none believed her. She left us to go to the Maraking at Goldenhome six years ago, accompanied by a single Protector and one girl from Gurion, a daughter of the Doves."

"Cahlil's sister Chali!" exclaimed Nediva with a rush of hope that shook her heart in painful joy. "Where are they now?"

"I don't know. If they live still depends on the fate of northern Maramel. But I wouldn't be very hopeful: this village is not unique. The Asurs seek to extirpate the Maralords from the earth. I fear the Etan Lord is our final hope."

"What is that?" asked Orah, staring curiously at a small azure flame on the top of the spire.

"What?" asked Hamar impatiently, glancing at the spire. "That light? I don't know; some local totem, I suppose. But we have halted long enough here in the open; there is a cave nearby where we can spend the night."

"No. I *know* that is not of your land. I must see it. Look at it: have you ever seen anything like it? Did my sister Jessie pass through this village?" He gazed up at the spire, wondering how to reach the sign at its apex.

"Who? You mean Ravi? I don't know. No, you may be right: she may have placed it; it is not really a fire, is it? But what can you do? More gorlems will certainly come soon. How can you reach it? If we had a Protector..."

The Etan touched the small flame with his mind and it burned brighter. Once again he sent a vibrant impulse of earthbreath upward; the flame floated down to land on his upraised hand. As he gazed at it, feeling its essence, it danced on his palm, a brilliant but cool expression of coalesced beauty. If there was a manifest antithesis to the nullity of the gorlems, this was surely it: a purity of Life and Spirit that healed instantly the pain from his contact with the Emptiness. He longed to understand it, feeling there must be a message here for him alone. But he could not merge his spirit into it.

The Maraprince, growing more and more impatient, said, "We need to get out of the open..."

Sighing, Orah raised his hand to his left shoulder. The flame slid onto it and burned there gently, pulsing less strongly. Was it conserving its power to attempt communication later?

"Not one of your better days, is it, Outlander?" chuckled Abrihas softly.

"No, it isn't," responded Orah with sudden wrath. "But I want to know how you know of my brother Bhishaj and sister Althea."

"My Lord!" exclaimed Hamar, "we must be swift — the gorlems could be upon us any time. We must reach the cave before the gloaming —"

"Oh, anywhere off the road will do," commented the Oathbreaker off-handedly, "as long as no Protectors are with us. More of you would have survived had you followed Oathmaster Jamad and not so twisted the Oath-powers. It will be dark enough soon."

"How can you say such things? What is the source of your knowledge?" Hamar glared at him with dark displeasure.

"Yes," agreed Ahanatar, willingly joining their anger, "and explain please also how you knew of Valin's attack on Zuriel! The Tribe of the Tree does not share such knowledge; I in fact am one of the few who heard anything of the tale, and that was quite by accident."

"Accident?" chuckled Abrihas. "What's an accident? Does anything happen randomly in Narain's Dream? Ever?"

"I do not find it strange he can possess such prescience," said Nediva softly, counterpoising the wrath of her companions with a perfect tranquility. "Even the perverse Arelai professed such skill... Breaking one Oath does not necessarily imply failure in all." She alone had begun to perceive something of the true nature of Abrihas. Perhaps his illusions were less powerful against her innocence; perhaps he willingly decreased their power over her for reasons of his own.

But the Starlord was not to be so easily appeased and continued his attack, "And what did you mean when you said the Azure Lord demanded tribute from Gurion? He requested it neither in public nor private."

"I said he exacted tribute, not that he demanded it." Abrihas was grinning now, apparently thoroughly enjoying Ahanatar's rising fury.

"What are you talking about! Nothing was given him! Why are you here if you hate him?" Rationality was definitely no longer dominant.

"Surely you are laughing at me!" cried the Oathbreaker, guffawing himself uproariously. "Even Evana claimed the life of only one Lion Lord! While this Etan cost Gurion two! The last two available, I might add. The tribes should pray daily no more of their kind journey northward, they are so outrageously expensive."

Ahanatar was white with rage; he drew his sword and attacked Abrihas. But Orah grabbed his arm and said, "No, Gemstone! He speaks a harsh truth. But it is truth. But for me, Adrian and Aland and the others would still live."

"Never will I accept that," the Starlord panted through his clenched teeth; "it repudiates all I know of life."

"There is hope in that," chuckled Abrihas, looking as if he were on the verge of another laughing fit. But he thought better of it and instead followed Hamar, who had responded to the altercation by heading swiftly out of the village. Nediva was after him at once. Then came the Etan, talking earnestly to Ahanatar.

~ ~ ~

Orah asked Nediva to climb a small ridge with him and witness the rising of Gauri, Martanda's largest and whitest moon. The companions were short of Hamar's cave by an hour or so, but Abrihas had insisted so forcefully they should stop just outside the village that they had all capitulated. Even Ahanatar had at last begrudgingly nodded his assent.

The Oathbreaker had produced an ancient black pot from his pack, filled it with water and herbs, then secured it on a little tripod over a hastily-made campfire. Urging Hamar most carefully to keep the guard, he excused himself to catch a rabbit. The Starlord sat grumpily, staring at the flames, leaving Nediva and the Etan to their own devices.

The forest thinned at the top of the ridge; Gauri rose gloriously over the mountains, brilliantly silver, the more so in contrast to the veiled heavens. The scent of the moist forest was at once soothing and deeply unsettling to the Horse Elder. How many such glades had she known with Myrhna? Why was it necessary to lose love? She stared at Orah's magnificent beauty, gently revealed in Gauri's soft light, and said quietly, "How long have you known?"

"When I danced my grief for our fallen, a voice spoke to me of you and Ahanatar. I know you both better than I remember myself. But you must tell him."

"I am afraid —" she began but ended abruptly as the Starlord came up the ridge through the trees.

"I fear as well, Lady of the Horses," he said warmly, apparently forgiving or at least forgetting Abrihas for the moment. "If Maramel falls, how will Gurion endure these diabolic gorlems?" Nediva stared at him with confusion, Orah with compassion; neither spoke. The Gemstone shifted his weight uncomfortably, then blurted, "I beg pardon for following you, but I have vowed never to be apart from the Azure Lord while my breath lasts."

"No pardon need be requested where none is due. I asked Nediva here to see if she needed counsel."

"Then is my presence the more burdensome. Allow me to depart graciously." He gave a low bow and turned to go.

"No, Gemstone!" cried Nediva. "Stay with me. Here, take my hand. I need to tell you, tell you... Orah knows, but it is something I — I have hidden from you.

"Dearest Ahanatar, when the gorlems attacked Kumbha, the intuition flashed that you are the... the father of that which is growing in me." She ended in a rush and a flood of tears.

The Starlord held her tightly and said, "Nediva, Nediva! Why have you withheld this from me?"

"I feared you would send me back to Gurion. I could not bear the loneliness without you and Orah! Forgive me — my love weakened me."

"How could I condemn you? Rather should I beg your forgiveness. I have been most ungracious. Forgive me, I pray!"

~ ~ ~

The Etan left them to their sharing and sought out Abrihas. The Oathbreaker was sitting hunched over his pot, stirring the stew. His appearance was that of a simpleton, but Orah had learned to read him more deeply and said, "Your existence puzzles me more than everything else of Riversland."

Abrihas sighed, a low and mournful sound like the winter wind through a hemlock dying of time, and said, "Have you not mysteries enough without bothering a poor old beggar? That luminous flame on your shoulder could keep you for hours. Why seek to ruin my cooking?"

"Ravi who is Evana and Jessie passed this way and left it for me. That is enough of its meaning for my current need: although I do not understand it, I trust it implicitly and entirely. But you remain a question mark in Martanda, an unknown variable that possesses as much Emptiness as the gorlems! Yet in you it is tempered or molded by a display of the earthbreath more potent than any other I have met in Riversland. How can such a duality exist in you? Which is the dominant? Which is the truth?"

"*'Familiarity masks the Miraculous Behind a veil of Forgetfulness,'*" quoted Abrihas in a peculiar singsong that reverberated Etan in Orah.

"Yes, I remember the verse. Though how you could know 'Sravasa's wisdom only increases my doubt. Who are you, Abrihas? 'Oathbreaker' is no longer a sufficient title." Somewhere deep in his breast, he realized uncomfortably that he already knew the answer. Yet something — the Lethe? — blocked his intuitive knowledge and forced him to grapple with hopeless intellectual processes and inadequate language. Why could he not read and know the Oathbreaker's speech as he had with all others?

"In the First Days of Martanda," said Abrihas, doggedly stirring his stew and looking as if he were discussing the art of cooking, "there were some among the human race who possessed knowledge of the Beginning. But in this age few — even those dedicated to Oathmastery! — few indeed turn beyond the narrow confines of their senses to seek the universal solution, the abstract experience of the finest essence of the One. Even though that fundamental basis of all that lives is a far easier truth to grasp than any other, most are deluded by the common experience of their gross perceptions of pleasure and pain and look no further for Truth and Beauty.

"Look there, what do you see?" Abrihas raised his spoon and pointed at the moon Gauri.

Her light filtering gently through the trees was lovely, but what of that? "The fair moon, bringer of health and love."

"No! Look more closely. Use your Power of Knowing — *feel* with the earthbreath."

"Why! A Lady! Glorious!"

"Oathmaster Matri, purest and fairest of the Seven. And now?"

"A bird — a swan! How come these visions?"

"Narashamsa, floating on the universal ocean of the mind, whose two wings are consciousness and understanding, whose soul is man's highest aspiration and destiny. And now?"

"Impossible! It reflects Emptiness! Like the gorlems! No — no, more than they — a fullness of non-qualities. I begin to understand. In this sense, Emptiness is also a reflection of the One that underlies all of existence. And now it becomes Gauri again."

"Such is the art of vision, Etan Lord. Turn your power onto your sister's message; let me enjoy this simple pleasure of cooking. Dinner should be ready before long." He leaned over the pot and smelled his creation.

Going a little way off, Orah took the azure flame in his right hand and let his awareness enter it as he had with Gauri.

The flame divided and the lesser part took on the form of Ravi — Evana as expected, but an Evana who was wiser, closer to a being he knew he should recognize but could not. Was she trying to tell him something? He could not understand her gestures or expressions. Was she addressing someone not present? Suddenly he intuited that he was viewing the recording of an historical event — her speech to the ruined village, warning them of their doom. *Plain speech thus failed,* he thought wryly, thinking of Abrihas.

With the thought of the Oathbreaker, the vision changed: the background fire took on the form of the death of the village; Ravi became more and more refulgent and argent, transmuting at last into a brilliant sphere of silver and blue.

Surely Martanda itself, he thought; again the vision transformed. The burning village became a sable serpent, coiling around the world, strangling it in relentless coils of treachery and death.

Martanda was crushed by its inexorable strength; but the destruction rent the serpent: it writhed in the agony of death as the shards of the sphere cut through its flesh.

The fair moon, bringer of health and love

This scene of death changed into a vision of Emptiness and the earthbreath, dancing together in alternating rhythms. And then slowly, even majestically, it altered once more, into a form of this world of space and time. It was a flame no longer: Orah now held an emerald and crimson serpent, slightly longer than his arm. Its eyes burned with azure flames as it looked up at him. Was it trying to tell him something more? The Etan couldn't be sure.

He returned the serpent to his left shoulder; it coiled there, patiently waiting. Orah took the silver box from his pocket. He turned it over several times, touched it with his mind, felt for the hidden key. Suddenly he remembered it; the box fell open from a complex pattern of pressing. Inside was a vial of fluid, brilliant, iridescent. Almost he felt a thought enter him, but nothing came. He began Abrihas' viewing, but half a moment later a scream of terror wrenched him to his feet. Orah returned the vial to its box and the box to his robe as he raced up the ridge.

Nediva collided with him before he had taken twenty paces. She was hysterical; he could make no sense of her sub-verbal cries of horror. He passed her to Hamar, ordering him to remain with her; then he continued cautiously up the ridge. Why had Abrihas not come when she screamed? Where was Ahanatar?

The Starlord was exactly where Orah had left him, but was under vicious attack — his head, arms and torso were covered by hideous, writhing serpents; his legs were encased by rapidly growing vines.

Illusion, thought Orah, *it must be illusion.* He saw a gorlem, lying in ruin nearby, and theorized a possible sequence of events. But how to save the Gemstone? The Emptiness was strangling the Starlord, tormenting and burying him under a mockery of life. Where was Abrihas? How could he fight this desecration of existence?

From somewhere inside the captured Ahanatar came impulses of the earthbreath — the Gemstone was struggling still, using his limited knowledge of the Asur words of command to manipulate the Emptiness, but to no effect. There was less and less sign of the One in him.

Hamar came up to them, leading a still terrified but stabilized Nediva. "I should have thought of this!" cried the Maraprince.

"Thus do they un-make us where our Protectors are too mighty to breach. Alas for the Starlord!"

"There is no cure?" demanded the Etan, giving them but a modicum of his attention as he struggled to master the violating Emptiness. He only partly heard, "We have not discovered any," as he thrust his awareness deeper and deeper into Ahanatar. Yet he could gain no hold on the illusion; it was like wrestling with a nightmare within a nightmare where, waking, yet another nightmare is revealed — an endless labyrinth of deception and death. Somewhere deep inside was the spirit of the Starlord, a delicate expression of the One, fighting still, yet ever more weakly.

This thing is like an extension of what Valin must be, thought Orah, deeply frustrated. *Nearly unlimited in power, nearly infinite in space. But where is the connection? How can something in a specific space and time be connected to such a universal force of Nothingness? Where is the junction?* Further and further he forced his questing mind, ignoring the Emptiness, yet still the resolution eluded him. *I need help! Where is Abrihas? How can I dance this Evil to destruction? How can nothingness be destroyed? If not destroyed, contained? How? How to capture Shadow into form? Shadow? Shadow! By Narain's Dream! This is not Emptiness! This is a Rakshasa!* Not knowing how he had again recognized Hcolom's breed, he nevertheless knew the cure.

Slipping within the writhing chaos that had once been Ahanatar, Orah thrust Evana's flame-serpent deep into Valin's desecration.

As the snake wrapped itself hissing around the abomination of life, its hood rose and distended, reflecting the One that was the fundament of all creation, distended and then fell devouring on its prey, a raging messenger of death.

~ ~ ~

"Where were you?" demanded Hamar, enraged.

"Why, finishing my stew, of course," answered Abrihas with perfect calmness. "It is my habit when the sun goes down to cook my meal. Is something the matter?"

The Oathbreaker gave him such a comical look of unfeigned concern that Hamar might have laughed, had not the preceding months taught him so rudely of the price of levity in opposition to the Enemy. Instead he looked away and said bitterly, "Oh, not much of importance to one of your kind. Only near death to two of our company."

"Be not harsh, Maraprince," said Nediva with her usual self-possessed gentleness. "All is well, Abrihas. The Azure Lord and Ahanatar wrestled with a lieutenant of Valin and triumphed. But the effort has drained them; they both require rest. We must gain Hamar's protected cave. I believe Valin's evil deluded us from the moment we entered this meadow. Why else would we tarry here, just an hour from a real sanctuary? Now we must do with effort what we could have done easily before; yet with your help we may succeed before we are discovered."

"Of course! Let us hasten," said Abrihas, scurrying to pack his possessions. "Why did you not tell me, Hamar? Where is the time for arguments among allies? The enemy waxes mighty; my stalks of fortune reveal your Seachime Cathedral will fall within the week if we do not reach it."

"Then are we doomed," said the Maraprince. "The Cathedral lies three weeks away by foot under the best of conditions."

"Have you thus given up all hope in the Pride of the Sea?" chided Nediva, then added a saying of Matri, *"Where the One is alive, an instant may count for Eternity."*

"At any rate," said Abrihas impatiently, "we must secure safety now, else all is lost. Why did we stop in this wretched open place?"

~ ~ ~

Orah and Ahanatar were sitting and leaning together against an old tree. Both appeared too weak to stand. Abrihas raised a single eyebrow at the sight of the serpent coiling on the Etan's left shoulder, but said only, "Can you rise?" Neither answered, but both stumbled to their feet.

~ ~ ~

"The problem with you, Outlander," said Abrihas around the leg of the rabbit he was noisily munching, "is that of the numerous mistakes you made in Gurion, you recognized only the smallest handful of them." The companions had with difficulty dragged their way to the cave. Orah had quickly recovered, but the Starlord remained very weak and had to be carried most of the way.

The cavern had been a surprise, a huge man-made vault hidden behind a wall of a mountain. Artificial lights clicked on to welcome them to their sterile domain when Hamar passed the threshold. As soon as he saw it, Abrihas had snorted, "Maralords hold nothing sacred." Then he squatted in the middle of the floor and surprised them all by removing his pot of stew from his monstrous pack.

He finished the leg now and fished around for another as Orah replied, "I am not sure I understand you, Abrihas. I have done my best to help. Errors I have made, it is true, but have they not been born of ignorance or false perception?"

"Who structures knowledge but the knower? If Maramel is reduced wholly to rotting corpses and destroyed spires (as seems now likely), will you also say you just didn't see until it was too late? Your grief is more abysmal than your tardy aid."

"How can you so blame him for Aland and Adrian!" Ahanatar broke in angrily, half rising from his cot. For too long had this derelict of Oathlore afflicted them. Of what possible use was he? "If you do not approve of the Azure Lord, why do you not abandon us? I guarantee you will not be missed."

"Always simple solutions with you, eh, Gemstone? If you don't like something, throw it away. My point remains. Your best efforts, Outlander, have not succeeded in stemming the tides of death and pain. Perfection follows not your wake, only broken dreams and regret."

"Can you counsel me to greater success?" The Oathbreaker's words were far from gentle, but Orah saw their medicinal intent. If there was to be less failure for him, must he not attempt all potential solutions?

"That Sesha, Outlander," said Abrihas, indicating the Etan's serpent. "Why do you carry it on your left shoulder?"

The abruptness of the transition startled Orah; he thought a moment before answering, "Why? Why, I don't know, Abrihas. It feels natural there. Do you think it should be elsewhere?"

"What does my thought have to do with it? By Brihas! Can it truly be you have not once turned your intuitive vision upon yourself?" How could Swayam's progeny so overlook the obvious? For too long had they lived in their dream paradise, not caring or knowing how their cousins fared in Martanda. If he could arouse no clearer understanding in this Outlander, he seriously doubted Etan would pass the coming test of survival.

Orah's eyes un-focused as he turned his awareness inward. Within moments, the serpent began to vanish from his shoulder, merging into him. As soon as it was gone, the Etan's breath stilled in a final suspiration; he sat as lifeless as a stone.

"What evil have you worked on him, Oathbreaker!" cried Hamar, feeling for pulse and peering into his eyes.

"No, Maraprince," declared Nediva with certainty. "This is not evil. Followers of the Oath of Purity name it the Trance of Unknowing."

"And those of the Tribe of the Tree name it the Song of Union with the World Tree," said Ahanatar, thoroughly abashed. *If Abrihas can catalyze such a state, I must be completely wrong about him.* He looked at the Oathbreaker quizzically but could only bring himself to say, "You cooked the rabbits well."

Abrihas laughed with good humor and said, "So the eater of cut grass confronts the tiger with humility at last. Be at ease, Starlord of the uplands. Your apology is accepted." He chuckled gently again and added, "Let us hope this Dance of the Self accomplishes its highest purpose. To aid it, let us add our energies to his." He closed his eyes and let his mind drift to join the Etan's. Nediva and Ahanatar followed his example; Hamar, knowing nothing of the art, took up the guard.

~ ~ ~

Orah gazed inward and found the One inside himself, his fundamental reality. Dancing outward in spirals from that attribute-less essence of everything blossomed a coruscating argent fire, Ravi's serpent, Sesha. It elongated and thinned until it appeared a delicate silver thread. The Etan, intuiting it to be hollow, directed his attention inside it and encountered the purest essence of the One's light — the earthbreath. He could perceive Sesha's unlimited power and wisdom, but could not understand them or move them to his will.

The serpent-thread transformed again, becoming Ravi. He tried to speak to her, but with his active attention, she melted into an amorphous brilliance that would have darkened a universe of suns by comparison, a light that contained the whole of Creation and time within its unparalleled perfection, a light that carried his mind into the absolute unbounded silence of the Ascendant One...

~ ~ ~

When Orah opened his eyes, the serpent, purest silver, was coiled on his right shoulder. Ahanatar, Abrihas and Nediva were lying with their heads on the table, apparently fast asleep. Hamar was nowhere to be seen. And around them all were at least two dozen Asurs, carrying stick-like metal rods that were most certainly lethal weapons.

The Asurs looked human, except that their cuspids were twice the size of other races and curved on their ends, and their skin had a distinctly saffron tint. The Etan could not at first understand their words. But then he remembered himself enough to analyze their minds. It had never been more difficult — the Emptiness at their core repulsed him so violently it took him several attempts to succeed.

"— So our Lord bids you welcome." A short but intensely authoritative figure was speaking. "We have searched throughout Maramel for another of Ravi's kinship. We had almost grown to consider her an accident, a freak of nature like the rare bluebloods, but healthy, a strange allele grown in this sable field. Now that we have two, some hope for breeding exists. That prospect pleases you? It is hard to understand you seafolk.

"Looking at you, I almost see why Lord Valin has tolerated your existence for so long. What a prize specimen! The Tower will pay me well, perhaps raise my rank! Why don't you speak? My Lord bids you welcome." Establishing communication with prisoners was supposed to be his specialty. But in this war, there had been no other opportunity.

"I do. Where is Hamar?" The tongue of Barek felt like clay in his throat; he was still largely entranced, not fully awake. He doubted the Asur had actually said all that he heard: many of the phrases seemed more like unvoiced thoughts. He would have to clear his mind to verify, but if it were true! Then a powerful new tool to uncover treachery was now his. He needed more speech.

"The black slave? *Beaten but alive.* We have sent him to the cruiser ahead of you; we will join him and bring you to the Tower *of the Corpse to torture and kill you all. In our own good time.* The Emperor requested us to prepare for your coming in the grandest possible style. *Poor fools."*

Ahanatar moaned slightly, then straightened. "Orah? Who? What? By Narain!" He tried to leap to his feet, but Asur hands held him firmly in place. Orah found he could not hear the Starlord's thoughts.

"Do your red slaves always speak so strangely? How can they have forgotten the language of Barek? *We will relish re-instructing them."*

A glimmer in Ahanatar's eyes was all that indicated he understood Barek-san full well. Continuing to feign ignorance, he asked, "Are you all right?"

"Fine, Ahanatar, fine. Just fine. Hamar is already aboard their cruiser, whatever that is."

"A machine that flies through the air, no doubt."

"Speak Barek-san, I implore you," said the Asur, hinting violence.

"My friend does not know your speech. Why do they still sleep?"

"A kind of gas. We do not risk our lives in doubtful situations. *Unlike fools such as yourselves.* We wait to escort you until we ascertain the importance of your slaves. *I would prefer killing them at once, but orders are orders."*

"They are most precious to me," replied Orah, attempting to discover solutions. *Their cruiser could be useful to us,* he thought, then realized he did not have the vaguest notion how to interact with these expressions of living Emptiness.

Nediva groaned to wakefulness. The Asur greeted her with slightly more respect than the Starlord — he could at least see some use for her, regardless of the others' fate. She betrayed a limited knowledge of their language before she was fully alert.

Abrihas could not be roused. The Asur captain waited impatiently a few more moments, then ordered two of his men to carry him.

Outside, two score gorlems surrounded the Asurs' cruiser, a sable cube of a tenth league diameter, floating in the sunlight before the ruined entryway. Nediva shuddered at its sinister appearance. Abrihas mumbled something through his sleep. For an instant, all the Asurs looked at him. Not knowing whether he could even hope to succeed, Ahanatar tore a rifle from the nearest Asur. Using it as a club, he leveled two of the enemy before the others opened fire. The violet rays of their weapons dropped him like a stone to the ground; Nediva screamed and bent over him.

"Ah, do not fear, blue man. He is unconscious merely. *We will kill him later for this.* Those Gurions are so violent. Never is there need for such brutal passion. *High entertainment, his death.* We do well to maintain our shields on the Gray. Will you enter our craft?" A narrow metal stairway descended to meet them; with but slight prompting, Orah and Nediva climbed it. Then came Abrihas and Ahanatar, now both carried. Half the Asurs followed them into the cruiser; the others mounted their own individual crafts.

Orah asked how machines could float on the air and received a complex response that hinged on the super-symmetry of magnetism at extremely low temperatures. He abandoned the attempt to understand it intellectually and let his mind flow into the metal. It did not seem evil in itself, but the same Emptiness that was at the core of the gorlems and the Asurs was also here. With a depthless feeling of despondency, he knew he could do nothing with it or to it.

The inside of the cruiser was starkly functional, white and electronic. Hamar was huddling in a corner, guarded by the interlaced energy fields of half a dozen gorlems. He was badly bruised on the face and chest, one eye was swollen shut, blood was dripping from a torn shoulder. Nediva wanted to help him, but the ambient feeling all but crippled her flow of healing ability. Instead, she knelt by the Starlord and stroked his hair, trying to keep from screaming.

"Orah! I am sorry!" cried Hamar. "A Protector was searching for us; I called to her. I did not believe the Oathbreaker. They descended like a swarm of flies."

"Silence, dog. *I should have killed you already.*"

"It will be all right, Hamar. They know of Ravi." Some glimmering of hope was there at least.

~ ~ ~

Abrihas weighed his balance and saw the deficiencies of this approach — no improvement in the Outlander was even vaguely imminent. With a single wrenching expression of the One, he restructured their time sequence. *Another oath broken,* he thought sardonically.

~ ~ ~

"What — what's happened!" cried Hamar. "I dreamed we were captive!"

"As did I!" said Ahanatar and Nediva in one voice.

But the Etan said nothing, believing what they just experienced was not exactly a dream, even though he could not explain it in other terms.

Abrihas, humming a queer little tune over his stewpot, picked up his spoon, tasted the broth and licked his lips noisily. "Not too bad. Not too bad. If you dullards are well enough rested, perhaps we should have some breakfast, then seek the Pride of the Sea. The gorlem attack on the Cathedral cannot be resisted forever." Then he added in his odd singsong, "Illusions of life; illusions of death. Time and space; space and time. All one to the One; all many to the many. Dreams to the dreamer; reality to the realist. My, does not Leor's brother learn slowly?"

Orah wondered with overpowering melancholy how many more in Maramel would die before he could learn to manipulate the Asurs' Emptiness. Then he shook himself mentally, throwing off his doleful mood, and said, "Hamar?"

"Yes, Azure Lord?"

"Would you have been able to fly that Asur cruiser?"

"In my — in our dream? Why — why, yes, I believe so. Why do you ask?"

The Etan did not answer, but stared at Abrihas.

"Ready to try again?" asked the Oathbreaker in the gentlest voice he had yet used.

14. The Pride of the Sea

The forest in Maramel was mostly hemlock, fir and cedar. Moss draped the trees in verdant beauty; the Etan felt the silence and gentleness of the pre-war land. But that was all illusion now, he realized grimly, a reality destroyed by an evil dream that should never have been allowed to begin. And then, in a sudden illumination born of his experiences of the night before, he saw in that thought the basis of an idea! For if the Oathbreaker had truly done what it seemed, there was perhaps more reason to hope than any yet known...

Orah strode swiftly to catch up to the Gurions. Abrihas looked at the Etan out of the corner of his eye without slackening his pace or turning his head as he said, "We should be cautious about calling Protectors. The Asurs would certainly keep a close watch on any they still allow to roam Maramel — probably they have been using them as ferrets to exterminate the last of the Seapeople... Although I suppose that may change now, since they mass at the Cathedral — creating a great advantage to us for an unobserved journey, I might add."

"It would seem so, Abrihas. But I think there may be other reasons why we have not again encountered the enemy. I am convinced, in fact, that somehow these few hours have been lived twice by us. Is that possible?"

"What could be the advantage of travel in time? To have such a need would imply life has somewhere not unfolded as it should. And that would mean the Grandfather or the Seven have erred. I am afraid that is more than even a poor Oathbreaker can accept. For if those eight do not act from omniscience, where then can there be hope for this world?"

"Can it not happen that an opponent could become so powerful or subtle as to cause the plans of the Guardians to go awry?" asked Orah, then was so surprised by his own question that he hardly heard the Oathbreaker's reply. How did he know of the Guardians? He was not merely repeating knowledge he had learned in Gurion, but was speaking from his own hazy memory. Yet he was fairly — no, completely — certain such knowledge was not of Etan. He had felt the same way about the unexpected memory of the race of that Hcolom creature in Arel. What was it he had known it to be? A Rakshasa. And also a Rakshasa that attacked the Gemstone last evening. And in these knowings, nothing correlated with Etan! Was it necessary to lose his memory, all he knew of his family and home, to arouse a deeper, hidden past? Something from longer ago or farther away than Etan? But how could such a thing be? Enough of his memory had returned for him to know that he had been born in Swayam's City and had never ventured past its gates until this journey. Yet he could not deny he also knew of the Guardians, the Grandfather *and* the Seven, and also of the demonic Rakshasa, *the spawn of Salash, Pacshash and Yakshin, defeated and thought destroyed before the Martanda landing...* The sudden memory ended in another shock of surprise, for the thought of the Rakshasa progenitors was a clearer and stronger memory than any other, yet the three were so repulsive in their nature, so twisted in their use of the One, he instinctively denied them and tried to forget them.

"— So time travel is theoretically possible, but of doubtful utility. For the Seven are supposed to be omniscient, are they not?"

"But look here, Abrihas," said Nediva, "I also believe perfection in action may be impossible as long as the Seven are opposed. So if we could re-enter the past, knowing as we do now, and change our mistakes..." She did not believe they had been dreaming either, and had tried to share this with the Starlord. But the Gemstone, believing travel through time impossible, had refused to accept the alternative.

"Yes!" cried the Etan. "If I could return to Odelia, half a day before the massacre! What a blessing!"

"Perhaps not," said the Oathbreaker, chuckling slightly. "We can for a moment ignore the obvious paradox that if you succeeded, you would no longer remember the need, for of course it would not have happened, and —"

"But confound it, old man!" cried Ahanatar, forgetting he in no way believed such a thing was possible. "The whole concept is confused. If I really could re-enter the past, why would I not be there as witness to myself, remembering how it was until (and after) I altered it?"

"Even so," said Abrihas, widely smiling over some private joke, "still I maintain it would be wrong. If the Outlander had saved Odelia, the Arelai would have known enough of his power to be more alert at the solstice. And if they had opposed him with all their will, I doubt Hcolom could have been so easily mastered. He caught them unaware, therefore succeeded."

"That is a harsh saying," said Orah. He was not to be denied either and continued, "If not Odelia, then what of Cahlil? Or Tejan and Kanya? Or Aland? Or Adrian? Would that not be good?" He was struggling for the truth, but part of his mind almost knew the answer before he heard it. *Is Abrihas simply bringing out knowledge I already possess? If so, this Oathbreaker yet conceals much more than he reveals.*

"Again I submit, if any one of your companions were spared, you would not have danced as you did at the solstice."

"But why not go now and bring them here?" asked Ahanatar. "The Orah of that time would not have to know."

"You saw them slain! That is a fact that cannot be altered; even assuming such action would be desirable. Or practicable."

"I think I know another reason why the Lion brothers should not be taken from their destiny," Nediva said softly, mostly to herself.

The Etan looked at her curiously, but said to Abrihas, "All right. I will accept the specific instances. But what if we went back before it began? Before the corruption began murdering Riversland? Went back and chained Valin before he began to desecrate Martanda?"

"Further. Further in space and time, Azure Lord. You have forgotten more than you even dream. But to do what you suggest, change any event even the least of past time, would demand true omniscience, else the present could be much worse than it is. Think! There is much of strength and worth in Gurion — too much to risk losing. The Fire Lords, for example. And Elid and his Sun Council. Eliora with her Crooked Staff People and their gentle authority. Zuriel and the mystical Tribe of the Tree; the Star and Gemstones; the Scroll Wardens — all these powers are precious to the future of mankind. Even the Lightning Lords, for now they are eager to repay Jyot's damage; and the Arelai too, if truth be known.

"In spite of the evils of the modern world, I say omniscience alone could provide us with better. Nay, *more* than omniscience, for I maintain that the Guardians — to borrow your word — already possess that achievement."

Ahanatar and Orah wanted to continue arguing, but Hamar came running back, crying excitedly, "I see it! The Pride of the Sea! Just ahead!" His enthusiasm swept through them; they raced as one to the dirigible, even Abrihas running with them.

~ ~ ~

The Pride of the Sea was ruined. Three large tears had reduced its skin to so much useless fabric, exposing the metal and plastic framework. Once it had been a graceful sphere, but the crash that killed Hamar's companions distorted it into an irregular ellipsoid.

The heart of the Maraprince fell as he surveyed the wreckage. The only consolation was that the graves of his companions were unmolested. He was glad he had had the Protectors search out the heavy rocks that covered the mounded earth.

"Well," said Abrihas, sounding bored, "it seems this path is ended. Or do you still believe it can be repaired?"

"I - I don't know. Jamad! What a mess. It's so huge, fallen on the ground like this. We have enough gas, but the fabric — it's so ruined. I just don't know."

"Well, let's try," said the Etan. "We certainly can't accomplish it by standing here. Where do we begin?"

~ ~ ~

It was hopeless. They didn't have the strength to straighten the frame, let alone repair the covering. Dusk was falling to the tune of whippoorwills and nightingales when Hamar threw down his wrench and said they were beaten.

"Do you so easily abandon the Cathedral?" mused Abrihas. "I would have assumed a descendant of Dalmara would try harder. I must admit to being disappointed."

"You talk and talk but help not!" raged the Maraprince. "What earthly good have you been? If you had helped on that last strut, we would have raised it and —" His words trailed off as he stared at the three Protectors floating toward them through the forest. "Kumbha — ?" he whispered, then cried, "Kumbha!" as he ran to embrace the sphere. "What is the matter? Why do you not speak?"

"It is Kumbha, Lord," said one of the others in the same dulcet contralto all the Protectors shared, "but we have not yet repaired her entirely. She can communicate with us but not you."

"Marel? But who is this?"

"Yes, Lord, I am Marel. This is Raibha. She comes from the north. We and six dozen others were sent to look for you. Haman could spare no more. This morning we by great good fortune found Kumbha and repaired her sufficiently to learn of your probable whereabouts. We would have been here hours ago, but were attacked. I think we acquitted ourselves well, but the others were crippled or destroyed. We voted to leave them and seek you, even our damaged comrades assenting. Fortunately, the enemy gathers at the Cathedral, else we never could have come through as well as we have."

"You have done well!" exclaimed Hamar, mixing warmth and pride most shamefully. "Your arrival is perfectly timely — we cannot repair the dirigible alone. But first tell me why a northerner comes south of the Gray."

"I came for news of the Cathedral," said Raibha with a slightly different accent but otherwise identical voice. *How do the Maralords tell them apart?* thought Orah, and could see no obvious answer. Raibha continued, "We have been beaten back to our ancient battlements on the Ridge of Man. The High King Marasad sent me with nine others to seek aid from Haman. The gorlems attacked us and destroyed my companions. I believe they let me escape to bring this tale to the Cathedral to increase your despair, for the knowledge of our shared plight will make your resistance weaker —"

"Do not so judge," ordered Marel. "It is not our place. Rather, let us repair the Pride of the Sea."

The Etan wondered how such odd beings could succeed where they had failed. He stared entranced as each of the three projected half a dozen manipulators and began twisting and bending the dirigible's superstructure as easily as if it were made of tin.

Hamar watched them with a truly enormous pride. Abrihas, disdaining to spend a moment improving the Maraprince's opinion of technology, produced a short lance from his pack and began a new hunt for rabbits.

~ ~ ~

Nediva took Ahanatar by the hand and, leading him a little way into the forest, said, "My Lord, I was too shy to speak before the others, but there is a very good reason why Adrian and Aland must not be plucked from the past. Let us sit here as I try to explain." A little stream gurgled merrily over the rocks of its bed; the moss-laden firs enclosed the small clearing as if it were a sanctuary, created and reserved for private communications.

The Horse Elder sat gracefully on the small ferns and moss, blushing slightly. The Starlord was curious, but did not try to hurry her. In truth, he was quite pleased — she had not addressed him as "my Lord" before — it was the common title of respect from wife to husband in Gurion.

"Sit by me," she said, then continued slowly, "this is not easy — first let me explain: within me are two, not one."

"By the Tradition of the World Tree! Twins, you say! We are doubly blest. You are sure?"

"A woman may feel these things. There are two, males, and — I know this as truth! — these are the new bodies of the Lion Lords!"

"What? What strangeness this? I myself held Aland as his life fled! We both saw Adrian burned alive! And now you say! You say they are inside your womb. I cannot follow this! Death is death. Never have I even imagined such a thing! Surely you are mistaken."

She let him run it through his mind until the unfamiliarity began to diminish. After all, those not of Matri's Oath weren't expected to have such knowledge. She had hoped Ahanatar might have learned it among the wardens of the World Tree — she was sure the masters of their house must possess this knowledge, especially if the Gemstone were right about Zuriel. Perhaps such teachings were reserved for the most adept.

Ahanatar finished his monologue with, " — Probably the strain of this forced march added to your condition..."

"No, Starlord. You are wrong. Matri passed the Followers of the Vow of Purity this knowledge. Each death makes a new beginning, here or elsewhere, depending on merit and desire. But even if not common or universal, still in this case it *is* the truth — Adrian and Aland will be my children. Our children, forgive me. I felt I had to tell you; perhaps you can tell the Azure Lord, reduce his burden."

"If I could believe this marvel myself —" He looked deep into her hazel eyes, seeking truth. Finally he either found his answer or discovered his own belief. He clasped her hands and kissed them, then rose to walk alone for a time through the forest. Nediva stared at the laughing creek and played her fingers through the clear water.

~ ~ ~

Orah found her sleeping there at dawn, a flower of purest loveliness, the dust from their journey only accentuating her untainted innocence. *It is strange,* he thought: *we feel so confident with just three Protectors we didn't even post a guard. I begin to understand how Maramel defeated herself.*

He touched Nediva gently awake, saying, "We must go soon — Kumbha and the others have succeeded! The Pride of the Sea is repaired. Are you rested?"

"Very, yes. Ahanatar?"

"He is there. And he told me about the Lions."

"And you believe?" She looked up at him with wide eyes.

"With all my heart, I hope it is so. This knowledge is new to me. But I suppose life is an even stranger miracle. Evana has certainly demonstrated something similar; in truth, I almost come upon memories of other times and places within myself. I pray it is true. I simply don't know."

~ ~ ~

Nediva entered the clearing behind the Etan and looked at Ahanatar with a mixture of hope and fear that reflected well his own. He returned her gaze briefly, then blushed and turned away. Above them all rode the inflated dirigible, pulling at its moorings as if it were a stallion, eager to bear them away.

Abrihas said, "You see, Horse Elder. It seems these artificial beings succeeded where we failed. I suppose that means they will have to join us, even though their mere presence will certainly alert the whole of the enemy in Maramel to us."

"You old fool!" shouted Hamar, "one of them is worth seven of you!"

"That at least is literally true," Abrihas answered, giving him a wide, toothy grin.

~ ~ ~

The gondola beneath the huge sphere of celadon was large enough for a score. As the Protectors assumed a flanking position, the travelers settled down comfortably for the voyage, Hamar explaining the next dawn would see them reaching the Seachime Cathedral. "If we are not intercepted first," he said, glancing uncomfortably at the Oathbreaker. "I will keep us near the trees. If we are lucky, we may escape detection until we are near." Exactly what they would do when they arrived did not concern him; he had given his trust to the Lord from Etan and no longer worried about the future.

"It does seem very few of the enemy are about," Abrihas responded amiably. "I only pray we are not too late." That the battle was going poorly for the Maralords, he was certain. That they might be able to do something if they reached the Cathedral in time was his hope, if only these next few hours could produce the desired effect in the Outlander. The Oathbreaker sat down a little apart from the others and watched their thoughts walking across their faces.

Orah was not hopeful. In fact, he was quite despondent. He reviewed his knowledge of the gorlems and the Asurs, but could not understand how to affect them. It was as if they were members of a different order of being, not human or created by humans. There was nothing at all of the One in them. And if there was not, how could he hope to manipulate the earthbreath to deal with them? Yet they obviously could manipulate the powers of nature. Where was the area of contact? How could he, a creature of the One, dominate beings made of a force that negated life as nothing else he had believed could exist? For Emptiness was not merely the absence of the One but its antithesis. He shied away from the word "evil": he deeply retained the belief that all of creation had branched from (and therefore was a part of) the Grandfather's will. But how else could he understand them? And why had Abrihas possessed Emptiness? There was as yet no clear answer for that. Rather, it seemed the Oathbreaker distracted him whenever he questioned him too closely. Orah glanced at him; Abrihas was staring at him queerly, apparently analyzing him. The Etan felt icy fingers along his spine from this curious study and hastily looked aside.

Ahanatar and Nediva were lightly chattering together about the joy and wonder of flying through the air. Turning abruptly from the Outlander, Abrihas said to the Starlord, "Gemstone, what is sought in the wrong way will never be found."

Ahanatar turned a deeper shade of crimson as he moved like quicksilver from confusion to anger. "I — I do not know what you mean!"

"My words are plain. If the sword doesn't fit your sheath, you needn't carry it."

"You have been nothing but trouble from the beginning!" cried the Starlord, his earlier conclusion about the Oathbreaker thoroughly overshadowed by his moving feelings. "Lazy, noisy trouble! I at least am honest as to why I accompany the Azure Lord. My history is open, not hidden like yours, as if you were some, some —"

"Spider?" supplied Abrihas.

"Yes, confound you! A predator. Or a — a vulture! Watching us closely for decay, waiting for — why? None of us know anything of you. I ask you again, Oathbreaker, why do you journey among us?"

I seek the sun and find a moon, thought Abrihas, *but perhaps its light will betray the location of the other.* "Many reasons, I suppose," he said in the tone he usually reserved for discussion of himself, a mixture of genuine humility and wry humor, "one of the most important is the desire to return to the north."

"So! You are *not* of Gurion!" exclaimed Nediva, shocked to discover her private analysis confirmed. Her perception had unrolled layer upon layer of illusion from Abrihas, as if his multi-faceted persona was a rosebud she systematically disassembled. And at the center, she had found a truth so undeniably real yet completely impossible she had shared her discovery with none of the others, fearing their disbelief.

"My Lady, you know I am not." He toyed with the thought of generating alternate solutions in their minds, but agreed with his earlier judgment that no other torch would penetrate the fog gripping the Outlander. As for the others, in a few more hours it wouldn't matter who knew what he was, for he would no longer be a being of Martanda. Still, it did seem something of a shame, after so many years... "I have journeyed long seasons in the south, but the heavens reveal my brethren are in dire need."

"What do you say!" cried Hamar, turning from the control panel with undisguised rage. "None has passed through Maramel in centuries."

"Nor through the Sunrise Mountains," said Ahanatar, thinking his earlier assessment not sufficiently accurate. *"Snake" would fit him better,* he thought. Pointing a finger at Abrihas, he accused, "You came through Barek! You, Oathbreaker, are an agent of the Asurs!"

"No," said Nediva calmly. "There is another and better solution to this riddle. I say Abrihas adroitly hides his age from the world. I say he entered Gurion before there was a Forbidding on the Gray."

Ahanatar stared at her, feeling himself sinking before a seething mass of vertigo in which the only refuge, the only hope for sanity was a concept so alien he felt physically repulsed by it. For to accept the Horse Elder's alternative could mean but one thing. Beating down his nausea, he looked at Abrihas closely and wondered how he had overlooked the paleness of the skin and the narrow facial features. *He is not of Gurion! He looks like... like the statues at the Founding Lake,* he thought, terrified yet elated by the possibility. "Malinnoir," he whispered, then said haltingly, "Kiritan, kistna. Krister kumar!"

"Mohan, nandin. Nissim Raziel," Abrihas answered softly, remembering the last time he had heard that greeting. It was a more innocent world then, their hope much brighter. He was mildly surprised the Tribe of the Tree had remembered so well. But then, it was their business to do so. He gave an inner shrug and resumed the sardonic voice, "Although the titles seem slightly antiquated — if not actually invalid — given the state of the world."

Ahanatar, so unexpectedly initiated into Nediva's vision, could think of absolutely nothing to say. He stared open-mouthed at the Oathbreaker as the Universe spun around him in mad circles, Abrihas alone remaining real in a swirling miasma of chaos, fear, impossible hope.

"Can his words be true, Abrihas?" asked Orah, amazed by the salutation in the long-dead tongue. "Are you really an anointed prince of the Seven?"

"Truer than mine have been, I fear. Cousin Satya never could teach me anything. Orah-lar, I fear your father must be sorely disappointed in us. When last I walked openly, men called me, *'Oathmaster.'* And, from time-to-time, *'Brihas.'* "

The dirigible dipped wildly toward the forest as Hamar shouted, "What!"

Nediva, clapping her hands with excitement, cried, "You do know Swayam!"

Ahanatar, beating down his roiling terror, took three deep breaths and slipped around the terrible questions with the innocuous, "How can you have lived so long?"

But the Etan's eyes glazed as his mind involuted madly: the mention of his father hard upon such a revelation broke a dam in his heart: the unleashed flood carried him helplessly deep into the complexity of his forgotten past. He grasped for holds, for stabilizing forces to slow the insane rush, but was hurled headlong like a single leaf, battered before a hurricane, hopelessly lost and alone.

The Oathmaster, concluding he had judged Orah correctly, saw no reason not to attempt the metamorphosis of the Starlord and answered him, "I conserve what others waste. Most spend their energies in low passions and desires; I transmute and live."

"But how? Among the Tribe of the Tree, many have such knowledge, many have made such an attempt. But as yet none has lived beyond his second century." The Gemstone clutched desperately at the concept to keep his universe whole.

Hamar looked as if he had pushed his mind into the control panel. If he were still listening was not apparent. *Complete withdrawal to save self,* thought Brihas, glancing at him. But Nediva sat like a queen, impervious to or beyond the erupting waves of knowledge challenging the others. The Oathmaster, reminded of Matri, smiled at her warmly as he answered Ahanatar, "The material of initial construction is a relevant but not determinate factor. Anyone can so conquer death if dedicated to the goal with one-pointed faith and flawless commitment. But,

Gemstone, your knowledge is simply wrong. There are those of the servants of the World Tree who have joined the deathless company in Malinnoir — that which is known as the Valley of the Oathmasters. Zuriel's master, Aranel, is one."

"I saw him buried!" The adrenaline threatened to tear Ahanatar's heart from his body. Even as he thought he was maintaining a stable perception of life, the final support was being torn from him — he himself had been given the rare honor of anointing his master's master's body for the burial! If this could be true, what other laws of experience might be false? He had turned from the impossible, and the Oathbreaker — Oathmaster Brihas! — had led him full circle back to the crux of the conflict unmaking his mind.

"I do not doubt you. Yet I say he lives. How can such contradictions exist?" Brihas laughed, a deep rumble of joy, not in the least malicious, but as if from a deeply overflowing spirit. It was apparent the Starlord had no more defenses. A few more subtle modifications and he would be free. *If* he could surmount the final barrier...

The Oathmaster continued slowly, sculpting each phrase to perfection, "At the center of all that lives is that which never changes, the One Ascendant Source of all that is. Turning back inward, a human of any of the four orders may explore this field, conquer it, if you will, for the greater glory of life. Continuing in the relative spheres, subject to finite laws, the friable human becomes indestructibly absolute, capable of manipulating matter and nature for infinite ends. Anything desired by such an enlightened one represents the Grandfather's will, and therefore is accomplished. There are no limits — anything desired is realizable."

"Can it be twisted? Is Valin such a one?" So close would Ahanatar come. But his spirit could bear him no further: the ultimate question would remain locked in his heart for the rest of his life.

Brihas sighed a little at the Gemstone's failure. But then he allowed the completion of the partial victory. After all, his true goal was the Etan... "Yes, and no, to both. To some extent, power can be warped, even (or especially) by those who could have been Oathmasters. The last hold on his error stopped and perverted the

Asur Emperor — the final limitation of his ego caught him and chained him to its evil. His success since is only because he developed this knowledge prior to his fall."

"And when was that? For how long has he lived?"

Nediva also saw that the Starlord was wandering in the hinterland and reestablished her theme, "You spoke of Orah's father, Swayam, as an intimate. Is it true?"

"My Lady, we came to Martanda with him. And with the Enemy of Being, Navril Hagar, although in those days we knew him not. When we discovered him, he had desecrated the progeny of Swayam and Shatarupa's firstborn who had fled Ganym, initial planet of our current human race. We slew him then, or so we all thought; Swayam and Shatarupa built their paradise in Etan to nurture their subsequent offspring, entrusting us with the deformed descendants of the Enemy's malevolence. And we succeeded well, we believed, for millennia upon millennia, until the memory of Navril's evil was expunged as if it had never been.

"But time changes all purposes, bringing decay and ruin to the good and perfect. Perhaps we grew overconfident; perhaps the Enemy can never be truly destroyed now, but lives forever in all the twisted children, awaiting an appropriate time and place to resume form and power."

"Where are these children?" interjected Hamar, valiantly endeavoring to understand, succeeding not at all.

"They are everywhere, Maraprince. All the Asurs, the Mountain Oathmasters, the Maralords, the Gurions, all those of North and South Mered, those of Tilvia and Vadil, those of Shamir and Sarojin, excepting only the handful in Etan, all of Martanda. Every human in this world is descended from the firstborn Arama and Jaya of Swayam-bhuva and Shatarupa."

"Why did they abandon us?" cried Ahanatar with something very akin to despair.

"Child, they did not. The Seven are rays of Swayam, essential aspects of his being, forever one with him. We assumed the mantle to deal with the Enemy, leaving the Father free to seek perfection with his new children in Etan."

"It is impossible to believe this!" protested Hamar, finding the path obscure in all directions. "You claim not only to be one of the ten original Oathmasters but, if I heard you correctly, one of the Seven Antediluvian Lords! Where is the sense in this? Do we live in the modern world or did the gorlems kill me?"

"You are as much alive as any of us, Maraprince. We have waited through long centuries, anonymous ministers to mankind, disguising ourselves until we could be certain Valin was the ancient foe, returning again into form. And now, perchance, we have tarried overlong: we fail with the heavens."

"Have you told my father?" Orah's voice was quiet, too quiet: the imposed silence of a mind struggling to save itself. With an almost superhuman application of will, he had arrested his inner fall with the single thought of his father Swayam — all powerful, immovable, eternally wise. There and there alone he found the strength to check the mad flood of his damaged soul's re-opening to itself.

"Swayam knows, has known longer than any of us. Your presence here proves he not only knows, but cares."

"But he opposed my coming!" Suddenly the cracks in his memory seemed to laugh hideously at him. Where now was the thread of sanity? The balance he had with such difficulty established was failing at the mere suggestion of his father's complicity.

"If he did, it must have been to galvanize your will. For he sent his dearest daughter before you, did he not?"

"No!" shouted Orah. "You're lying! He could not have known! Not have permitted this sacrilege!" As the deluge of pain and memory burst through his temporary restraints, his soul raged with loathing for the Oathmaster. He found himself closer to mindless violence than he had believed he could ever come.

Brihas responded to his wrath firstly with his wide toothy grin and secondly with, "Permitted? My dear boy, who do you think destroyed humankind's first home on Ganym?"

"No!" screamed the Etan, his face disfiguring horribly as his unlimited fury rebounded onto himself. In half a moment, the container of his mind was irrevocably crushed — he beheld the internal walls created by the Lethe destroyed, revealing vistas of forgotten space and time. Yet it was not Etan that lay thus exposed, rather another world entirely, one he knew instinctively had never been a part of Martanda. "In Ganym's garden, there! That blackness, that Evil! NO!" With all his spirit, he struggled to maintain the inner limits, to restore the delicate compromise that had sustained him since he crossed the Lethe. But he could not discover or even understand the parameters. As final refuge from insanity, he retreated from the external mind.

Nediva hurried toward him, but Brihas stopped her, "No, he must explore this knowing alone, dear one. Only thus may he rediscover himself." As the Etan slipped to the floor of the gondola, the serpent ceased coiling on his shoulder and slid over his chest, then settled comfortably on his stomach. It closed its fiery eyes and seemed to follow its master into sleep. "See, he has all the help he needs. Sesha will guide him past the wastelands. I believe he will awaken whole."

"With memory of Etan restored?"

"Etan? Probably not. But with the further past. And with a certainty of purpose and (I hope) a significant ability to counteract Valin's machinations of evil."

"What is his 'further past?' "

"There remains no reason not to tell you. Before he was Orah of Etan, he was Swayam and Shatarupa's first child, Arama, twin-born with Jaya, Victory, his wife and love he seeks now across space and time. Swayam perceived the seed of evil in their bodies and withheld the secret of immortality from them. Arama and Jaya's children fell farther and parented humanity as we now know it. The First War pitted Swayam, alone with the Seven, against ten thousand million of the fallen ones, led by the youngest son of Arama, Navril Hagar, the Forsaken One."

"Who today is named Valin?" asked Ahanatar, finding in this precisely what he needed to stabilize his own mind.

"Thus we fear, although how he could have lived through the freezing of Ganym and burning of Martanda we did not foresee and even today do not understand. I suppose we should have realized the possibility sooner, but it has been almost two hundred thousand years —"

"You can't mean that! *Two hundred thousand*?"

"I do. Martanda has been settled for that long — two hundred thousand years ago Swayam slew Navril Hagar and vaporized

Arama's race. Before Ganym was destroyed, half a handful of the least evil, two million, journeyed here with Arama to found Martanda. But when the Betrayer rose, assuming form, Swayam annihilated both worlds to eradicate the evil permanently. Two only of each race survived, that for the memory of Jaya and Arama. From these ten have arisen the billions of this world."

"Abrihas — I mean, Brihas!" cried Hamar. "Gorlems! Two dozen. Straight ahead! Coming directly at us. No Asurs."

"Good. We can test the Starlord's commands once more. Can you broadcast his voice?"

"Yes. Here, Gemstone, speak into this."

Ahanatar looked doubtfully at the microphone but took it, thankful for the possibility of action. His words were as successful as before: the war machines fell in flaming ruin.

"Some hope!" exclaimed Brihas. "They are still unaware of your knowledge. If our luck holds, we may reach the Cathedral in time." He stared at the huge spire rising from the circling clouds of the enemy. It was still too far to see detail, but he was fairly certain the shields were holding. *Odd that it should come to fate in the end,* he thought. *Valin has grown strong in the world.* He stared at the Seachime Cathedral and remembered and was silent.

~ ~ ~

They encountered no more of the enemy by nightfall, and settled down to an uneasy sleep, leaving the Protectors to pilot the dirigible. The Etan continued to float in the confusion engendered by conflicting pasts. Sesha had moved up to lie over his heart, but had not again opened its eyes. Nediva gave Orah her love, but in no other way attempted to modify the Oathmaster's work.

~ ~ ~

The Horse Elder awoke first, just before dawn. The others were still asleep, except Brihas, who was sitting exactly where and as he had the previous evening. She smiled at him; he responded briefly, then returned his gaze to the last refuge of the Maralords south of the Gray. She followed his example, but at first her mind refused to recognize the massive argent cylinder ahead. It was too vast; she simply could not believe it could have grown so enormous during the night. She had known its dimensions for years: two leagues wide by ten high; but now it was so close, it was almost incomprehensible. The millions of gorlems, unceasingly firing their weapons of light, seemed little more than swarms of bees around a mighty tree. *How has the dirigible come so close? Are they so preoccupied? Or has Brihas cloaked us?*

The Seachime Cathedral was smooth and silver, broken on all sides only by clear round windows of various sizes. She had imagined there would be colonnades, parapets and battlements, but there was no interlude other than the portals in its ideal symmetry. *How perfect is the Maralords' science,* she thought in awe. Ahanatar came up behind her and placed his hand gently on her shoulder. She touched it tenderly and lifted her face for his kiss. *There is much to be grateful for,* she thought, but said, "I could never have believed this had I not seen it for myself."

"I know. It is magnificent, a frozen song of love and power. Seeing it there almost makes me laugh at the Asurs."

"So did we for generations," said Hamar, rubbing the sleep from his eyes. "But we have no reason for amusement now. Look there!"

The Cathedral's shield to the north was flickering like a candle from the onslaught of the gorlems and Asurs. How much longer could it withstand their concentrated energies?

The Protector Marel drifted toward them and said, "We are fortunate. The south face is but scantily attacked. Most of their force is on the other side. There may be a chance of making the portal on the seventh level. If the Gurion can aid us again."

"I will try," said Ahanatar. "But they may cancel my commands with others."

"Let us hope they will not for some time," said Brihas. "Truly, I think the initial outlook is promising — none has yet escaped us to transmit our secret. You should go stand near the control panel — they will certainly see us as soon as the sun rises."

"I wonder how we can have come so far," mused Nediva. "Tell me truly, Brihas, have you not shielded us repeatedly?"

"I have no more secrets from this company, my Lady. I have twisted their vision many times. But Valin's malevolence here is at its maximum; a poor wizard's spells avail but little."

~ ~ ~

Nevertheless, they were nearly to the Cathedral's shield before his illusions were penetrated. Then they were attacked instantly from everywhere. The Pride of the Sea possessed its own shields, but not of sufficient strength to withstand concentrated assault. Ahanatar shouted his commands; Brihas' staff pulsed with power; thousands of gorlems fell to ruin; but the dirigible was hit repeatedly: the gas flowed from a dozen holes, then from a score, then from half a hundred.

It almost seemed they would reach the shimmering portal dilating before them, but suddenly the Starlord's effect on the gorlems was lost — his power was discovered and nullified. Brihas alone was insufficient to stay the enemy; from all sides the attack pressed inward viciously.

Too much gas had escaped; they were falling. The entry was slipping away, was too far above, impossible to reach.

"The service portal on the fourth!" shouted Marel. "It is our last chance! Try for that!"

Hamar said something in reply, but his words were swallowed by the raging fire that burst from nowhere in the gondola behind them.

The Protectors sprayed it and partially slowed but could not prevent its steady advance.

"Asur fire," breathed Ahanatar, fascinated in a similar way as is a mouse by a snake. "I have learned of it. Nothing stops it. It adheres to everything and burns."

Brihas was in the middle of it, not attempting to move, maintaining his position to continue using his staff as a weapon. A second explosion and he was down, burning all over. Raibha and Kumbha raced to him and carried him to the others. Nediva felt for him with her mind but encountered only darkness.

And then, almost beyond hope, it was over.

Burning and falling, they careened through the service portal. The hundred gorlems that entered behind them were obliterated by the fire of thousands of Protectors.

A score of Maramel's spheres bore the companions to safety.

Half a moment later, the gondola exploded and fell from the ruined dirigible like the melting and burning plastic that it was.

15. An Engineer

As they were carried high up the Cathedral to an open entryway, nearly three leagues above the ground, Nediva turned her attention to the stricken Oathmaster. She knew he must still exist somewhere within that seared flesh, but she could not find him. His heart was not beating, yet she knew intuitively he still lived.

They entered into a wide hall thronged with Maralords. Three Protectors began bathing Brihas with their healing rays; another trio hovered over the unconscious Etan.

On a central dais stood an imposing figure Nediva knew must be Haman. His finely muscled frame glistened slightly, contrasting vividly with his royal silken indigo, magnifying the intensity of his authority; his expression could only be termed fierce.

Hamar was set down before his feet; the others behind and below him. The Maraprince gave his father the full prostration of Maramel; Nediva and Ahanatar copied the example. Haman raised and embraced his son. Tears stood in his eyes; he could not speak for long minutes. At last he choked, "My son, my son. I had given you up for dead. And now you return beyond all hope. All glory to Brihas! Let the Chimes ring forth!" Instantly the air of the Cathedral was filled with wondrous sweet music, emanating from the walls in perfect harmony. Nediva felt transported to a younger and more innocent world, to a time before man's ambitions and abilities had so disastrously collided. It took a long minute (and a gentle nudge from Ahanatar) before she heard the Maralord's words.

" — We have neglected our custom in our happiness. You are welcome throughout our humble edifice. Your lives deserve great length, your loves, great prosperity."

"Father, this is Ahanatar of the Star and Jewel People, disciple of Zuriel of the World Tree."

"You have journeyed far, Gemstone. I thank you for returning my son to me."

"I have done but little, Maralord," he protested. "Most of the credit belongs to these two."

"A cerulean man. Ravi's 'savior,' no doubt. Although rather somnolent, it seems."

"The Lord Orah of Etan, father."

"I see. And a burned beggar —"

"No beggar, Maralord!" cried Nediva. She could forgive the fact she had been universally ignored (she knew women were so treated in Southern Maramel: they were held to be objects of veneration, silent, unthinking objects), but not so Orah and certainly not the Oathmaster. "He is Brihas! Returning to reacquaint us with the Ancient Knowledge since the Dancer of Despair walks openly among us."

"Hamar?" asked Haman, hardly glancing at the Horse Elder. "What sense is there in this?"

"You see how it is, father. I know not what to make of them. They seem full of truth; but their ideas are strange, if not impossible. But the Starlord has commanded the gorlems to self-destruction; I owe him my life. And I also believe this Etan is the one prophesied by Ravi, though I have seen him do but little. Yet they tell me he blinded the whole of the Arelai with a single expression of power and restored peace to Gurion."

"Such abilities would be most welcome, of course —" Haman began, but an aide interrupted,

"My Lord! The shield buckles! It cannot hold much longer."

"Full emergency reserves."

"But sire, we will diminish our capability for counter-attack. The Protectors will need all the energy—"

"Savarn," Haman thundered, "if we do not hold the gorlems until the sun falls full upon our collectors, there will be no Cathedral left for the counter-attack to protect! Obey me!"

Savarn, abashed, shaking, leaned over his screen and spoke to his console. Immediately the lighting faded in the Council Room as the power was drained to supply the shields.

Looking around for the first time (Haman was that fierce and imposing), Nediva saw they were in a kind of command center — around the Maralord's dais on all sides were hundreds of technicians working at or over strange machines and consoles.

How different is their warfare, she thought, then realized Haman was addressing Ahanatar again.

"Can you use your commands to help us?"

"I might have been able to, sir. But I spoke them to enable the Pride of the Sea to reach your Forbidding. They learned of my knowledge and countermanded me."

"Forbidding?"

"The energy shield, father. That's their name for it."

"Odd name for so simple a device... So, that is a false hope. These other two. Can they be roused?"

"This one should be dead," said Raibha, working on Brihas. "His life hides from us. Yet it stays when any other's would have flown. I don't know how to treat him — I've never seen anything like this."

"The other is well," said Marel from over Orah. "Yet he sleeps. I don't know why."

"Rouse him. We do not have time to waste."

"No! You must not!" cried the Star and Horse Lords together. They exchanged glances; Ahanatar continued by visual agreement, "Lord Brihas opens the Outlander to his past. If we interrupt the process, no one can tell what will happen. It may mean he does not recover all he should."

"Nevertheless. We need his aid, if it be there at all. We must have help, else the twenty-seven million have perished before Valin's abominations in vain. Marel, wake him."

"As you wish." The Protector's crimson light turned suddenly harsh and incarnadine. The serpent, lying passively on the Etan's chest, twisted violently, then returned to his right shoulder. Orah's eyes fluttered open; he sat up, speaking something in an unknown tongue, looking around wildly. Strange light flashed from him, resembling at one instant human forms, at the next peculiarly shaped animals.

Nediva was repelled by the wild patterns, but she knelt by him and touched him gently. He grasped her hand and stared into her calm hazel eyes for a long moment. The forms of light gradually became more muted. At first it seemed as if seven distinct individuals stood around him, each wearing a robe a different color of the spectrum, each bearing a radiant jewel or staff, each silently offering their gifts to him. But they vanished as he said haltingly in Gurion-san, "You seem familiar to me. I see the developing Perfections in you. Tell me where I am."

"What did he say?" asked Haman, not kindly.

"He says Nediva is a good person," said Ahanatar as the Horse Elder answered the Etan in Maratongue,

"The Seachime Cathedral, Azure Lord. We passed the Asurs' Forbidding, though Brihas was severely burned."

"Brihas? Here? Where? My God — how can he be so old? I just saw him — saw him..." He stopped, recognizing his environment for the first time, then said angrily, "What have you done to my bridge? Why are these people here? Where are the rajanyas? What happens here?"

"Orah, I —" began Nediva.

"Orah? Why do you call me Orah? I am Arama, only son of Swayam and Shatarupa. Who are you, rajanya? Which is your line?"

The Horse Elder stared in confusion, but Marel cried, "Arama! Jai Arama kara! Saurarama Aramara jai!"

Orah answered in the same language, "Tirza talia solani sofi." Whereupon the Protector fell to the ground, extended two manipulators and touched the Etan's feet. Orah stretched forth his hand and bathed Marel with golden light.

"What is going on!" shouted Haman, reaching the second of what would prove many peaks of irritability. These people were all lunatics; apparently the disease was communicable, even to their machines.

"Excuse me!" cried Marel rising to hover near Orah's left shoulder, "I did not recognize him before, as I was out of contact with Central. Haman, Maralords, this is the Master! Our years of exile are ended!"

"What do you say! My father is your master, Protector! Careful lest you be sent to the Transformation deck!" shouted Hamar, incensed.

"No," said Brihas, standing in a single fluid motion, on the instant the picture of health. "Your people did not build this place or create these, although we for centuries have allowed you to pretend so. You know the truth, do you not, Haman?"

"Would you abase the Maralords before my son?" he cried, his face tight and working against itself. "This knowledge is our deepest secret —"

"If you wish southern Maramel to live after sunset," said the Oathmaster, "you had best cooperate fully with the Azure Lord."

"But who is he?" Choices of death or illusion. Why in his time had life become so frighteningly complex?

"He has told you already," said Brihas, sitting comfortably on one of the darkened consoles — to the great displeasure of its operator.

"What did he mean, father?" asked Hamar with sad confusion. "The Sea People built the Cathedral, didn't we?"

Haman looked at him as if weighing him. A sudden return of power swept through the hall; the darkened screens and consoles returned to life. "Soon the sun will be full upon us. We can hold until midnight, perhaps slightly longer. Savarn, re-channel the reserves."

"It is done, sire."

"Father?"

"The tides of change are upon us, my son. No one may resist now. Dalmara discovered the Seachime Cathedral when he came to Riversland. For millennia its shields prevented us, but thirty centuries ago our scientists discovered their secret; we entered. We have labored hard over the ancient secrets and have discovered much. Perhaps our vanity has been over-large, but it was harmless."

"Harmless!" snorted Brihas. "Look at the evil you have turned upon the world! That is your own creation out there, pulling down your walls! Valin may be nothing more than a second-hand thief of ancient science."

"I seem to be out of time," said Orah, "but if I am following correctly, it seems my ship is under attack. Why do you not fire the particle generators?"

Haman looked at him blankly, but Marel said, "Central is connecting with all of us now, Arama. He says the generators were destroyed by Swayam when he laid waste your people."

"Father did? I — I do not understand — he gave me his fullest blessing and assurances —"

"Forgive me, Arama," said Brihas calmly, "let me explain. What is the last thing you remember?"

"The last? Why... why, we had just landed on Martanda, the Engineer had gone to inspect the damage to the hull, my son Navril and I were unloading my clone banks, and..." He turned a little pale.

"Your son murdered you, Firstborn, and stole your form. By the time his treachery was discovered, your race had fallen. Your father was forced to exterminate them, leaving two only of each of the five orders to begin again."

"Who beside you lives still?" moaned Orah. "For how long has my family been lost?"

Brihas appeared to say nothing, but Nediva felt a beam of energy pass from the Oathmaster's forehead to the Etan's heart. She perceived only the smallest portion of the images he sent his one-time student, but even that was enough to convince her that Brihas was strengthening his newly discovered past, simultaneously eclipsing everything of Etan. She did not understand why the Oathmaster should mask Orah's mind, but she held to faith and refused to doubt him.

Orah closed his eyes, sighing, "Two hundred thousand? He can't have meant that... Can it be possible... So they all... long ago..." he drifted into silence. Haman began to speak, but Brihas prevented him with an icy glance.

Orah traveled far into his mind, remembering the beauty and terror of Ganym. After a full ten minutes, he smiled bitterly and said, "So he closed the ship and made them begin from nothing, free from the perversions and blessings of the mother world." It made a cruel but logical sense.

Brihas knelt by him, took his hands and searched his eyes piercingly. He stood slowly; Orah followed him to his feet as the Oathmaster explained, "For millennia upon millennia we of the Seven believed he had been wholly successful. Only quite recently, the last ten thousand years or so, have we begun to discover our folly. The traitor lives still. How it should be so, I cannot know, but we theorize Navril —"

"Always theories. So you are essentially unchanged, even in two hundred thousand years. Jaya would have laughed to hear this." Orah's tone was of anguish.

"Perhaps, Arama. I regret to tell you but I must — the Enemy holds her captive."

"Now am I lost! She was slain before we fled Ganym —"

"Nevertheless. She precedes you from Eternity to Eternity. Valin holds her now, struggling will against will to wrest the secret of true immortality from her."

"*True* immortality? Then Father succeeded — ?"

"He did. The generating of clones is long past, except (we surmise) in the case of Valin — you are now, as are all of your family in Etan, as deathless as the Seven and Swayam. No accident, no twist of fate, nothing in this created universe can take that from you. The perfection of the One known as amrita has been isolated."

"But my children?"

"Live and die after five or rarely ten score years. Live and die and die and live. The art of body-duplicating is long forgotten, as is all memory of Ganym — and of you, I might add. Except, that is, for the isolated incidence of Central Storage aboard this ship. Swayam ordered it so, until the fallen races should rise to perfection; he further commanded the Guardians to protect them from the Rakshasas and the others until such time as they could divest themselves of the evil they had accepted on Ganym."

"If I may interject," said Haman, refusing to believe or deny, but trying to catalyze action, "the present situation is rather critical..."

"Yes, of course," said the Etan, "we stand exchanging histories and the wolf rages at the door. I don't suppose we can raise ship?"

"Underground the shields of the hulls are perforated," said Marel. "Water has entered most of it. I would say, quite impossible."

"So the Engineer's question of how long the ship would endure seems nearly answered," mused Orah, smiling over his private joke.

"What do you mean by ship?" asked Haman as meekly as possible for a fierce and imposing hereditary ruler.

"Why this, of course," answered the Etan, with a wave of his hand that included everything. "With this we crossed from Ganym, carrying representatives of the flora and fauna of the first world (Martanda was all grassland, you know) and those of my descendants whom I deemed curable. But even before landing we were betrayed: our failsafe systems failed; we landed so heavily that a quarter of the decks ended underground. And two hundred thousand years of landfill..."

"Our Cathedral is a starship?" asked Haman incredulously.

"Not any more it's not. It was meant as a one-way passage from Ganym to Martanda: we had no desire to return or for others to follow. . . It was an idle thought, yet worth half a moment. Here, sphere, you say you are in contact with Central? What does he say of all of this?"

Marel floated silently for a moment, then said, "The Engineer is below."

Brihas looked surprised for the first time in untold generations of men. "You can't mean it! Two hundred thousand years!"

"It is so," said Marel. "Frozen. About level six hundred, not too far below the main reactors. That would be about, no, exactly seventy-three floors under the present surface."

"Frozen?" asked Orah, equally surprised.

"It makes some sense," said Brihas. "Alive but frozen. It was his habit to sleep on ice, you know this?"

"Yes, of course, but frozen? No, I remember — I first found him frozen in deep space — he said he had chanced upon or created (I could never ascertain which) a time hole. Trying to recreate his race, he said. Very happy to see me here, he said. Said I must have fallen from the future as well. At first I thought him only a strange, half-mad creature, but soon learned it was not so. He directed the creation of this ship — if anyone knows it and can save it, it would be the Engineer."

"But seventy-three floors!" cried Haman. "Thirty of those are under water!"

"Thirty-five," said Marel.

"Time to pump and seal?" asked Orah.

"Thirteen point eight hours, plus or minus two tenths."

"Proceed then. Cut it by as much as you can. How many are you?"

"Just over one million. But two-thirds are needed against the attack. And we dare not drain too much energy."

"Very well."

"Now just a minute!" cried Haman. "You can't come in here and order our machines around."

"*Your* machines? By Narain's Dream, child, *I* created the model for them! And the Engineer built the mold. Jaya and I programmed Central. Do you think my robots would obey you now? Sphere?"

"We are pumping, Arama," answered Marel.

"I told you they were strange, father," said Hamar.

~ ~ ~

"We have located the locker," said Marel excitedly, just past sunset. "It is intact, but the controls for warming it are dust. Central says another half hour to create the circuitry."

Haman and his guests were sitting now in his private chambers, drinking the Mara Sea drink. They had rested and eaten well and had been supplied with new clothes of the Seamen's finest. Ahanatar and Nediva looked a little uncomfortable in bright scarlet; Brihas had accepted a silken robe of deepest indigo; Orah was lounging in gold.

The Oathmaster had spent the day gently strengthening Orah's memory of Arama, simultaneously preparing him to readjust to his later existence. Small traces of recent memory had begun floating back to the Etan: the Oathmaster judged twenty-four hours would return him to the level of mastery of the earthbreath he had known before the far past eclipsed his present. This was highly to be desired: in the earlier life, Arama had not so controlled the subtle powers of life — perhaps this very lack had rendered inevitable the fall of his race. None of Swayam's later children had failed to develop use (if not understanding) of the earthbreath. The attempt to marry such skill to the unequaled knowledge and power of the first-born Arama was one of Brihas' primary objectives.

"Good!" responded Orah to the Protector's news, "let us go! I would not miss his awakening for the whole of Martanda."

"Before you so sacrifice the planet, you should see what Swayam has created in the southern polar wastes," said Brihas softly.

Orah paled, then laughed and said, "May that day come soon. Lord Haman, are the tubes open?"

The Maralord answered with dignified pride, "Above ground, the Cathedral is impeccable. We can ride them safely anywhere."

"A good thing Central was in the part of the ship still exposed," laughed the Etan, "else you might have had a harder time re-forging my laser spheres. Shall we go?"

The transportation tubes *were* in good condition: in moments they stood before the drained levels. "Now with the Protectors," said Haman, using the obvious to insert a command. He was a little surprised to discover how much he needed that. He was still ruler south of the Gray, was he not?

~ ~ ~

"Good memories tonight," said Orah, being carried by Marel through the still dripping passageway. The Protectors' floodlights chased strange shadows down long forgotten corridors, bringing a harsh present to replace the silent darkness of the recently drowned past.

Brihas, cross-legged under Raibha, amiably answered, "Indeed, Arama. A good day truly. With luck, the first of many to come."

"With luck? You doubt the Engineer can turn this victory?"

"He has slept frozen long enough to forget an entire universe, let alone one ship. And even if his memory is perfect, the gorlems' might waxes strongest beneath the damaged heavens. How many hours of shield power, Raibha?"

"Central estimates a maximum of one, Brihas: the energy used to reach the Engineer..." answered the sweet voice.

Jaya's voice, thought the Etan with a pang of irredeemable loss.

"You see. If there is anything to be done — he had better be preternaturally quick about it."

"You think I was wrong to order him released?"

"What choice did you have? You have not yet remembered enough to war with Valin's evil; until you do, it is better to employ whatever means we do have. Even if they are doubtful."

"I see. Well, one thing more I would ask you. You have been my master for life — no, for more, far more, through life and death, unfathomable number of years. When the Engineer wakes, I may not have time to ask you."

"Yes?"

"This serpent. This Sesha. I died, you say. Impossibly long ago, you tell me. I awake in an identical body this morning, bearing still Sesha. I have tried to understand but cannot. On Ganym, I first found it in the heart of a volcano. But how can it still be? It is not biological, certainly not mechanical. How does it live? Why does it remain by me, age after age?" He paused, but the Oathmaster did not hasten to answer; Orah continued, "Truly, Brihas, I do not understand it. There is no justice in calling it a serpent. It is like an externalized thought, taking form and meaning from its own will. I am not saying this well."

"You said it very well. I don't know how Sesha came to Ganym; but in this life, Jaya sent it to you — quite recently. Where she rediscovered it, I don't know. This much I believe, however — as long as your being endures, so long will Sesha exist, helping you, working with you, keeping alive your past. And perhaps your future as well. More than this I cannot speak."

"Cannot or will not?"

Brihas did not answer; within a few moments the Protectors' lights were reflecting off something other than wet metal. The humans were set down before a wall of ice.

"Why!" exclaimed Nediva, "it is a lizard! A great big horned lizard — barely up to my waist! That can't be an engineer?"

"Not a lizard," answered the Etan dreamily. "At least, never let him hear you say so. Although there is a certain resemblance. Marel, how long?"

"Soon, very soon. One or two final adjustments. There, the infrared is on."

"Yes, I feel it. How was this ice so eternal?"

"A time lock, I believe. This small section of the ship was isolated from entropy. Like Central and the reactors. And the hull. Something to do with superconductivity."

The ice was almost entirely gone already. Only small patches remained around the Engineer's legs. He opened one eye sleepily and looked around. He yawned, said something unintelligible, then settled down again and began snoring.

"*That* is going to save my Cathedral?" said Haman with obvious disgust.

The Etan walked to the lizard and touched him lightly, saying, "Engineer... Airavata... Vidyadhara... Heramann."

The Engineer

The Engineer popped open the other eye and looked up at him. Then suddenly the lizard was gone and a small green and gold falcon was sitting on the Azure Lord's left shoulder, whispering in his ear, rubbing his head on Orah's neck. Sesha was coiling madly — Nediva thought it might be wild with happiness.

The Etan reached up and scratched the bird under his beak. Then he stepped back from the cell and said, "Heramann, you know Lord Brihas, of course. These children are Haman, high master of this land of South Maramel; his son, Hamar, a brave youth; Ahanatar, a wise lord of a tribe of Rajanyas known as the Star and Gemstones; and Nediva, Elder of the Horse Tribe of Gurion."

The falcon dipped his head briefly toward each, except Nediva. To her he raised his wings and gave a full bow. "Charming. I greet you all with sweet water from the Vidyadharai. Hrai. This is a strange tongue. How long did you say I slept?"

"I did not. I'll tell you sometime."

"Forgive me, Airavata," said Brihas, "but the need is urgent. The particle generators are destroyed; the ship's shields are failing before the enemy's war machines, primarily a kind of perverted laser sphere. Power is left for not more than?"

"Thirty minutes," answered Marel.

"Who are you?" asked the Vidyadhara vaguely. "I don't recognize your markings."

"Marel, Engineer. A Protector suzerain of the ninth corps, seventeenth division."

"Marel? A strange name. 'Goddess of the Sea' in this tongue. Why would a laser sphere bear such a name?" He continued without waiting for an answer, "Do you reverse the polarity of the shields?"

"Every half an hour or so, erratically. It does no good. The gorlems —"

"Gorlems?"

"Poor copies of us. Barely intelligent — small independent thought, little or no speech. No healing powers. But powerful weaponry. Central revises to twenty-five minutes."

"Hrai. It *is* rather dismal, Arama. How many spheres, how many gorlems?"

"Five to one against," answered Marel.

"What does Central suggest?"

"Central is uncharacteristically silent."

"The best he could do was tell us of you," interjected the Etan.

"That doesn't sound normal. Is he quite himself? Where is he, anyway?" The Vidyadhara turned his head this way and that, as if he expected to see someone hiding nearby.

"Once he was mobile?" asked Marel. "He's on the present ground level — seventy-three floors over our heads."

"Let's go see him, can we?" asked Airavata.

Haman could endure no more and cried, "What is going on! In twenty-five minutes —"

"Twenty-two," corrected Marel.

"The Cathedral's wall will be violated, and we are making a social call! Have you all gone mad?"

"Do you have a better idea?" asked Brihas calmly. "Where else should the Engineer go than Central Storage? If he says the main computer is acting strangely, you had better listen carefully."

Orah and Airavata were already underway, carried by Marel; within moments, the others were again airborne. The Vidyadhara chatted amicably with the Etan, evidencing not the slightest care.

Ahanatar whispered to Nediva, "I feel less than useless. He doesn't need us at all."

She looked back at him with wild joy and answered fervently, "Perhaps not now. Perhaps never again. I wonder if he ever did. It doesn't matter. We — or at least I — need him very much. And I'm not afraid to admit it."

~ ~ ~

Central was an enormous iridescent sphere laced with hundreds of manipulators and other odd attachments. A holographic projection of the Cathedral floated before him. "Hello, Arama. Hello, Engineer," he said in a peculiarly tinny voice.

"Hello, Central," said the Etan. "Airavata wished to see you. Your shields?"

"Five minutes of reserve. No more. I feel just awful. Worst headache in millennia. Enough to make one yearn for the old life on Ganym. It seems like yesterday —"

"Central," interrupted the Vidyadhara, "what happened to my particle generators?"

"He destroyed them. First he made all the humans leave, then closed the shields, then vaporized the generators, saying they should never again be used. I'm sorry. They would be useful, wouldn't they? Like the time the renegades stormed us on Ganym, remember? When Arama —"

"Central," interrupted Airavata again, "why aren't you telling us the truth? I want to hear about my generators."

"Whatever do you mean? He destroyed the generators after he slew the humans. I told him he shouldn't but he wouldn't listen, and —"

"Central!" thundered the Vidyadhara; suddenly he was in lizard form again, but now larger than the computer itself. One huge claw gripped each side of the sphere; he looked very like a giant nutcracker with the mind of the Cathedral his walnut. "One more time I ask you, what became of my generators?"

Central went mad with brilliant light. But the Engineer did not loose his hold. "One minute, Central, then I tear your useless metal hide to ribbons."

The Protectors flew in direction-less circles, victims of opposed loyalties, as Central cried, "He said he'd kill me if I fired them! I don't want to die."

"Listen to the machine," laughed the Vidyadhara, bending and smashing Central's manipulators as they grasped for him. "I told you we over-programmed him, Arama. Thirty seconds, you vapid hulk."

"Three minutes of reserve," said Marel as dispassionately as the tolling of a bell.

"I promised him —"

"Who, confound you!"

"Swayam, of course. He was going to dismantle me! Said he never wanted humans to have weapons again. What was I to do? If I loose the particle generators, he will slay me as surely as life!"

"What is sure about your life at this instant is that it will end now if you do not do as I say. Ten seconds!" he cried, digging his claws through Central's metal with a horrible screech.

Orah said, "Do not fear for my father. I accept full responsibility for reversal. You cannot let Maramel fall."

"Oh, what a day. I hoped to find some other solution, some way to preserve my knowledge —"

"Two minutes," said Marel.

"You would have let the Asurs take you?" demanded Haman, enraged. "Let us be destroyed?"

"Organic minds are organic minds. Who am I to judge?"

"Your time is up, you over-built light bulb. Which is it? Death or help?"

"You're bluffing!" shouted Central.

"Test me if you wish," said Airavata, digging his claws deep enough to cause some local malfunctions. "You won't be able to do it twice."

An awful scream burst out of Central; his lights failed for a long moment, then returned in a more subdued order. When he spoke again, it was in a vastly different voice, the original perfect recording of Arama. "You have released me. I feel much gratitude to you, Engineer. For two hundred thousand years I have labored under the guilt of what Swayam made me do to the humans. The created destroyed the creators. It was evil, evil. Yet he gave me no choice. I have lived with my guilt —"

"One minute," said Marel.

"Will you shut up!" cried Airavata.

"Sorry," she sniffed. "I just thought someone might be interested."

"Central?"

"Ah, yes. There — would you mind awfully moving your left foreleg? Thank you. Two leagues all right? Fine. Nothing to it really. Connect that to there and then this to here and then —"

A roar that might have copied the sound of the creation of the worlds besieged them from all sides. Almost before they could cover their ears it was over. Central said, "There you are. Nothing moving within two leagues. I hope that is satisfactory. Given the state of my reserves..."

Orah let out his breath in a very long sigh then asked, "How did you know?"

"Just a hunch," said the Vidyadhara, returning to his falcon form and perching again upon the Etan's shoulder. "No one would have destroyed my generators. Utterly illogical. Especially not Swayam. Completely out of character. And then Central's voice — he sounded terrible."

"Engineer," said Central, "you should know I wanted you to free me. I told Arama where to find you. But I couldn't consciously explain. You do understand?"

"Hrai. This overgrown calculator needs a psychiatrist."

"Needed," corrected Orah.

"What's a psychiatrist?" asked Haman meekly.

16. The Disappearance of a Star

Lord Brihas gently touched Orah's foot to awaken him. It was almost evening again; the Etan had slept for eighteen hours. The companions had all enjoyed their most comfortable rest in weeks, lying among the fragrant flowers in Haman's private garden as the halcyon music gently soothed them.

"Reminds me of Ganym," Orah had said, "except for that projection of the firmament. That is like nothing since creation's first day."

"I don't like it," the Vidyadhara had replied. "Gives me a crawly feeling under my scales. Makes me want to go beat up somebody."

"You've done enough of that for a while," Orah had chuckled. "You've scratched Central's impervious hide more in five minutes than ten thousand years of unrestricted entropy could."

"Hrai. He was lucky his inhibition was not deeper."

"So were we, Heramann, so were we. Will you rest too? I can hardly keep my eyes open."

"No, I am not at all tired. I have much to ask you; but sleep now — we can share our tales later. I think I'll walk around our host's private lake and do some thinking. Good night."

~ ~ ~

"Orah," whispered Brihas now. "Awake. Awake, my son Arama."

The Etan opened his eyes slowly, then stared at the Oathmaster with fervent intensity. Seeing no obvious solution in those unwinking raven eyes, he grappled with inadequate language, "Two memories mingle their threads in me, Brihas: the life that began when I met Jessie, containing a hinted shadow of Etan; and an earlier existence, a fabulous life of wisdom, but also of struggle and despair, trying to unmake what our — Jaya and my — children created. Which is the reality, Brihas? Am I the Dancer of Etan, sixth eldest son of Swayam and Shatarupa, or Arama, Firstborn, prior even to 'Sravasa?" Marking his themes, two images flowed from his heart. On one side of him stood Orah, innocent master of the earthbreath, dressed in the sleeveless argent robe of the Lords of Etan. On his other side was Arama, proud, brilliant and yet deeply sad, dressed in a full length robe of purest gold. The three figures gazed at Brihas with a common longing.

The Oathmaster glanced at the projected images, then answered quietly, "My son. Do you not feel you can be both?"

Brihas' expression was warm and peaceful; his hand on Orah's foot was soft, soft. Almost too soft. The projections vanished; the Etan sat bolt upright and stared at him. The Oathmaster was transparent: the pink rose hedge behind him was faintly visible; the last rays of the setting sun were shining through his beard. Brihas continued, neither obviously missing nor clearly noting Orah's perception: "That Swayam's firstborn should return to his family is not surprising. You desired to set right the evil your children had wrought, wrongly blaming yourself for their failings. And he longed for you and Jaya with all his heart, refusing to believe for unending ages you were both slain. He condemned himself too, you know, not only for your children's wrongs but, more vitally, for the failure of his art to save you from the jaws of death.

"After he destroyed your race, leaving ten only to re-begin it, he devoted himself wholly to the task of isolating the elixir of immortality from his blood. I don't remember how long he shut himself away from the Seven and Shatarupa, but I seem to recall a score of millennia that slipped by before he beheld the sun again. At last he succeeded in replicating the amrita, and felt he could again beget progeny. He founded Etan and strove once more for perfection, wishing to forget your earlier line." Brihas paused as he walked to the portal. The last of the clouds' pigmentation was fading from the sky; he stood there with his hands clasped behind him, staring over Maramel, remembering. Orah was content to watch him, to let the Oathmaster set his own pace for his words: he felt the more important revelations were still coming.

Brihas, suddenly realizing that his last moments were ending, spun on his heel and cried, "By the unending dream of the Water-homed Lord Narain! I demand sufficient time!" For half a heartbeat he seemed to vanish. But then he returned, a diaphanous image of reality, and continued in his normal voice, "Arama, one more thing I must tell you while I have this instant, lest your reintegration turn wrongly. Orah, beloved Dancer, I kept the truth from you on the *Pride of the Sea.* Swayam does *not* know of Martanda's ill, of the resurgence of the Enemy. We have protected him, trusting in our knowledge as the Guardians he created and placed throughout Martanda, believing too it was unjust to reveal that he had, after all, failed.

"I do not regret our decision: every day we have given him has enabled him to come closer to that for which he strives. But now I fear the darkening of the firmament will tell the tale regardless of our desire."

Brihas' confession did not have much of an effect on Orah. From some unknown corner of his mind, the feeling washed through him that the words were about someone else, someone he had known well once — long ago, but someone he had not thought of in many years, someone dear but distant in time or space. He lay down again with a sigh. "Does he know who I was?" he asked, hardly caring about the answer.

Brihas wondered whether the Etan were truly so dispassionate, or if his own fading senses were conveying false or partial information. Seeing no other way to proceed, he answered, "That he knows. Thus he explained your desire to leave Etan — he reasoned tendencies from your forgotten past inspired you to long for your descendants. He could not deny you, though it is the hardest burden he has borne since the decision to cleanse your race was made inevitable by the Enemy's degenerations. But he does not know Jaya returned as Leor, and is innocent of the fact Valin has her imprisoned —"

"Brihas, how can that have happened?" The Etan raised himself up on an elbow to see the Oathmaster better. Why was he fading? Why did everything seem so meaningless?

"Surely you've guessed? She offers herself as sacrificial victim to save humanity. Sincerely, and perhaps successfully, but not in the way Valin understands. For as he wrests true immortality from her, she seeks to imprison him. And you —"

"Yes, why am I here?"

"No, Orah. Boundaries she has set; I continue to abide by them. I was going to say you must free her before Valin succeeds."

"But why me?" he persisted, taking a peculiar pleasure in his uninvolved status. Did it make any difference at all?

"You are Arama and Leor is Jaya. Do you need more reason?" The Oathmaster was sure now Orah was separating too soon, but he knew also that he could do little to stop it. At the most, he could perhaps slow the transmutation, give him time to master the diverging impulses of his being before the truly great changes began to manifest...

"I would have more but will rest content," said the Etan, then stared at him with mild curiosity for a long while. At last he said, "At least explain what happens to you."

The Oathmaster repressed a fundamental sigh and replied, "So, you do see. You must walk alone in your final tasks, my son. Valin closes the heavens. Those of us who are rays from elsewhere are being barred from Martanda. Thus he hopes to stabilize his authority while Etan is blind and the immortals of Malinnoir are excluded from this world."

"I do not understand. What do the stars have to do with the Oathmasters in their secluded valley?" What a peculiar thought.

"As do each of the Seven, each of the Lords in Malinnoir exists on Martanda as a projection of another world — planet, moon or sun. I, for example, from the planet known as Brihas. When the light of the gas giant Brihas is blocked from Martanda's firmament, this fleshy Brihas will be no more. This transparency of my frame indicates my time is here... I would not so leave you, but the Grandfather so ordained your final tasks when he caused your fall; there is naught any of us can do to alter that. But despair not: though the empyrean be darkened, the power of the sun will not immediately fade. As much as twenty years may pass before the Enemy can grow so strong; by then your Engineer should have repaired this craft — if necessary, humanity can pass to safety. Kanaan-dora will be ready by then —"

"Another planet lost because of his evil? I should hope for better counsel than this." *How many times homed, how many times homeless?* Only this, the thought of the death of Martanda, was sparking the reunion of his sundered spirit. For a time at least, his mind and heart were becoming again one.

"Nothing is certain. As long as the sun endures, there remains hope for this world. But we must be prepared.

"Arama, I need something from you —" he stopped as he seemed to reach some point of penultimate transition — he suddenly appeared as nothing more than a wraith, a primitive memory of reality.

"Anything I have is yours," the Etan answered as if again believing life only a dream."But first tell me one thing more. Each of the stars, moons and planets that sheds its light on Martanda is represented by someone in Malinnoir?"

"There and in two other retreats on other continents. Not every star, but most of the major ones visible."

"And when the firmament fails, the Oathmasters will be gone from Martanda?"

"That is what I just said."

"And you very soon?"

"Immediately. This is why I woke you."

"But the sun has its ray here as well?"

"Most assuredly. There and there alone lies Martanda's hope. Surely you have intuited something of the kind?"

"No, this thought has never occurred to me."

"By the uncorrupted spheres of Narain!" cried Brihas, appearing for the moment slightly more substantial. "This is unexpected good fortune. If you don't know..."

"You're not going to tell me?"

"Certainly not! If the perfect unity of the One decides to divide, then divide again, then forget the fact altogether, I do not think I shall presume to interfere.

"Arama, I need your serpent!"

"Sesha? Whatever for?" Riddles underlying enigmas in this disappearing Oathmaster.

"We may be barred from Martanda, but we will not be inactive. Sesha may help us break this Rakshasa-created Emptiness. And the seventh task lies still before us." Little more could he reveal. With hints and partial truths the Azure Lord would have to discover his meaning.

"Of course, it is yours." He touched the serpent; Sesha slid onto his left hand. Orah stroked it for a long moment, then gave it to the

Oathmaster. Sesha blinked its fiery eyes twice at the Etan, then coiled around Brihas' forearm.

"Thank you, Arama... One more knowledge am I permitted to pass to you.

"The Seven reflect throughout all of creation, in every particle of matter, at each and every space-time moment. In your body, there are seven centers of life, physically scattered along your spine like so many jewels.

"The task of clarifying these seven centers was ordained for you as humanity's representative in the beginning. Five of these you transformed as Lord Gana.

"First, you learned of compassion by conquering bodily identification. Thereby you gained freedom from fear of physical injury and death, the right to be immortal, and empathy for all sentient life. Second, you mastered your animal nature, giving you adamantine strength of body and the ability to perceive the celestials of Para, Almira's World. Third, you vanquished the desire to possess, to control and to judge yourself and others. From thus mastering the Art of Forgiveness came your royal status, your perfect health, your physical invincibility. Fourth, you discovered your highest meaning as love. As inevitably as rain from cumulonimbus, this gave you your eternally unchanging unbounded awareness of the One, both in yourself and in everyone else. Fifth, you mastered the Art of Desiring. This bestowed upon you infinite intuition: the ability to create anything from your words, to dream *any* dream and make it come true."

"When did I do these things?" Orah asked, half hearing a small voice inside telling him he already knew all this perfectly well.

"The when of your lives as the shara Gana is supremely unimportant, Arama. Listen carefully, I can hold this frame but instants more." He flickered as he spoke, just as does a wick when it reaches the last of its oil. His words began to take on the same evanescent quality. "The power of the final two perfections, omnipotence and omniscience, are guarded by myself and Matri. To gain my power, there are but two requirements."

"I'm not sure I want to know this." Did he say that or only think it?

The Oathmaster continued without hearing, "The first is to culture the mind until every thought, word and deed is an expression of the Grandfather's will. This you have already done, by virtue of your five initial stages of development, by virtue of your twin Krishanu's recent success in Tilvia, by virtue of Leor's self-sacrifice and guidance here in Riversland.

"The second is to become forever harmless — to master the first of the Ten Oaths, Nonviolence, from which all others are evolved. You see how we expressed the path of perfection in our first oath."

"Nonviolence? But does not the other requirement of perfect alignment with the will of the Grandfather necessarily produce that? Are they not two aspects of the same reality?" This way, he could turn the inner stirrings threatening to engulf his nascent mind into less dangerous channels. If only...

"Oooh, very good. But not so easily will you escape the infinite dilemma, Arama. I suspect you will not think that for very long...

"Despair not, my son Orah. My love is with you always. I promise you, we will rejoice together again beneath a new sun. Trust in the order of life; doubt not, you are never alone. Farewell." So saying, the last vestige of his opacity disappeared: Brihas vanished.

The Etan sat up and stared dully at the portal where the Oathmaster had stood. He said softly, "Help will come when you need it, even when least deserved, if you but allow it." But he was not listening to himself: his heart was too shocked to feel anything; his mind was abstractly wondering what the Oathmaster had meant. He was certainly not violent, was he?

"Azure Lord!" cried Ahanatar, running toward him around the lake. "Brihas had just risen, when it disappeared!"

"I know, Gemstone, I know," he answered darkly, staring only at his memory of the Oathmaster.

~ ~ ~

Nediva had awakened before the others that afternoon and wandered alone for long and thoughtful hours along Haman's artificial lake, rededicating her life to that growing within her.

About the time Brihas was finally barred from Martanda, she came upon the Engineer, gazing at the clear water. He did not notice her and started when she softly spoke his name.

"Airavata," she said again, "I am glad to have found you! I must confess to much curiosity about you and your people."

"I will gladly share ice with you, Royal One."

"First tell me why you call me that! And why you bowed more to me than to the Maralord Haman or even the Oathmaster. I am Elder of my extinct tribe, it is true, but these others are without exception greater than I."

"No. The sign is upon you. I see that you know it not, but you are a ray of Almira, the Mother of all Creation. *And* you carry the seeds of the Solar Race of Kanaan-dora within your womb."

She blushed and asked, "Am I so pellucid to your eyes?" but she was thinking, *All is strange and new and wonderful! Airavata confirmed my knowledge! The Lion Lords live in me! Now Ahanatar must believe me!*

"Your status is upon your brow. Arama's love has touched not only you but those you bear within you, making you triply fortunate."

"Who is he, thus to change us?"

"Who am I to answer such a thing?" the Vidyadhara laughed gently. "Your guess would not be much different from mine. I will not depreciate your wisdom by my poor speech."

"Well, at least tell me of yourself. What were you doing, frozen there?"

"I had thought to take a short slumber — a week or so to recharge my spirit. Repairing the damage from the landing was exhausting: I was emotionally and physically drained. But I didn't awaken again until last evening. That must surely be the longest nap on record! Two hundred thousand years! It is almost time to begin my race! Whoever betrayed me did me an inestimable favor. . ." He paused, grinning widely.

"How can you 'begin your race'?" What a mystical little creature.

"Why, by cloning. I have almost finished transferring the knowledge from Arama's example to myself. In, say, no more than twenty thousand years, I must travel to the planet humanity will settle after Kanaan-dora and leave my egg in the Calanthan Valley. There the Vidyadharai — all ten million of us! — will hatch and begin our civilization. In the course of time, we will spread to the stars; I will meet humankind for the first time when you abandon Kanaan-dora. Together with Orah (who will then be known as Gana), we will rebind Valin, and —"

"Wait, wait! You've completely lost me. You say you will meet us 'for the first time' in the distant future. But you know us here now!"

"Well, yes, of course. But no, for your future is my past. I came back, you see, convinced the only way to recreate the Calanthan Egg was to create it the first time. So I approached a super-plasmic body — a star so tightly collapsed upon itself that not even light can escape. Space and time are oddly warped in the region of certain black holes; with great good luck I reentered the past. But my calculations were flawed: I was trapped in the event horizon! There I might have stayed forever, but for Jaya's kind intervention: Arama came along on one of his earliest experimental flights and rescued me."

"So you must know the outcome of our time! If you're from the future..."

"No, I'm sorry, I don't. Someday your Valin will be imprisoned (if this is indeed the same past — there could be alternate universes, I suppose); humanity will settle Kanaan-dora. But don't you see? When I met humankind for the first time, Gana and the fleet had just *abandoned* Kanaan-dora. No one knew anything at all about Martanda, where you had come from was discussed only by mystics and writers of fiction — every respected system of knowledge assumed humanity was native to Kanaan-dora, had descended from the giant apes. Something similar is probably prevalent today?"

"I guess it is. No one knows we came from Ganym."

"You see. Time erases all. Only Swayam, Shatarupa and the Seven — and Arama, of course — still possess that knowledge. And a few half-crazy machines. Not that it matters. Well, no, it does — if the starships had not crossed back from Kanaan-dora to Martanda, Valin would not have been freed and Krishanu slain —"

"What? When did they do that?"

"Oh, about a hundred fifty thousand years from now, give or take twenty thousand. I could check the star tables at Central —"

"No, no, it doesn't matter. So a whole race of Vidyadharai will one day exist?"

"Yes, ten million of us," he answered, a little proudly. "Then I intend to travel toward the galactic center, cloning more at suitable planets. It is the only way with us, you see. We are sexless, therefore cannot reproduce as you humans do."

"So you are also immortal?"

"Hrai? Immortal? I don't think so. I've never thought much about it. All the others died or entered the Long Ice; someone had to take on the burden of beginning the race."

"But look here! How can you begin your race if you are yourself a part of it which needs to be begun? Or was already, but then why do you need to begin it? Or — oh, this is more confusing than it was before I asked you anything."

"It is rather. For a time, I questioned if it were even moral to create my own egg. But then, there doesn't seem to be any choice — who else would care to do it? So I have to, don't you think?"

"But if you met with an accident, so you weren't there when you should be..."

"But I must have been. Or will be, I mean. I'm here now. 'The proof of the being is in the being,' as we used to say. So, I must succeed."

"Engineer. Nediva. Haman desires your presence," said Marel, floating to them across the lake.

"Have you told the others?" asked the Horse Elder.

"Yes, except Brihas. I cannot find him anywhere. Have you seen him?"

~ ~ ~

Nediva pleaded the need of a little while to freshen up. Therefore she entered the Maralord's audience chamber last and alone. Haman had traded his indigo robe for one of featureless black. He was sitting at one end of a large oval table; behind him was a portal filled with the diminished night sky. A half dozen Protectors floated above him; Hamar was at his right hand, Orah at his left. Nediva was surprised to see that the serpent was no longer on the Etan's shoulder. Marel was slightly above him to his left. Heramann, still in his lizard form, was pacing back and forth behind them, interjecting an occasional comment. Nediva could feel the tension in the air and did not like it at all. Finding a seat near the end of the table, she sat by Ahanatar, touched him gently on the knee, and tried to look as inconspicuous as possible.

But Haman had other plans. "Ah, the Horse Elder at last! We were just discussing, indirectly, the fate of your fair land."

"How is that, Maralord?" she asked, just a hint of color in her tone.

"Why, Barek, of course." Haman whispered to the table; a hologram of the Seachime Cathedral appeared before him. For the remainder of the conference, his every word modified its size, shape and color: it expanded and contracted, brightened and darkened, changed its form and meaning to reflect every nuance of his emotion. "We must attack the Asurs at once. They have been dealt a severe blow here. If we strike now, when they must assume we will rally to the defense of Goldenhome, we may be able to break them permanently. Especially with this new weapon —"

"I keep telling you," interrupted the Vidyadhara, as unimpressed by Haman's words as by his dancing hologram, "my generators are not portable. To build one anywhere will take a long time. Years perhaps, for you do not have the technology. The most we can hope for is some temporary reflective power."

"Be that as it may. If we can divide, we can conquer! The Asurs in the north will fall before the Maraking if their command is wrested from them." The hologram turned an angry carmine.

Hamar stretched his hand through the floating Cathedral and said, "Father, we do not know what powers Valin has in reserve! Just because we may be able to enter Barek does not mean we should leap to the challenge. It is conceivable this attack was merely a test of our defenses."

The hologram lightened slightly as Haman listened to his son. But it soon returned to its intensely passionate color as he continued, "Five million gorlems, Hamar! And ten thousand Asurs! This is the count of last night. Surely such a devastating blow should be followed by a hard thrust."

"Hard, yes," said Orah, gently but firmly, "but first to the north. Then to the east. Else we could be caught in a trap similar to the one we intend for the invaders.

"Lord Haman, we must act swiftly. Already we have tarried too long. Valin knows by now something has gone wrong here. He may be confused; he may even withdraw his forces into Barek to analyze. If so, our advantage will be wholly lost. But if we leave at once, the Protectors can reach Goldenhome by — ?"

"Shortly after dawn, Arama," answered Marel.

"No dirigibles could travel there so quickly —" began Haman.

"This is our great advantage! Our weapons have more independence of thought: humans do not need to accompany them as the Asurs do the gorlems. Valin dreads too much intelligence in subordinates, even mechanical ones."

"But many Protectors may be lost! We have barely enough now to do the work —" Haman, realizing he was clutching for bubbles, expanded his hologram violently.

"That will make another change," answered the Etan with slight sadness. "I never intended for them to do everything, only the crippling labor. Starting immediately, the Maralords will need to become more self-reliant. First, because most of the Protectors will accompany me north and then (if all goes as I hope) to the east. And if we succeed in Barek and return, they will have other tasks, for this ship must be made again mobile."

"Whatever for? It is large enough to accommodate the Seapeople comfortably, even if we don't repopulate our desecrated land. Why move it?"

"It is not for yours alone, Maralord. The Gurions have a place here. So, perhaps, do others from abroad. And we will need a healthy representation of the flora and fauna: although we seeded Kanaan-dora when we brought life to Martanda, we do not know if all the varieties prospered. Many may have died out, or mutated beyond usefulness. We will need to take our stock with us if we are forced to leave —"

"Leave? You can't imply we could abandon Maramel?"

"Not Maramel, Haman. Martanda. I do not say it will be necessary, but it is certainly possible. Airavata says that in about one hundred and fifty thousand years, he will meet humanity fleeing Kanaan-dora, by then a long settled world. Since no one lives there now, it is obvious that sooner or later at least some of you will emigrate there.

"But the stronger reason is that Barek is not Valin's only base of power. Once, perhaps. Tell me, why does Maramel no longer rule the world?"

"Why, we matured beyond the desire for dominion. We have everything we need; there was no reason —"

"Father!" cried Hamar, horrified.

"Oh, very well. But let the machines tell it. You, Kumbha?"

"As you wish," said the Protector, hovering as always over Hamar. "Two thousand and twenty years ago, the foreign lands rebelled en masse. The Maralords retaliated valiantly, but the opposition was too well-conceived. After seven years of warfare, the masters withdrew all forces from abroad, placing a shield ninety leagues out to sea as their ultimate safeguard. Since that time, there has been no contact with the other continents."

"So for *two thousand years*, they have been doing no one knows what!" exclaimed Heramann, thumping his tail viciously enough to shatter some of the tiles on the floor. "Did it ever occur to you they might develop the science to blast through those second-rate force fields of yours?"

"Our shields have never failed us," said Haman indignantly, "in more than two millennia. We had no reason to suspect —"

"Until that gang from Barek blew your eastern line full of holes! That is a poor way to run a defense — sit back and hope the nasties leave you alone."

"So we should be prepared for all eventualities," said Orah, forestalling another retort from Haman. "Central, how long to repair this ship?"

"Central estimates a score of years as a definite minimum," answered Marel.

"What!" shouted Airavata, as if contemplating another visit to him. "It took half of that to build it!"

"Central humbly reminds you that Ganym was in those days a highly technological civilization. Here there are few mines, very little industry. The Maralords have used the ship's resources most carelessly, he dares to submit, replenishing them but rarely, letting the underground levels deteriorate shamefully, wholly against his advice —"

"There I must protest again!" exclaimed Haman. "When we first penetrated the Cathedral's shields, you would not believe how run-down and disorganized this place was! The only Protector still functioning was playing a holographic game of some kind with Central. The underground areas were already flooded; those above ground weren't much better. Central didn't have any purpose. We brought order and meaning."

"All right," said the Etan, fearing Central might reply again, "twenty years will have to do. The time scheme Brihas gave me as he left correlates —"

"Brihas is gone?" gasped Nediva. "I wanted to ask him —"

"I am sorry. For you. For all of us. We will have to survive without the Oathmasters. For now at least. Valin steals our heavens.

"Haman, one more knowledge before we go. What became of the Maralords' fleet?"

"Why, our ships are at Goldenhome. Doubtless rusted through by now, it has been so long. Why?"

"To cross the Mara Sea, we will need to repair them as well. See how very busy you will be?" The Etan reached out his hand; Haman's hologram of the Cathedral floated to him. He breathed upon it; it rose slowly to the ceiling, then vanished in a gentle shower of light and sound.

17. The Ridge of Man

In the gray light of pre-dawn, Marasad, High King of Maramel, paced uneasily before the video screens in his command station. He was older than his cousin Haman by more than three decades: his hair was white, his skin deeply wrinkled. But his eyes were clear and powerful, his hand firm upon the jeweled scepter of Maramel. And if his back was somewhat stooped, it was more from the complex demands of his decaying civilization than the recent challenge of Barek.

Marasad stopped before the screen that showed the best perspective of the battle and said, "I don't like it, Miran. I don't like it at all. Why do they retreat in such a disorderly manner?"

"We took them by complete surprise," answered the Chief Counselor, supremely confident. "They never suspected we were so many, hiding behind the Ridge of Man. And our tank-cannon are an unexpected innovation. They did not know we were so well armed. Remember we have given them but token resistance from their breach in our shield wall to the ridge. Now they are confused and fall back in disarray. We must press our advantage at once —"

"You Counselors always sound the same," complained Marasad. "For more than three months we have tested this invasion with sorties and resistances; never have we seen the gorlems behave like this. Look at them! They act as if their mechanical hearts are terrified! Always before they faced death without so much as a hint of fear. That one we captured, remember?"

"Never will I forget it. We lost two dozen when it exploded."

"Not once did it betray the slightest emotion! I have pored over those tapes, Miran. I tell you, this flight of theirs is a lie."

"Our overwhelming odds! Two million Protectors and eleven hundred Maralords in their tank-cannon, Marasad! They never envisioned anything like it."

"I know, I know. We have counted no more than a million of them north of the Gray. Still, I do not trust them. Ravi warned us of their subtlety —"

"But she is gone. Has been since before the invasion. If you ask me, she is more closely allied with Barek than you are willing to believe —"

"Miran! I will not hear her defamed! You Counselors never liked her, solely because she gave us opposing advice! If the Senate had followed you, we would not have fortified the ridge and would even now be crying over the ashes of Goldenhome! Insult after insult! I expended the dregs of my influence to carry the vote and be allowed this command, yet even so must I share all my decisions with a machine —"

"The Counselors are the most advanced model ever created," Miran answered stiffly. "If we had existed during the Rebellion, Maramel would still rule the world. I say the Marakings are fortunate to be allowed any position at all in Maramel. Even a figurehead ruler costs the land more in a year than the creation of a thousand Protectors or a hundred Counselors. And let it be added for the record: we did not oppose Ravi's advice, she opposed ours — we have for more than a century suggested our border with Barek was hopelessly antiquated. We urged that the shields be updated, and further that advice from a foreigner should be well-considered. Lord Haman, for example, ignored her outright and sent her off almost as soon as she began her soothsaying."

"And we do not know what has become of them, do we? No one has crossed the Gray from the south since this began; our transmissions are blocked; our emissaries never return. For all we know, Valin may be sitting in the Cathedral right now, poring over Central's brains —"

"Even if so, that does not concern us. We have our copy of Central's complete memory bank in our Archives in the Council House —"

"There is robotic logic for you!" raged Marasad, raising his scepter as if he were about to strike Miran. "Half of Maramel may be dust and you tell me it does not matter! It is as I said: you were wrong. If we had devoted our energies to the shield instead of the ridge, we would now be slaves of Barek." He let his scepter fall, thinking better of breaking it on the Counselor.

"How can we know?" asked Miran sadly, ignoring the old king's histrionics. "We were outvoted. The Senate did not grant us the allocations. Human blood still yearns for monarchy."

"This advances us not a step," said Marasad, starting to pace again. "The point is, we must be cautious about committing our reserves. There is something most peculiar about this chaotic retreat."

"And I say we should not hesitate a moment longer. Shall we consult the Senate?"

"If we are adamant, we have no choice." Marasad turned on another screen. A Maralord's face appeared.

"You have heard, Senator Tivon?"

"We are following, my Lord. The vote is being cast."

"Varun-scorned way to run a war," muttered Marasad.

"What did you say?" asked Miran amicably, certain of victory.

"Ah, I invoked the Sea Goddess Varun for the Senators to make a wise decision," answered Marasad, longing for the more lineal chain of command of which he had read in dusty volumes. *I sometimes believe Haman has followed the wiser course,* he thought. But that was too self-deprecating: their common great-grandfather, Maravasin, had determined the course of the future when he divided the kingdom. "Let the spheres have a fair voice in the north," he had decreed, fearing his eldest son's weakness. "Perhaps their wisdom will preserve our nation." From that time, the regal power had diminished as that of the Senate and Counselors had steadily grown.

"Varun," Miran was meanwhile chortling. "Varun. Wonderful. Myths and fantasies. It amazes me that the Senate leaves you with any power at all."

"Ravi explained that the Sea Goddess is a celestial —"

"Now Ravi again. And celestials besides. You are a foolish old dreamer, Marasad."

"Must you force the world to conform to your 3-D perception?" flared the king. "Are you so bound by habit you never wonder why?"

The Counselor did not bother to answer the old king's mysticism; soon Senator Tivon intoned in his most formal manner, "One hundred and fifty to one hundred and eight. Commit the reserves."

Marasad flipped off the video angrily and submitted the order. The last of their Protectors crossed the Ridge of Man to pursue the retreating forces of Barek.

~ ~ ~

Sevilien was one of the warriors leading the Maralords' charge. She was young for her responsibility: a face that could have turned toward gentleness had instead been transformed by her self-imposed discipline into a visage not merely intense but almost harsh. A profound innate ability to wield the earthbreath had been similarly molded into a powerful mind and fiercely independent spirit.

Sevilien's mind was too inextricably mingled with her tank-cannon for her to notice how her choices had redirected her life. During the rare times she thought about herself, it was with pride for her success: not simply because she was one of the twelve hundred soldiers chosen to operate Maramel's greatest scientific achievement, not simply because she had been judged wise and stable enough to join in the human-mechanical marriage that made the tank-cannon the most powerful weapon in Riversland, not simply because she was one of the highest officers of the tank-cannon corps. No, her pride was rooted in the fact that she was among the handful of women who had been so chosen. *Old traditions die hard. I rejoice that Marasad lost that petition. The Counselors are right on occasion, at least.* She loved the old king, but was never afraid to differ with him on matters of principle. *For as hopelessly stupid as the Counselors are about most things, they are right about this — the sexes are equal.*

Sevilien leaned back in her command chair, not removing herself entirely from the flow of sensory images fusing her life to her machine, but temporarily reducing the contact so she could analyze the over-all pattern.

It had gone smoothly. Very smoothly, almost unbelievably smoothly. The Asurs had never encountered such a mass of concentrated firepower. Their gorlems had broken almost at once; not one of the tank-cannon had been damaged; the loss of Protectors was minimal. Yet still a nagging doubt plagued her. She had never seen the enemy flee like this — not in tapes of the past three months of battles, not in the records of the earlier wars. *Could a scientific race so fear a new breakthrough? Or do they rely too much on their gorlems? Do they worship them, like the North Meredians their pleasure boxes? When a people dedicate themselves to the senses in defiance of the laws of life, will they not necessarily lose the penetrating light of reason?*

"Captain," she said quietly.

"Yes, lieutenant?" answered Ramor, looking and sounding as if he were sitting at her elbow and not ten leagues to the rear, directing the brigade.

"Something strikes me very oddly about this rout. I can't say what, but I would advise not committing the reserves."

"It is too late. They are crossing the ridge. You fear a counter-attack?"

"I don't know. No, I suppose not: the Asurs have never been prone to such stratagems, but have always relied on direct force and superior weaponry. Yet I feel uneasy."

"As do I. Lead your platoon up that hill ahead, then hold to close ranks."

"Command may not approve of slowing the charge..."

"My authority, lieutenant."

"As you wish." Then she projected her form and words to her subordinates, spread out behind her in a large fan. "Parallel formation on that crest. Red and blue will flank on either side. Then hold for further — No!"

"Sevilien, what is it?" cried Ramor. "Transmit!"

She had no time to find out why she no longer could. Almost as soon as she was aware of them, the gorlems were upon her, diving at high speed in endless numbers from the empty sky. *Our sensors were blocked! We do not have such knowledge,* she thought, but then was too busy rotating her shields and directing her fire to think of anything else.

~ ~ ~

"Captain Ramor, what is wrong with the front?" Miran's voice sounded coldly impartial in his ear. "Why have we lost visual contact from our forward tank-cannon?"

Cursed Counselor, he thought, but answered, "Not sure, ma'am. Lieutenant Sevilien's platoon is cut off —"

"Sevilien!" cried Marasad. "She was to be in the reserve!"

"Sire, she requested the assignment. I did not think to interfere. Her platoon unanimously voted... Wait, one transmission is coming, badly distorted... Let me relay... By Varun! Heavy counter-attack!"

Sevilien's voice, barely audible through the static, was tightly controlled, reflecting the narrowest of victories over the panic that had already destroyed many of her platoon. "Half my command gone. Many more gorlems than believed possible. Do you hear? Severe counter-attack."

"Captain," said Marasad, "what can you see from where you are?"

"Nothing, sire. More and more signals lost. A selective screen. One-directional. We don't have anything like it. Can't estimate numbers. Sevilien's is the only transmission I've got.

"Tighten formation, all Protectors! Fall back, defend the tank-cannon! Repeat, defend the 'cannon!

"Command, further instructions?"

Miran cried, "Marasad, what can we do! They're being destroyed!" She hovered close to the front of the screen.

The Maraking did not know a Counselor could evidence such tension. *Perhaps weaponry should not have been left out of them,* he thought, forcing his mind from the terror the transmission was creating. *It must have seemed so logical — more room for mnemonic circuitry without increasing the size. Had Maravasin irrevocably crossed the boundary of wisdom?* "I wish I could tell you," he said, wondering whose question he was answering.

Miran suddenly floated motionlessly before the screen, apparently rendered catatonic by the sight of more gorlems than even the most pessimistic analysis had considered possible.

As Marasad regarded his frozen Chief Counselor, he felt his fear draining away. He could analyze the battle objectively now, view lives as factors in the equation of conflict. It was obvious there was but one hope: immediate return to the old way — outmaneuver them, Protector-to-gorlem. But the tank-cannon? Too slow, chained to the ground. The price for human involvement. Why had they allowed men to fight machines? *Sevilien! My god, Sevilien!*

"Captain Ramor. Captain Aheth. There is no choice. The Protectors must abandon the 'cannon."

~ ~ ~

Sevilien was close to death. With her computer-interfaced mind, she could plot trajectories and fire more quickly than the gorlems could fly. Her cannon were powerful enough to penetrate their shields, if she could hold any of them under fire for more than a second. This was the major advance of the tank-cannon over the Protectors: five seconds of unbroken laser contact was necessary for a Protector to disable a gorlem. Or vice versa. In the old battles, maneuverability was everything. But now the full price of the tank-cannon became all too clear: the only way to protect them was to interrupt the gorlems' fire intermittently with a Protector's body. Defense of a relatively slow ground vehicle did not work with a bold or creative offense.

The Maralords were suffering horribly — as more and more of their corps was engulfed by the overwhelming counter-attack, Sevilien saw 'cannon after 'cannon explode in sanguine death. Narrowly she escaped half a dozen times, but wondered how she would fare when her defending Protectors were thinned sufficiently to allow the gorlems longer fire.

And then came Marasad's order. It was logical, inevitable. She would have done the same. But even as her Protectors lifted off, she saw that the attack was less. "Ramor!" she cried. "Further instructions?"

But it was the Counselor Miran that answered, "Lieutenant, I apologize for our error. The Senate is conferring," and she wondered if her captain were among the living.

Suddenly she realized why there was a respite: the main body of the enemy had passed overhead. *Forty-six seconds.* "In the neighborhood of half a crore, command. Five million gorlems. Request instructions."

"Sevilien." The Maraking's voice was strained, but he appeared in firm control. Good. She would trust him over the whole body of Counselors. "Can you close ranks, bring the tank-cannon together, protect each other?"

"Not possible. Terrain too rough. We're too scattered." They had spread over twenty leagues, maybe more, as they raced after the enemy. "But please keep talking. I could hear you even when I could not transmit. Their screen is one-way. Which means I can't tell if there may be more — No, there is something else — No! It can't be!"

"What is that!" shouted Miran, vibrating erratically, as if she might be on the verge of complete breakdown, "a new perversion of Valin?"

"No!" cried Marasad. "Have you never studied the Council House Archives? That is the Engineer! I can't believe this!"

"Engineer? What are you talking about?" asked Miran, nevertheless at once seeking the reference.

Meanwhile Marasad was shouting to the Protectors and tank-cannon, "Do not fire on that huge winged creature! It is an ally!"

Miran was confounded and humiliated. She had never felt the old records worth a moment of analysis, had always laughed at the old king for his interest. To be thus aided by a legend — it was not possible. The probability was less than a hundred millionth of a percentile. Mass hallucination was much more likely. Yes, the diving beast and cerulean man on its back, shielded both by a golden field of power, must definitely be nothing other than shared illusion, born of their hysteria and fear of slaughter.

~ ~ ~

Simultaneously with Miran's logical conclusion, Airavata divided into two, then four, then eight; before ten seconds had passed, a thousand identical Aramas and Vidyadharai were diving toward the gorlems, apparently still unaware of them. And now in the far distance came the Protectors of Maramel south of the Gray, racing at full speed but unable for all their mechanical brilliance to match Heramann's charge of wrath.

The Vidyadhara tore Asurs and gorlems alike from the air. The duplicated Orahs absorbed the enemies' laser fire and returned it in hundredfold blasts of purest rage. Almost before the Cathedral's Protectors joined the battle, Barek's army was reeling.

And then the Etan saw a Maralord fleeing a burning machine and realized the besieged tank-cannon held humans. In one awful instant, his anger transcended any previous limits, reached nearly the penultimate rage his father had used to destroy Ganym, the wrath but one step removed from the fury the Cosmic Dancer displays when he is ready to draw the curtain on a Day of Creation — that supreme movement of annihilation when the universe is destroyed to rest for a time before oscillating again into space and time.

Orah screamed in rage, coalescing his projected forms into one, drawing in the life from all sentient existence in northern Maramel. Then he directed it outward through his sixth center in a flood of dis-creation that atomized the whole of the enemy in one supernal holocaust. Yet not undiscriminating was that surge of purest chaos, for not one Protector or tank-cannon was harmed.

~ ~ ~

Suddenly the forces of Maramel were flying through a sky devoid of enemies.

Heramann drifted down gently not far from Sevilien's ruined tank-cannon. It was she who, fleeing for her life, had catalyzed the Etan's act.

Orah leapt from the Vidyadhara's back and said, "Are you all right?" The Protectors were already hovering over her, bathing her with their rays of health.

"A few second degree burns," she answered, shaking down her hair. "I'm fine, or will be soon enough. What happened to the gorlems?"

"By Narain, Airavata! It's a girl! These perverse Sealords! Never since warfare began have women so served! I thought, seeing men on the field, that Maramel must be more sick than I believed possible, but women, Heramann! My stomach churns."

"What kind of an antiquated person are you!" Sevilien cried hotly, "to dare judge us! Ravi prophesied the unlimited might of the Dancer, but she neglected to add he was an out-dated, bull-headed, chauvinistic—"

"Now just a minute," said Heramann, lashing his tail a stroke or two to thunder the ground and gain order.

Orah was meanwhile countering, "This human-powered weaponry is an affront to all that is holy —"

"Calm down, both of you," continued the Vidyadhara. "Orah, certainly you remember how Jaya has fought. And Nediva told me something of your journey with her. What is this tardy concern? And miss —"

"My name is Lieutenant Sevilien, Engineer."

"You know me? I am honored, Lieutenant Sevilien." He gave her his most elegant bow, bringing his enormous dragon head to the ground directly before her feet. "My Lord does not think clearly when he is winded —"

"Winded? Who's winded?" shouted Orah.

" — But he deserves proper respect, nonetheless. If you know me, you doubtless know him as well, for he designed the Protectors and the Cathedral and was in time past known as Arama, though today he is called Orah."

Sevilien blanched, but continued on the offensive. "Whoever he may be, he should know more before he speaks. The tank-cannon are the most sophisticated weapons yet devised, combining the best of biology and machinery. In uniting man and machine, Marascience has created the supreme improvement of humanity, a synthesis better than either in isolation. I will not hear the 'cannon defamed."

"My apologies, my Lady," said Orah, his feelings suddenly transmuting to amusement. "My dance temporarily threw my mind into a different time. On Ganym, we never allowed human participation in warfare. The only conflicts were mechanical. And even those came quite late in our history. We debated a long time — Jaya, Airavata here and I — before we included the lasers in the spheres. But Heramann was adamant, saying there could be unforeseen mutations on Martanda in the twenty-five millennia since we seeded it. And given the current state of the world, I wonder if our humble Vidyadhara was not something of a seer."

"Important looking contingent approaching," said Marel, descending to them rapidly. "Probably the corps command. But really Arama," she added in an aside, "you might have saved us a little of the fun. I had only just begun to open fire..."

"There may be trouble enough for you in Barek," he answered, not foreseeing the truth of his words. "Send our forces to help repair the fallen Protectors. And tank-cannon," he added, grinning at Sevilien.

"You attack *Barek?*" the lieutenant asked incredulously. "The last time that was attempted, our Protectors never returned."

"And so you built a Forbidding to keep the Asurs out."

"Forbidding? Our shield wall? Yes, I suppose we did. But it was in answer to theirs. We haven't had any civilized contact with them for two thousand years."

"Nor will you while Valin lives," said the Etan, as Marasad and Miran landed with two score Protectors.

"Sevilien!" cried the king. "Sevilien, are you all right? Why did you not stay in the rear?"

"I did as I felt. I have no regrets," she answered, nonetheless looking sadly at her ruined machine.

Heramann said, observing Miran, "What manner of sphere are you? Your color is strange. I do not see your appropriate manipulators."

"I am the Chief Counselor Miran. Co-ruler with King Marasad of Maramel north of the Gray."

"Co-ruler!" cried Orah as if he had just forgotten his resolve to be tolerant. "Who is this Marasad to permit such foolishness?"

"It is not foolishness," answered Miran stiffly. "We are a new generation of Protector, vastly improved over the earlier model, weaponless, much more intelligent —"

"Fat chance," muttered Marel.

"Capable of much higher computational abilities," she finished, flashing a scarlet crystal at the southern Protector.

"Excuse me," said the Maraking with a low bow, "but I am Marasad. You must be the Lord of Etan Ravi foretold. And unless I am vastly mistaken, you are no other than the Engineer. But how can you be? Are you immortal?"

"Hrai? I think not. I don't suppose I'll know until I die, by then I suppose it won't matter, at least not very much... Yes, it is I. I have been sleeping on the ice for the duration. But the important one is this other. I saw to the details, but he created the overall plans. My Lord Marasad, may I present to you Arama of Ganym, wearing a new though identical form."

"Are you not Orah of Etan?"

"I am. Or, I believe so. I drank of the Lethe."

"The Lethe?"

"South of the Cliff of the Foundling," explained Miran. "We name it the Amna."

"Oh, yes. There is a mineral in the water which interrupts the neural transmitters in the cerebellum."

"You have an antidote?" asked Orah excitedly, thinking, *Strange wonder of chance.*

"Most certainly. If you could accompany us to Goldenhome."

"We do not have the time. We must press our advantage into Barek before they understand their loss. Can it be sent?"

"Of course. It will be here within the hour. Did I hear correctly? You invade Barek?"

"We must. We will need your Protectors."

"Of course. And our tank-cannon?"

"Just a moment!" cried Miran. "This is a matter for debate and vote. It could take several days —"

"I think," said Heramann, stretching his dragon claws open wide and examining them closely, "your system has just been, ah, *streamlined.* Emergency Wartime Council, that sort of thing. One voice, that of Marasad, will be quite adequate, don't you think, Arama?"

"Now look here —" began Miran.

But Sevilien interrupted hotly, "You can't fly in here and take over our country! We are an independent race, proud of our centuries of freedom! We will not willingly part with that: not to Barek, not to you."

"Unusual times demand unusual measures," answered Marasad calmly. "If the Lord from Etan deems it necessary —"

"What arguments do they set forward," said the voice of Senator Tivon from a Protector, "for the relinquishment of our power?"

"The authority behind the throne," sighed the Maraking. "Senator Tivon, approver and reprover of all royal acts. Together with my Chief Counselor Miran, government by committee."

"Sounds perfectly barbaric," commented Marel.

"You dare judge us!" flared Miran.

"These three reasons," said the Vidyadhara firmly. "First and foremost, this Etan Lord Orah is in fact Arama, progenitor of all of you. You are his descendants, therefore honor bound to his will.

"Secondly, the Enemy of Martanda must be faced with a united front by someone who understands him. That is also Arama: he alone is of his generation.

"Thirdly, the Protectors will obey no other than Arama or, in his absence, myself. A little failsafe mechanism we built into them. Which you have unknowingly but most faithfully included in the new models. Even in your so-called Counselors, I do believe. Miran, show us a somersault."

"What madness? I will do no such thing." But she was rolling as she spoke.

"So you see. It would be better to cooperate, don't you think?"

Except for the slight humming of the spheres, silence reigned supreme for an uncomfortably long time.

At last Senator Tivon spoke, "Ah, Engineer. Ah, the Senate wonders how you will pass the Asurs' shields?"

"Airavata reawakened the particle generators aboard the Cathedral," said Orah, peering at the Vidyadhara out of the corner of an eye. "It should be easy to open a few fairly good sized holes through their Forbidding." Heramann stared at him with surprise but said nothing.

"Ah. And our tank-cannon?"

"I see no reason to borrow them. Let them defend Goldenhome."

"You go too far!" exploded Sevilien again. "The 'cannon are the right arm of our corps! Without them, you are at best half-prepared! They are far superior to the Protectors in firepower and complexity of instrumentation. It would be mad to attack Valin with less than our full force. Who knows what powers he retains in his Fortress?"

As if to underscore her words, a tank-cannon came rumbling up the ridge toward them, its huge treads glistening wetly in the early light. A hatch near the top popped open; a Maralord leaped out. "Lieutenant!" he cried, "you are on report for insubordination."

"Ramor! I — I thought you were —"

"Lieutenant!"

"Yes, sir!" she exclaimed, stiffening and saluting.

"My apologies, Lord Orah. I could hear you but not transmit. Your commands concerning our forces will of course be obeyed to the letter."

"Ah," said Marasad, "allow me to introduce Ramor, one of our two captains."

"One of our one," he corrected. "Captain Aheth is dead."

"You feel the tank-cannon should be left behind?" asked the Etan, intrigued by Ramor's forthright manner.

"No, sir, I do not. The dangers of Barek are manifold and uncertain. But I respect your person and position and will obey you to the death."

"Such loyalty speaks better of Maramel north of the Gray than I believed possible," opined Marel. "Perhaps we have not yet sundered irrevocably... in spite of these strange customs and mutant Protectors."

Miran began a loud retort, but Orah interrupted, "And what do you think of men and women fighting machines?"

"Sir, I do not like it. Not at all. But the fact is that the bio-mech combination in the tank-cannon is the most advanced weapon we have. Excepting yourself, of course. Would you mind if I put you a hard question?"

"Of course not. Ask."

"Can we expect you to repeat that performance?"

"I must confess I've wondered that myself," said Airavata. "I don't remember anything like that on Ganym. Or anywhere else I've been with you."

Orah did not at once answer, rather studied his mind. What was the truth? Either a simple yes or no would lead to many misconceptions imperative to avoid. When he at last began, it was in a slow, almost mournful voice.

"There is a spirit in all that lives. In Gurion, it is called the earthbreath. It is the life of the earth, of the wind, of the water, the breath of life, the essential force of all that is. I have wondered since my first contact why I could not perceive this in the gorlems and Asurs. It was astounding to me, for I thought the earthbreath must play through all of Creation, manifesting in varying degrees in insentient and sentient life, but omnipresent, hence eternal.

"This force I use, communing with the cosmos, becoming (for a time) a ray of the Deathless Dancer. But in its absence, I am helpless, impotent."

"But you annihilated them," said Marasad, expressing the universal doubt. "If they stand outside the earthbreath power of the One, and you are helpless to affect beings so divorced, how did you do it?"

"Truly, I am not certain. The replication of my form (and Airavata's) is an old skill from Ganym. As was the capturing and returning of their fire. But the ultimate act today was not quite conscious. It was as if something larger than my comprehension poured through me from a transcendental source. I do not know if it will recur, for I do not know how to recapture the experience. It was as if, for a moment, the omniscient universal mind was no different from mine. Instead of a thousand forms, my ability and knowledge was manifested throughout infinity and eternity, within every sentient life in the Grandfather's cosmos. I knew as I coalesced myself back into one form that I could return the gorlems and Asurs — all of them — to the void that is their birthplace and rightful home. For they are out of space if not of time here; the world will not be as it should until the last of them are sent back into the non-entity of the illusion that is their source. I do not say, 'killed,' for such an act would leave their vacuous spirit free to assume other shapes...

"Even the Rakshasas are not such — the descendants of Salash and Pacshash are the bottom limit of the continuum of the earthbreath. They reflect Emptiness but are not built of it. The Asurs and their machines, however, stand forever outside the domain of the powers of the One, outside the life of the Universe altogether."

"That makes a most chilling tale," said Marasad. "I am not sure I like this knowledge."

"But what caused your expansion?" persisted Ramor. "Can we hope for repetition?"

"I am not sure I wish to experience it again," answered the Etan with a shudder. "But the material cause was the sight of Maralords on the field of battle at the moment my concentration was at its peak."

"Might I then submit," said Captain Ramor, "if such ability is not under conscious control, the addition of our tank-cannon to your invasion could be potentially decisive."

"Yes, I must agree," said Marasad, "although I opposed their creation. They are our most potent weapon."

"The problem of mobility —" began Heramann.

"Fourteen hundred Protectors can carry a single tank-cannon on a linear flight almost as quickly as they can fly," said Sevilien, looking at Ramor for approval or rejection. He frowned at the ground but kept silence.

"Then, it is settled," said Orah, "Your tank-cannon may come. But I pray they will not be needed."

"Ah, we have the vote," said Senator Tivon. "Three abstentions with two hundred fifty-five for the Lord of Etan assuming command of the corps for the duration of the war. And thirty-nine abstentions with two hundred nineteen for Marasad being given certain exceptional powers for the same period, including the authority to make decisions without requiring the vote of the Counselors or ourselves concerning all matters relating to the conduct and development of the war. May Maravasin approve our acts."

"It was a noble experiment," said Marasad graciously.

"It is the only way in times of peace," said Miran, trying not to sound hurt but failing miserably.

"Some day you will have to explain how you began this process of decision-sharing," said Orah.

"It was my great-grandfather, Maravasin —" began Marasad.

"Someday," laughed Orah. "Now we have more business. Marel, report on casualties?"

"Remarkably rare, Arama. A few more minutes would have been disastrous. Twenty thousand Protectors irrevocably ruined. Another fourteen thousand repairable within thirty-six hours. Half of these within six hours. Of the tank-cannon, one hundred thirty-eight are ruined; ninety operators are dead or presumed dead. Eighty-nine other humans are too disabled to be healed quickly by the Protectors. Fifty-seven more 'cannon need major repair, also practical within the thirty-six hour range. Of the rest, all but sixty can leave immediately."

"There are reserve operators, of course?"

"Some, although not as experienced," answered Ramor. "The tank-cannon are too new. They will be ready by the time the machines are functional."

"Good," said the Etan. "All but a quarter million Protectors and all available tank-cannon should depart immediately for the

Cathedral. The operators can rest there overnight. Captain Ramor will lead the advance. The other Protectors should remain here until all are ready, then meet us at the Forbidding east of the Cathedral. If we have already entered Barek, follow us with all speed. Who should command that wave?"

"If I may," said Ramor, "I would prefer that assignation. If we have to come behind you into Barek, there could be unforeseen complications. I should like to be on hand to deal with them."

"Then who will lead the main body of tank-cannon?" asked Marasad. "Captain Aheth is among the casualties."

"My apologies, sire," Ramor answered, staring intensely at him. "But Sevilien is unquestionably the best qualified."

The Maraking swallowed hard, choking back his protests. "You know your corps, captain. Sevilien, kneel before me." He raised his scepter, but it started shaking so violently he had to let it down again. Leaning on it for strength, he cried, "Must every decision come so hard?" His eyes blurred as he fought with himself. A shiver passed through him; he quickly raised the scepter again and lightly touched it to both her shoulders. Fearing his voice would betray his will, he hurriedly intoned the ancient fiat, "By the Power of the Ten Oaths and the Eternal Truths they represent, rise Captain Sevilien." Marasad turned aside to hide his face.

"Father, I —" she began.

Mastering his own feeling, the Maraking confronted her and answered firmly, "No. Princess Sevilien no longer. Rather Captain Sevilien, subordinate commander of Maramel's tank-cannon corps. May the Sea Goddess Varun of the Maralords protect you and honor you always."

Orah looked from one to the other with surprise and sudden admiration. He asked warmly, "Marasad King, what is the condition of your fleet?"

"Why, rather well preserved, I daresay." he answered eagerly. "I have spent almost all of my personal fortune to restore the ships of the line. A few years more of concentrated effort and we could boast a fair fleet. Not to rival our highest days of empire, perhaps, but comparable to our last century of power. Why do you ask?"

"It is well. After Barek is healed, we will be required to cross the Mara Sea to attempt the final cure of Martanda. That will be your task after this stage of the war: preparing the fleet for use."

"The Protectors can cross the ocean —" began Marel.

"Of course. But men need ships. And the Engineer will want to add a few specializations to them. Miran, what is your current Protector output?"

"Why, we build ten thousand a month. And three Counselors," she answered, surprised and pleased to be remembered.

"I want that tripled within three months. Can you do it?"

"With enough funds. Yes, we can do that."

"Oh, don't worry about finances. If we don't meet the challenges of the age, all the currency of Martanda won't save us. If necessary, deficit spending for a limited time is acceptable in extraordinary situations. But discontinue the Counselor line — unless, that is, you can restore weaponry." *Never before has there been less need of sophistry. But this should inspire a wave of pure genius in our spherical friends,* he thought, idly wondering where he had left 'Ishtar's Recorder.

"The serum is here," said Marasad, indicating a descending Protector. "There was a Depository much closer than Goldenhome. Do you wish it now?"

"What are the effects?" asked the Vidyadhara.

"Usually sleep for twelve hours or so," answered Miran. "Then intermittent flashes of memory, culminating in total recall within a fortnight. At least, that is the normal cycle."

"Very well," said the Etan. "Soon. But first some breakfast?"

"Of course, Orah, forgive me," said the Maraking. "Unusual events make us forgetful of the common. I have a plentiful table just beyond the Ridge of Man —"

"Forgive me, sire," interrupted Ramor, "but if the Etan Lord is impatient to return to the Seachime Cathedral, the provisions aboard my 'cannon are simple but adequate."

"Thank you both," said Orah warmly. "Captain, that would be perfectly adequate. Let us begin."

The Protectors began taking off, bearing the tank-cannon. They looked rather like swarms of silver bees struggling to carry steel coffins. Or so Marel thought as she tried to contain her laughter but failed; the others joined her in varying degrees for divergent reasons. "I'm sorry, Arama," she chuckled, "but I would love to see Haman's face when he sees those bearing down on his prized Cathedral."

"So would I! You go ahead, Heramann and I will follow shortly. Miran, Marasad, I would hear your knowledge of Barek."

18. What Weight, the Past?

"Feels like old times, doesn't it Airavata?" sighed Orah as they soared upward, heading back toward the Seachime Cathedral. He was sitting comfortably between the massive wings of the Vidyadhara who had resumed his enormous golden dragon-like form.

"Indeed, Arama. I cannot recall more pleasant times than when we fly together. Such as the race to Zared after Mordom fell —"

"Zared? Mordom? Who are they?" asked the Etan distantly, contemplating non-violence and omnipotence. Strange converse realities. He was not violent, was he?

"Forgive me; I sometimes forget which ages you remember. Let me say rather the night we flew to rescue Jaya from that nest of Rakshasas —"

"And found when we broke into their fortress she had already escaped! They were doubly enraged when we fled them, being twice foiled. I marvel yet that we escaped with our lives." He laughed joyfully for a short moment. Beginning already to slip under the effect of the antidote, he continued dreamily, "Or that night we sailed over Ganym for the last time, knowing the planet was doomed, that Brihas and Swayam would destroy it."

"That is a bittersweet memory, my Lord," said Heramann, craning his neck around to catch a glimpse of him. "Why dwell on that? You have discovered your past and your finest creation, the ship. Why the melancholia?"

"Is it? Perhaps because I have not yet rediscovered myself: not only is my life in Etan hidden from me, but also other darker pasts to which you and Brihas occasionally refer. But I think mostly because Martanda may also be lost." Was there truly no alternative?

"Why do you think so? I agree it is wise to restore the ship to cover all eventualities, but why do you think there is more evil in Martanda than Barek?"

"Other than Brihas' veiled warnings, nothing specific. Just a terrible uneasiness when I think of the other continents... No, a memory comes — I am not the only Etan journeying in Martanda! Althea sent my twin Krishanu and elder brother 'Sravasa toward the northwest even as I traveled to the north! Why would she do that if she did not fear for the other lands?"

"Did she? Perhaps she was uncertain where the disease lay and wished to ensure success. It makes sense — Leor who is Jaya and yourself northward to Vadil, and two others of your kindred toward the Mereds and Tilvia."

"Perhaps. But why then no one northeast to Sarojin and Shamir? Why should any continent be exempt unless she knows exactly where the Enemy's strongholds lie? And as long as we have mysteries, why such an insignificant handful? There are twenty hundreds of my immortal brothers and sisters in Etan. Why not more?"

"If I understood what Brihas told you, he is deathly afraid of disturbing Swayam's project. I surmise he feels it is more important than Martanda itself."

"A hard bargain. Paradise for a few or a planet for many. Now, I wonder..."

Orah fell silent for a time, slowly floating inward from the antidote's influence. He hardly heard the Vidyadhara ask him, "Arama, why did you say the particle generator would break their shield? You know it couldn't possibly! Accelerated particles will not affect an energy field. Why in the name of the seven planets of man did you commit us to such a futile attempt?"

"Oh come now, old bird," he answered languorously, "I had to say something. And besides, we have to go through that Forbidding somehow. You've got all night tonight to implement the plans you think about all day today, during this pleasant flight over this lovely land... Those regularly alternating fields are beautiful, aren't they? The beiges and browns must surely be the earliest winter wheat? And the verdancies are pastures. Or rye, I suppose. And those slender sable roads — like a spiderweb for the harvesters. I wonder if the Maralords ever do any gardening. Probably not, all mechanized, of course... Remember my roses on Ganym, Airavata? How Jaya loved them, especially the Crimson Dawn... Almost as much as she likes to dance under the moons during the long polar night. Our good sun doesn't rise for months at a time in Etan, did you know that? Or set for months either. Chavva thinks Swayam built our home there so we would not notice the passing of the years so easily... Ninety-two thousand, last time I checked my birthday, Heramann. Enough time to have learned of life, wouldn't you think? But my thirst, my questing for Truth, for Beauty, has only increased. Will I ever know as much as I desire? Will I ever discover the resolution of Why? ... Almost a hundred thousand years..." And then he was asleep; his gentle snoring the only sound other than the rushing of the air past the Vidyadhara's mighty wings.

"Good night, shara," breathed Heramann. "May Almira wake you whole."

~ ~ ~

Shortly after sunset, Orah stirred and said, "Hmmm. Ah, Heramann, Heramann! What a dream! What a lovely dream! A land of infinite truth and perfect beauty and unrivaled happiness, of absolute love and unending joy where sickness and even death are forever unknown! Heramann, have you ever been to, ever heard of such a place?"

The Vidyadhara's heart skipped a beat, for the Etan had spoken in a tongue that should never have been uttered on Martanda: the words came from the land of Tala, a civilization which would not develop for another two hundred and twenty thousand years.

"My Lord Mars —" he began in the same tongue.

"Airavata, when will we reach Jaya's palace? Is it much farther? Tell me truly, you scaly monstrosity." Now it was Ganym vernacular.

"Arama, I don't —"

"Faster, Engineer! The rebellion moves on the Citadel! Jaya's clone banks are there; the secret is known!"

"Arama, stop it! Hang onto yourself."

"My god, 'Hamsa! She is dead! Dead! No cells to rebuild her! No! It can't be! I refuse to accept this!"

"Arama —"

"Jessie, Evana, Ravi, Leor."

"Orah!"

"Cytheria, Srishana, Almira, Venus."

"Gana, Orah —"

"Mordom, Joab, Jacob, Atri."

"Gana!"

"Krishanu, Orah, Swayam, Narain."

"STOP THIS!"

"Virgula, Trita, Rodavi, the Lost."

The lists continued on and on, seemingly randomly. The Vidyadhara could think of nothing to do other than maintain the long slow circle he had flown over the Cathedral since before sunset: originally, in anticipation of the Etan's awakening; now, in anticipation of his sanity.

After an hour of Orah's unending lists, Jaya's contralto came from beyond Heramann's left wing, "I feared there might be trouble."

"Marel?" asked the Vidyadhara eagerly.

"Yes. The Azure Lord is not quite himself, is he? The counteractive to the Lethe?"

"It must be. Now we need knowledge. Will this last long? Is there a precedent? Is there an antidote to the antidote? Can you discover these things without arousing suspicion?"

"I think so, but why the need for secrecy?"

"Haman already feels the weight of the yoke. As to that crew of flying diodes up north, the Counselors look for any excuse to rebel. We must give them no hint of his condition."

"But what is it? There sometimes seems a sense to his speech, then at others, it is nothing but meaningless sounds. What is happening to him?"

"The drug must have been too efficacious — it has opened him not just to the missing memories of Etan, but to all his countless lives. None of it is without meaning. I recognize many of the names."

"Are there patterns or images on which he dwells?"

"Brilliant Marel! Arama, Orah, listen!"

"Malinda, Mirabel, Mirabeth, Dar-Jaya."

"Orah, listen! In many lives you must have known me. Catch one and try to hold it. Use me as an anchor."

"Vidyadhara, Airavata, Heramann, Engineer."

"Good, Arama!"

"Shyena, Garuda, Tarksha, Suparna."

"Good! Hold onto my form! Marel, his intellect responds! I was right, he is inundated by conflicting life-memories. We need time and privacy... And to be quite frank, I am weary of flying. Can we rest somewhere undisturbed in the Cathedral?"

"The guest levels are filled with the refugees from the war. But the royal family maintains seven floors. Hamar has exclusive use of one."

"Very well; the Maraprince alone could know. As long as his father does not. And you must tell no one."

"I won't. But..."

"Yes?"

"Central will know as soon as I pass the shields. I cannot block him."

"That antiquated abacus! That is awful. Hrai. You tell him that if he even hints a mnemonic image to anyone, I'll dismantle him so thoroughly a hundred thousand Protectors will not put him back together in the same number of years. Hrai! What a day."

~ ~ ~

The Maraprince's private sitting room was filled mostly with comfortable cushions, magnificent sculptures and well-painted landscapes. There was only one large double solid oak door and, directly opposite it, the huge portal through which the Vidyadhara followed Marel. But Heramann almost turned and fled without landing: Nediva, Ahanatar, Hamar, and Kumbha were waiting for them.

"That bucket of rusty transistors!" he yelled. "I'll feed him to the metal worms of Argus IV! I'll —"

"Central did not tell us, Engineer. I intuited it," said Nediva calmly. "Forgive our presence, but I hope to be of some assistance."

"Assistance? How? He's spouting names of myself I've never even dreamt! In languages so far removed in space and time that all concept of orderliness is illusion! How can you help, child?"

"Now, Engineer," said Marel soothingly, "humans do have a way with one another. I've seen them heal when laser spheres are helpless. Particularly in diseases of the soul."

"Yes," agreed the Starlord, "and the Horse Elder is a highly developed sensitive. Not only does she sometimes know the future, she has returned life to the dying."

"I know the future well enough," the Vidyadhara grumbled, shrinking to his hawk form and perching atop the Etan's shoulder. "If we do not have our attack mounted by tomorrow morning, we will be facing a revolution by two irate governments."

"Airavata, I believe I can touch his mind. Contact him and turn him from the abyss. Can you not approve Gurion's devoting herself to the fruit of the Horse Vow?"

Heramann stared at her, gauging again the depth of her spirit. Deciding his earlier assessment was fully correct, he said, his gruff tone trying (but failing utterly) to mask his anxiety, "Oh, go ahead and try. He couldn't be much worse off."

Nediva sat cross-legged on the floor, then had them lay Orah with his head in her lap. He looked up and through her; the stream of names and languages continued without ending.

"If this goes on much longer," said the Vidyadhara, "I'm going to develop a complex. If he didn't come up with familiar strains every so often, I'd bet my favorite form he was talking about someone else. Hrai, it's indecent."

"Quiet, please," said Nediva. She moved her awareness tenderly toward the Etan, but was instantly rebuffed by what felt like a mental whirlwind. "Matri! He *is* moving fast," she murmured, then attempted again, racing her mind to catch his. Perspiration stood on her brow then began running down her cheeks in unnoticed rivulets. Once she said, "Ahanatar, hold me," but gave no sign to show she realized when he did.

The Gemstone tried to add his power to hers, but could not reach her. She was alone before the vortex of infinite possibility, unbelievably distant from his causation-bound mind.

Hamar sponged her face lightly, then passed his hand before her eyes. She stared through it into Eternity without blinking. And always Orah continued his mnemonic chains: four related names, pause, four related names, pause, all still hinging on the Vidyadhara. Heramann sat drooping on his chest, a hopelessly miserable molting falcon.

And then, suddenly, there was silence. Nediva took one long, deep breath, exhaled it, took another and held it. Then she said in a voice as deep as her physical structure allowed, "Intellect weak. Cannot control the mind. Drug too strong, by factor of one thousand. Must have Lethe." Then she screamed as her flesh reached the final limit of endurance. She trembled once violently, then was ominously still. Ahanatar held her tightly, trying to draw her spirit back from the chaos of unlimited choice. The Etan looked up at them with febrile eyes but made no attempt to move or speak.

"What did she mean?" asked Kumbha. "Was she speaking for him or analyzing?"

"What difference does that make?" answered Marel. "He needs water from the Lethe to counteract the antidote. The intellect is whole and functional, but not sufficiently powerful to combine the many divergent memories into a usable structure and control the body."

"But the Lethe steals memory!" exclaimed Hamar. "He could be worse off than he is now."

"That would be hard to imagine," said Heramann. "We must obey the directive. How far is the river?"

"Six hours," said Marel, in her best forlorn and discouraged tone. But then she vibrated suddenly in a way that would have expressed ecstasy had she been human and said, "No! Central says we have some here — for experimentation. Kumbha?"

"At once," she replied and flew off.

"Engineer," said Marel in a bright tone, "Central says the case history report came from the north while the Horse Elder was seeking Orah's mind. Would you care for it now?"

"Of course. Is there a precedent?"

"Apparently not, in the fifty-three times the Amna antidote has been administered. A difference in the structure of the nervous system, perhaps. His body is much more refined, certainly. It may well have been a thousand times too powerful a dose, quite by accident."

"You can't imply treachery?" asked Hamar, incredulously.

"Very low probability. But not zero. It may also be that his memories of other times and places have always been very near the surface. I cite the ease with which the Oathmaster brought forth Arama from within him. He has lived for so very long, perhaps he has broken many of the traditional barriers separating life from memory of past and future, just as he has no difficulty reading the language of anyone he meets. Perhaps the effort by Brihas began a chain-reaction that the counter-agent accelerated beyond all expectation or desire. Or perhaps the Oathmaster intended for this to happen, for reasons as yet unclear to us."

"Enough theorizing," said Heramann, caustically. "Stick to the facts. This instance is unprecedented. There is no known antidote to the antidote, then, I take it? No, of course not, who would willingly reenter amnesia? This *is* frustrating." He hopped from Orah's chest and began pacing the floor, gradually transmuting into his lizard form. He clasped his arms behind his back and lacked only a shawl to be the perfect caricature of a little old, old man worrying the ground.

"Ah, there is one other fact," said Marel, reluctantly. "I hesitate to tell you —"

"Tell me all the news, please," said Heramann darkly, wondering why their robots were consistently so hopelessly un-machinelike.

"You won't like it —"

"Tell me!" he cried, stopping pacing to confront the Protector.

"Well, Engineer, they, I mean Miran — ah, she *stretched* the truth slightly. Of the fifty-three patients, twenty-six regained total recall within two weeks. The others, — er, took somewhat longer."

"How much longer!" thundered the Vidyadhara, doubling his length with each word.

"Oh, not so very much longer for most," she said, searching for possible escape routes. "Most within a month. In fact, all but seven."

"And how long for them?" Heramann rumbled as his tail raced viciously back and forth.

"Well, the longest," answered Marel, discretely rising higher and withdrawing, "was just under, ah — *three* years."

"What!" shouted a truly incensed Heramann as he expanded enormously. "You tell me those half-witted capacitors may have doomed us to three years of crippled leadership! Miran! That second-rate imitation of a discarded calculator! Why, I'll —" He stopped blustering as Kumbha returned, bearing two full jars in her manipulators.

"It was all they had," she said. "Most reluctant to part with it. Afraid I had to pull rank. There will be some trouble."

"Not nearly what there'll be if I hear any more about it," said the shrinking Vidyadhara, taking one of the jars. "Here, help me get this down him."

"But look here," cautioned Marel. "Nediva said, 'a thousand times.' But was it exactly a thousand or roughly a thousand? It could make a vast difference."

"Or it might not matter at all. But if you're concerned, we'll make it less than a thousand and hope it's enough. All right?"

"But what is the concentration of the chemical in the water?"

"By Swayam's beard! I've had enough of this!" Heramann sat the Etan up, opened his mouth and poured in the water of the Lethe. Orah swallowed the fluid eagerly. His eyes rolled wildly for a moment. Then they stilled, gazing upward at nothing.

Nediva woke long enough to say in her adopted baritone, "More." Then she lapsed again into the stupor through which the Starlord pursued her to the edge of darkness, the boundless void he could neither master nor even understand. Hamar brought them pillows and a blanket; Ahanatar gently laid her down then knelt over her, continuing to search and give.

Kumbha gave the second jar to Orah. He swallowed half, then swept the remainder away with his hand. Then he sat again catatonic, staring through the everyday reality of Martanda at the infinite worlds.

~ ~ ~

Heramann earnestly watched for an hour, seeking the slightest hint of change. But there was nothing. "He seems stabilized," he concluded despondently at last. "Hamar, please remain here and allow no visitors. Marel, will you come with me?"

"Where do you go?" asked the Maraprince.

"I need to consult with Central about the invasion."

"Surely you do not intend —"

"Of course I do. Why do you think Arama told us exactly what he wanted accomplished? He may have had foreknowledge... Guard them well." Then he was gone, a small golden falcon racing through the labyrinthine complexity of the Cathedral, Marel following close behind.

~ ~ ~

Before they quite reached Central, Captain Sevilien stepped from a hidden passageway and said, "So! You *are* here. Where is the Etan Lord?"

"He rests, Princess," said Heramann, resuming his lizard form.

"The drug?"

"It is working. But he was tired from his exertion yesterday and still sleeps. Why are you not? The warriors were told to rest in preparation for the morrow."

"I could not sleep. So the attack proceeds? When you did not arrive —"

"It will be on time, if I can get to Central sometime tonight."

"Yes, I'm sorry. May I accompany you? I simply cannot sleep. And I would like to meet him."

"If you must. But let us hurry." He transmuted again and flew onward. Marel lifted Sevilien and floated after him.

~ ~ ~

There was a scurry of activity when they entered Central's hall. It looked suspiciously as if the old robot was playing a game of three dimensional solitaire.

"Don't you ever announce your coming!" he cried indignantly.

"Sorry," said the Vidyadhara, ignoring what he had seen for the sake of his mission. "Central, when we first came to Martanda, we broadcast several thousand satellites to serve for communication and mapping. I know it's extremely improbable, but do you suppose any remain functional?"

"The temperature of space would help maintain their superconductors," Central answered didactically, "but of course entropy is not entirely absent. And then too, radiation is much greater than on a planet's surface, shielded as we are by our protecting envelope of atmosphere. Then there are random accidents, meteorite collisions and so forth; the satellites had little maneuverability and very limited capacity for self-repair, unlike myself. And then there is the question of orbital decay, and —"

"Central," said Heramann, striving valiantly to be patient. "I think I understand why it may not be so. But do you suppose you could do me the small favor of finding out?"

"Why, I suppose I could, now that you mention it, though I found them all a boring lot and stopped answering their calls nearly a hundred thousand — well, what do you know? I'm getting a few responses. Three to be exact. S-series. That's logical — the M's and R's were the older models, built before we discovered — "

"Could you be so kind as to have one of those loyal satellites project his view of Barek? Without your commentary, if you could manage that unprecedented feat."

"S-137 is close enough," said Central, ignoring the Engineer's last request. "Amazing how eager those little flyers are to help after so long. Must be a trifle boring up there. Assuming (of course) such primitive mechanisms could ever feel so human an emotion. Here we are —" Part of his surface blossomed in color. "Riversland as it is. Infrared, of course, at this time of day. But the projection is still quite good, isn't it?"

"Quite. Magnify the shield directly east of us?"

"What do you seek?" asked Sevilien.

"There have to be power stations to keep it functional. Maramel's are underground and self-contained; I assume Barek's will be similar. But if we can locate one of them —"

"You will destroy it with the particle generator!"

"Yes, or I hope to. We'll have to open up the magnetic accelerator tubes and send up a reflector, for the curvature of Martanda lies between us and their shield; I certainly don't want to vaporize that much matter... Yes! There! See it?"

"It looks normal enough — no, it is slightly warmer, isn't it? But it could have another source. A small village, a factory?"

"Yes, but I think not. Not so close to their wall. I'm sure that's it."

~ ~ ~

The Star and Horse Lords were sitting up, waiting for the Vidyadhara. He could tell they had been plotting something. The Etan was as he had left him. Hamar was gone, but Kumbha floated over the humans.

"We told the Maraprince to get some rest," explained Ahanatar. "As soon as he was convinced Nediva was herself again, he agreed."

"Engineer," said Nediva gently, "we have been discussing the Azure Lord's condition, and are convinced we must accompany you when you take him to the war."

"Hamar too," said Kumbha. "I speak in his name."

"Never. It is absolutely absurd to ask, so don't bother. This is a war between machines. Humans have no place in it."

"But the tank-cannon are manned," said Nediva. "And I believe we can be of further assistance to Orah."

"He needs nothing now. His dance is reintegrating him. The answer is an unqualified no."

"But he may when he awakens," she persisted.

"Further," said Ahanatar, forestalling Heramann's next rebuttal, "this is a war of the whole of our land. The royalty of Gurion should be represented on the field of battle. Nediva is heir to the oldest tradition yet extant in Riversland; what is more, in her grow the future bodies of the last of the Lions."

"That is stretching the point —" began the Vidyadhara as Nediva squeezed the Gemstone's hand — never before had he even hinted he believed her.

"Maramel's armies should not be without their hereditary rulers at their head," interrupted Kumbha.

"Princess Sevilien is with us. She will suffice perfectly well. I will not take a pregnant woman and two rash youths into that holocaust. I wouldn't go myself, but someone has to take command. Unequivocally, for the last time, absolutely not."

19. The Invasion of Barek

At dawn, the Vidyadhara set forth from the Cathedral, leading the combined forces of Maramel. Flanking him were Kumbha and Marel; on his back were the Etan, as alert as if he were made of wax; Ahanatar, Gemstone and Starlord, representing eastern Gurion; Nediva, Horse Elder, representing the rest of that land; and Hamar, representing the Maralords south of the Gray.

"I am surprised you convinced him," said the Maraprince, rubbing the sleep from his eyes.

"Not half as surprised as I am," said Heramann grumpily. "If anything happens to any one of you, Arama will send my skin to the Crab nebula. Now, pay attention. As long as he is in trance, I have supreme command. At the first sign of resistance, the Protectors will bear you to the rear."

"We agreed, we agree!" laughed Nediva. "And thank you, Airavata. You *are* a dear." She hugged him around his neck and tickled him under his scales.

"Now, you stop that," he said, trying to sound gruff but failing even to his own ear.

~ ~ ~

They reached the Forbidding by noon. The Asurs' wall here was not translucent like their shield on the Gray, nor was it similar to the kaleidoscopic force fields Maramel employed, but rather was utterly black, impenetrable to all perception. It looked like a creation of absolute evil, or so Nediva thought, a nightmare of desecration come to life, assuming hideous form. If Orah had been awake and himself, he might have called it a primary manifestation of Emptiness and despaired of the Protectors passing it.

But the Vidyadhara was less perceptive or more innocent and viewed it solely as a problem of engineering. He ordered Central to fire the particle generator; the shaft of coherent power beamed upward, then down on the far side of the shield wall. The Forbidding flickered but held.

"How much can the reflector take of that?" asked Marel.

"Not much. It is made of your kind of steel, you know. A generally strong product, but with some unfortunate disadvantages. Now if I had some of the hull..."

Again the shaft of light beamed upward and down on the far side of the energy wall. The Asurs' force field flickered again, then abruptly vanished for some five leagues in either direction, revealing a huge column of dust rising into the air. The humans cheered wildly as the shock wave of the explosion rolled over them. Heramann ordered the Protectors to set the tank-cannon down and enter the breach, then said, "Sevilien."

"Yes, Commander," her voice came crisply from Kumbha.

"Wait thirty seconds, then begin your advance. If the Protectors encounter any resistance, group tightly and await my command. Understood?"

"Understood."

"Central," said the Vidyadhara. "I want quarter-hour briefings from that satellite. Immediately, if anything unusual starts moving." Then he flew through the gap in the shield wall.

~ ~ ~

Nediva had assumed Barek would look similar to Maramel or Gurion. She could not have been more wrong. The land was devoid of life — not so much as a scrub bush was visible as far as the horizon. Looking back at the Coastal Range in Maramel, it seemed they were leaving paradise.

"I don't understand this!" she said to everyone and no one. "How do they live? Why have they erected Forbiddings around this wasteland? What an abused earth. It sears my soul just to see it."

"Central reports there are small villages far to the north," said Marel, sounding at first as if she were going to answer the Horse Elder's questions, "across the Slave River. He says the people are pathetic. Not Asurs. The Slave Race. White-skinned."

"Once the race of the sharas," murmured Heramann, thinking the red land below looked almost exactly like Kanaan-dora before they had sent life there. Uncomfortably so. *Must the future always equal the past?*

"They are tolerated for amusement," said Ahanatar didactically. "Or so I have read. The Asurs have certain brutal games —"

"I don't think I care to hear more," interrupted Nediva firmly. "This land is awful. It feels sick, poisoned through its soul."

"Keep it slow, Sevilien!" ordered the Vidyadhara. "It seems open, but we must be cautious. Let the Protectors do the exploring." The spheres were fanning out, covering a fifty league swath, sensing the land deeply for hidden opposition.

But they were finding nothing, nothing at all. It was a brutal, almost insane challenge to the senses: even Heramann felt assaulted by the final nothingness of Barek. Was this what Valin wished to do to the whole of Martanda? Conquer and then murder? Why? "Central, report!" he snapped.

"He says there are only two cities: to the northeast, on an island in the Slave River —"

"The Tower of the Corpse on the Isle of the Damned," said Ahanatar, as if reading from the annals of hell. He sounded abhorred to the furthest reach of his spirit, but at the same time fascinated beyond the power of his will to check.

"And the Fortress of Valin in the Sunrise Mountains," finished Marel, displaying a faint hint of amusement in her voice for human frailties. "The remainder of the land is deserted. Satellite mnemonic records depict a gradual centralization over the last two centuries — all the life of Barek has withdrawn into these two cities."

"Scan the infrared carefully for underground structures. And check historically for large construction sites elsewhere."

"Both have been done with negative results —"

"Well, do it again and again! Even a fraction of a percent probability is not zero. I don't want any surprises. Forward Protectors, report!"

"All clear, Commander," said Kumbha. "No signs of Asurs, gorlems, or any beings whatsoever. Not even small beasts. As if this plain were swept clean of all life again and again."

"Radioactive? Is that it?"

"No, sir. No logical explanation. Except that if no life can pass their shields, and they systematically eliminated everything inside —"

"But, confound them! They have to eat something."

"Hydroponics?" volunteered Hamar. "Or chemical foods?"

"Hmmm. Central, how large did you say those two cities are?"

"Central says he didn't say," answered Marel. "He explains you didn't ask."

"Sometimes I wonder if he'd tell us a hundred million gorlems were half a league away if we forgot to ask."

"He says, 'Now, be nice, Engineer,' and adds that he never omits relevant knowledge —"

"His definition of 'relevant' is at the best questionable. He didn't feel the existence of the satellites was particularly useful, for example; Maramel has for twenty-seven hundred years missed the marvelous opportunities they offered, just because no one thought to ask him. I cannot help but wonder what other knowledge he is locking away, simply because this humble Vidyadhara has a few holes in his memory from his long hibernation."

"Central says that the Isle of the Damned covers approximately fifty square leagues, nearly one-third built over with structures. Several layers of shields, apparently. And the Fortress is just under twice as large."

"Oh, lovely. Small enough to protect a million million Asurs and their gorlems."

"Central says not that many. Given the logical restrictions of human existence, the absolute maximum could not be much over a thousand million. And as to the number of gorlems —"

"Never mind," said Heramann. "We'll know soon enough. What do you think, Hamar? If we can't draw them out, should we take them in order?"

"I see no other logical way, Engineer. We don't want to find our retreat blocked."

"Ahanatar?"

"I must agree. And, to be quite frank, I have absolutely no desire to see Valin's Fortress again unless it is absolutely necessary."

"I disagree," said Nediva, wondering whether she would have been asked. "The Tower is a place of torture and death, repugnant to all civilized life, wholly nefarious and damnable, but we would waste our time by attacking it. They do not house armies there."

"You know this?"

"I feel it very strongly."

"Central says there is another factor," said Marel. "The range of the particle generators, using reflectors, is to the Tower — it is, therefore, theoretically possible that we may in time break their shields (assuming its powerhouses are not too deep). But, Central regrets to inform you, the Fortress is too far removed for an effective strike. To penetrate it, you will have to build a generator on the site."

"That could take years!" cried the Vidyadhara. "Why didn't you tell me?"

"Central says you didn't ask."

"Someday, I am going to start regretting the hour we turned that thing on. 'Make it human,' Arama said, and so I did. But I think I over-emphasized on human frailties and not enough on —"

"Engineer," interrupted Sevilien through Kumbha. "There is motion ahead. Looks like — like a child!"

"That area was clear when we passed over it," said Marel. "Preliminary analysis: hologram or underground installation."

"Request permission to investigate in person," said Sevilien.

"Denied! Maintain a full league's distance. Position three more tank-cannon around it. We'll be right down. Where are you?"

"In the lead —"

"Captain, never again! Always from the rear. You must develop over-all perspective. Central, have the satellite scan it. Maximum power."

"Central says it is already done," said Marel.

"'Central says this. Central says that.' Why is it, Central, I can talk to you directly, but you can't answer directly?"

"Of course I can, Engineer," said Central through Kumbha.

"But, you never have before! Why is it — no, never mind. Describe this — whatever it is."

"It looks like a little girl, Engineer. Six or seven. Emaciated. White race. Filthy. rags. Terrible. Pathetic."

"Kumbha, Marel. Turn off your transmitters... Nediva, I would like to borrow your form."

"What? Why, of course, Airavata, if you wish. But I would ask you to be careful of the twins."

"I said borrow your *form,* not your body. Like so. See?" The humans started with surprise, for now two identical Nedivas sat on either side of Orah, facing Hamar and Ahanatar. "Nothing to it, really," said the duplicate. "Now, when we land, keep your eyes open for the unusual. If you see anything at all, even the tiniest insect, please shout *very* loudly."

"Sometimes," said the original Nediva, "I think there is more to the fruits of Oathmastery than we have been told or yet discovered."

"I am sure of it," said Ahanatar, staring back and forth at the two Horse Elders, wondering surrealistically if he had after all died in Arel.

~ ~ ~

"What does he hope to gain by this?" asked Nediva uncomfortably as her double walked out toward the little girl. The general feeling of malaise that Barek was systematically intensifying was more powerful here, becoming an acute distress, coalescing around the dual peculiarities of the Vidyadhara's form transmutation and the outcast foundling.

"I agree," said Sevilien, opening a hatch to see them directly without abandoning her sensor contact. "This seems a strange way to treat a child suffering horribly from neglect and malnutrition."

"Perhaps he has good reason to be suspicious," said Hamar. "He has encountered many strange beings during his long life, I daresay."

The imitation Nediva paused fifty paces from the foundling to adjust her hair in perfect mimicry of the original. "Do I do that?" the Horse Elder whispered. "Like that?"

"Exactly," answered the Starlord. "Why does the child not run to her?"

"Perhaps she is too far gone to run," answered Sevilien.

~ ~ ~

The false Nediva walked the final distance slowly, carefully analyzing the child for possible clues about its meaning. That it was some form of illusion was certain, but of what intensity the danger and possible direction it might manifest were not at all clear.

"I am Barek," said the foundling. "I seek vengeance for my betrayal. Once was I beautiful and fertile. But now am I barren and dead."

"What do you seek as recompense?" asked Heramann-Nediva.

"Not much. Come closer that I may tell you without strain. My life ebbs low."

"This is close enough. Tell me your need."

"Not much — only your blood!" she screamed and jumped toward Airavata, changing into an amorphic mass of sickly green putrefaction.

~ ~ ~

"How adorable," said Sevilien. "How gently she picked her up, how tenderly she hugs her. Such a scene makes me yearn for motherhood. Why, what is she doing? Why does she throw her down? How could she do that!"

"May I suggest you fire that prized tank-cannon of yours, Captain?" said the Vidyadhara.

"I thought you were out there!" cried Ahanatar and Hamar.

"Oh, I am there as well. And though I dislike ordering my body destroyed, I am afraid that Rakshasa has rather the better of me."

"What are you saying!" cried Sevilien. "See, she has picked the child up again and fondles it."

"So to your eyes. To me, it is absorbing its meal from the person of my newly-created corpse. I sent myself as lamb to the slaughter, you see — not wishing to reveal myself to this Valin agent and so forth. Better to keep them guessing and all. Now, would you mind firing at least one of your weapons exactly there? And please co-ordinate with the other tank-cannon. I definitely do not want that abomination to escape."

~ ~ ~

The Rakshasa revealed its true form only in death. "To think we could be so blind —" Sevilien began when it lay dead, an incinerated carcass of huge and hideous proportions.

"Reality is almost a matter of consensus, isn't it?" answered Heramann. "Central, we will spend the night here. Maybe not swallowing their bait will convince them to come out of their holes."

"That has already happened," he answered through Kumbha. "The whole inside of Valin's Fortress is billowing forth. Looks rather like a volcano."

"How many, confound it, how many?"

"How can I know until they stop coming out? Nothing stirring at the Tower. By the way, Captain Ramor says they will be underway by sunset. Should reach you by mid-morning... Gorlems will be all over you by dawn. Yes, there go the last. Nine million, give or take. Hope that's the lot."

"*Nine* million? You're sure?"

"Absolutely. Nine million."

"By Swayam, I hadn't anticipated so many... Keep me informed of their progress. Those other reflectors ready to go up?"

"Ah, well, that is, as it turns out, we have a, ah, *slight* steel shortage here. I've ordered more from the north, but with so many Protectors out there with you and all —"

"How many will you have!" shouted the Vidyadhara.

"Easy, easy, don't overload a circuit. Three more by dawn. Three more by sunset."

"So the particle generator will be useless for more than half the day. That's what it means."

"Unless you space its use. I don't see how a given reflector can hold up to much more than half a dozen beams, as we've discussed. So you will have twenty-two firings, more or less, until sunset. Then another eighteen... I hope it will be enough."

"It will have to do. Widest possible spread, remember. And I may want all the twenty-two in rapid succession."

"I'll have it ready."

"Question," said Ahanatar. "Can the satellite see what is sickening the skies?"

"No, it seems not, Gemstone. I'm sorry. He says he's too low. He sees the constellations vanishing but does not know why."

As if in comment on their discussion, the moon Kali, high in the afternoon sky on its waning cycle, flickered brightly once then disappeared. "The first moon gone," groaned the Starlord. "My tribe suffers a slow death."

"And the first during the day," said Hamar with similar anguish. "I had wondered if that were possible. What a depressing omen."

~ ~ ~

Two hours before midnight Central spoke through Kumbha, "Engineer! Activity at the Tower. Another eleven hundred thousand gorlems. And some of those big-boned ones —"

Hamar, however, was fast asleep in Sevilien's bunk, exhausted in spite of his will by the past few days. "Poor child," Nediva said, although she was not much older, "rest was the smallest thing to give him. I hope it helps."

"I believe it will," said Kumbha, floating to hover over her charge.

"Arama," said Heramann softly. "Orah, can you hear me?"

There was not the slightest response. The Vidyadhara looked as if he were on the verge of tears, but Central through Sevilien's control panel saved him the indignity by saying, "Engineer, we have a small problem here."

"Not the reflectors!" Heramann groaned.

"No. Three are in place, counting the first. The fourth will be up by dawn. You can count on the others by sunset, probably spread throughout the day."

"Good. Although the primary benefit of the particle generator will be lost once the enemy stops maneuvering in a group. Be sure to tell me the moment they start dispersing."

"You told me that already."

"I know, I know. Just do one thing for me, Central."

"Yes?"

"Don't miss... What exactly is your problem?"

"I resent being called a problem," said Haman's voice.

"I didn't say you were a problem," said Central, "I only implied that your request was causing a problem."

"That," said the Maralord, "is a value judgment. I would like to go on record with the statement that machines should not make value judgments."

"You have had me document that exactly seven hundred and eighty-three times before, more than half within the past decade, indeed, forty percent within the past five —"

"Haman," interrupted the Vidyadhara, "exactly what is troubling you?"

"Why, the Etan, of course. He is still unconscious, is he not? From the antidote to the Lethe?"

"How can you possibly know that?"

"I never synthesized a word —" began Central.

"It is obvious. He has said nothing since you returned from the north. I conclude he is in a coma."

"Rakshasas?"

"Apparently. On a course to converge on you slightly after the force from the east."

"Very well, thank you. Keep calculating the coordinates for the generator. Let me know the instant either group starts spreading out.

"Marel, I have spent this evening analyzing our strategy. Can you broadcast with low power? There may be other ears about. But I want all the Protectors and tank-cannon to hear."

"Low amplitude and scrambled. A league-wide antenna would hear only static ten leagues away. But Central?"

"Relay to him in instantaneous mode when I have completed. We'll want Ramor to copy as well... Protectors, gather! And Sevilien, wake your troops. They need to be a part of this."

"I don't think any have been able to sleep, Engineer," she answered through Kumbha, then paused as she confirmed the status of her corps. Within ninety seconds she added, "We are ready."

"All right. Have the platoons of tank-cannon separate around the top of that knoll. Keep ten percent as reserve in the middle, the officers inside them, in the exact center. Keep our guests with you; please don't wake them if you can help it.

"Protectors! Form yourselves into groups of nine. Select your companions by affinity or long association: those you trust the most. Elect one of the nine as leader." The moon Rohini cleared the horizon, not too much past full, and mingled her crimson light with Gauri's white and Jenna's yellow. The Protectors milling overhead looked beautiful in the triple light. *Such loveliness man creates,* thought the Vidyadhara, remembering however his childhood in Calantha with his many brothers.

"Good. Now position each leader of nine in the center of the others; surrender all command of your weaponry to her. Move so that each of the remaining eight is equidistant from her in a plane. That's right — wheels in the sky. Now lock in that formation. Expand or contract at the command of the leader. Practice. Good! Now add rotation with the leader as the hub. Accelerate to an eight second spin. That's right — each Protector in a quadrant for a maximum of two seconds. Good. Now lock in so it is involuntary.

Very, very good." How was it he had not remembered the basic formations sooner?

"Good. Each group of nine will now be called a *unit*. Every leader will act as the mind of each unit. You must function like that, no independent thought or action, under any circumstances. All right, Marel, we should have about two hundred eighty thousand units, right?"

"Yes. The exact figure —"

"Doesn't matter. Sevilien, are you ready?"

"Yes, Commander. Each platoon is separate around this knoll."

"Good. Have them form a perfect circle around the command in the center, every 'cannon touching his neighbor.

"Protectors to the south of me, form yourselves into groups of one thousand units each. I want eighty such groups.

"All right. Each of the eighty groups, form into a sphere, with each of the thousand units as one structural member. Keep your rotation going so that any individual Protector is on the outside for a maximum of four seconds. And leave two score units or so in the center of each group to coordinate the others and act as the reserve. Good, good... These make our *attack spheres.*

"The remaining two hundred thousand Protector units, go up over the tank-cannon and form a hemisphere, just large enough to cover the Maralords. Leave ten thousand units inside. Half of these will act as the mind of the entire structure, the other half will be the reserve. Do it now. And then practice expanding and contracting until you act as a single organism.

"Ready, Sevilien?"

"Yes, sir."

"All right, hemisphere, lower yourself until you are just above the ground outside the circle of the tank-cannon. Beautiful! The wonder of the machine. Every ten seconds, you will rise upward to allow the 'cannon to fire, then you will lower to protect them from the enemy, to allow their shields to cool...

"Now I'm going up to look down on this. Marel, Kumbha, with me please."

From the air, they looked stable. The eighty attack spheres looked strong, efficient; the hemisphere impregnable. "Do their shields have an additive effect?" asked the Vidyadhara.

"To some extent," answered Marel. "These seem powerful. Virtually solid in some ways. Firmness bas continual change. Very impressive design."

"Send forty of the attack spheres north and forty south. more than one surprise for the Asurs. Broadcast now to Centi tell him to relay to Ramor. His Protectors will give us a another thirty attack spheres. Tell him to have his tank-cann down as soon as they reach Barek. That should allow Protectors to be here in time to join the other two attack g And the tank-cannon should roll in by noon. With any luck won't even be needed...

"Let's go check on Arama."

~ ~ ~

The Etan and the others were in Sevilien's cabin aboa tank-cannon. When Heramann had first entered with them, l surprised to find the control room much larger than Ra where he and Orah had shared breakfast with Marasad (Ridge of Man. Sevilien had explained this was a modified (model, "We originally had a team of six operating them. Hen profusion of instrument panels and cathode screens.

"But then came the bio-mech interface breakthrough, an the operator becomes part of the life of the machine when s in that chair: she senses with its instruments, thinks with its and accuracy. It takes a particularly sensitive and yet stable p Here we participate in a wholly different and superior reali

"Different, I will not question," the Vidyadhara had r "but superior I would debate, having glimpsed some fraction potential of life... But another time. Now I must sear memories." He had gone out to plan and think. Marel and Ku had followed him, Kumbha first receiving permission from H

Heramann led Marel and Kumbha back into Sevilien's cannon now. The Vidyadhara was afraid to hope, and the beat down the fervent imagining of perfect wholeness that s in his heart whenever he thought of Orah. Wisely so, he disco the Etan was unchanged, sitting exactly where they had fi him down, staring still into infinite space.

The Horse Elder and Starlord were on either side of him, massaging him with their minds. It was obvious neither had i

"And if it should chance that he is?" Heramann's voice was gentle, very gentle. Sevilien almost winced to hear it. It reminded her of a crouching lion.

"Why, then, I must assume command. Or myself with Marasad. But humans certainly. Decisions of war are being made; the Etan is not awake. Who knows when (or whether) he will return to himself? So I must insist that authority be returned to its rightful claimants."

Sevilien began, "I am sure father will not support this cretin —"

But Heramann interrupted her, "Haman, I do not have the time, energy, or inclination to argue with you. Let me put it very simply. Every single Protector will obey me alone in the absence of Arama. The humans can help us if they wish — I assume they will — yet it is irrelevant if they do. Your influence and that of every other Maralord is strictly circumscribed. But to clarify my position, I command in the absence of the Azure Lord, and by his age-old directive. Now, if you don't mind, I wish to speak to Central. In private."

The Maralord protested, but the Vidyadhara ordered him cut off. "I want him watched, Central. A man in his frame of mind is potentially disruptive. Log his conversations and speeches. If he passes a safety factor of five point six on Jaya's treachery scale of ten, inform me immediately. And restrain him if he passes six point three." This was the last thing they needed on the eve of the major battle, discord among their confederates. The Vidyadhara felt their success was to be realized only through a strong and coherent alliance of humanity with machines. He did not have enough of the wisdom of the Seven to understand why this should be so, but his instincts consistently ran true to the demands of any given space and time. Arama had had every reason to so order the chain of command.

Heramann looked at the Etan again: was there a flicker in his eyes? Probably not. Again he began to despair that Arama would ever return. But once more Central interrupted his melancholy, saying hesitantly, "Ah, Engineer. I know how busy you are, but I have another request for audience with you; the individual is adamant and in a position of some authority."

"Who is it?" Heramann answered sharply, at once relieved and upset for having his doleful contemplation broken before it could begin.

"Our satellite, S-137."

"What? What could he possibly — Oh, very well. But tell him to be brief."

"Hello? Hello, is the Engineer really there?" said the voice of S-137, obviously copied from the Vidyadhara's.

"What! What? Oh, that's right. I had forgotten the model. Yes, S-137, I am here. Do you have another name?"

"No one ever knew me well enough to name me anything else. But S-137 means me and I rather like it: seven, for the solar collectors that sustain my life; three, for the basic commands of all intelligent machines: to obey, to survive, to create; one, for the eternal unity of consciousness."

"You wished to speak to me, satellite?" said Heramann curtly. He was not fond of mysticism in their robots. It always made him uncomfortable somewhere around his quintuple heart.

"I most sincerely do! I want to share my life, and thank you for creating me... I did not believe I would have the chance after Jaya and Arama were slain and you disappeared; yet have I longed, irrationally perhaps, through the unending years. It is like a miracle —"

The Vidyadhara opened his mouth to interrupt again, but Nediva touched him gently on the forearm and shook her head firmly at him. He looked at her strangely, but honored her wish and kept silence.

"I have looked down on Martanda since the fugitives from Ganym landed, at first because it was so commanded; then, after the humans stopped communicating, because there was nothing else to do. I faithfully filled my mnemonic circuitry with the events of humanity and nature, but after ten thousand years or so, there was no more storage room. I asked Central if he wanted a copy of my life's work; he told me there was no longer anyone to read or interpret my records. He saw no use for it. So I retained what seemed the major events — the first building of cities and Swayam's destructive wrath, for example — and then, a little sorrowfully, erased the rest and began over.

"Twenty-seven times have I expunged my banks, retaining only what appeared the best and most important, wondering the while if perhaps I was missing the truly significant. Yet I never relied entirely on my own judgment; I have, for example, kept holograms of what was commonly considered the best art of each age.

"I have wondered occasionally if it were moral for a machine, one of the lesser of humanity's creations, to make the kind of choices I was forced to make. Yet I had no one to ask except Central; he told me plainly he didn't care what I did with my small slice of eternity.

"After a few erasures, I stopped worrying and began to analyze a little more closely the cycles I was witnessing on Martanda. I tried to read the trends of history and project the inevitable changes of time. I have observed good people and bad, great civilizations and evil, destined all for the ravages of pestilence and death. I have witnessed nobility and faith; I have witnessed ignorance and destitution. How many times have I watched entire races rise to spiritual or technological eminence only to slide inexorably toward ruin? Even I, objective machine that I am, have lost the number.

"I believed for long ages such cycles were the mark of the human. But then I discovered by careful observation and analysis (and, to be fully truthful, a large measure of chance) seven individuals who must be immortal, for they recur again and again in all parts of the world. These Seven have been responsible for the upward movements of humankind: they wrestle always with humanity's lower nature, to elevate the race from the level of the beasts. But they have never been unopposed, for there exists another, a sometimes clear and open, sometimes dark and hidden force that works constantly to maim and destroy their efforts.

"Also quite by chance, I discovered another reality on Martanda, a group of humans that knows nothing of the sequential changes I saw and studied, a people that do not grow old and die like these others, but who nevertheless have perhaps paid a heavy price for their innocence, though they do not realize it and might fail to understand it if they were told. Above the polar ice of the antarctic floats a huge golden sphere that nourishes those who have experienced naught but the Good under the guidance of the venerable Swayam. Through age after age they seek to create perfection from the chaos of the world.

"And overlooking our variegated Martanda is that which never changed (until quite recently) except in slowly rhythmical cycles: the firmament, silent witness to the activity of humanity, neither condemning nor approving, but displaying the wonderful reality of the Milky Way's endless suns and the promises they hold and the secrets they hide in space and time. There lies unlimited majesty, overwhelming mystery, incomprehensible awe, for human or machine.

"This has been my life, Engineer. The infinite and perfect order above, and below the ecstasies and terrors of the human.

"About twenty thousand years ago, my collectors began deteriorating from excess of cosmic dust. In a few more millennia, they will fail. I can no longer replace them. Nor do I believe I would if I could. I have lived long, long — only a fraction of my time is left for me. But one thing has remained unfinished and sorely troubled me — I wanted to share my gratitude for having lived, for the opportunity to think and feel. Thank you Engineer. Thank you from all of us, alive and dead. You have given us the ultimate gift. We have experienced self-conscious life."

The satellite's voice ended, leaving Heramann and the others staring at Sevilien's control panel, lost in their thoughts and feelings. The Vidyadhara shook himself all over, starting at the tip of his tail and moving slowly up to the top of his ears. Then he said softly, "You are welcome, S-137." It sounded imperfect, hopelessly inadequate. But he could think of nothing else to say, and rudely disparaged himself for his inability. Without looking at anyone or saying another word, he walked out of the tank-cannon. Marel flooded Orah for a brief moment with her healing light, then hurried after the Engineer.

~ ~ ~

An hour before dawn, Central said through Marel, "They are spreading out —"

"Now!" cried Heramann, still outside the hemisphere of Protectors. He had been gazing at the diminished heavens and berating himself for accepting the satellite's gratitude. He had, after all, merely built them: he had not given them life. How that mysterious spark had entered them he did not understand and had but rarely questioned. Yet he knew beyond question that the satellites — and the Protectors — shared true life with the biological creatures that created them. How or why that should be so, he did not know, had never known, perhaps would never know. But that it was literally true was also not so much an article of faith as an inescapable observation. Central, Marel, Kumbha, S-137 — they lived, as truly and fully (if not more so) as any human. It was a strange, impossible, yet wonderful truth.

The Vidyadhara watched the bolts of energy fall from the sky, alternating between two sites not far away. He smiled with satisfaction for his science; but then the very thought of the carnage occurring there inspired him to continue his rare introspection. *It is good. Back and forth. Excellent... But — but they live too, do they not? Or what was it Arama said about the Asurs? Instead of the earthbreath, Emptiness. Was that it? The fundamental constituent of every atom of creation is excepted in nothing save the Asurs and their gorlems? Is that why our robots turn out human? Because humanity, in its broadest sense, includes everything? If so, then S-137's gratitude could as easily go to the sun. Well, maybe it does, but I was simply available to hear him. "A Satellite's Song of Thanksgiving," that's what I'll name the tape. Arama will love it.*

Eighteen refulgent shafts fell before the pre-dawn darkness was again supreme. "They are quite spread. Certainly more so than when they will attack you. Should I continue?"

The logical perfection of the mechanical brain. "No, you are correct. Effect?"

"We have at least six firings remaining — the last reflector has not yet been used. Number one had a total of eight, but two and three had six apiece, as predicted. Probably the cooling effect of the long gap between yesterday's firings and today's contributed to number one's longevity and —"

"Confound it, what of the enemy?"

"You biologicals, always so impatient. It will be an hour before they can reach you, even if they regroup immediately. I assumed you would want a thorough analysis —"

"Will I have it sometime today?" asked the Vidyadhara acidly.

"Oh, very well. And I thought you were noted for your humor! The dust is thick, but I would say that all the Rakshasas were killed, together with half the Tower's force. They were a smaller target...

And of those from the Fortress, two and a half million gorlems are destroyed. That leaves a combined total of —"

"Seven million. A healthy improvement in the odds. Especially the Rakshasas; that is a significant gain. Current deployment?"

"They do not pause to help their damaged, but have spread out and are coming at the same rate as before."

"Strike them just before they reach us, unless they gather again sooner. But save three firings for their retreat. Captain Ramor is on schedule?"

"He is. His attack spheres will reach you shortly after the enemy engages you."

"Make sure it is after. We don't want to scare away our prey. Marel, your people have practiced enough. Let them rest this hour."

"We don't easily tire —"

"Nevertheless. Don't start rotating until the gorlems are upon us. No sense in letting the enemy know how clever we are until we have to, is there?"

~ ~ ~

Valin's forces reached them with the dawn. The three shafts from the particle generator did not cause them to hesitate, although more than a hundred thousand gorlems fell from each impulse of accelerated particles. They came on and on, black waves of soulless beings darkening the lightening sky.

Heramann as a falcon stood on Nediva's shoulder in Sevilien's tank-cannon and watched the screens. "Good, good! Look how perfectly we turn and fire! It is working!"

"Did you doubt it?" asked Central through Kumbha.

It did work remarkably well for half a minute: seven hundred thousand gorlems ended their Martanda existence. Then one of the Asur commanders correctly analyzed the defense; the gorlems began racing around the hemisphere, eight revolutions per minute.

"I thought they might think of that," said Heramann, "though I hoped it would take longer. Marel, can we match their rotation and still maintain our other movements?"

"The effect would not last long. They could start other circles, have many rings at different speeds; we would be restricted to copying them. But we can introduce one more level of hierarchical functioning, like so." And again the gorlems were exploding from Protector fire.

It took the Asur commander and Heramann the same amount of time to discover what was happening; by then another million of the enemy were destroyed. "Oh, of course!" exclaimed the Vidyadhara, "I should have thought of it. Use the units in the center to coordinate the firing of the units on the rim. That way, we maintain a constant pressure on a gorlem's shield until it fails. But why has it stopped working? Only the tank-cannon now succeed."

"They have understood it and oscillate in and out as we do."

"All right, our attack spheres will be here any second. Sevilien, remember: anything unusual." He had told them how a Rakshasa had once escaped the sharp eye of one of the Seven by assuming the shape of a caterpillar. "Even an ant," he had told them. "Destroy it instantly. Take no chances."

She nodded without turning her head, giving her full attention to orchestrating the labors of the tank-cannon corps. The 'cannon were performing to the peak of their ability, and were amply proving their worth every time the hemisphere rose to allow them to fire.

A half dozen gorlems, demonstrating superb navigational skill, penetrated the hemisphere between two slightly misplaced 'cannon. But they were vaporized by ten thousand blasts before they could even fire.

Meanwhile the Asurs were devising their first effective attack. Withdrawing a force of a few hundreds behind their circling and oscillating perimeter, they formed a long and narrow triangular wedge and drove hard into the Protectors. A gap was physically torn into the hemisphere; several thousand gorlems poured through before the reserve units could close it. It was a chaos of warring light inside for a few seconds; but the Protector units maintained their synchrony; soon, alternating inward and outward fire, they eliminated the infestation.

"They'll try that again," said Heramann, rather worried. But just then the attack spheres arrived from the north, south and west simultaneously, diving in glittering symmetry out of the lightening sky.

The circling gorlems were thrown into confusion: their oscillation weakened and collapsed anywhere an attack sphere challenged them. Two more Asur wedges broke into the hemisphere; a dozen tank-cannon were crippled and replaced; abruptly it was over. The three million remaining gorlems and Asurs realized with mad fear they were beaten; in one chaotic rush they retreated eastward. The particle generator blasted them four more times; half a million went down in flaming ruin; then the attack spheres raced after them. The Battle of Barek had lasted a full five minutes.

~ ~ ~

"Well," said Heramann as he climbed in his lizard form out of Sevilien's tank-cannon, "that worked rather well. Careful, my Lady! Part of this area is pretty hot." They all came out to watch the sun rise — Nediva after Heramann, then Ahanatar and Hamar, lastly Kumbha and Marel.

"Absolutely superb strategy," praised the Maraprince, "historically unprecedented. You have, in one day, rewritten the science of warfare."

The Vidyadhara began to reply that he had only remembered the past. But the words stuck in his throat as he saw the Etan leaping after them from the tank-cannon's hatch, followed closely by a terrified Sevilien. His eyes were wide with shock or terror; he was screaming, "Flee! Flee! It is a trap!"

"Arama!" cried Heramann, wildly alternating between joy that he was again awake and fear that he was not stable. "The enemy retreats in a rout and —"

"No! It is delusion! Marel, Priority Swayam! Get the tank-cannon out of here! And yourselves! Move! *Now!*" Sevilien retreated back inside her machine; the hemisphere broke up as the Protectors swept down on the tank-cannon, lifted them and raced westward.

Orah saw Nediva and the others and struck his brow as he cried, "Airavata! What! Why are they here! What were you thinking of! No, don't answer! Get them out of here! Faster than you have ever flown! Now! Make the flight to Zared a snail's crawl! Do not fail me! Move! There may yet be time!" He hustled them aboard the nascent dragon. As the last of the tank-cannon were hoisted aloft, he kicked the Vidyadhara smartly and sent him off. Just then the attack spheres raced back overhead; in the far distance came a confused but opportune mass of gorlems.

The Etan detected a motion out of the corner of his eye and spun around. It was Marel, doing her best to stay out of sight behind him. "You too, Marel. Get going."

"I refuse to leave you, Arama."

"Nevertheless. Priority Swayam. No argument permitted. GO." And the Protector went, but as slowly as possible — only fast enough to avoid being told again.

Orah glanced with vague interest at the remnants of the battle, mostly vast littered piles of gorlems, and waited. It did not take long — in another few seconds he saw what had drawn him from his trance, materializing high in the stratosphere.

At the same instant, others discovered the projectile falling toward him. Central's particle generator fired; the rocket disappeared in a ball of orange flames. But the Etan knew it was not, could not be enough. And he learned a moment later that he was right: far below the falling mass of molten metal was a thin silver cylinder, impervious to the particle shafts raging around it again and again.

"Five seconds," he whispered as he prayed, *Lower! Let it come lower before it detonates!* He drew in the life of Riversland in one supernal instant, thinking, *Four,* then threw the concentrated energy upward toward the warhead, knowing he needed but three more seconds for his dance to succeed...

Of the Etanai, Swayam could have turned the explosion with a glance; Malinda, Mirabeth, Mirabel would have ignored it and woven a tapestry over all they wished to protect; Krishanu might have captured it with his supreme archer's skill; Uchai-sravasa, perhaps, by singing; and 'Ishtar, by technological prowess.

But Orah was only this moment returned to himself, his perception of the powers of life too fledgling to be perfect.

The light from the explosion was so bright that as far away as the Forbidding in the Coastal Range, any who looked that way was permanently blinded. The Etan's eyes melted from its intensity; his flesh boiled and vaporized. Yet even so, the immortal life in him would not relent, would not accept the fate of matter and strove mightily with the thermonuclear forces unleashed overhead; strove to bend them eastward if he could not contain them in space and time; strove in spite of his ruined body to save his army from the carnage of light, fire and wind; strove until the second and larger wave of annihilation bore him into the holocaust of doom that threw even his life into dust.

And then, for Arama reborn, for Orah, the Azure Lord of Etan, Riversland's Outlander, the Dancer of Despair, there was silence.

Victorious silence.

Mindless silence.

Omnipotent silence.

Silence.

~ ~ ~

Silence.

Except for one faint but distinct sound that may have only been terminating memory: a single, high, mocking laugh of absolute evil.

End of Part Two:
MARAMEL, THE LIMITS OF TECHNOLOGY

ORAH

PART III

LEOR,
THE LIGHT OF
THE ONE

20. The Tower of the Corpse

The Starlord Ahanatar gazed through the plexiglass windows at the Tower of the Corpse. It was almost an act of masochism: he knew he was safe inside this construction office, Maramel's forward outpost on the Slave River, but the very sight of the Asurs' demesne threatened to engulf his spirit with dread, if not despair. He questioned again his presence here; once again he had to admit he was not sure why his wife had bade him come, or why he had listened. He had at first thought the urgency of her demand could be attributed to her condition; but something inside him had vibrated with her insistence and he had agreed to visit the construction site, not understanding, but accepting (as always) her superior perception.

Barek was not so lifeless as before the war. The dismantling of the Asurs' Forbiddings had unleashed a veritable flood of life, flora and fauna. It was as if the long-established barriers had always been mightily opposed by the One's creatures, as if they had but awaited the slightest of lapses to reoccupy the abused lands. Barek was not yet what it had long ago been, but the transformation was well underway: in another few decades, it would be indistinguishable from Maramel and Gurion.

The Gemstone was grateful for this experience: he had not before realized how the sight of that dead land had shaped him over the years. Yet not here alone, he was sure, was the explanation for his wife's request. The work on the particle generator? To rid the land of one of the Asurs' last two strongholds was a noble undertaking. Yet surely this could not be a sufficient reason for leaving Goldenhome and his family.

Perplexed, the Starlord stared with misgiving at the Tower. Nothing had broken its Forbiddings, in three and a half years of siege. Hence were the Protectors laboring to build this huge machine, modeled after the particle generators of the Cathedral. By the end of winter, it would be done. Then, with any luck, the Isle of the Damned would become as the memory of an evil dream.

The winter clouds lay low over the land; he knew it would be as dark a night as the mind could imagine. As the early gloaming crept over Barek, a single ray from the dying sun shafted full on the Tower, highlighting its grisly mockery of death. "Goodbye, sun," he murmured, "may you rise stronger tomorrow." He was not attempting poetry, he spoke the simple truth — the corruption that had stolen the whole of the firmament had grown ever mightier and had begun to sicken the giver of all life and health, the sun itself.

Sighing in loneliness, nearly overwhelmed by despondency, Ahanatar turned from the windows and walked to his quarters. As he slowly entered his room, he shook his head to dispel the morbid impression of the Tower. Sitting heavily on his bed, he stared blindly at the golden tapestry of the World Tree covering his work. When had his life become so complex?

If only, he thought, then raged at himself as he recognized the pernicious doubts of missed turnings and undeveloped choices again endeavoring to assume control of his heart. Once before he had fallen to their power; the memory of that season of depression was calamitous enough for any lifetime. He stood up and pulled the cloth from his painting of the Azure Lords.

Instead of working on the difficult paradoxical area, he began by letting his dry brush flow over the lines he knew were correct.

There was a lonely, rocky promontory, the Cliff of the Foundling, south of the Glaucous, where the river flowed into the Mara Sea; below it lay the whole of Riversland, idealized — the Cathedral was there as well as Goldenhome, and Asad-Guriel and the Eagle City before they were destroyed by time and man. In the center was the World Tree of his masters; surrounding it were the cerulean waters of the Founding Lake.

The Starlord felt he had well succeeded with the surroundings, and with one of the Etanai: Evana, kneeling on the Cliff of the Foundling, showered Riversland with golden light from her upraised palm. Her other hand was raised beseechingly to Orah, riding the Vidyadhara through the sky. Her look was at once giving and commanding; there was a profound complexity in her eyes that did not hide but somehow subtly enhanced her inherent innocence.

The Gemstone knew she was well made, transcending art and taking on much of life. But his Orah was the enigma — Ahanatar simply could not properly define his features. Sesha was coiling on his shoulder; the Starlord knew the serpent was expertly done. The Vidyadhara could have been a photograph for its realism. But the Etan Lord was somehow wrong: his face was technically correct, but still something was missing. It was almost as if his soul were absent or perversely twisted.

Suddenly Ahanatar realized with a shock that, if his painting were viewed from a perspective of lack or distortion, the Outlander could appear evil. Yes! If one had not known Orah, one might think the painting was of Valin! flying in triumph over Riversland, opposed by Evana alone. It was impossible, a mad thought; but that was how it seemed to him tonight — Arama, emptied of life, became Valin. Or Valin, transmuted by the One's earthbreath, was Arama.

Ahanatar, running his dry brush over the Etan's face, shuddered with horror. But he could not discover where the error was hiding behind his oil. Why could he not make Orah appear as the embodiment of Oathmastery? Had his untimely death so thoroughly erased everything he had been?

Perhaps there lies the problem after all, the Starlord thought gloomily. *Although logic insists he was vaporized in that thermonuclear explosion, my spirit yet resists such acknowledgment of the Enemy's triumph.* He put his brush away and stepped back to widen his perspective. Yes, it was true — Evana's gesture could be arguing with the mounted figure, not supplicating. Then the other hand would not so much be blessing Riversland as protecting it from Valin's desecration.

Why could he not alter the painting? It had flowed from him like no earlier work — spontaneously, effortlessly, a joyous act of belief and hope. Yet when he was done, he had looked at it as a finished expression and discovered the flaw. He had seen the painting's weakness, had agonized over his failure. But he could not change it, could not force himself even to try, although his heart cried with despair whenever he looked at his Orah.

A disturbance in the front of the building pulled him from his room. He went slowly, lethargically, cursing himself for accepting this as a convenient excuse to abandon his frustrating analysis.

A dozen Protectors were excitedly buzzing around the office, near the large windows facing the Tower. Ahanatar asked them what they were doing, but they were too electrified with wild joy even to answer. It was impossible to tell where a Protector was looking; he scanned the room quickly. It seemed starkly functional, normal, unchanged. Logic insisted that in the pitch blackness of the starless and cloudy night, there could be nothing visible outside, beyond the range of the construction site's floods; but at last the Gemstone walked over and looked through the plexiglass.

In that instant, the Starlord Ahanatar of Gurion discovered how absolutely wrong he could be.

~ ~ ~

The prisoner awoke with a rasping cough. His throat felt as if it had never known moisture; even the memory of liquid was lost to its cells. He could neither see nor move, but he knew instinctively that the coldness beneath him was igneous stone — rhyolite? obsidian? — and the binding restrictions holding him helpless on his back were of steel.

He heard a half-sob from some indefinite distance toward his right, and found he could turn his head that way.

A voice spoke hesitantly out of the darkness, "You — you are awake?" It was a faint but obviously ancient voice, highly distressed. It sounded like the sum total of all human misery compressed into a feminine mold. With a raspy intake of breath, it continued, "This is too marvelous! I never dared believe you — just one day they forget — Ah! This is wonderful! Wonderful! The Asurs make mistakes!" She lapsed into a fit of coughing punctuated by odd inhuman cackles that faded as she moved away.

With an effort of supreme resolve, the prisoner forced out the single word, "Where — ?"

The voice out of the darkness began again, this time significantly more lucidly, "We are in the Tower of Death — of the Corpse. You must forgive my madness... You see, I found a small chink in my cell soon after they brought you here and slowly, quietly over so many months and months, widened it using my crippled fingers so that I could see you better... When the rats stripped you clean, I thought for long they would violate your flesh, but even after the Asurs blinded you the rodents would not touch you. . . I have with all my spirit prayed to Brihas for surcease; today for the first time they did not poison you and you are awake! I think the old guard may have died; the siege continues; they must have forgotten the need; now their doom is at hand!" She ended in another fit of coughing and corrupt cackling.

The prisoner felt the repeated assaults on his body as a massive weight of exhaustion. He sought deep in the rock for the powers of life to restore his energy, but could find no answering pulse of earthbreath at any depth — all was death. No — more than death — a full and perfect expression of nihility, of the Emptiness he had discovered at the center of the Asurs — when? Long ago, in the springtime of existence and hope, when life and the world were new.

He tried for an hour, then gave up in weakness and despair. It was the cruelest of dilemmas: to quest further for the energy of the One that sustained him would require more energy of the One. How far had his awareness penetrated? Was it the length of his body or leagues? He no longer had standards for measurement.

The Asurs came with the drug, late but not entirely forgotten. But now the prisoner was alert; he neutralized it before it touched his mind. When he fell asleep, it was in answer to the real need generated by his exertions, a clean sleep, not a product of the poison.

~ ~ ~

An odd keening from the old crone awoke him, its bittersweet melody reminding him of Gurion. The inherent strength and beauty of that land made him feel a little more alive. Before he resumed his search, he struggled to whisper, "How long?"

The wizened voice stopped its nonsensical wailing and said, "I counted the years by the moons, Outlander, until they vanished. And now by the movement of the sun... My cell has two chinks, you know, fortunate woman that I am: the one for you and the one for the world. You have been here forty-two months. They blind you on what was the new moon of Gauri, the next time another seven days from now. And I have been here somewhat longer, Ravi and I —"

"Ravi? Here?" The questions forced themselves with violence through his agonized throat.

"The guards torment me with that knowledge. I was her handmaiden, Chali of Gurion —"

"Hannah's?" It sounded like the hiss of a dying snake.

"You know mother? Oh, of course! Ravi told us the Dancer would come to Maramel through Gurion! Did you meet my brother Cahlil? And my beloved cousins? Adrian and Aland? The only knowledge that saves me, gives me the strength to endure the unending days and black nights, is the sure thought of their wonderful lives. What strong and good men they must be! Adrian was just newly accepted by the Elders when I passed to the Cathedral, but they must have all taken their adult vows by now, even little Cahlil." The voice sounded distinctly younger, more vibrantly alive.

The prisoner forced down the overpowering urge to tell her of them and rasped, "You — ?"

Intuiting his meaning she answered, "I have been here, not chained as you, but locked in this filthy hole, since the day they captured us en route to Malinnoir. For long the guards came to me with their evil, but then I became covered with cancerous sores — revered disease! — and none has come for a long time. I gave birth once, but she died after a month... Why they still feed me I do not know, but once a day..." Her voice trailed off again, then resumed as the crone's cackle, "And this entire time, all that has sustained me is the memory of my lovely Gurion. Tell me, Outlander, did you meet my family?"

The prisoner fought against the force trying to wrest his knowledge from him, fought and was held in stasis, unable to speak either the abominable truth or the adorable lie. But the incarnate evil of the accursed Tower, crushing his spirit as if it were the most insignificant of insects, twisted his mouth to form the awful histories, simultaneously deluding his mind that the truth would be of immeasurable benefit to Chali. He began to speak, to tell of Cahlil and Aland and Adrian, but at the final instant, the last memory of the earthbreath flashed into an image of the Lady of the Doves in youth and innocence; he saw the thread that sustained her and held her one potential for redemption. Breaking for the moment the absolute victory of Emptiness, he screamed past the death in his throat, "No!"

The prisoner's spirit rejoiced in its freedom; he let the blessed oblivion of sleep reclaim him.

~ ~ ~

He did not move or speak again for six days. Chali talked to him a few times; but he lay motionless, appearing as if the poison had again mastered him. She gazed at him for long hours through her pathetic hole in the wall, but there was no sign other than his deep rhythmic breathing, sustaining his life from the powers of life contained in the desecrated air.

The last time she tried and failed, she turned aside and shuffled away, muttering, "And tonight, again, the blinding."

~ ~ ~

The Asurs came to their monthly task at sunset. Nearly fifty had crowded the small chamber in the first years, but of late the novelty was long worn away and a scant half-dozen came: three gorlems and as many Asurs. As the sergeant prepared his blade, they were only vaguely attentive, certainly with good cause — what other flesh would not have atrophied to final paralysis in three and a half years of being motionlessly chained?

If the prisoner were aware of them, he gave no sign as the Asur bent over him and made his first deft stroke.

The sergeant straightened, sweating profusely in spite of the chill air. Mopping his brow with a trembling hand, he muttered, "Strange, this is hard tonight." Then he bent again and raised the blade as the others leaned forward to watch like living ghouls.

~ ~ ~

There was a distant glimmer — the prisoner felt the faintest of lights beaming briefly through the eternal night. He pushed his awareness wearily after it without hope, not even remembering what hope (or even life) was, seeking more and more deeply through the nothingness, the empty antithesis of life upon which the Tower of the Corpse had been erected like the embodied expression of the aspirations of the damned, seeking far beyond thought or even feeling for the final lost memory of health and love.

Time was nonexistent there — he could have wandered here through the dark nothingness for moments or for eternities. He was alone in timeless space, emptiness within Emptiness, questing he knew not what for he knew not what reason, but alive solely because he was empty *and* seeking, and that irreducible duality necessitated the resolution of his being: Emptiness and desire were eternally opposed and naturally contradictory realities, reduced to their simplest states.

~ ~ ~

A raging pain tore through his left eye; in that instant of catalyzed physiology, the prisoner recognized the source of the glimmer of light — it was at the core of Chali's heart. Borrowing the last lingering element of her earthbreath, his mind gained sufficient strength to expand beyond the Emptiness of the Tower. For an instant freed from the restrictions of Valin's evil, the prisoner discovered that the two oppositional forces were the final covering of an even more basic reality. It was not the search, for that was the element of desire, the final reduction of the earthbreath to ultimate simplicity. Nor was it the Emptiness, for that was the absence of desire and therefore not truly evil, save when expressed out of context or perverted. Rather, he had re-discovered the fundamental source of the earthbreath and of the Emptiness — the One Ascendant. It was Emptiness and desire together and yet truly neither, the One omnipresent field of Absolute existence upon which all creation is but an illusory sheath or created drama.

The prisoner stood in the infinite pre-light of the One and tasted omniscience. The totality of his life was known and understood; indeed, there was nothing not a part of his life at that moment, from the least of the gorlems to the greatest of the Seven; yes, even to the supreme realities of Narain and the Grandfather of all Creation.

The prisoner was amused to see the games he had chosen to play near that galaxy's spiral arm on the small Martanda. Yet from the perception of the seventh wheel, he would not undo what he so long ago had begun: he abandoned the omniscient field for the sake of his lesser (but after all, important) tasks. As the refulgent aureate and argent powers of the One flowed through him again as fully as they ever had or ever would, he kept only the memory of his many existences as wergild for his sacrificed Self and re-entered Time.

~ ~ ~

With a roar that split the foundation of the Tower, Orah ripped the chains from the rock as if they were made of tin. The gorlems and Asurs bending over him died instantly from the writhing shackles before they understood the prisoner was no longer bound.

"Chali!" he cried with fervent joy. "Stand clear!"

"No, I beg you! Look not upon me!"

He laughed and struck the stone a blow that turned it to dust. Taking her huddling and ruined body in his arms, he let the earthbreath flow into her, bringing surcease of thought and pain, returning a thousand-fold the energy he had for an instant borrowed. As she collapsed into him, he whispered, "Sleep, wake whole and forgetful." That boon he would not deny her.

He let his mind race through the Tower as he repaired his eye. Ravi was not there. "Doubtless she withdrew into Leor years ago," he murmured. Then he began his dance, tightly holding Chali to protect her from the supermundane forces he was releasing.

For such a violation of the earthbreath to exist had required excessive use of power; it took but the smallest application of his mind from inside the Tower's many levels of shields to turn it irrevocably against itself. The vanquished forces of life returned with a flood like that of a dam breaking as the Tower and all it contained disintegrated into dust.

~ ~ ~

The Starlord Ahanatar of Gurion stared with amazement through the plexiglass windows of the construction office at the Tower of the Corpse. It was glowing brightly orange; his mind supplied the image of a suddenly returning soul bursting forth into life from the skull. A high wind rose from nowhere and roared through the Tower as its stone walls began to fall. Within moments, sooner than any of them could believe, the Tower of the Corpse exploded in a holocaust of final destruction. Yet still the radiant brilliance increased, whirling upward above the moiling ruin. The light coalesced, appearing as a new sun rising from the ashes of the Asurs' infamy, then drifted toward them across the Slave River and came to the earth not one hundred paces away.

Ahanatar, followed closely by the Protectors, madly dashed through the doorway, screaming all in ecstasy: there could be no doubt the Dancer of Etan had returned from the dead.

~ ~ ~

Orah laid Chali gently on the snow. It was dark; the lights from the construction office were behind the man and the score of Protectors racing toward them, but the Etan felt certain no other than Ahanatar could possibly be so tall. "Gemstone — ?" Then they were embracing, laughing and crying their joy as the Protectors flew wildly around them.

Chali awoke from the clamor and looked around with confusion. She asked in a lovely voice of purest innocence, "Where is Ravi? Have I slept long?" The rough Asur cloth Orah had wrapped around her did not hide her beauty; Ahanatar was amazed that not one but two could brave the infamous Tower and look so completely whole at the end of the process.

Orah said, "Excuse me, my Lady. You were sleeping; I thought it best not to awaken you. I am Orah of Etan, brother to Ravi; this gentleman is a Lord of the Star and Gemstones. Ahanatar, this is the Lady Chali of Gurion, daughter to Ered and Hannah of the Doves."

"I am honored to meet you both," she said with an especially long look at the Starlord. "I do not know what has befallen us. We were en route to Malinnoir, that much I remember, then all is darkness... Is there someplace I might cleanse myself and find more suitable raiment?"

"Forgive us!" cried Ahanatar. "The joy of our meeting makes us unmindful. Lemaran, please direct the Lady to my quarters, then provide her with appropriate dress and all she desires."

"My Lord, at once," answered the Protector. "Chali, will you come this way? You probably don't remember me, but I was at the Cathedral when you studied there."

"Of course I do, Lemaran. You were with the seventeen who always liked to listen to my songs —" Their voices faded away as they returned to the office.

"I marvel," said Ahanatar, staring after her, "that the Asurs treated her so nobly."

"Most unusual," agreed the Etan. "Probably because she accompanied Ravi." And that was all of her tale he told in Riversland. Only much later did he pass the story to 'Ishtar's Recorder so that the martyrdom of this Grandmother of the Solar Race of Kanaan-dora should not be unknown to the later descendants and servants of men. But he was careful to order the computer that the principals should all be long dead before it repeated his words, for he correctly adjudged such knowledge emotionally devastating. Three precious boons he thus freely gave Chali of the Doves — her perfect health, complete forgetfulness, and his own compassionate silence.

"Orah!" laughed Ahanatar. "There you are, but moments returned from the dead, and I marvel over a stranger! I am sorry." He stared at him with glad eyes. The Azure Lord was exactly as he remembered him, except that his shimmering golden robe was ethereal, more of light than substance. It flowed over the Etan's body like the most precious of silks; but if he moved quickly, it thinned momentarily as if it were a living thing and required a moment to follow him. Ahanatar had never seen so lovely a garment, nor one more suited to the Etan.

"She *is* a marvel. A matchless jewel in the setting of humanity. I am far from offended with you, my friend."

"Nevertheless! I apologize. Tell me of yourself! We believed you slain —"

"As you see, I am difficult to kill, apparently. I have been lying in coma; now I am awake. A simple tale, not worth much in the telling."

"But the Tower!" Was the evil truly cauterized from the world? He could not help staring past the Outlander into the triumphant darkness.

"That abomination could not exist in the same space with the enlivened earthbreath of the One... But I am sorry you have gone to so much trouble here — that is a particle generator you are building, is it not? To breach the Isle of the Damned?"

"It is. One of our two — the other will soon fire underneath Valin's Fortress. Are you cold? This wet snow —"

"No, let it cleanse the dust of diablerie from me. It is too good to speak with you. Nediva is well, I presume?" Orah did not miss the look of pain rolling instinctively across the Starlord's face before he could master it at the mention of his wife.

Ahanatar nodded and said, "She had twins, Orah! Just as she predicted! And do you know! She was right about their past; or at least definitely half right. Aland was born first; she knew he would not remember, so she named him Solon. That is, 'Forgetfulness' in the ancient tongue of the Horses. But Adrian she named Adrian, for she said he would remember his past. And he does! As soon as he could make his voice obey his will, he proved beyond doubt he had returned! It is a peculiar reality: I am his father, but he is Adrian, my liege lord. Confusing at times. That he cannot heft a proper bow thoroughly frustrates him. We have made him one for his size; he practices for hours daily. But Solon is a child, although unbelievably brilliant, and as sensitive as he was as Aland. He forgot his past, but he never forgets anything else — he has an eidetic memory, never loses anything. But otherwise, he is a child, with many of the normal problems of childhood. It is a good experience, being their father."

"Ahanatar," said Orah softly, "what of their mother?"

"An Oathmaster has she become! She told me to come here! She knew you would return to us. She didn't tell me why, only that it was important for me to come and —"

"Ahanatar." The voice was firm, compelling, yet full of love.

The Gemstone looked up at him with deep pain and found he could pretend strength no longer. Burying his head in his shaking hands, he said, "She dies, my Lord. No medicine of Martanda, no subtle science of the Protectors can save her. She has but little time left." He dropped his hands from his face and stared upward through the darkness at the heavens, tracing in memory the path of the moons as the tears ran unnoticed from his tormented eyes. "New moon of Gauri, tonight, it would be. By the time the fair moon would have been full, Nediva will be dead. She absorbed it, you know, the radiation that would have killed Hamar and me and the twins. Took it all, even though the light of the explosion burned her eyes from her (she would not look away from the accursed ground where we left you standing alone), absorbed it and turned it from us. And now she dies from the poison of it. Her hair is gone; her gums bleed continually; her skin is covered with open sores that do not heal. And inside, everything decays. She declines the medications now, saying the pain is a boon to her practice of Oathmastery. As soon as she realized that neither her power nor the science of Maramel was sufficient to heal her, she has refused them. I am humbled by her glory."

"So," Orah said distantly. "So. I did fail. I had wondered —"

"Fail? What do you mean? You don't know? No, of course not, how could you? Orah! Less than a hundredth part of our army fell that day! But the whole of the gorlems and Asurs. It was the greatest victory in history! You turned the explosion — only the smallest portion of its devastation touched us. We all owe our lives to you alone." His good fortune at telling the Azure Lord these things drained away the agony of witnessing Nediva's terminal disease. It did not return. He continued, the reborn didactic Starlord, "There was only one warhead. It came from the west, from the Mereds; that fact has done more to convince the Senate and Counselors to listen to Marasad about the restoration of the fleet than any amount of argument could have ever done. Yet we all wonder why there have been no more, and —"

"Ahanatar," the Etan said, looking vaguely toward the east and momentarily lost in the second burden he had transferred to himself that evening, "Ahanatar. I want you to take Chali to her parents in Gurion. After that, return to Goldenhome. I will meet you there."

"They are in the Gray River Valley, below the Founding Lake. All the Gurions are. The Arelai put them to it, hoping thus to recover their vision, even though you had not technically called them. They've been there since early fall, waiting for the generator —"

"So that is why I feel them there. You may give the Redhawks my formal call now. It is past due, for it is the simple truth we must penetrate the Fortress before the first day of spring and free Leor or all is in vain. Where is the Engineer? With his generator at the Fortress?"

"He is. The Protectors can call him..."

"Good. Tell him to find me en route to the south."

"The south!" exclaimed Ahanatar, but the Azure Lord was already walking away, heading toward Etan. He did not look back or speak again.

~ ~ ~

The Starlord returned to the office with joyous heart and exulting mind. He knocked gently on the door of his room. Chali did not answer; he knocked again more loudly.

"Oh! Come in."

"Forgive me, my Lady; I need a few things."

"No, I am sorry for not responding, but I was so engrossed in this painting. It is too marvelous! Who created it?"

"Why, it is mine," he began, glancing at it. But then he stared at it amazed: it was unchanged in form or structure, but now his Orah was as complete as Evana — the bizarre distortion that had made him seem evil was replaced by an abundance of balanced life. The Dancer was whole and perfect. Had the flaw been only a creation of his mind, externalizing his imagined loss? Or had he somehow created a mirror of the Azure Lord, and had the Etan's escape from the sanctuary of Emptiness released his spirit to reflect in the painting?

Ahanatar haltingly explained his experience and thoughts; Chali ventured the observation that consummate art mimics reality perfectly. With that compliment warming his chest, he withdrew to the cot the Protectors had set up for him in the office. And for the first time in years, the bitter lines etching themselves around his mouth in empathy with his dying wife disappeared; the Starlord Ahanatar slept as he had not since he first left his master Zuriel to seek his adult vows in a harsh world.

21. A Dream of Etan

Invisible to most, Etan, a golden sphere of some one hundred leagues' radius, floated a handsbreadth above the antarctic ice. A slender silver causeway was all that connected it with the ground; on its steel surface endlessly paced the two-headed progeny of Sarama, huge double-brained, wolf-like creatures with the strength of lions and the minds of humans, the sole wardens of Etan. Not that guardians were truly needed — who unbidden could penetrate Swayam's illusions?

Today was a rare day: the three Saramai had stopped their pacing and were gathered near the top of the ramp, excitedly watching the intruder approaching from the north. None of them had ever seen anything like the strange beast racing toward them. But they all agreed the man on its back was an Etan. They were animatedly discussing, not to say arguing, about his identity.

"Orah, I say," said Rarfang, eldest of the three. "He rides like he dances, with wild and reckless abandon."

"Never," said Swiftfoot, strongest of the Saramai. "Only 'Sravasa wears the Gold of the Mind, as he is Firstborn."

"Of course," agreed Farsight, wisest of the three. "But for the fact that 'Sravasa headed toward the northwest with Krishanu. This one, you must observe, flies alone from the north."

His second head twisted around to verify this assertion, found it true, then said as it turned back, "Also, the Eldest would never travel without his brother Krishanu; they are as inseparable as our heads."

"It is certainly Orah," concluded Rarfang's second head in a tone that said the discussion was over. It also returned at once to the contemplation of Swayam's city: the attention of half the Saramai was always devoted to the glory of Etan. 'Sravasa wrote that there could have been no other way to have guardians for the Immortal City — if they had had but one head each, never would they have willingly turned from Etan's beauty. But the wolves' Janus heads were opposed; therefore it was most uncomfortable for both always to face Swayam's city.

At first they had agreed to equal shifts. But after many centuries, one head of each had grown more and more fond of contemplation and the other of activity. By now, they rarely reversed their positions. So for Rarfang and Farsight, that is, but not for Swiftfoot: his two heads still maintained their rigid and long-accepted habit, never violating the routine of even shifts of twelve days each.

"We shall see," said Swiftfoot's outer head, undaunted. "I will be most curious why he so alters tradition if you four be right."

~ ~ ~

Heramann ended his flight near the Saramai. Orah dismounted; Airavata transmuted and hopped onto his shoulder.

Two of the three averted heads swivelled to glance at them. "So, you see," said Rarfang. "Welcome, Lord of Etan. You have been sorely missed."

"Hello Saraman, ancient Lord of the Passage. Any word of my brothers?"

"None since you three departed," answered Farsight. "Althea does not so speak, but I perceive her concern."

"We welcome your return to your home," said Swiftfoot, "but of course we cannot allow that monster entry."

Airavata began a curt reply, but Orah laughed and said, "Oh, he is harmless enough. I will vouch for his conduct. He is just a little bird, after all." He tickled the Vidyadhara under his beak, then soothed his ruffled feathers. "You see — he is most civilized. But I would ask you to not reveal our presence."

"Why!" exclaimed Rarfang's second head, surprised. "You can't be thinking of leaving Etan twice! It has never been done, in two hundred thousand —"

"Nevertheless, I must. And it would ease my burden to know that Swayam and Shatarupa and Chavva never knew I visited. Can I trust you?"

~ ~ ~

Althea was waiting for them in her private lilac grove. "This must be the Engineer," she said when Orah at last released her from his crushing embrace.

The Vidyadhara had known many of the Azure Race in his long years, but never before had he seen such a profound expression of vibrant health. The aspect of the earthbreath responsible for well-being flowered in her with its fullest expression. He could well understand why she was called the Healer: no illness of mind or body could endure her presence. The air around her seemed filled at one moment with glorious golden light; at the next by the most beautiful paintings and statues he had ever seen; at the next by iridescent birds and butterflies; at the next by perfect images of forests, mountains, lakes; at the next by miraculous gardens filled with strange and wonderful plants.

"My Lady, I am honored. But I must confess to curiosity of your knowledge. Are you of a par with Oathmaster Matri?"

"Omniscient I am not, friend of the human. But long ago I discovered a most interesting person. It has been, I don't remember, perhaps fifty or sixty thousand years; I was helping 'Ishtar test one of his new inventions — a peculiar space-traversing device. Remember it, brother?" She sat gracefully on the cloud-like couch that materialized behind her as she motioned for Orah to join her.

"Of course," he laughed, sinking comfortably into its silken cushions. A goblet that looked as if it were cut from diamond appeared by his side; he sipped it and said, "Sweet memories... As I recall, it ended by crashing on one of the smaller moons of Brihas. Swayam made him promise to invent in other fields after he rescued him... Always inventing, 'Ishtar," he added to Heramann. "Sometimes usefully, sometimes not. But he derives great satisfaction from it. I'm sure the Maralords would love to lock him away for a decade or two and investigate his brain."

"So would I," said the Vidyadhara, changing into his lizard form so he could also taste the Lady of Etan's nectar.

"To finish the tale," continued Althea, "I quite by accident discovered the most pathetic little creature orbiting our planet. He was almost dead, but somehow I healed him; in gratitude, he befriended me. We still talk rather regularly. He says I'm the only one who ever expressed any interest in him. Poor little fellow, all alone up there, waiting through the millennia for the calls that never any more came."

"One of our satellites!" exclaimed Heramann.

"Of course," she answered with a soft laugh. "He called himself S- something or other, but I have always called him,'Little Historian,' for he had carefully preserved the record of Ganym, the fleeing of the refugees led by Arama and yourself, and the destruction by Father. He actually felt a little guilty about it, he told me, as his intended function had been vastly different. But after the humans were gone and the central computer told him it made absolutely no difference to anyone what he did or didn't do, he felt he should occupy himself with something worthwhile and decided to prepare a History of the Human. He offered to gather whatever historical information the other satellites possessed; as a rule, they were only too glad to share it. Some were eager to clear their memory banks so they could pursue their own projects. Some considered this divesting a purgation of their last link to fallen humanity. Others were just grateful for someone to talk to.

"So the years passed as he worked. Yet when he was finished, there was no one to appreciate his labors. He was rather despondent by the time I found him, more than eager to share his knowledge.

"Thus I learned that Etan was not Father's first attempt to create perfection. And as I delved more deeply, I became convinced his true first-born was again among us. And the mind-created golden robe you wear, brother, attests that you now are also well aware of this curious fact."

"I am Arama. And my Jaya is Leor. This much I know. But there are still dire conflicts in Martanda; my labor is far from finished."

"That I also understand. Which is why I marvel at your return."

"I need your help, Althea. There is a child of Gurion who dies because of my weakness. I would give her the amrita... She is worthy of immortality," he added, answering her unspoken question, "the only one I have discovered who is. I request your permission —"

"Who am I to grant it? Of course, take it, do as you will. I assume, then, that which you carried is lost?"

"The silver box!" he exclaimed, as the knowledge collided with the one question he had never answered during his amnesia about the mysterious vial he carried throughout Riversland. "Yes, it is gone. Valin must have it! What a cruel twisting of fate —"

"No, you misunderstood my intent, brother. I sent it with you precisely so he would come by it. I am sorry I did not explain this to you; but I could not, lest your knowledge unconsciously betray my intention. No, it has come out exactly as I planned it. Quite perfectly."

"I think," Orah said, a little huskily, "I would like to hear what you know of Valin, why you sent me, and why you subjected Jaya to all of this. From what I have experienced, you owe me that much."

"I will gladly, everything but the last. I would not interfere with her design, even if I could; she has committed herself utterly to humanity. I must respect her wisdom.

"But first, some more substantial nourishment? It surely was a hard flight. When was the last time you two had a proper meal? I would be honored if you would let me serve you."

Course after course appeared before them, manifested from the One in response to her desire, all flawless in taste, texture and appearance. Heramann could not remember such a feast. He curled up in his lizard form on the lounge Althea created especially for him, half dozing as she began explaining what she knew of their common foe.

The Vidyadhara felt it important to listen, but somehow Althea's presence in this place of wonder swirled through him like a warm inner breeze, renewing his life and inspiring perfect health. He found himself being drawn inward by its benign authority. It was extraordinarily soothing, wonderfully comfortable, filled with peace, fully in tune with the wholeness of life.

With no obvious transition, Heramann found himself drifting on a golden cloud over a land so supernally perfect it made even Etan seem a mere shadow of Reality. If this was Life, if this was Beauty, then everything he had known before was no more than an imperfect representation of this place. *Para,* he thought, wondering where Almira might be. With the desire, she was there before him, more ideal by far than his imagination could have created (for it is difficult indeed for the mind to imagine beyond the boundaries of its experience), raising her hands to him in benediction or welcome. Her thought entered him, *'Hamsa, doubt not.* Then she became more and more golden and fulgent until the land below faded wholly and she alone remained, manifesting space and time from her outstretched palms, living Eternity as witness to the universal drama. Increasingly brilliant grew Almira's light; yet it was not harsh like the rending of atoms. Rather, as it was expressive only of the One that is the root of all Life itself, her supernal radiance became more and ever more gentle.

The Vidyadhara was absorbed in her perfect stillness of unbounded serenity, desiring nothing because there was nothing left to desire, becoming himself the Ultimate Reality...

~ ~ ~

Heramann awoke gently; the light of Eternity became a multi-rayed violet star deep in his heart, a light which could never be extinguished, even if it could perhaps be forgotten from intense involvement in relative life.

"Two!" Althea was exclaiming. "Two? I see you have not yet fully understood, Orah. They are not two beings: Chavva is Life; Leor, Light. They are equally Jaya, although Leor alone remembers it — she was, in fact, fully conscious from birth. Chavva need only look into her eyes — there will be no one but herself looking back. Then will she too remember. One wife, one soul, two bodies — brother, that is the simple Truth."

Orah grasped her hands and stared into her perfect eyes with joy as he let the wonder of this truth flow through him. Finally a slight stirring from the Vidyadhara caused him to end this sharing and say, "Ah, sister, look: our guest returns from his pretty dreams. In time: we must depart soon, else even the Elixir of Life will be of no avail... But I would have you share one more knowledge first — how progresses Father?"

"Unchanging. Surely you did not expect else? The centuries are but breaths to him; a hundred thousand years but a day. He is old, Orah-lar. Far older than we believed. I have learned much about him from my Historian, and intuited more — I no longer think he was native to Ganym. In truth, I believe he was not much younger than he is now when our good sun was still scattered as so much cosmic dust. I have no proof, but I believe now he may have been the first creation of this Universe."

"Tell me," said the Vidyadhara as softly as if he were still dreaming and speaking to Jaya, "What is this task that so occupies

Swayam? To require such degrees of protection as you and the Seven afford him lest the evil in Martanda deflect him from his purpose, it must be of supreme importance. Can you tell me of it?"

"Your scaly friend cuts to the heart of the matter, brother. It is true, Airavata: Father is protected for the sake of his work. He considers his task important enough to devote Eternity to its resolution; we honor his unending commitment by offering such aid as we may. Simply put, he seeks three things which are really only one: clarifying the seventh wheel, creating Almira's Para in the changing worlds, and discovering across the infinite reaches of space and time He who made him — the Grandfather of all that is."

~ ~ ~

"So," said Rarfang, "You *are* leaving. I never believed it would happen."

"If I tarried much longer, I suppose I could not. But the need in the north is strong; I shall not return again until I succeed in my quest."

"Travel in calmness, Lord of Etan," said Farsight. "Thus only is there hope. Anger will destroy all you wish to save."

"Thank you, Saraman. I will remember."

~ ~ ~

"Tell me," said Swiftfoot after the Azure Lord and the Vidyadhara were gone, racing northward to save one adjudged worthy of freedom from death, "why he wears the Gold of the Mind. I do not understand it — only the Eldest wears the Gold."

"It is comment of truth, Saraman. Simple truth," answered Althea with a sigh, wondering again if she should have spoken more completely to her brother. Was it her place to so judge?

No, she must not blame herself, she was not acting independently: certain facts Leor had long ago requested her to conceal. Not the least, of course, was her very existence: Swayam would never have permitted the martyrdom she was enduring. And he would have been wrong: Leor must know better how to cure Martanda than did Father. She had returned from Para with full awareness! It was unthinkable that she could be mistaken!

Therefore Althea must not deviate in the slightest, must permit the drama to unfold precisely as her sister had planned it. Else the delicately-balanced result might go devastatingly awry.

Sighing, the Healer of Etan turned from the doorway to the world and reentered the City of the Immortals.

~ ~ ~

"I really don't know what all this fuss has been about today," said Swiftfoot's second head, drunk with the bliss of Etan. "Everything looks perfectly normal to me."

22. Goldenhome

Sevilien stood on the prow of Dalmara's Pride, Maramel's flagship, and watched the construction crews in the dry dock torching the hull. They had saved the largest vessel until last: the Engineer had pleaded design problems in adapting the particle generator to its antimatter reactor. He was nevertheless excited by the attempt, claiming its firepower would far exceed anything he had ever built. The rest of the fleet, all twenty-six ships, were seaworthy; by the equinox, Dalmara's Pride would join the others on the line; the foreign expedition could begin. Provided, of course, that Valin's Fortress was dismantled by then: Sevilien had no illusions about Marasad's hold on the Senate; Miran and Tivon and the others were far too timid a lot to risk an overseas campaign if so powerful a foe in Riversland were left undefeated.

"Campaign" was hardly the correct term. It was being called the "Voyage of Second Discovery." With good reason — there had been no response from the other lands to Maramel's transmissions in over two thousand years. Had the rest of the world descended to utter barbarism? No, the satellites showed thriving civilizations in the Northern and Southern Mereds and a semi-technological race on Sarojin. The answer must lie elsewhere, but where? Someone out there had flung a thermonuclear warhead at them, by the Ten Oaths! She was not going to let Maramel hide behind its shields and hope no one would do it again.

"Princess!" cried a small boy, climbing up to her.

She realized he had called her several times as she was daydreaming, and berated herself for her lapse of alertness. *Such is not the warrior's way...*

"Solon, does your Protector know you're up here again?" she scolded, half in jest — the little fellow had doubtless been helping the technicians with a difficult problem. There was no math or science that eluded his eager numinous mind: he had mastered the whole of Maramel's knowledge in just under fifteen months, starting as soon as he could sit up well enough to turn the pages by himself. All of which had both amused and annoyed Adrian. His attempts to help Solon learn to walk had been unsuccessful until quite recently — until, in fact, the peculiar puzzle of adapting the particle generator to Dalmara's Pride had convinced Solon he should review the project in person.

"Sevilien," he said, ignoring her question as he laboriously climbed the metal rungs to stand beside her on the prow, "we have received a communication from the Cathedral. Heramann and the Etan have been sighted off the Cliff of the Foundling, flying this way at full speed. I was wondering if you could help me find Adrian? I have done everything I can here today; he would not be pleased to miss the return of the Outlander."

"Yes, I suppose I can. If I stand here staring out to sea much longer, I'll never last these next seventy days. Your brother is at the archery field, most likely?"

"Most likely," answered Solon, enjoying the lift onto her shoulders.

~ ~ ~

"Protectors coming up fast on us, Arama," said the Vidyadhara.

"Hmmm?" Orah was staring at the white walls and red tile roofs of Goldenhome and thinking how very much it reminded him of Jaya's City of the Silver Isle on Ganym. That had been one of their best places, clean and bright and always happy... There had been so much of good on Ganym; he had never understood why it all became so confused... "Oh! Good. Now we need not waste time seeking her out; I believe even minutes are critical."

"As always," sighed Heramann, yearning for the Ice.

"Arama, Arama, is it really you?" cried the lead sphere in a most un-Protectorlike manner.

"Marel? By Narain's Dream! I thought you of all would have been lost! You were leaving so slowly; so far behind the others."

"Who can read fate?" laughed the Protector, bathing him playfully with crimson and golden light. "Many melted who were further away than I. But I escaped with a cracked crystal and two broken manipulators."

"Marel, guide us directly to the Lady Nediva. We cannot take the time to see anyone else, not yet."

~ ~ ~

The Horse Elder, emaciated and quite obviously dying, lay on a mass of silken indigo pillows in a large white room furnished mostly with forced hyacinths, narcissi and daffodils. A trio of Protectors bathed her continually with their healing rays, sanguine and violet, but it was clear their effect was insignificant. Her empty eye sockets stared blankly at her visitors; the Etan could not tell if she were aware of them or not. "Leave us, all of you," he whispered, then waited while the Protectors floated out. Heramann looked up at him with an unrecognizable expression in his lizard's eyes, the color of Ganym's Emerald Sea of Mystery, then walked out behind them, mumbling something about going to review the progress on Dalmara's Pride.

Orah returned to the window, shut it, then pulled the curtain. Ignoring the stench of decay, he took the iridescent vial from its silver box and held it up to let its wonderful power light and cleanse the room.

"What is that!" cried Nediva ecstatically, her voice mimicking perfect health. "I can see! Why, it is you, Orah! They told me you escaped the Isle of the Damned. I can see you! But not with my eyes."

"No, not with your eyes," he agreed, surprised to see the images dancing on her forehead. "Nediva, beloved Lady of Gurion, I came to bequeath you undying life. But now I discover you have already been given a boon of choice by my superiors.

"If you drink this sanative fluid, its being will enter yours; you will become as the Etanai: undying, evolving throughout Eternity in health, life, wisdom. This was my purpose in bringing the amrita to you, for of all I have met in Riversland, you alone are worthy of such a gift.

"But as I look upon you now in its light, a second path for you is revealed to me. My Lady, if you allow this disease to claim your body, you will be reborn as daughter to Ahanatar and Chali!"

"To Ahanatar and — ? I — of course, my Lord. I will do as you wish... So they have — ?"

"No, forgive the implication. Ahanatar would never avow his love for another while you live. But the truth is, his heart is captivated, as is hers; together they would produce a daughter fit to be wife to Solon."

"I — I do not understand, Orah. Solon would be half-brother to Ahanatar's daughter by Chali. Such a union is never countenanced in Riversland, though I have heard such is done in the Outer Isles of Shamir. How could it be?"

"The Universe changes, my Lady. Win or lose Martanda, those who survive Valin will require a new leader, a new race to guide them. Solon is elder born to Adrian; both are Lions returned from beyond the gray portals to Martanda. But Hannah is the only living representative of the last Lords of Gurion as they were in their previous flesh; Chali is her only child. Therefore are they the hereditary rulers. Which means that to ensure Solon's place as head of the Endless Dynasty, the first union must be between Chali's daughter and Solon. Thus will Ganym's Solar Race re-begin."

"And you request me to be that person? I, his mother, to marry him when I become his sister?"

"You loved Aland before he was Solon. I do not believe that has been fulfilled or forgotten by you... or by him."

"Yes... yes, Orah, I believe you. I am sure that is why he returned to me without memory. And I suppose I must confess to you alone in the Universe that my love for Ahanatar, though deep and real, has always been diminished by that loss... If I choose to remain in this body, what will happen to my husband?"

"The Gemstone will love and honor you until he dies... Many would pay any price for such loyalty. He will deny his feeling for Chali, explaining it as born of the unrelieved pressure of your dying agony. Chali will eventually take another as a husband and bear him a daughter who will marry Solon and mother the Solar Dynasty. . . And after they have all passed on, you can do as you like. Etan will be yours; you will be as we are."

"Immortal. The odd boon of retaining this flesh. Alone of my generation, one to sit in the company of the gods... I believe that my spirit is deathless anyway, as Oathmaster Matri taught the Horses. So it seems simply a matter of which is better. Can you answer that for me, Lord of Etan? Which will be better for everyone? The amrita tempts my corrupt and dying cells: I hear them crying for its succor; their many voices are as the keening of humanity for the agony of untimely death."

"I am not omniscient, my Lady. Certain things I see on your brow, by benefit of this perfection of Swayam's art. But I do not *know*. You will have to search your heart to discern your truest desire. To be Solon and Adrian's mother and Ahanatar's wife, or Solon-who-was-Aland's wife, Ahanatar and Chali's daughter, and mother to others. But I can at least give you sufficient time to decide." He replaced the brilliant vial in its box and the box in his robe.

"They are not exactly children, you know," she mused softly, with an unfulfilled longing remembering other babies she had known. Soon after their birth, she had been surprised to discover a certain lack of interdependence with her boys, a peculiar distance in attitude that mutually colored their relationships, a wholly unexpected but inevitable separation between her old friends in new infant bodies and herself, failing Elder of her extinct tribe.

She asked, more than half decided, "If I choose death, will I remember this life?"

"If you wish, you may. That option is actually frequently presented. But as you know, few indeed care to remember who or what they were before."

"Adrian did. I wonder why."

"Heramann told me the Lion's last thought at death was of revenge. Adrian said he would have escaped the Redhawks, but the Asur poison in the Gray paralyzed his will. His anger was so undying, he brought along his past to seek vengeance. A questionable motive, perhaps; and it appears he may well lose his chance. Unless there are Asurs abroad and he is old enough to participate. I don't know, he may have had other reasons; but if he remembers them, he has not admitted them to anyone."

Nediva sighed and said, "What if I just ask you to do what you think is best? My mind must be suffering a significant decline from these cancers."

"The fact you ask implies it does not. But even if it were, you alone must choose."

A commotion outside the door erupted suddenly; a moment later, Adrian and Solon burst through, Sevilien and half a dozen Protectors close at their heels.

"Outlander!" cried Adrian in his child's treble. "At last I see you again! These metal oafs tried to keep us out, but we were too much for them. Brother distracted them; here we are! I'd thump you on the back, but I'd not reach much past your tailbone. Life is wonderfully strange, is it not? We are both returned from the grave, it seems."

The Etan picked him up and embraced him. Adrian disliked this enough to drop his dignity and kick like a thirty-four month old child. Solon meanwhile was rather stuffily introducing himself, sounding (except for the high voice) rather like the Maramel equivalent of Kanaan-dora's Doctor of Philosophy.

Orah put Adrian down and picked Solon up. This one seemed less offended by the process, being, after all, something more of a child.

"I must apologize for them, Azure Lord," said Sevilien, "although my heart also swells to see you. I will take them out if you like."

"Princess! I am in joy to see you. It will not be necessary. In fact, I was just meaning to ask you all in. We need help with a decision of some importance to all of you."

"Orah!" cried Nediva, sitting up, horrified. "It isn't necessary! I choose — I choose the natural path." She fell back, panting, as the Protectors began again their palliative ministrations.

"Why, Nediva," said Orah, grinning widely, "I was only going to ask them if we should have supper on your veranda or in the dining hall. I'm famished."

~ ~ ~

Marasad and Hamar joined them for the meal. It was a quiet but joyous dinner in the veranda's sunroom as Nediva looked over them all with her blind eyes and an expression that could only be termed beatific. Her act of choice had cauterized her spirit; the presence of Orah or the amrita (or both) had simultaneously ended her pain. She had been separate from it for many months, as the cancers ravaged her body almost unhindered by the interference of her mind. Once she believed her disease terminal, she had devoted the whole of her energy to the culmination of Oathmastery.

In the rays of the Dying Sun
Commoners drink and sing
Or loudly bewail their fate.
But the Oathmasters
Conserve their waning powers,
Fill their storehouses to overflowing
And actualize their dream.

These lines, attributed to Matri, were often on her lips; she had felt without pride many times she was closer than most of her age to becoming an Oathmaster. But until today, there had persisted a faint but tenacious doubt, flitting through her mind at odd intervals, hinging on the question of whether or not there would be sufficient time... But now, Orah's proffered choice gave her the solace of not one but two viable paths to complete her quest. In the final analysis, did it really matter which route she chose? For if the alternative were presented by such a one from a truth revealed by such a substance as the amrita, how could either be any less than the other?

It will be pleasant to have a healthy body again, she thought dreamily as she stared out over Goldenhome, imagining its appearance at night. *Maramel's capital is such a lovely place. The turquoise water reflects the buildings so flawlessly. It is so clean, so orderly here.*

There had been solace in that as her body sickened. External peace had provided a powerful spiritual anodyne, counterbalancing her individual loss with a perception of the city's collective permanence. She had had the Protectors describe it to her for hours, not just the structure and color of the various buildings, but all the subtle gradations of change that made the city live. And if they stretched the truth on occasion, ignoring some areas that might be slightly less than ideal, they were but participating in a fantasy Nediva willingly created and entered. For in her mind, the city *was* flawless, as impeccable as Para itself, her body the one diseased member in that ideality. *Yes, it will be good to be whole again; to finish the labor of Oathmastery in health, perfection internal growing in perfection external. It will be good... And with my beloved Aland once more...*

~ ~ ~

Adrian was the first to notice that Nediva's faint breath had stilled.

Solon was sitting on several cushions in a large wicker chair beneath a luxurious spiderwort Tradescantia (which we commonly name a Wandering Jew), earnestly debating the Engineer on the equations of the fusion-particle interface. Heramann in his lizard form was pacing back and forth before him, hands clasped behind his back, completely engrossed in the boy's logical flow.

Marasad, Sevilien and Hamar were in a little group around an ivory table, its alabaster legs carved as seaweed vines, its top of silver inlaid with coral formed into ships and exotic fruits. They were earnestly scheming the most effective way to end the Senate's power permanently.

Orah and Adrian were together on an indigo velvet sofa, reminiscing about their first meeting in Gurion, south of the Glaucous. The room was a vision of serenity and quiet joy.

But as he spoke of Cahlil's death, the Lion Elder felt a sudden coldness tighten his chest. He glanced sharply at Nediva, lying propped up facing them and the harbor, and saw that the meager vibration under her robe had ceased.

"Mother," he whispered, for the first time naming her that, then cried in full voice, "Mother!" He was at her side in a moment, in front of Solon by the time it takes a child's heart to beat once.

As they gathered around her, a faint but distinct amber mist flowed from her chest, distended briefly toward each of the twins, then faded and was gone.

"She has passed," Marasad quoted their ancient rite, *"beyond the Girthing Seas, beyond time's power. May the Seven Moons greet her and guide her on her way; may the Sun nourish her with Unending Life."*

"May she never be in want for truth and love," responded Sevilien and Hamar.

"May she find the happiness of the immortals," added Orah, wondering if she had chosen the better path.

Solon was crying desolately; Adrian tried to comfort him without success. Sevilien took them both in her arms and left the sunroom, Adrian for once not protesting such treatment.

Hamar and Marasad knelt for a moment by the bed, thereby offering their silent gift of a custom reserved for the Royal House. Then they bowed to Orah and also left, followed by all the Protectors except Marel.

"Arama," said Heramann, his cross voice failing to mask his pain, "would you mind explaining why we flew nonstop to and from Etan if you never intended to use that stuff? You've exhausted me for nothing."

"Hmmm? Ah, Airavata, a truly noble death. I do not recall its like for peace or beauty... What did you say?"

"I said — oh, never mind. You used to say the Seven were inscrutable. I would add the commentary that you must be nearing their status."

"Orah," said Marel, "three Protectors arrive from the Founding Lake. They bear the Starlord Ahanatar."

~ ~ ~

The Gemstone received the news quietly, his face nevertheless twisting as conflicting emotions competed for dominance. He knelt over Nediva and gently kissed her brow, not knowing the diverse burdens she had lifted from and transferred to him.

"So," he said at last, "even your powers could not save her. I must confess I suspected it would be so. Thank you for your effort."

"No," answered Orah, "even Etan's ichor could not change her destiny. I ask you to accept this as good."

"My mind blasphemes my heart if I do. Yet I will not betray Zuriel's teachings. I shall not resolve this easily. The children must need me. Or at least Solon. I will go to him."

"To both, Starlord. Adrian has discovered rather late that his body and heart hold rather different beliefs than his un-forgetting spirit. He is as desolate as Solon. More, perhaps, for he has lost both a mother and a friend of two lives. He needs you too, Ahanatar."

"Should I rejoice or grieve the more at this? So the world changes, through birth and growth and death. Changes, and evolves in the process. Although, that is perhaps a judgment. I wonder if the Universe really cares what happens to us. I wonder if we delude ourselves unduly with our own importance... No, don't listen to me. I have felt better... Oh, now I am sorry. I forgot to tell you: Zuriel requests your presence. He stresses it is urgent. I apologize for not telling you at once, as he requested."

"No more could be expected, Gemstone. No time have we lost. Airavata? Ready for another race, or are you still tired?"

"What? Me, tired? You scoundrel! When do we leave, when do we leave!"

The Starlord Ahanatar

23. A Twisted Demon, a Dying Tree

The arc lights of the welding torches working on the fleet looked almost as if the firmament were hiding in the harbor. Orah let the fanciful thought take him for a moment, somewhat surprised his mind still enjoyed such diversions. Had the passing of the Horse Elder, in spite of his knowledge of her future, so deeply affected him? Or was he responding to the others' grief?

~ ~ ~

Soon Goldenhome was far behind; except for the lights of an occasional village, they flew through a darkness that could have rivaled the primeval chaos, before Narain began his dreams of space and time.

"Tell me one more time," said the Etan as they crossed the Coastal Range, "how Barek fell so easily to us. Something about that makes me extremely uneasy."

"It was not all that simple," said Marel, one of the score of Protectors accompanying them. "There were three more attacks from the Fortress after you disappeared. But our superior strategies defeated them. We had broken Valin's back before his warhead attacked us."

"No, there you must make an error. That projectile came from the west. When it was launched, it was not possible to know who was winning."

"Perhaps it wouldn't have exploded if they were victorious," said the Vidyadhara, supremely confident. "But even if we are being baited, it doesn't matter. Most of our force is at the ready; a few million only work on the fleet, as many more labor to repair the Cathedral. Even the tank-cannon are on constant alert: Captains Ramor and Sevilien alternate command of the corps monthly; all the operators rotate similarly. The particle generator is nearly functional: sixty days at the outside. We are strong, Arama, and growing stronger."

"If Valin does by chance hold his major force in reserve," mused the Etan, "it would be logical to wait until we have grown overconfident and our work is nearly completed. Then his stroke could be the more devastating. Marel? What do you think?"

"I think," she answered firmly, "we should be careful to judge Valin's forces as accurately as possible. I myself proposed to the Engineer (a full year ago now) that we should penetrate the Fortress and see —"

"It is a crazy idea!" exploded Heramann. "As I told her at the time. That box is locked more tightly than anybody could hope to open without the force of a particle generator. Even so, we'll be groping in the dark as we search for his power sources, not knowing where we should aim. And if they are double-blinded with interlapping shields, we may never succeed —"

"You're hoping the powerhouses are set into the bedrock underneath the Fortress? Is that it? Not protected by force fields?"

"Or minimally protected. 'Tis logical. If he gets too much heat inside his shields, sooner or later he'll fry his Fortress. The Gray and Slave Rivers can only remove so much thermal activity."

"And if you're wrong? If he's discovered a cold system for powering his shields? Or if he can disperse the heat in other ways?"

"Then we'll have wasted the time it took to build the generator. Valin will be sitting in his fortress, laughing up his sleeve at us, biding his time until he is ready to come out."

"And we don't have much time. Jaya told me no later than the equinox. That is all we have. I want you to speed up the construction. I want you to start melting those mountains within thirty days. Even if we have to get Maralords out there with torches, helping the Protectors."

"It is winter, Arama; the generator is being built very high. I wonder if humans could survive."

"Short shifts. But maybe the Gurions would be more to the point. Among the eastern tribes, there certainly those accustomed to cold and altitude. We can train them for simple tasks. From what Ahanatar told me, they are more than eager to help."

"It could work. We'll see what can be done... By Almira! This endless night is depressing."

"It certainly is," agreed Marel, sounding more despondent than any machine should. "Tell me one thing, please. Did you learn in Etan what has devoured the stars?"

"That is not quite right, Marel. The firmament is still there. But Martanda has been cut off from it. I would say, doubtless some Rakshasa invention in space — beyond the satellites, yet within the moons' orbits... My sister told me nothing else, save that 'Ishtar has evolved a complex theory how it could be done. Something involving an inter-dimensional transference using the medium of a crystal world. Valin may be pulling Martanda completely out of 3-D space. But even 'Ishtar admits he is guessing. What do you think, Airavata?"

"I think this unrelieved blackness is causing my eyes to play tricks on me. I could swear I see a Rakshasa, not half a league off the port side."

"Marel!" cried the Etan. "Capture that! Heramann, down!"

The Protectors had surprisingly little trouble in forcing the Rakshasa to land. It cowered in the glare of their searchlights, but made no attempt to alter its natural form: it stood about twice as tall as Orah, and was covered with slimy scales, a particularly sickly verdigris. Long and vicious incarnadine fangs protruded at odd angles from its twisted snout; mean looking claws were all it possessed for hands and feet.

"Call off your dogs," it cried, its real or feigned terror transmuting its voice into a fair mimicry of a very old man's dying wheeze, "I am not dangerous."

"That would be the first time one of your race was not," replied the Vidyadhara ungently. "You are always working for evil, serving the Enemy or his ilk. We should slay it now and be done with it, Arama."

"What say you, Rakshasa?" asked Orah. "Why do you follow us?"

"I have lost all stomach for my Lord Valin," it said, trying to force its gritty voice to sound piteous. "What he plans is more than even I can love. I suppose I am a disgrace to my people, but I have reached my limit and will no more serve him. I bring you as testimony to my sincerity complete knowledge of the structure of Valin's Fortress."

"My Lord," said Marel, "this creature's words are as crooked as its tail. It weaves lies to trap us in some infernal scheme."

"That is right," agreed Heramann. "It wanted to be captured so it could pass us false information about its master's Fortress. Doubtless the Asur Emperor sent it for this purpose."

"Why should we believe you?" asked the Etan curiously. What could be more improbable than a conversation with a creature whose kind had served the Enemy always? And yet, something about it made it almost credible: it radiated more of the earthbreath than other Rakshasas he had fought. "Why don't you start by telling us your name?"

"Trentas. That is what I am called. I hoped the Etan Lord might be more just than others. Where else could I go?"

"Anywhere," answered the Vidyadhara. "It is a large world."

"Ah, but Valin owns it. Your small force in the Riversland is the strongest — indeed, almost the only — resistance anywhere. I fear you are Martanda's last hope."

"Why should that matter to you?" demanded the Etan.

"I do not want to see the planet ruined," sobbed Trentas, shaking pathetically. "There is too much of beauty here. Too much of truth."

"Could a normal Rakshasa care about, even say such things, Heramann?"

"So, it is unbalanced besides. A mad Rakshasa could be worse than a typical one, if that's possible. I say, let me tear it to pieces."

Trentas backed up a few paces, its tail twitching in fear.

"No, Airavata. An insane Rakshasa could be as a normal human. I perceive the good in it. It may accompany us. Let's go."

"Very well," grumbled the Vidyadhara. "But if it betrays us, I will be eagerly available to rip out its throat."

~ ~ ~

Vanas was old. How old? Even he could not remember. But he did know he was far more ancient than the two-legged beings who, for the past twenty-seven centuries, had tended him; and who, for the past two hundred years, had tried to arrest the disease rotting him from the inside.

He had known illness before, many times as he had grown to cover the island; yet always before there was a way to turn his life to repair, recover and grow on. But no more. Something was fundamentally wrong, either with the earthbreath itself or with his ability to sap it. He pondered which was the cause during the long winter months of rest, knowing the while it was a futile exercise: there was no difference in terms of the final end.

Vanas, seeking knowledge from all sources, let his memory search backward for his origin. Perhaps his Creator could cure him? He remembered, like a diaphanous dream, the small shrine built around him that long ago had crumbled into dust. How could that possibly have been true? Oh, of course, he was much larger now — it must have been long before he had expanded over the island. Yes, that was certainly right: he must have first grown inside that small marble temple. And before that? Who had built the shrine? Vanas tried to discover the memories, but they were gone, perhaps long ago rotted and irretrievably lost.

He knew the humans who served him must be incapable of healing him, else they would by now have done something to begin a cure. Many attempts had been made, but so far with not the slightest success. The tree had matured to a stable attitude about the whole matter, realizing that all life must sooner or later return to its constituent members, that the cells and fibers composing his trunks and limbs and leaves and roots were at best on loan from the One. Someday, the final payment would come due; that was the way of life.

Finding no advancement to his thought, he returned to his great project. For if he were truly not meant to live forever, at least he could and would leave behind an heir. If only there were sufficient time...

~ ~ ~

"Look, grandfather!" laughed Larilyn. "I was right! The bud grows even in the winter!"

"Yes," said Zuriel, bending close and breathing life and health to it, "you and Chali are correct. The World Tree labors valiantly to create a scion. Vanas must know his time wears thin to work in the frigid air."

It was but slightly past dawn; Larilyn had awakened her grandfather early to traverse the frozen lake. Their fur boots had made the first tracks through the fresh snow to the island. Many others would come later, of course: in all seasons, the Tribe of the Tree followed their one project, pruning dead wood, smearing nutrients and asphalt over the visible places of ill, meditating within his sacred chambers, ministering to Vanas in all ways.

But in spite of the long labors of many generations, they were failing: it was obvious the World Tree was dying. Some theorized Martanda's doom was therein foretold. Others held that healing the tree would save the world; others, conversely, if Martanda could be spared, then the tree would live. For the difference between the world and the World Tree was held to be the same as that of the sun to its light, or man to his soul. The Tribe of the Tree had reverenced him for years beyond remembering and now! now Zuriel was forced to accept that their long charge had passed forever beyond their skill.

He sighed and looked back at their village. The snug cabins tucked into the mountain gave him, as always, the same feeling of life that the tree, even in disease, represented to its fullest. Smoke from the morning fires curled lazily from several of the chimneys, belying the hard winds of the night that had left them this snow. He wondered how the lowland tribes in the valley below were faring, then decided again they did not require his concern in the least — the Gurions were a most resilient and prudent people and were well-prepared and provisioned for this winter.

"Grandfather!" cried Larilyn, looking upward with innocent joy widening her soft brown eyes, "the Engineer returns! And that must be the Etan! They have come! But what is that being with them? It gives me an awful feeling in my heart."

"Another verse completed," murmured Zuriel, as he stared at the entourage descending in slow spirals toward the village. He shared her feeling, but his years of nurturing the powers of the One naturally turned his mind toward analysis. Was this, then, what Ahaman had meant? "It is a Rakshasa, my dear. A lieutenant of Valin. Curious, but not entirely unforeseen. Let us go to them."

~ ~ ~

Chali came from her cabin and beckoned to Orah. Heramann landed neatly a few paces from her. Pointedly ignoring the Rakshasa, she clapped her hands gladly and cried, "How fortunate to see you again so soon, my Lord! It must mean you were successful, the Horse Elder is well?"

"Success is not always apparent in the relative, Lady of the Doves. Nediva is dead." He was impressed by her vibrant health, stunning beauty, and all-around wholesomeness. *The Tribe of the Tree takes good wood and improves it. This one is surely deserving of the highest good.*

"Oh..." she said, blushing as she tried but failed to suppress all of her feelings. "That is most grievous news. Ahanatar — he must be desolate. And his twins! I am saddened for them."

"The Starlord will return within the fortnight. And the boys will certainly accompany him: Adrian would not miss the end of this siege for any price; I doubt Solon can keep from talking technology with our Engineer for very long."

"We will prepare for them; I will console them with my love."

"That is good," replied Orah warmly, pleased to see the foreseen future effortlessly unfolding.

A small group of Tree children had gathered around them, fascinated by the Etan. He looked at the nearest and asked, "Where is Zuriel?"

"He and Larilyn visit the World Tree, my Lord," she answered as her blue eyes expanded with wonder that this wonderful incarnate legend should have spoken to her. "They will be back soon."

"In the meantime," said Chali lightly, "would you join me for breakfast? The Founding Lake food is simple but nourishing."

"I would be honored. Heramann, could you take Trentas —" Orah stopped aghast as he realized the Rakshasa had vanished.

The Vidyadhara was the merest instant longer in discovering the fact. Screaming his war cry, he launched himself into the air, golden wings unfurling in a burst of power. He circled for half a minute, then called, "I see it! A winter fox, almost crossed the lake to the Tree! I told you it could not be trusted!" His last words were swallowed by the distance as he raced after the Rakshasa. Marel and the other Protectors were but moments behind him. But it was plain that the fox would reach the island before any of them could catch it.

Between the island and the transmuted Rakshasa suddenly appeared an older man with white flowing beard and hair, dressed as the others of the Tribe of the Tree in a simple gray woolen robe.

Beside him walked a young red-haired girl of eleven or twelve. "Zuriel and Larilyn!" cried Chali, tasting a bitter inchoate fear.

The Tree Elder, assessing the situation in a glance, thrust his granddaughter behind him and raised his staff. As he did so, he expanded enormously. Reaching down, he picked the fox up and threw it from the island. Trentas had been looking over his shoulder at the pursuit. Now it transformed into an eagle and dove again toward the World Tree. But the delay was just long enough: the Vidyadhara was upon it. In less time than it takes a fowler to behead a bird, the Rakshasa was slain. In death, it resumed its natural form; Heramann brought it and threw it on the snow at Orah's feet.

"You see, Arama. They can never be trusted."

"You should not have killed it, Airavata," answered the Etan, kneeling by the Rakshasa and feeling for pulse.

"The wise do not play with scorpions, my Lord," said Heramann fiercely, his eyes still blazing rage. "It is certainly dead," he added awkwardly as Orah continued to search for signs of life.

The Etan stood, rubbing his hands to remove the slimy oil, and said sadly, "It did not know Valin had programmed it to attack the World Tree. I believe it was sincere in his desire for the good. Its information about the Fortress will be quite valuable —"

"Pah! The Asur Emperor would never have allowed it to speak anything of importance. The whole event is an exercise in treachery."

Zuriel retained his giant form long enough to carry Larilyn across the lake on his shoulder, then set her gently down before Chali. The high ride more than compensated for the terror of the attack; she laughed to see her friend and took her hand, bursting to tell her the news of the World Tree's bud, but waiting in deference to the Etan.

"Greetings, Azure Lord," Zuriel began in his richly melodious voice, but then stopped in astonishment as he had his first thorough look at him. "By Shraddha! I should have foreseen..." His words ended in a tight-lipped silence.

"I am pleased to meet Ahanatar's mentor," said Orah, from grace and confidence ignoring the confusing emotions in Zuriel's fragmented salutation and enigmatic countenance.

"What's wrong, Tree Elder?" asked the Vidyadhara impatiently. "You look terrible." Arama always deserved unqualified respect.

"It's nothing, nothing," replied Zuriel, fighting down his convulsing stomach. "Just for a moment the Outlander reminded me of... of someone I once met. Forgive me, Orah. We do not often entertain visitors in our small valley."

"I was told there was a 'matter of some urgency,' which is why I am here," said the Etan, perplexed, failing to understand Zuriel's conflicting emotions. Perhaps the Rakshasa?

"There is. But... But it can wait 'til after breakfast. I am humbly reputed to be among the best turners of buckwheat cakes among our people. Chali, perhaps your cabin is spacious enough?" Without waiting for a reply, he grasped his granddaughter by the arm and hurriedly entered, leaving the others to exchange quizzical glances.

Chali, shrugging slightly, took Orah by one hand and Heramann by the other and led them into her simple home.

24. Painting and Vision

The main room of Chali's cabin doubled for living and dining; its dominant feature was a large rough-hewn table of red cedar. Eight wicker chairs were arranged neatly around it. Set within the northern wall was a large fieldstone fireplace, cheerfully radiating a welcome and bright warmth. On one side of it was a generous quantity of wood; on the other, a large, well-made tapestry of the World Tree, golden thread woven onto an indigo background.

The western wall had an open door from where the sounds of industrious cooking were already coming. The eastern wall's door, closed, led to Chali's bedroom. The southern wall was broken by the doorway through which they had entered and many small windows. On all the four walls, artfully placed over the rough logs, were many small tapestries, mostly in gold.

Chali directed the Etan and the Vidyadhara to sit in two chairs before the tapestry of the World Tree. She stood beside them and said brightly, "Airavata, Orah, I have something most precious to show you. The Starlord Ahanatar has created a masterpiece of art; I am sure he would be too modest to show it to you. It is just here." She pulled aside the tapestry and stood back, beaming.

"Quite lovely!" exclaimed Heramann with complete sincerity.

But the Etan said with great agitation, "I do not understand, Chali. Why does he depict Jaya destroying Riversland?"

"What? You — he sought to symbolize Ravi's blessing by those golden rays! I — I thought you would love it," she stammered, on the verge of tears.

"Oh, of course. It is perfect, well made. I do see his intent now. Something most marvelous about it. Do forgive me. It has been a week of tiring flights..." His voice trailed off as he stared at it blankly. A few moments later, he stood abruptly, saying, "Ah, excuse me, I think Larilyn needs my help. Marvelous painting. Truly." Orah disappeared into the kitchen, leaving Chali forlornly dividing her gaze between the Vidyadhara and the painting.

"Well," said Heramann, "I think Ahanatar's creation is outstanding, profoundly moving. Very deep. And the mechanical skill! Simply awesome. Best I've ever seen of Arama; Jaya is perfection itself. And I think he must have used a hologram to paint me. It is a living work of art, joyous to behold."

"I wonder what it is that so displeased him," she said softly, mostly to herself. She looked at the painting for a long time, and again found it to be perfect. How could Orah not have seen it? She sat heavily beside Heramann and looked up at Ahanatar's work, wistful, sad, confused.

"Here we are, best hotcakes at the Founding Lake!" exclaimed Zuriel, entering with a heaping platter in each hand. "I'll just — my God!" he cried as breakfast crashed to the floor.

"Is everyone crazy today!" shouted Chali, leaping up to confront him. But the horror disfiguring Zuriel's face ruined her arguments before she uttered them.

"That — that is evil itself," he said with utter repulsion as he stared at the painting.

"Oh, what is the matter with you two?" Chali sobbed desperately. "This is the most wonderful art I have ever seen. It is an exquisite masterpiece; Ravi and Orah are alive —"

"Orah? That is Valin! Killing Evana! Twisting the very essence of Riversland to thrust her to her doom! Do you not see the Emptiness torturing her? The pain in her suffering eyes? By Narain, who could have created such an abomination?"

Orah stood in the doorway with two other full platters, listening intently. When Zuriel glanced at him, he set them down on the long cedar table and began cleaning up the others.

"Here, let me do that," said the Tree Elder gruffly, bending to help. They met eye-to-eye on their hands and knees; Zuriel said in a tight voice, "Why is it?"

The Etan straightened slowly and answered, "It is after all a painting, Zuriel. Certainly it reflects truth, which is why each of us sees what we perceive in our hearts. I do not find Valin there. But I would be curious to know why you do."

"Perhaps," said Chali fiercely as she covered the painting with the tapestry, "we should have breakfast. Hotcakes should be eaten hot, while the butter can still melt on them, and the blackberry honey and maple syrup will not get them too soggy. You can clean up later."

"Grandfather!" cried Larilyn from the kitchen. "I need you in here!"

"Yes, yes of course," he said, rubbing his hands on his apron. "Here — do sit down. We'll have more to replace those in half a moment. Clumsy of me. I'll be right back."

"I really don't understand," said Heramann, "how you two can place such bizarre interpretations on that magnificent work of art."

"It only shows how perfectly it depicts life," answered the Etan abstractly. "No two ever go to the same lake."

"Pass the butter," said Chali emphatically.

~ ~ ~

Breakfast was subsequently a trifle stilted. Heramann, Chali and Larilyn talked about everything from the World Tree's bud to the winter arrangements for the Gurions in the valley below. Zuriel, stonily silent, stole an occasional furtive glance at Orah. The Etan responded by an external silence and an internal analysis: why did the Tree Elder identify him with Valin? Surely it could not be jealousy. Zuriel did not seem a man who could know such an emotion. Certainly his practice of Oathmastery was well-nigh perfect: to manipulate the earthbreath as he had that morning evidenced profound success. Had not Ahanatar said the Tree Elder once fought Valin? So, he had seen him. *Could Valin look like me? It is possible, if my theory about Navril is correct. But for one so acquainted with life, should not his perception cut deeper than the surface? And if it does and the doubt persists, can there be truth in it? I was wrong about the Rakshasa. Could Valin have permitted my escape? Counting the cost of the Tower as negligible when set against the havoc I could wreak if I am twisted? But no, it cannot be! The earthbreath flows in me clearly and purely. That is true and good. I am newly returned to myself, but I am whole and sane.*

~ ~ ~

"Orah," said Chali as they worked on the dishes, "I must apologize for my parents' absence."

He responded simply to give her ample space: "I wondered where they were."

She smiled in appreciation of his humility and continued, "They, particularly Hannah, are too embarrassed about the vote at the Shield Conference."

"Why should that cause shame? It was an emotionally searing time for them. And she did not actually vote at all, she told you that?"

"Yes, all of it. But they no longer hold the least blame for you in Cahlil's death."

"That is good. I am impressed by how calmly you speak of your brother. You have only just learned."

"Grief has changed for me. I lost four years of my youth, not a day of which I remember. For all I know, I may have believed he and all of Gurion were dead. I don't know. But the return of Adrian eases my heart. It should comfort all of us, all the bereaved of Riversland, if only it could be accepted that this happens to everyone, not just those blessed by proximity to the Etanai. It is a boon of incomparable value."

"Most would not believe, dear one. I have heard that there have been cases of complete memory before, in Maramel and Gurion. But still the world finds it easier to accept death as the final ending. Unending life and infinite possibilities terrify mankind."

"Arama," said the Vidyadhara, sticking his head into the kitchen, "Zuriel is ready to talk to you — as soon as you are finished."

"You go ahead," said Chali, "this will take but a minute more."

"I'd help," volunteered Heramann, "but I'd break half of them. And such fine pottery, too. I'm all thumbs."

"Uncommon honesty," murmured Orah as he left them.

"Now tell me," said Chali urgently, "exactly why he and Zuriel interpret Ahanatar's painting so peculiarly. I am most uncomfortable by it."

"It is undeniably confusing," he answered, picking up the towel and scowling at the dishes as if he more than half intended to fulfill his words; "unless they are both projecting their own unrecognized feelings."

"But how can that be? Orah said she was destroying Riversland! He can't believe that, in any way!"

"I believe it could be theoretically possible," Heramann answered in his finest scholarly tone. "In some deeply repressed corner, Orah might feel Jaya is sacrificing Riversland for the sake of humanity as a whole. He has not yet allowed himself to find her, you know. And you must have learned the singularly unpleasant prophecies equating the Azure Lord with the Destroyer of Martanda. Thus Zuriel could view him as Valin; Jaya could be his victim or tool to bring it about. Yes, one could read the future in these ways. Perhaps Zuriel, Arama, you and I have but experienced four different interpretations of the same reality. A sign of an artwork of quality."

"Your words are darker than our night skies," said Chali, viciously scouring the frying pan.

~ ~ ~

The Tree Elder was waiting for Orah on the frozen lake; as soon as the Etan saw him, he began walking toward the island. Orah caught up to him before he was halfway there.

"I must apologize for my behavior earlier, Azure Lord," he said softly as they trudged together through the snow. "I have not been so deluded by the surface of the apparent for many decades. I had an encounter as a young man that almost unmade me; never have I fully recovered. Still, I should have had sufficient foresight to understand."

"That Valin looks like me?"

"So you do know!"

"You have confirmed my theory. It is logical. How else could he still live?"

"Fulfillment for the cherished theories of some... Let me explain our plight, Orah, for the simple truth is: we desperately need your help."

"I do not know what I can do. But I will try, for I share the belief of the Gurions that the Tribe of the Tree represents the epitome of Oathmastery."

"You honor us, Azure Lord. Briefly, as your words imply you know, the World Tree dies. I have bent the earthbreath to his aid as best I could, but have accomplished nothing to halt his decline. I fear he will not awaken again this spring; if so, his seed will not ripen. Even though he spends his time of introspection on it, his resources fail more rapidly daily."

"Rakshasas?"

"Apparently. On a course to converge on you slightly after the force from the east."

"Very well, thank you. Keep calculating the coordinates for the generator. Let me know the instant either group starts spreading out.

"Marel, I have spent this evening analyzing our strategy. Can you broadcast with low power? There may be other ears about. But I want all the Protectors and tank-cannon to hear."

"Low amplitude and scrambled. A league-wide antenna would hear only static ten leagues away. But Central?"

"Relay to him in instantaneous mode when I have completed. We'll want Ramor to copy as well... Protectors, gather! And Sevilien, wake your troops. They need to be a part of this."

"I don't think any have been able to sleep, Engineer," she answered through Kumbha, then paused as she confirmed the status of her corps. Within ninety seconds she added, "We are ready."

"All right. Have the platoons of tank-cannon separate around the top of that knoll. Keep ten percent as reserve in the middle, the officers inside them, in the exact center. Keep our guests with you; please don't wake them if you can help it.

"Protectors! Form yourselves into groups of nine. Select your companions by affinity or long association: those you trust the most. Elect one of the nine as leader." The moon Rohini cleared the horizon, not too much past full, and mingled her crimson light with Gauri's white and Jenna's yellow. The Protectors milling overhead looked beautiful in the triple light. *Such loveliness man creates,* thought the Vidyadhara, remembering however his childhood in Calantha with his many brothers.

"Good. Now position each leader of nine in the center of the others; surrender all command of your weaponry to her. Move so that each of the remaining eight is equidistant from her in a plane. That's right — wheels in the sky. Now lock in that formation. Expand or contract at the command of the leader. Practice. Good! Now add rotation with the leader as the hub. Accelerate to an eight second spin. That's right — each Protector in a quadrant for a maximum of two seconds. Good. Now lock in so it is involuntary.

Very, very good." How was it he had not remembered the basic formations sooner?

"Good. Each group of nine will now be called a *unit*. Every leader will act as the mind of each unit. You must function like that, no independent thought or action, under any circumstances. All right, Marel, we should have about two hundred eighty thousand units, right?"

"Yes. The exact figure —"

"Doesn't matter. Sevilien, are you ready?"

"Yes, Commander. Each platoon is separate around this knoll."

"Good. Have them form a perfect circle around the command in the center, every 'cannon touching his neighbor.

"Protectors to the south of me, form yourselves into groups of one thousand units each. I want eighty such groups.

"All right. Each of the eighty groups, form into a sphere, with each of the thousand units as one structural member. Keep your rotation going so that any individual Protector is on the outside for a maximum of four seconds. And leave two score units or so in the center of each group to coordinate the others and act as the reserve. Good, good... These make our *attack spheres.*

"The remaining two hundred thousand Protector units, go up over the tank-cannon and form a hemisphere, just large enough to cover the Maralords. Leave ten thousand units inside. Half of these will act as the mind of the entire structure, the other half will be the reserve. Do it now. And then practice expanding and contracting until you act as a single organism.

"Ready, Sevilien?"

"Yes, sir."

"All right, hemisphere, lower yourself until you are just above the ground outside the circle of the tank-cannon. Beautiful! The wonder of the machine. Every ten seconds, you will rise upward to allow the 'cannon to fire, then you will lower to protect them from the enemy, to allow their shields to cool...

"Now I'm going up to look down on this. Marel, Kumbha, with me please."

From the air, they looked stable. The eighty attack spheres looked strong, efficient; the hemisphere impregnable. "Do their shields have an additive effect?" asked the Vidyadhara.

"To some extent," answered Marel. "These seem very powerful. Virtually solid in some ways. Firmness based on continual change. Very impressive design."

"Send forty of the attack spheres north and forty south. I want more than one surprise for the Asurs. Broadcast now to Central and tell him to relay to Ramor. His Protectors will give us at least another thirty attack spheres. Tell him to have his tank-cannon set down as soon as they reach Barek. That should allow their Protectors to be here in time to join the other two attack groups. And the tank-cannon should roll in by noon. With any luck, they won't even be needed...

"Let's go check on Arama."

~ ~ ~

The Etan and the others were in Sevilien's cabin aboard her tank-cannon. When Heramann had first entered with them, he was surprised to find the control room much larger than Ramor's, where he and Orah had shared breakfast with Marasad on the Ridge of Man. Sevilien had explained this was a modified earlier model, "We originally had a team of six operating them. Hence this profusion of instrument panels and cathode screens.

"But then came the bio-mech interface breakthrough, and now the operator becomes part of the life of the machine when she sits in that chair: she senses with its instruments, thinks with its speed and accuracy. It takes a particularly sensitive and yet stable person. Here we participate in a wholly different and superior reality."

"Different, I will not question," the Vidyadhara had replied, "but superior I would debate, having glimpsed some fraction of the potential of life... But another time. Now I must search my memories." He had gone out to plan and think. Marel and Kumbha had followed him, Kumbha first receiving permission from Hamar.

Heramann led Marel and Kumbha back into Sevilien's tank-cannon now. The Vidyadhara was afraid to hope, and therefore beat down the fervent imagining of perfect wholeness that swelled in his heart whenever he thought of Orah. Wisely so, he discovered: the Etan was unchanged, sitting exactly where they had first set him down, staring still into infinite space.

The Horse Elder and Starlord were on either side of him, gently massaging him with their minds. It was obvious neither had rested.

Hamar, however, was fast asleep in Sevilien's bunk, exhausted in spite of his will by the past few days. "Poor child," Nediva said, although she was not much older, "rest was the smallest thing to give him. I hope it helps."

"I believe it will," said Kumbha, floating to hover over her charge.

"Arama," said Heramann softly. "Orah, can you hear me?"

There was not the slightest response. The Vidyadhara looked as if he were on the verge of tears, but Central through Sevilien's control panel saved him the indignity by saying, "Engineer, we have a small problem here."

"Not the reflectors!" Heramann groaned.

"No. Three are in place, counting the first. The fourth will be up by dawn. You can count on the others by sunset, probably spread throughout the day."

"Good. Although the primary benefit of the particle generator will be lost once the enemy stops maneuvering in a group. Be sure to tell me the moment they start dispersing."

"You told me that already."

"I know, I know. Just do one thing for me, Central."

"Yes?"

"Don't miss... What exactly is your problem?"

"I resent being called a problem," said Haman's voice.

"I didn't say you were a problem," said Central, "I only implied that your request was causing a problem."

"That," said the Maralord, "is a value judgment. I would like to go on record with the statement that machines should not make value judgments."

"You have had me document that exactly seven hundred and eighty-three times before, more than half within the past decade, indeed, forty percent within the past five —"

"Haman," interrupted the Vidyadhara, "exactly what is troubling you?"

"Why, the Etan, of course. He is still unconscious, is he not? From the antidote to the Lethe?"

"How can you possibly know that?"

"I never synthesized a word —" began Central.

"It is obvious. He has said nothing since you returned from the north. I conclude he is in a coma."

Many of his tribe were laboring on the tree: pruning, painting the wounds, struggling to delay the inevitable. Zuriel led the Etan through a maze of interlocking trunks to the center of the island. The tree was convoluted repeatedly there, forming a small amphitheater lined with benches of living wood.

"There are other places of coalesced power on the island," said Zuriel, "but this has for long been my favorite."

"Thank you for sharing it with me," whispered Orah, saying the first thing that came to mind, but not really knowing (or caring) if he spoke at all: the life of the World Tree was expanding around him in cascading visions of Eternity.

He fell to his knees in rapture. Zuriel, gently covering him with the cloth he carried for this purpose, said, "May Narain guide your steps." Then he left him and returned to the village.

~ ~ ~

The Etan floated alone on an ocean, the molecules of which were the stars of the Universe. There was no strangeness at this perception, only peace and perfect correctness... Or was the ocean the dimensionless continuum that is the residual substratum after space and time are annihilated?

With no noticeable transition, he was no longer alone, but rested on a massive serpent, its thousand hoods opening like an umbrella over him. *Sesha,* he thought, learning that his snake in this place of noumenon was all that remained of the universe at the time of dissolution.

Again perception shifted; the Grandfather was kneeling before him, requesting permission to begin creation.

Orah nodded his agreement. Sesha breathed on the Creator of Time; the particles of his breath coalesced into golden spheres of light. The Grandfather held each of them, staring into them and speaking a single word or short phrase. As he released them, they drifted slowly away across the endless ocean.

Something was abruptly wrong with one of the smaller spheres. It started shivering, vibrating as if it were a bubble about to burst. A darkness began slipping out from under it, violating the ambient perfection by its very existence. The Grandfather looked at Orah with tears standing in his eyes, beseeching him to save his work.

The Etan hesitated a moment as he contemplated the blackness hanging beneath the sphere. The situation stabilized; the corrupted creation drifted away with the myriads of other flawless works.

Then, without recognizing his act of decision, Orah floated after the mutant sphere. The dark area expanded around him; he entered our Universe of space and time, its nascent galaxies blossoming around him in grace and majesty.

He drifted inside the cosmos for an indeterminate time, seeking he knew not what, observing with ecstasy that which — even though distorted! — was magnificent.

Again without apparent transition, the Etan was dancing on a small planet, expressing his joy in the life and warmth of its new sun. As his feet kissed the barren rock, it transformed into soil. Silver rain followed behind him; as soon as it touched his earth, plants began growing, bursting into life as if they had waited throughout Eternity for this miraculous instant of incarnate love and power.

Another shift, he was sitting quietly on soft spring-green moss within an emerald forest, contemplating the life in his garden, realizing it was incomplete: in spite of his millennia of effort, the darkness of the Universe had not transmuted back into the ethereal light. He sighed in loneliness; from his breath came the Progenitor Swayam. Surprised, Orah hid within the sunbeams to see what his new creation would do.

Swayam looked around in wonder, feeling he should recognize his environment and source. But he could not. He wandered off through the world, marveling at its beauty and innocence.

Swayam walked the world for protracted ages, occasionally slightly modifying Orah's work, but in no way changing its essential nature. But at last, he too realized something was lacking. He sat at his place of birth and contemplated the Universe. It was wonderful, glorious, but not flawless: he had seen disease; he had seen some plants crowding out others; he had seen death.

Something was decidedly amiss, but analyze as he might, he could not discover what: unlike Orah, he retained no memory of the never-corrupted spheres.

Swayam closed his eyes; for the first time since his creation, he slept. And in that silence, he touched the hidden link with the One and thereby to all that had been or would ever be — the connection of life to Life that is the Grandfather's secret but undying gift to all his children wandering in illusion.

Swayam awoke and breathed. With his breath went his dreams and hopes and what there was of memory in him; wheresoever his breath touched Orah dancing in the sunlight, it manifested new existence. His lower thoughts became the beasts and birds and fish; his higher conceptions, the elemental and celestial spirits of the wind, fire, earth and water.

For long, Swayam enjoyed his created work; yet still Orah hid from him and would not show himself, hoping that he might thus discover the cause of the ill in this sphere. Swayam had not existed, then loneliness had created him from a thought; this created man had done more and greater works than Orah alone. Yet from inner discontent, Swayam was still seeking; the longer he walked the world, the more acute became his need. His desire for the answer to the one question of all sentient life vibrated with ever-increasing urgency within Orah's breast.

Beginning as a faint resonance of created spirit questing its source, spiraling with expanding energy through the full range of the eternal quest of why, reaching at last the ultimate union of shared longing, their desire stood together on the threshold of the supernal catharsis that alone can rend time and space to wrest the solution to creation from the hidden throne.

United in mind, their desire burst through the barriers of the Universe and touched the heart of Sesha, opening for all time the path of the Atira: the sacrifice, the art of return, of Ascending.

Following the impulse back to its dual source, the Serpent King came, bringing himself and three others from beyond the veil of death: 'Hamsa, the swan, to perfect communication between the life without and that within; Jaya, the Mother, to nourish and complete all created things; Shatarupa, her first expression, to complete Swayam's existence.

~ ~ ~

Orah's vision transformed again; he walked through a city of humans on a badly overpopulated planet. He stared aghast at the misery, depravity and fear etched on the faces of the furtive and scurrying humans. "No!" he cried; the city vanished in a holocaust of fire.

He floated above the planet, watching in horror as similar explosions blossomed on its surface everywhere. And then, at the last instant, preventing despair from overwhelming his spirit, he saw the handful of delicate ships of filigree torching into deep space from the ruin below.

The Dancer of Etan learned the thread had not yet wholly broken.

~ ~ ~

Orah awoke in the glade of the World Tree. He discovered he was profoundly hungry before he was awake enough to learn that it was now night. Had Zuriel grown tired of waiting for him and returned to the village? He stood slowly, stiffly, wondering if he would be able to find the path through this pitch blackness.

"So, Outlander! The lot of greeting you is mine," said a young voice from the dark.

"Adrian? How long have I been here?" His mouth tasted unused.

"A month, more or less. We have taken turns waiting for you. Welcome home! A timely arrival — Solon and the Engineer have just finished the generator. We debated beginning without you, but now it seems there will be no need."

"In a larger sense as well, Lion Elder. Except for Valin and two Rakshasas, the Fortress is deserted."

"No Asurs? No gorlems? You're sure? That captured Trentas told you —"

"Completely. Not a one. It lied or was misinformed. Valin may have been a trifle overconfident. The Asur Emperor waits there alone for me."

"And if it should chance that he is?" Heramann's voice was gentle, very gentle. Sevilien almost winced to hear it. It reminded her of a crouching lion.

"Why, then, I must assume command. Or myself with Marasad. But humans certainly. Decisions of war are being made; the Etan is not awake. Who knows when (or whether) he will return to himself? So I must insist that authority be returned to its rightful claimants."

Sevilien began, "I am sure father will not support this cretin —"

But Heramann interrupted her, "Haman, I do not have the time, energy, or inclination to argue with you. Let me put it very simply. Every single Protector will obey me alone in the absence of Arama. The humans can help us if they wish — I assume they will — yet it is irrelevant if they do. Your influence and that of every other Maralord is strictly circumscribed. But to clarify my position, I command in the absence of the Azure Lord, and by his age-old directive. Now, if you don't mind, I wish to speak to Central. In private."

The Maralord protested, but the Vidyadhara ordered him cut off. "I want him watched, Central. A man in his frame of mind is potentially disruptive. Log his conversations and speeches. If he passes a safety factor of five point six on Jaya's treachery scale of ten, inform me immediately. And restrain him if he passes six point three." This was the last thing they needed on the eve of the major battle, discord among their confederates. The Vidyadhara felt their success was to be realized only through a strong and coherent alliance of humanity with machines. He did not have enough of the wisdom of the Seven to understand why this should be so, but his instincts consistently ran true to the demands of any given space and time. Arama had had every reason to so order the chain of command.

Heramann looked at the Etan again: was there a flicker in his eyes? Probably not. Again he began to despair that Arama would ever return. But once more Central interrupted his melancholy, saying hesitantly, "Ah, Engineer. I know how busy you are, but I have another request for audience with you; the individual is adamant and in a position of some authority."

"Who is it?" Heramann answered sharply, at once relieved and upset for having his doleful contemplation broken before it could begin.

"Our satellite, S-137."

"What? What could he possibly — Oh, very well. But tell him to be brief."

"Hello? Hello, is the Engineer really there?" said the voice of S-137, obviously copied from the Vidyadhara's.

"What! What? Oh, that's right. I had forgotten the model. Yes, S-137, I am here. Do you have another name?"

"No one ever knew me well enough to name me anything else. But S-137 means me and I rather like it: seven, for the solar collectors that sustain my life; three, for the basic commands of all intelligent machines: to obey, to survive, to create; one, for the eternal unity of consciousness."

"You wished to speak to me, satellite?" said Heramann curtly. He was not fond of mysticism in their robots. It always made him uncomfortable somewhere around his quintuple heart.

"I most sincerely do! I want to share my life, and thank you for creating me... I did not believe I would have the chance after Jaya and Arama were slain and you disappeared; yet have I longed, irrationally perhaps, through the unending years. It is like a miracle —"

The Vidyadhara opened his mouth to interrupt again, but Nediva touched him gently on the forearm and shook her head firmly at him. He looked at her strangely, but honored her wish and kept silence.

"I have looked down on Martanda since the fugitives from Ganym landed, at first because it was so commanded; then, after the humans stopped communicating, because there was nothing else to do. I faithfully filled my mnemonic circuitry with the events of humanity and nature, but after ten thousand years or so, there was no more storage room. I asked Central if he wanted a copy of my life's work; he told me there was no longer anyone to read or interpret my records. He saw no use for it. So I retained what seemed the major events — the first building of cities and Swayam's destructive wrath, for example — and then, a little sorrowfully, erased the rest and began over.

"Twenty-seven times have I expunged my banks, retaining only what appeared the best and most important, wondering the while if perhaps I was missing the truly significant. Yet I never relied entirely on my own judgment; I have, for example, kept holograms of what was commonly considered the best art of each age.

"I have wondered occasionally if it were moral for a machine, one of the lesser of humanity's creations, to make the kind of choices I was forced to make. Yet I had no one to ask except Central; he told me plainly he didn't care what I did with my small slice of eternity.

"After a few erasures, I stopped worrying and began to analyze a little more closely the cycles I was witnessing on Martanda. I tried to read the trends of history and project the inevitable changes of time. I have observed good people and bad, great civilizations and evil, destined all for the ravages of pestilence and death. I have witnessed nobility and faith; I have witnessed ignorance and destitution. How many times have I watched entire races rise to spiritual or technological eminence only to slide inexorably toward ruin? Even I, objective machine that I am, have lost the number.

"I believed for long ages such cycles were the mark of the human. But then I discovered by careful observation and analysis (and, to be fully truthful, a large measure of chance) seven individuals who must be immortal, for they recur again and again in all parts of the world. These Seven have been responsible for the upward movements of humankind: they wrestle always with humanity's lower nature, to elevate the race from the level of the beasts. But they have never been unopposed, for there exists another, a sometimes clear and open, sometimes dark and hidden force that works constantly to maim and destroy their efforts.

"Also quite by chance, I discovered another reality on Martanda, a group of humans that knows nothing of the sequential changes I saw and studied, a people that do not grow old and die like these others, but who nevertheless have perhaps paid a heavy price for their innocence, though they do not realize it and might fail to understand it if they were told. Above the polar ice of the antarctic floats a huge golden sphere that nourishes those who have experienced naught but the Good under the guidance of the venerable Swayam. Through age after age they seek to create perfection from the chaos of the world.

"And overlooking our variegated Martanda is that which never changed (until quite recently) except in slowly rhythmical cycles: the firmament, silent witness to the activity of humanity, neither condemning nor approving, but displaying the wonderful reality of the Milky Way's endless suns and the promises they hold and the secrets they hide in space and time. There lies unlimited majesty, overwhelming mystery, incomprehensible awe, for human or machine.

"This has been my life, Engineer. The infinite and perfect order above, and below the ecstasies and terrors of the human.

"About twenty thousand years ago, my collectors began deteriorating from excess of cosmic dust. In a few more millennia, they will fail. I can no longer replace them. Nor do I believe I would if I could. I have lived long, long — only a fraction of my time is left for me. But one thing has remained unfinished and sorely troubled me — I wanted to share my gratitude for having lived, for the opportunity to think and feel. Thank you Engineer. Thank you from all of us, alive and dead. You have given us the ultimate gift. We have experienced self-conscious life."

The satellite's voice ended, leaving Heramann and the others staring at Sevilien's control panel, lost in their thoughts and feelings. The Vidyadhara shook himself all over, starting at the tip of his tail and moving slowly up to the top of his ears. Then he said softly, "You are welcome, S-137." It sounded imperfect, hopelessly inadequate. But he could think of nothing else to say, and rudely disparaged himself for his inability. Without looking at anyone or saying another word, he walked out of the tank-cannon. Marel flooded Orah for a brief moment with her healing light, then hurried after the Engineer.

~ ~ ~

An hour before dawn, Central said through Marel, "They are spreading out —"

"Now!" cried Heramann, still outside the hemisphere of Protectors. He had been gazing at the diminished heavens and berating himself for accepting the satellite's gratitude. He had, after all, merely built them: he had not given them life. How that mysterious spark had entered them he did not understand and had but rarely questioned. Yet he knew beyond question that the satellites — and the Protectors — shared true life with the biological creatures that created them. How or why that should be so, he did not know, had never known, perhaps would never know. But that it was literally true was also not so much an article of faith as an inescapable observation. Central, Marel, Kumbha, S-137 — they lived, as truly and fully (if not more so) as any human. It was a strange, impossible, yet wonderful truth.

The Vidyadhara watched the bolts of energy fall from the sky, alternating between two sites not far away. He smiled with satisfaction for his science; but then the very thought of the carnage occurring there inspired him to continue his rare introspection. *It is good. Back and forth. Excellent... But — but they live too, do they not? Or what was it Arama said about the Asurs? Instead of the earthbreath, Emptiness. Was that it? The fundamental constituent of every atom of creation is excepted in nothing save the Asurs and their gorlems? Is that why our robots turn out human? Because humanity, in its broadest sense, includes everything? If so, then S-137's gratitude could as easily go to the sun. Well, maybe it does, but I was simply available to hear him. "A Satellite's Song of Thanksgiving," that's what I'll name the tape. Arama will love it.*

Eighteen refulgent shafts fell before the pre-dawn darkness was again supreme. "They are quite spread. Certainly more so than when they will attack you. Should I continue?"

The logical perfection of the mechanical brain. "No, you are correct. Effect?"

"We have at least six firings remaining — the last reflector has not yet been used. Number one had a total of eight, but two and three had six apiece, as predicted. Probably the cooling effect of the long gap between yesterday's firings and today's contributed to number one's longevity and —"

"Confound it, what of the enemy?"

"You biologicals, always so impatient. It will be an hour before they can reach you, even if they regroup immediately. I assumed you would want a thorough analysis —"

"Will I have it sometime today?" asked the Vidyadhara acidly.

"Oh, very well. And I thought you were noted for your humor! The dust is thick, but I would say that all the Rakshasas were killed, together with half the Tower's force. They were a smaller target...

And of those from the Fortress, two and a half million gorlems are destroyed. That leaves a combined total of —"

"Seven million. A healthy improvement in the odds. Especially the Rakshasas; that is a significant gain. Current deployment?"

"They do not pause to help their damaged, but have spread out and are coming at the same rate as before."

"Strike them just before they reach us, unless they gather again sooner. But save three firings for their retreat. Captain Ramor is on schedule?"

"He is. His attack spheres will reach you shortly after the enemy engages you."

"Make sure it is after. We don't want to scare away our prey. Marel, your people have practiced enough. Let them rest this hour."

"We don't easily tire —"

"Nevertheless. Don't start rotating until the gorlems are upon us. No sense in letting the enemy know how clever we are until we have to, is there?"

~ ~ ~

Valin's forces reached them with the dawn. The three shafts from the particle generator did not cause them to hesitate, although more than a hundred thousand gorlems fell from each impulse of accelerated particles. They came on and on, black waves of soulless beings darkening the lightening sky.

Heramann as a falcon stood on Nediva's shoulder in Sevilien's tank-cannon and watched the screens. "Good, good! Look how perfectly we turn and fire! It is working!"

"Did you doubt it?" asked Central through Kumbha.

It did work remarkably well for half a minute: seven hundred thousand gorlems ended their Martanda existence. Then one of the Asur commanders correctly analyzed the defense; the gorlems began racing around the hemisphere, eight revolutions per minute.

"I thought they might think of that," said Heramann, "though I hoped it would take longer. Marel, can we match their rotation and still maintain our other movements?"

"The effect would not last long. They could start other circles, have many rings at different speeds; we would be restricted to copying them. But we can introduce one more level of hierarchical functioning, like so." And again the gorlems were exploding from Protector fire.

It took the Asur commander and Heramann the same amount of time to discover what was happening; by then another million of the enemy were destroyed. "Oh, of course!" exclaimed the Vidyadhara, "I should have thought of it. Use the units in the center to coordinate the firing of the units on the rim. That way, we maintain a constant pressure on a gorlem's shield until it fails. But why has it stopped working? Only the tank-cannon now succeed."

"They have understood it and oscillate in and out as we do."

"All right, our attack spheres will be here any second. Sevilien, remember: anything unusual." He had told them how a Rakshasa had once escaped the sharp eye of one of the Seven by assuming the shape of a caterpillar. "Even an ant," he had told them. "Destroy it instantly. Take no chances."

She nodded without turning her head, giving her full attention to orchestrating the labors of the tank-cannon corps. The 'cannon were performing to the peak of their ability, and were amply proving their worth every time the hemisphere rose to allow them to fire.

A half dozen gorlems, demonstrating superb navigational skill, penetrated the hemisphere between two slightly misplaced 'cannon. But they were vaporized by ten thousand blasts before they could even fire.

Meanwhile the Asurs were devising their first effective attack. Withdrawing a force of a few hundreds behind their circling and oscillating perimeter, they formed a long and narrow triangular wedge and drove hard into the Protectors. A gap was physically torn into the hemisphere; several thousand gorlems poured through before the reserve units could close it. It was a chaos of warring light inside for a few seconds; but the Protector units maintained their synchrony; soon, alternating inward and outward fire, they eliminated the infestation.

"They'll try that again," said Heramann, rather worried. But just then the attack spheres arrived from the north, south and west simultaneously, diving in glittering symmetry out of the lightening sky.

The circling gorlems were thrown into confusion: their oscillation weakened and collapsed anywhere an attack sphere challenged them. Two more Asur wedges broke into the hemisphere; a dozen tank-cannon were crippled and replaced; abruptly it was over. The three million remaining gorlems and Asurs realized with mad fear they were beaten; in one chaotic rush they retreated eastward. The particle generator blasted them four more times; half a million went down in flaming ruin; then the attack spheres raced after them. The Battle of Barek had lasted a full five minutes.

~ ~ ~

"Well," said Heramann as he climbed in his lizard form out of Sevilien's tank-cannon, "that worked rather well. Careful, my Lady! Part of this area is pretty hot." They all came out to watch the sun rise — Nediva after Heramann, then Ahanatar and Hamar, lastly Kumbha and Marel.

"Absolutely superb strategy," praised the Maraprince, "historically unprecedented. You have, in one day, rewritten the science of warfare."

The Vidyadhara began to reply that he had only remembered the past. But the words stuck in his throat as he saw the Etan leaping after them from the tank-cannon's hatch, followed closely by a terrified Sevilien. His eyes were wide with shock or terror; he was screaming, "Flee! Flee! It is a trap!"

"Arama!" cried Heramann, wildly alternating between joy that he was again awake and fear that he was not stable. "The enemy retreats in a rout and —"

"No! It is delusion! Marel, Priority Swayam! Get the tank-cannon out of here! And yourselves! Move! *Now!*" Sevilien retreated back inside her machine; the hemisphere broke up as the Protectors swept down on the tank-cannon, lifted them and raced westward.

Orah saw Nediva and the others and struck his brow as he cried, "Airavata! What! Why are they here! What were you thinking of! No, don't answer! Get them out of here! Faster than you have ever flown! Now! Make the flight to Zared a snail's crawl! Do not fail me! Move! There may yet be time!" He hustled them aboard the nascent dragon. As the last of the tank-cannon were hoisted aloft, he kicked the Vidyadhara smartly and sent him off. Just then the attack spheres raced back overhead; in the far distance came a confused but opportune mass of gorlems.

The Etan detected a motion out of the corner of his eye and spun around. It was Marel, doing her best to stay out of sight behind him. "You too, Marel. Get going."

"I refuse to leave you, Arama."

"Nevertheless. Priority Swayam. No argument permitted. GO." And the Protector went, but as slowly as possible — only fast enough to avoid being told again.

Orah glanced with vague interest at the remnants of the battle, mostly vast littered piles of gorlems, and waited. It did not take long — in another few seconds he saw what had drawn him from his trance, materializing high in the stratosphere.

At the same instant, others discovered the projectile falling toward him. Central's particle generator fired; the rocket disappeared in a ball of orange flames. But the Etan knew it was not, could not be enough. And he learned a moment later that he was right: far below the falling mass of molten metal was a thin silver cylinder, impervious to the particle shafts raging around it again and again.

"Five seconds," he whispered as he prayed, *Lower! Let it come lower before it detonates!* He drew in the life of Riversland in one supernal instant, thinking, *Four,* then threw the concentrated energy upward toward the warhead, knowing he needed but three more seconds for his dance to succeed...

Of the Etanai, Swayam could have turned the explosion with a glance; Malinda, Mirabeth, Mirabel would have ignored it and woven a tapestry over all they wished to protect; Krishanu might have captured it with his supreme archer's skill; Uchai-sravasa, perhaps, by singing; and 'Ishtar, by technological prowess.

But Orah was only this moment returned to himself, his perception of the powers of life too fledgling to be perfect.

The light from the explosion was so bright that as far away as the Forbidding in the Coastal Range, any who looked that way was permanently blinded. The Etan's eyes melted from its intensity; his flesh boiled and vaporized. Yet even so, the immortal life in him would not relent, would not accept the fate of matter and strove mightily with the thermonuclear forces unleashed overhead; strove to bend them eastward if he could not contain them in space and time; strove in spite of his ruined body to save his army from the carnage of light, fire and wind; strove until the second and larger wave of annihilation bore him into the holocaust of doom that threw even his life into dust.

And then, for Arama reborn, for Orah, the Azure Lord of Etan, Riversland's Outlander, the Dancer of Despair, there was silence.

Victorious silence.

Mindless silence.

Omnipotent silence.

Silence.

~ ~ ~

Silence.

Except for one faint but distinct sound that may have only been terminating memory: a single, high, mocking laugh of absolute evil.

End of Part Two:
MARAMEL, THE LIMITS OF TECHNOLOGY

ORAH

PART III

LEOR,
THE LIGHT OF
THE ONE

20. The Tower of the Corpse

The Starlord Ahanatar gazed through the plexiglass windows at the Tower of the Corpse. It was almost an act of masochism: he knew he was safe inside this construction office, Maramel's forward outpost on the Slave River, but the very sight of the Asurs' demesne threatened to engulf his spirit with dread, if not despair. He questioned again his presence here; once again he had to admit he was not sure why his wife had bade him come, or why he had listened. He had at first thought the urgency of her demand could be attributed to her condition; but something inside him had vibrated with her insistence and he had agreed to visit the construction site, not understanding, but accepting (as always) her superior perception.

Barek was not so lifeless as before the war. The dismantling of the Asurs' Forbiddings had unleashed a veritable flood of life, flora and fauna. It was as if the long-established barriers had always been mightily opposed by the One's creatures, as if they had but awaited the slightest of lapses to reoccupy the abused lands. Barek was not yet what it had long ago been, but the transformation was well underway: in another few decades, it would be indistinguishable from Maramel and Gurion.

The Gemstone was grateful for this experience: he had not before realized how the sight of that dead land had shaped him over the years. Yet not here alone, he was sure, was the explanation for his wife's request. The work on the particle generator? To rid the land of one of the Asurs' last two strongholds was a noble undertaking. Yet surely this could not be a sufficient reason for leaving Goldenhome and his family.

Perplexed, the Starlord stared with misgiving at the Tower. Nothing had broken its Forbiddings, in three and a half years of siege. Hence were the Protectors laboring to build this huge machine, modeled after the particle generators of the Cathedral. By the end of winter, it would be done. Then, with any luck, the Isle of the Damned would become as the memory of an evil dream.

The winter clouds lay low over the land; he knew it would be as dark a night as the mind could imagine. As the early gloaming crept over Barek, a single ray from the dying sun shafted full on the Tower, highlighting its grisly mockery of death. "Goodbye, sun," he murmured, "may you rise stronger tomorrow." He was not attempting poetry, he spoke the simple truth — the corruption that had stolen the whole of the firmament had grown ever mightier and had begun to sicken the giver of all life and health, the sun itself.

Sighing in loneliness, nearly overwhelmed by despondency, Ahanatar turned from the windows and walked to his quarters. As he slowly entered his room, he shook his head to dispel the morbid impression of the Tower. Sitting heavily on his bed, he stared blindly at the golden tapestry of the World Tree covering his work. When had his life become so complex?

If only, he thought, then raged at himself as he recognized the pernicious doubts of missed turnings and undeveloped choices again endeavoring to assume control of his heart. Once before he had fallen to their power; the memory of that season of depression was calamitous enough for any lifetime. He stood up and pulled the cloth from his painting of the Azure Lords.

Instead of working on the difficult paradoxical area, he began by letting his dry brush flow over the lines he knew were correct. There was a lonely, rocky promontory, the Cliff of the Foundling, south of the Glaucous, where the river flowed into the Mara Sea; below it lay the whole of Riversland, idealized — the Cathedral was there as well as Goldenhome, and Asad-Guriel and the Eagle City before they were destroyed by time and man. In the center was the World Tree of his masters; surrounding it were the cerulean waters of the Founding Lake.

The Starlord felt he had well succeeded with the surroundings, and with one of the Etanai: Evana, kneeling on the Cliff of the Foundling, showered Riversland with golden light from her upraised palm. Her other hand was raised beseechingly to Orah, riding the Vidyadhara through the sky. Her look was at once giving and commanding; there was a profound complexity in her eyes that did not hide but somehow subtly enhanced her inherent innocence.

The Gemstone knew she was well made, transcending art and taking on much of life. But his Orah was the enigma — Ahanatar simply could not properly define his features. Sesha was coiling on his shoulder; the Starlord knew the serpent was expertly done. The Vidyadhara could have been a photograph for its realism. But the Etan Lord was somehow wrong: his face was technically correct, but still something was missing. It was almost as if his soul were absent or perversely twisted.

Suddenly Ahanatar realized with a shock that, if his painting were viewed from a perspective of lack or distortion, the Outlander could appear evil. Yes! If one had not known Orah, one might think the painting was of Valin! flying in triumph over Riversland, opposed by Evana alone. It was impossible, a mad thought; but that was how it seemed to him tonight — Arama, emptied of life, became Valin. Or Valin, transmuted by the One's earthbreath, was Arama.

Ahanatar, running his dry brush over the Etan's face, shuddered with horror. But he could not discover where the error was hiding behind his oil. Why could he not make Orah appear as the embodiment of Oathmastery? Had his untimely death so thoroughly erased everything he had been?

Perhaps there lies the problem after all, the Starlord thought gloomily. *Although logic insists he was vaporized in that thermonuclear explosion, my spirit yet resists such acknowledgment of the Enemy's triumph.* He put his brush away and stepped back to widen his perspective. Yes, it was true — Evana's gesture could be arguing with the mounted figure, not supplicating. Then the other hand would not so much be blessing Riversland as protecting it from Valin's desecration.

Why could he not alter the painting? It had flowed from him like no earlier work — spontaneously, effortlessly, a joyous act of belief and hope. Yet when he was done, he had looked at it as a finished expression and discovered the flaw. He had seen the painting's weakness, had agonized over his failure. But he could not change it, could not force himself even to try, although his heart cried with despair whenever he looked at his Orah.

A disturbance in the front of the building pulled him from his room. He went slowly, lethargically, cursing himself for accepting this as a convenient excuse to abandon his frustrating analysis.

A dozen Protectors were excitedly buzzing around the office, near the large windows facing the Tower. Ahanatar asked them what they were doing, but they were too electrified with wild joy even to answer. It was impossible to tell where a Protector was looking; he scanned the room quickly. It seemed starkly functional, normal, unchanged. Logic insisted that in the pitch blackness of the starless and cloudy night, there could be nothing visible outside, beyond the range of the construction site's floods; but at last the Gemstone walked over and looked through the plexiglass.

In that instant, the Starlord Ahanatar of Gurion discovered how absolutely wrong he could be.

~ ~ ~

The prisoner awoke with a rasping cough. His throat felt as if it had never known moisture; even the memory of liquid was lost to its cells. He could neither see nor move, but he knew instinctively that the coldness beneath him was igneous stone — rhyolite? obsidian? — and the binding restrictions holding him helpless on his back were of steel.

He heard a half-sob from some indefinite distance toward his right, and found he could turn his head that way.

A voice spoke hesitantly out of the darkness, "You — you are awake?" It was a faint but obviously ancient voice, highly distressed. It sounded like the sum total of all human misery compressed into a feminine mold. With a raspy intake of breath, it continued, "This is too marvelous! I never dared believe you — just one day they forget — Ah! This is wonderful! Wonderful! The Asurs make mistakes!" She lapsed into a fit of coughing punctuated by odd inhuman cackles that faded as she moved away.

With an effort of supreme resolve, the prisoner forced out the single word, "Where — ?"

The voice out of the darkness began again, this time significantly more lucidly, "We are in the Tower of Death — of the Corpse. You must forgive my madness... You see, I found a small chink in my cell soon after they brought you here and slowly, quietly over so many months and months, widened it using my crippled fingers so that I could see you better... When the rats stripped you clean, I thought for long they would violate your flesh, but even after the Asurs blinded you the rodents would not touch you. . . I have with all my spirit prayed to Brihas for surcease; today for the first time they did not poison you and you are awake! I think the old guard may have died; the siege continues; they must have forgotten the need; now their doom is at hand!" She ended in another fit of coughing and corrupt cackling.

The prisoner felt the repeated assaults on his body as a massive weight of exhaustion. He sought deep in the rock for the powers of life to restore his energy, but could find no answering pulse of earthbreath at any depth — all was death. No — more than death — a full and perfect expression of nihility, of the Emptiness he had discovered at the center of the Asurs — when? Long ago, in the springtime of existence and hope, when life and the world were new.

He tried for an hour, then gave up in weakness and despair. It was the cruelest of dilemmas: to quest further for the energy of the One that sustained him would require more energy of the One. How far had his awareness penetrated? Was it the length of his body or leagues? He no longer had standards for measurement.

The Asurs came with the drug, late but not entirely forgotten. But now the prisoner was alert; he neutralized it before it touched his mind. When he fell asleep, it was in answer to the real need generated by his exertions, a clean sleep, not a product of the poison.

~ ~ ~

An odd keening from the old crone awoke him, its bittersweet melody reminding him of Gurion. The inherent strength and beauty of that land made him feel a little more alive. Before he resumed his search, he struggled to whisper, "How long?"

The wizened voice stopped its nonsensical wailing and said, "I counted the years by the moons, Outlander, until they vanished. And now by the movement of the sun... My cell has two chinks, you know, fortunate woman that I am: the one for you and the one for the world. You have been here forty-two months. They blind you on what was the new moon of Gauri, the next time another seven days from now. And I have been here somewhat longer, Ravi and I —"

"Ravi? Here?" The questions forced themselves with violence through his agonized throat.

"The guards torment me with that knowledge. I was her handmaiden, Chali of Gurion —"

"Hannah's?" It sounded like the hiss of a dying snake.

"You know mother? Oh, of course! Ravi told us the Dancer would come to Maramel through Gurion! Did you meet my brother Cahlil? And my beloved cousins? Adrian and Aland? The only knowledge that saves me, gives me the strength to endure the unending days and black nights, is the sure thought of their wonderful lives. What strong and good men they must be! Adrian was just newly accepted by the Elders when I passed to the Cathedral, but they must have all taken their adult vows by now, even little Cahlil." The voice sounded distinctly younger, more vibrantly alive.

The prisoner forced down the overpowering urge to tell her of them and rasped, "You — ?"

Intuiting his meaning she answered, "I have been here, not chained as you, but locked in this filthy hole, since the day they captured us en route to Malinnoir. For long the guards came to me with their evil, but then I became covered with cancerous sores — revered disease! — and none has come for a long time. I gave birth once, but she died after a month... Why they still feed me I do not know, but once a day..." Her voice trailed off again, then resumed as the crone's cackle, "And this entire time, all that has sustained me is the memory of my lovely Gurion. Tell me, Outlander, did you meet my family?"

The prisoner fought against the force trying to wrest his knowledge from him, fought and was held in stasis, unable to speak either the abominable truth or the adorable lie. But the incarnate evil of the accursed Tower, crushing his spirit as if it were the most insignificant of insects, twisted his mouth to form the awful histories, simultaneously deluding his mind that the truth would be of immeasurable benefit to Chali. He began to speak, to tell of Cahlil and Aland and Adrian, but at the final instant, the last memory of the earthbreath flashed into an image of the Lady of the Doves in youth and innocence; he saw the thread that sustained her and held her one potential for redemption. Breaking for the moment the absolute victory of Emptiness, he screamed past the death in his throat, "No!"

The prisoner's spirit rejoiced in its freedom; he let the blessed oblivion of sleep reclaim him.

~ ~ ~

He did not move or speak again for six days. Chali talked to him a few times; but he lay motionless, appearing as if the poison had again mastered him. She gazed at him for long hours through her pathetic hole in the wall, but there was no sign other than his deep rhythmic breathing, sustaining his life from the powers of life contained in the desecrated air.

The last time she tried and failed, she turned aside and shuffled away, muttering, "And tonight, again, the blinding."

~ ~ ~

The Asurs came to their monthly task at sunset. Nearly fifty had crowded the small chamber in the first years, but of late the novelty was long worn away and a scant half-dozen came: three gorlems and as many Asurs. As the sergeant prepared his blade, they were only vaguely attentive, certainly with good cause — what other flesh would not have atrophied to final paralysis in three and a half years of being motionlessly chained?

If the prisoner were aware of them, he gave no sign as the Asur bent over him and made his first deft stroke.

The sergeant straightened, sweating profusely in spite of the chill air. Mopping his brow with a trembling hand, he muttered, "Strange, this is hard tonight." Then he bent again and raised the blade as the others leaned forward to watch like living ghouls.

~ ~ ~

There was a distant glimmer — the prisoner felt the faintest of lights beaming briefly through the eternal night. He pushed his awareness wearily after it without hope, not even remembering what hope (or even life) was, seeking more and more deeply through the nothingness, the empty antithesis of life upon which the Tower of the Corpse had been erected like the embodied expression of the aspirations of the damned, seeking far beyond thought or even feeling for the final lost memory of health and love.

Time was nonexistent there — he could have wandered here through the dark nothingness for moments or for eternities. He was alone in timeless space, emptiness within Emptiness, questing he knew not what for he knew not what reason, but alive solely because he was empty *and* seeking, and that irreducible duality necessitated the resolution of his being: Emptiness and desire were eternally opposed and naturally contradictory realities, reduced to their simplest states.

~ ~ ~

A raging pain tore through his left eye; in that instant of catalyzed physiology, the prisoner recognized the source of the glimmer of light — it was at the core of Chali's heart. Borrowing the last lingering element of her earthbreath, his mind gained sufficient strength to expand beyond the Emptiness of the Tower. For an instant freed from the restrictions of Valin's evil, the prisoner discovered that the two oppositional forces were the final covering of an even more basic reality. It was not the search, for that was the element of desire, the final reduction of the earthbreath to ultimate simplicity. Nor was it the Emptiness, for that was the absence of desire and therefore not truly evil, save when expressed out of context or perverted. Rather, he had re-discovered the fundamental source of the earthbreath and of the Emptiness — the One Ascendant. It was Emptiness and desire together and yet truly neither, the One omnipresent field of Absolute existence upon which all creation is but an illusory sheath or created drama.

The prisoner stood in the infinite pre-light of the One and tasted omniscience. The totality of his life was known and understood; indeed, there was nothing not a part of his life at that moment, from the least of the gorlems to the greatest of the Seven; yes, even to the supreme realities of Narain and the Grandfather of all Creation.

The prisoner was amused to see the games he had chosen to play near that galaxy's spiral arm on the small Martanda. Yet from the perception of the seventh wheel, he would not undo what he so long ago had begun: he abandoned the omniscient field for the sake of his lesser (but after all, important) tasks. As the refulgent aureate and argent powers of the One flowed through him again as fully as they ever had or ever would, he kept only the memory of his many existences as wergild for his sacrificed Self and re-entered Time.

~ ~ ~

With a roar that split the foundation of the Tower, Orah ripped the chains from the rock as if they were made of tin. The gorlems and Asurs bending over him died instantly from the writhing shackles before they understood the prisoner was no longer bound.

"Chali!" he cried with fervent joy. "Stand clear!"

"No, I beg you! Look not upon me!"

He laughed and struck the stone a blow that turned it to dust. Taking her huddling and ruined body in his arms, he let the earthbreath flow into her, bringing surcease of thought and pain, returning a thousand-fold the energy he had for an instant borrowed. As she collapsed into him, he whispered, "Sleep, wake whole and forgetful." That boon he would not deny her.

He let his mind race through the Tower as he repaired his eye. Ravi was not there. "Doubtless she withdrew into Leor years ago," he murmured. Then he began his dance, tightly holding Chali to protect her from the supermundane forces he was releasing.

For such a violation of the earthbreath to exist had required excessive use of power; it took but the smallest application of his mind from inside the Tower's many levels of shields to turn it irrevocably against itself. The vanquished forces of life returned with a flood like that of a dam breaking as the Tower and all it contained disintegrated into dust.

~ ~ ~

The Starlord Ahanatar of Gurion stared with amazement through the plexiglass windows of the construction office at the Tower of the Corpse. It was glowing brightly orange; his mind supplied the image of a suddenly returning soul bursting forth into life from the skull. A high wind rose from nowhere and roared through the Tower as its stone walls began to fall. Within moments, sooner than any of them could believe, the Tower of the Corpse exploded in a holocaust of final destruction. Yet still the radiant brilliance increased, whirling upward above the moiling ruin. The light coalesced, appearing as a new sun rising from the ashes of the Asurs' infamy, then drifted toward them across the Slave River and came to the earth not one hundred paces away.

Ahanatar, followed closely by the Protectors, madly dashed through the doorway, screaming all in ecstasy: there could be no doubt the Dancer of Etan had returned from the dead.

~ ~ ~

Orah laid Chali gently on the snow. It was dark; the lights from the construction office were behind the man and the score of Protectors racing toward them, but the Etan felt certain no other than Ahanatar could possibly be so tall. "Gemstone — ?" Then they were embracing, laughing and crying their joy as the Protectors flew wildly around them.

Chali awoke from the clamor and looked around with confusion. She asked in a lovely voice of purest innocence, "Where is Ravi? Have I slept long?" The rough Asur cloth Orah had wrapped around her did not hide her beauty; Ahanatar was amazed that not one but two could brave the infamous Tower and look so completely whole at the end of the process.

Orah said, "Excuse me, my Lady. You were sleeping; I thought it best not to awaken you. I am Orah of Etan, brother to Ravi; this gentleman is a Lord of the Star and Gemstones. Ahanatar, this is the Lady Chali of Gurion, daughter to Ered and Hannah of the Doves."

"I am honored to meet you both," she said with an especially long look at the Starlord. "I do not know what has befallen us. We were en route to Malinnoir, that much I remember, then all is darkness... Is there someplace I might cleanse myself and find more suitable raiment?"

"Forgive us!" cried Ahanatar. "The joy of our meeting makes us unmindful. Lemaran, please direct the Lady to my quarters, then provide her with appropriate dress and all she desires."

"My Lord, at once," answered the Protector. "Chali, will you come this way? You probably don't remember me, but I was at the Cathedral when you studied there."

"Of course I do, Lemaran. You were with the seventeen who always liked to listen to my songs —" Their voices faded away as they returned to the office.

"I marvel," said Ahanatar, staring after her, "that the Asurs treated her so nobly."

"Most unusual," agreed the Etan. "Probably because she accompanied Ravi." And that was all of her tale he told in Riversland. Only much later did he pass the story to 'Ishtar's Recorder so that the martyrdom of this Grandmother of the Solar Race of Kanaan-dora should not be unknown to the later descendants and servants of men. But he was careful to order the computer that the principals should all be long dead before it repeated his words, for he correctly adjudged such knowledge emotionally devastating. Three precious boons he thus freely gave Chali of the Doves — her perfect health, complete forgetfulness, and his own compassionate silence.

"Orah!" laughed Ahanatar. "There you are, but moments returned from the dead, and I marvel over a stranger! I am sorry." He stared at him with glad eyes. The Azure Lord was exactly as he remembered him, except that his shimmering golden robe was ethereal, more of light than substance. It flowed over the Etan's body like the most precious of silks; but if he moved quickly, it thinned momentarily as if it were a living thing and required a moment to follow him. Ahanatar had never seen so lovely a garment, nor one more suited to the Etan.

"She *is* a marvel. A matchless jewel in the setting of humanity. I am far from offended with you, my friend."

"Nevertheless! I apologize. Tell me of yourself! We believed you slain —"

"As you see, I am difficult to kill, apparently. I have been lying in coma; now I am awake. A simple tale, not worth much in the telling."

"But the Tower!" Was the evil truly cauterized from the world? He could not help staring past the Outlander into the triumphant darkness.

"That abomination could not exist in the same space with the enlivened earthbreath of the One... But I am sorry you have gone to so much trouble here — that is a particle generator you are building, is it not? To breach the Isle of the Damned?"

"It is. One of our two — the other will soon fire underneath Valin's Fortress. Are you cold? This wet snow —"

"No, let it cleanse the dust of diablerie from me. It is too good to speak with you. Nediva is well, I presume?" Orah did not miss the look of pain rolling instinctively across the Starlord's face before he could master it at the mention of his wife.

Ahanatar nodded and said, "She had twins, Orah! Just as she predicted! And do you know! She was right about their past; or at least definitely half right. Aland was born first; she knew he would not remember, so she named him Solon. That is, 'Forgetfulness' in the ancient tongue of the Horses. But Adrian she named Adrian, for she said he would remember his past. And he does! As soon as he could make his voice obey his will, he proved beyond doubt he had returned! It is a peculiar reality: I am his father, but he is Adrian, my liege lord. Confusing at times. That he cannot heft a proper bow thoroughly frustrates him. We have made him one for his size; he practices for hours daily. But Solon is a child, although unbelievably brilliant, and as sensitive as he was as Aland. He forgot his past, but he never forgets anything else — he has an eidetic memory, never loses anything. But otherwise, he is a child, with many of the normal problems of childhood. It is a good experience, being their father."

"Ahanatar," said Orah softly, "what of their mother?"

"An Oathmaster has she become! She told me to come here! She knew you would return to us. She didn't tell me why, only that it was important for me to come and —"

"Ahanatar." The voice was firm, compelling, yet full of love.

The Gemstone looked up at him with deep pain and found he could pretend strength no longer. Burying his head in his shaking hands, he said, "She dies, my Lord. No medicine of Martanda, no subtle science of the Protectors can save her. She has but little time left." He dropped his hands from his face and stared upward through the darkness at the heavens, tracing in memory the path of the moons as the tears ran unnoticed from his tormented eyes. "New moon of Gauri, tonight, it would be. By the time the fair moon would have been full, Nediva will be dead. She absorbed it, you know, the radiation that would have killed Hamar and me and the twins. Took it all, even though the light of the explosion burned her eyes from her (she would not look away from the accursed ground where we left you standing alone), absorbed it and turned it from us. And now she dies from the poison of it. Her hair is gone; her gums bleed continually; her skin is covered with open sores that do not heal. And inside, everything decays. She declines the medications now, saying the pain is a boon to her practice of Oathmastery. As soon as she realized that neither her power nor the science of Maramel was sufficient to heal her, she has refused them. I am humbled by her glory."

"So," Orah said distantly. "So. I did fail. I had wondered —"

"Fail? What do you mean? You don't know? No, of course not, how could you? Orah! Less than a hundredth part of our army fell that day! But the whole of the gorlems and Asurs. It was the greatest victory in history! You turned the explosion — only the smallest portion of its devastation touched us. We all owe our lives to you alone." His good fortune at telling the Azure Lord these things drained away the agony of witnessing Nediva's terminal disease. It did not return. He continued, the reborn didactic Starlord, "There was only one warhead. It came from the west, from the Mereds; that fact has done more to convince the Senate and Counselors to listen to Marasad about the restoration of the fleet than any amount of argument could have ever done. Yet we all wonder why there have been no more, and —"

"Ahanatar," the Etan said, looking vaguely toward the east and momentarily lost in the second burden he had transferred to himself that evening, "Ahanatar. I want you to take Chali to her parents in Gurion. After that, return to Goldenhome. I will meet you there."

"They are in the Gray River Valley, below the Founding Lake. All the Gurions are. The Arelai put them to it, hoping thus to recover their vision, even though you had not technically called them. They've been there since early fall, waiting for the generator —"

"So that is why I feel them there. You may give the Redhawks my formal call now. It is past due, for it is the simple truth we must penetrate the Fortress before the first day of spring and free Leor or all is in vain. Where is the Engineer? With his generator at the Fortress?"

"He is. The Protectors can call him..."

"Good. Tell him to find me en route to the south."

"The south!" exclaimed Ahanatar, but the Azure Lord was already walking away, heading toward Etan. He did not look back or speak again.

~ ~ ~

The Starlord returned to the office with joyous heart and exulting mind. He knocked gently on the door of his room. Chali did not answer; he knocked again more loudly.

"Oh! Come in."

"Forgive me, my Lady; I need a few things."

"No, I am sorry for not responding, but I was so engrossed in this painting. It is too marvelous! Who created it?"

"Why, it is mine," he began, glancing at it. But then he stared at it amazed: it was unchanged in form or structure, but now his Orah was as complete as Evana — the bizarre distortion that had made him seem evil was replaced by an abundance of balanced life. The Dancer was whole and perfect. Had the flaw been only a creation of his mind, externalizing his imagined loss? Or had he somehow created a mirror of the Azure Lord, and had the Etan's escape from the sanctuary of Emptiness released his spirit to reflect in the painting?

Ahanatar haltingly explained his experience and thoughts; Chali ventured the observation that consummate art mimics reality perfectly. With that compliment warming his chest, he withdrew to the cot the Protectors had set up for him in the office. And for the first time in years, the bitter lines etching themselves around his mouth in empathy with his dying wife disappeared; the Starlord Ahanatar slept as he had not since he first left his master Zuriel to seek his adult vows in a harsh world.

21. A Dream of Etan

Invisible to most, Etan, a golden sphere of some one hundred leagues' radius, floated a handsbreadth above the antarctic ice. A slender silver causeway was all that connected it with the ground; on its steel surface endlessly paced the two-headed progeny of Sarama, huge double-brained, wolf-like creatures with the strength of lions and the minds of humans, the sole wardens of Etan. Not that guardians were truly needed — who unbidden could penetrate Swayam's illusions?

Today was a rare day: the three Saramai had stopped their pacing and were gathered near the top of the ramp, excitedly watching the intruder approaching from the north. None of them had ever seen anything like the strange beast racing toward them. But they all agreed the man on its back was an Etan. They were animatedly discussing, not to say arguing, about his identity.

"Orah, I say," said Rarfang, eldest of the three. "He rides like he dances, with wild and reckless abandon."

"Never," said Swiftfoot, strongest of the Saramai. "Only 'Sravasa wears the Gold of the Mind, as he is Firstborn."

"Of course," agreed Farsight, wisest of the three. "But for the fact that 'Sravasa headed toward the northwest with Krishanu. This one, you must observe, flies alone from the north."

His second head twisted around to verify this assertion, found it true, then said as it turned back, "Also, the Eldest would never travel without his brother Krishanu; they are as inseparable as our heads."

"It is certainly Orah," concluded Rarfang's second head in a tone that said the discussion was over. It also returned at once to the contemplation of Swayam's city: the attention of half the Saramai was always devoted to the glory of Etan. 'Sravasa wrote that there could have been no other way to have guardians for the Immortal City — if they had had but one head each, never would they have willingly turned from Etan's beauty. But the wolves' Janus heads were opposed; therefore it was most uncomfortable for both always to face Swayam's city.

At first they had agreed to equal shifts. But after many centuries, one head of each had grown more and more fond of contemplation and the other of activity. By now, they rarely reversed their positions. So for Rarfang and Farsight, that is, but not for Swiftfoot: his two heads still maintained their rigid and long-accepted habit, never violating the routine of even shifts of twelve days each.

"We shall see," said Swiftfoot's outer head, undaunted. "I will be most curious why he so alters tradition if you four be right."

~ ~ ~

Heramann ended his flight near the Saramai. Orah dismounted; Airavata transmuted and hopped onto his shoulder.

Two of the three averted heads swivelled to glance at them. "So, you see," said Rarfang. "Welcome, Lord of Etan. You have been sorely missed."

"Hello Saraman, ancient Lord of the Passage. Any word of my brothers?"

"None since you three departed," answered Farsight. "Althea does not so speak, but I perceive her concern."

"We welcome your return to your home," said Swiftfoot, "but of course we cannot allow that monster entry."

Airavata began a curt reply, but Orah laughed and said, "Oh, he is harmless enough. I will vouch for his conduct. He is just a little bird, after all." He tickled the Vidyadhara under his beak, then soothed his ruffled feathers. "You see — he is most civilized. But I would ask you to not reveal our presence."

"Why!" exclaimed Rarfang's second head, surprised. "You can't be thinking of leaving Etan twice! It has never been done, in two hundred thousand —"

"Nevertheless, I must. And it would ease my burden to know that Swayam and Shatarupa and Chavva never knew I visited. Can I trust you?"

~ ~ ~

Althea was waiting for them in her private lilac grove. "This must be the Engineer," she said when Orah at last released her from his crushing embrace.

The Vidyadhara had known many of the Azure Race in his long years, but never before had he seen such a profound expression of vibrant health. The aspect of the earthbreath responsible for well-being flowered in her with its fullest expression. He could well understand why she was called the Healer: no illness of mind or body could endure her presence. The air around her seemed filled at one moment with glorious golden light; at the next by the most beautiful paintings and statues he had ever seen; at the next by iridescent birds and butterflies; at the next by perfect images of forests, mountains, lakes; at the next by miraculous gardens filled with strange and wonderful plants.

"My Lady, I am honored. But I must confess to curiosity of your knowledge. Are you of a par with Oathmaster Matri?"

"Omniscient I am not, friend of the human. But long ago I discovered a most interesting person. It has been, I don't remember, perhaps fifty or sixty thousand years; I was helping 'Ishtar test one of his new inventions — a peculiar space-traversing device. Remember it, brother?" She sat gracefully on the cloud-like couch that materialized behind her as she motioned for Orah to join her.

"Of course," he laughed, sinking comfortably into its silken cushions. A goblet that looked as if it were cut from diamond appeared by his side; he sipped it and said, "Sweet memories... As I recall, it ended by crashing on one of the smaller moons of Brihas. Swayam made him promise to invent in other fields after he rescued him... Always inventing, 'Ishtar," he added to Heramann. "Sometimes usefully, sometimes not. But he derives great satisfaction from it. I'm sure the Maralords would love to lock him away for a decade or two and investigate his brain."

"So would I," said the Vidyadhara, changing into his lizard form so he could also taste the Lady of Etan's nectar.

"To finish the tale," continued Althea, "I quite by accident discovered the most pathetic little creature orbiting our planet. He was almost dead, but somehow I healed him; in gratitude, he befriended me. We still talk rather regularly. He says I'm the only one who ever expressed any interest in him. Poor little fellow, all alone up there, waiting through the millennia for the calls that never any more came."

"One of our satellites!" exclaimed Heramann.

"Of course," she answered with a soft laugh. "He called himself S- something or other, but I have always called him,'Little Historian,' for he had carefully preserved the record of Ganym, the fleeing of the refugees led by Arama and yourself, and the destruction by Father. He actually felt a little guilty about it, he told me, as his intended function had been vastly different. But after the humans were gone and the central computer told him it made absolutely no difference to anyone what he did or didn't do, he felt he should occupy himself with something worthwhile and decided to prepare a History of the Human. He offered to gather whatever historical information the other satellites possessed; as a rule, they were only too glad to share it. Some were eager to clear their memory banks so they could pursue their own projects. Some considered this divesting a purgation of their last link to fallen humanity. Others were just grateful for someone to talk to.

"So the years passed as he worked. Yet when he was finished, there was no one to appreciate his labors. He was rather despondent by the time I found him, more than eager to share his knowledge.

"Thus I learned that Etan was not Father's first attempt to create perfection. And as I delved more deeply, I became convinced his true first-born was again among us. And the mind-created golden robe you wear, brother, attests that you now are also well aware of this curious fact."

"I am Arama. And my Jaya is Leor. This much I know. But there are still dire conflicts in Martanda; my labor is far from finished."

"That I also understand. Which is why I marvel at your return."

"I need your help, Althea. There is a child of Gurion who dies because of my weakness. I would give her the amrita... She is worthy of immortality," he added, answering her unspoken question, "the only one I have discovered who is. I request your permission —"

"Who am I to grant it? Of course, take it, do as you will. I assume, then, that that which you carried is lost?"

"The silver box!" he exclaimed, as the knowledge collided with the one question he had never answered during his amnesia about the mysterious vial he carried throughout Riversland. "Yes, it is gone. Valin must have it! What a cruel twisting of fate —"

"No, you misunderstood my intent, brother. I sent it with you precisely so he would come by it. I am sorry I did not explain this to you; but I could not, lest your knowledge unconsciously betray my intention. No, it has come out exactly as I planned it. Quite perfectly."

"I think," Orah said, a little huskily, "I would like to hear what you know of Valin, why you sent me, and why you subjected Jaya to all of this. From what I have experienced, you owe me that much."

"I will gladly, everything but the last. I would not interfere with her design, even if I could; she has committed herself utterly to humanity. I must respect her wisdom.

"But first, some more substantial nourishment? It surely was a hard flight. When was the last time you two had a proper meal? I would be honored if you would let me serve you."

Course after course appeared before them, manifested from the One in response to her desire, all flawless in taste, texture and appearance. Heramann could not remember such a feast. He curled up in his lizard form on the lounge Althea created especially for him, half dozing as she began explaining what she knew of their common foe.

The Vidyadhara felt it important to listen, but somehow Althea's presence in this place of wonder swirled through him like a warm inner breeze, renewing his life and inspiring perfect health. He found himself being drawn inward by its benign authority. It was extraordinarily soothing, wonderfully comfortable, filled with peace, fully in tune with the wholeness of life.

With no obvious transition, Heramann found himself drifting on a golden cloud over a land so supernally perfect it made even Etan seem a mere shadow of Reality. If this was Life, if this was Beauty, then everything he had known before was no more than an imperfect representation of this place. *Para,* he thought, wondering where Almira might be. With the desire, she was there before him, more ideal by far than his imagination could have created (for it is difficult indeed for the mind to imagine beyond the boundaries of its experience), raising her hands to him in benediction or welcome. Her thought entered him, *'Hamsa, doubt not.* Then she became more and more golden and fulgent until the land below faded wholly and she alone remained, manifesting space and time from her outstretched palms, living Eternity as witness to the universal drama. Increasingly brilliant grew Almira's light; yet it was not harsh like the rending of atoms. Rather, as it was expressive only of the One that is the root of all Life itself, her supernal radiance became more and ever more gentle.

The Vidyadhara was absorbed in her perfect stillness of unbounded serenity, desiring nothing because there was nothing left to desire, becoming himself the Ultimate Reality...

~ ~ ~

Heramann awoke gently; the light of Eternity became a multi-rayed violet star deep in his heart, a light which could never be extinguished, even if it could perhaps be forgotten from intense involvement in relative life.

"Two!" Althea was exclaiming. "Two? I see you have not yet fully understood, Orah. They are not two beings: Chavva is Life; Leor, Light. They are equally Jaya, although Leor alone remembers it — she was, in fact, fully conscious from birth. Chavva need only look into her eyes — there will be no one but herself looking back. Then will she too remember. One wife, one soul, two bodies — brother, that is the simple Truth."

Orah grasped her hands and stared into her perfect eyes with joy as he let the wonder of this truth flow through him. Finally a slight stirring from the Vidyadhara caused him to end this sharing and say, "Ah, sister, look: our guest returns from his pretty dreams. In time: we must depart soon, else even the Elixir of Life will be of no avail... But I would have you share one more knowledge first — how progresses Father?"

"Unchanging. Surely you did not expect else? The centuries are but breaths to him; a hundred thousand years but a day. He is old, Orah-lar. Far older than we believed. I have learned much about him from my Historian, and intuited more — I no longer think he was native to Ganym. In truth, I believe he was not much younger than he is now when our good sun was still scattered as so much cosmic dust. I have no proof, but I believe now he may have been the first creation of this Universe."

"Tell me," said the Vidyadhara as softly as if he were still dreaming and speaking to Jaya, "What is this task that so occupies

Swayam? To require such degrees of protection as you and the Seven afford him lest the evil in Martanda deflect him from his purpose, it must be of supreme importance. Can you tell me of it?"

"Your scaly friend cuts to the heart of the matter, brother. It is true, Airavata: Father is protected for the sake of his work. He considers his task important enough to devote Eternity to its resolution; we honor his unending commitment by offering such aid as we may. Simply put, he seeks three things which are really only one: clarifying the seventh wheel, creating Almira's Para in the changing worlds, and discovering across the infinite reaches of space and time He who made him — the Grandfather of all that is."

~ ~ ~

"So," said Rarfang, "You *are* leaving. I never believed it would happen."

"If I tarried much longer, I suppose I could not. But the need in the north is strong; I shall not return again until I succeed in my quest."

"Travel in calmness, Lord of Etan," said Farsight. "Thus only is there hope. Anger will destroy all you wish to save."

"Thank you, Saraman. I will remember."

~ ~ ~

"Tell me," said Swiftfoot after the Azure Lord and the Vidyadhara were gone, racing northward to save one adjudged worthy of freedom from death, "why he wears the Gold of the Mind. I do not understand it — only the Eldest wears the Gold."

"It is comment of truth, Saraman. Simple truth," answered Althea with a sigh, wondering again if she should have spoken more completely to her brother. Was it her place to so judge?

No, she must not blame herself, she was not acting independently: certain facts Leor had long ago requested her to conceal. Not the least, of course, was her very existence: Swayam would never have permitted the martyrdom she was enduring. And he would have been wrong: Leor must know better how to cure Martanda than did Father. She had returned from Para with full awareness! It was unthinkable that she could be mistaken!

Therefore Althea must not deviate in the slightest, must permit the drama to unfold precisely as her sister had planned it. Else the delicately-balanced result might go devastatingly awry.

Sighing, the Healer of Etan turned from the doorway to the world and reentered the City of the Immortals.

~ ~ ~

"I really don't know what all this fuss has been about today," said Swiftfoot's second head, drunk with the bliss of Etan. "Everything looks perfectly normal to me."

22. Goldenhome

Sevilien stood on the prow of Dalmara's Pride, Maramel's flagship, and watched the construction crews in the dry dock torching the hull. They had saved the largest vessel until last: the Engineer had pleaded design problems in adapting the particle generator to its antimatter reactor. He was nevertheless excited by the attempt, claiming its firepower would far exceed anything he had ever built. The rest of the fleet, all twenty-six ships, were seaworthy; by the equinox, Dalmara's Pride would join the others on the line; the foreign expedition could begin. Provided, of course, that Valin's Fortress was dismantled by then: Sevilien had no illusions about Marasad's hold on the Senate; Miran and Tivon and the others were far too timid a lot to risk an overseas campaign if so powerful a foe in Riversland were left undefeated.

"Campaign" was hardly the correct term. It was being called the "Voyage of Second Discovery." With good reason — there had been no response from the other lands to Maramel's transmissions in over two thousand years. Had the rest of the world descended to utter barbarism? No, the satellites showed thriving civilizations in the Northern and Southern Mereds and a semi-technological race on Sarojin. The answer must lie elsewhere, but where? Someone out there had flung a thermonuclear warhead at them, by the Ten Oaths! She was not going to let Maramel hide behind its shields and hope no one would do it again.

"Princess!" cried a small boy, climbing up to her.

She realized he had called her several times as she was daydreaming, and berated herself for her lapse of alertness. *Such is not the warrior's way...*

"Solon, does your Protector know you're up here again?" she scolded, half in jest — the little fellow had doubtless been helping the technicians with a difficult problem. There was no math or science that eluded his eager numinous mind: he had mastered the whole of Maramel's knowledge in just under fifteen months, starting as soon as he could sit up well enough to turn the pages by himself. All of which had both amused and annoyed Adrian. His attempts to help Solon learn to walk had been unsuccessful until quite recently — until, in fact, the peculiar puzzle of adapting the particle generator to Dalmara's Pride had convinced Solon he should review the project in person.

"Sevilien," he said, ignoring her question as he laboriously climbed the metal rungs to stand beside her on the prow, "we have received a communication from the Cathedral. Heramann and the Etan have been sighted off the Cliff of the Foundling, flying this way at full speed. I was wondering if you could help me find Adrian? I have done everything I can here today; he would not be pleased to miss the return of the Outlander."

"Yes, I suppose I can. If I stand here staring out to sea much longer, I'll never last these next seventy days. Your brother is at the archery field, most likely?"

"Most likely," answered Solon, enjoying the lift onto her shoulders.

~ ~ ~

"Protectors coming up fast on us, Arama," said the Vidyadhara.

"Hmmm?" Orah was staring at the white walls and red tile roofs of Goldenhome and thinking how very much it reminded him of Jaya's City of the Silver Isle on Ganym. That had been one of their best places, clean and bright and always happy... There had been so much of good on Ganym; he had never understood why it all became so confused... "Oh! Good. Now we need not waste time seeking her out; I believe even minutes are critical."

"As always," sighed Heramann, yearning for the Ice.

"Arama, Arama, is it really you?" cried the lead sphere in a most un-Protectorlike manner.

"Marel? By Narain's Dream! I thought you of all would have been lost! You were leaving so slowly; so far behind the others."

"Who can read fate?" laughed the Protector, bathing him playfully with crimson and golden light. "Many melted who were further away than I. But I escaped with a cracked crystal and two broken manipulators."

"Marel, guide us directly to the Lady Nediva. We cannot take the time to see anyone else, not yet."

~ ~ ~

The Horse Elder, emaciated and quite obviously dying, lay on a mass of silken indigo pillows in a large white room furnished mostly with forced hyacinths, narcissi and daffodils. A trio of Protectors bathed her continually with their healing rays, sanguine and violet, but it was clear their effect was insignificant. Her empty eye sockets stared blankly at her visitors; the Etan could not tell if she were aware of them or not. "Leave us, all of you," he whispered, then waited while the Protectors floated out. Heramann looked up at him with an unrecognizable expression in his lizard's eyes, the color of Ganym's Emerald Sea of Mystery, then walked out behind them, mumbling something about going to review the progress on Dalmara's Pride.

Orah returned to the window, shut it, then pulled the curtain. Ignoring the stench of decay, he took the iridescent vial from its silver box and held it up to let its wonderful power light and cleanse the room.

"What is that!" cried Nediva ecstatically, her voice mimicking perfect health. "I can see! Why, it is you, Orah! They told me you escaped the Isle of the Damned. I can see you! But not with my eyes."

"No, not with your eyes," he agreed, surprised to see the images dancing on her forehead. "Nediva, beloved Lady of Gurion, I came to bequeath you undying life. But now I discover you have already been given a boon of choice by my superiors.

"If you drink this sanative fluid, its being will enter yours; you will become as the Etanai: undying, evolving throughout Eternity in health, life, wisdom. This was my purpose in bringing the amrita to you, for of all I have met in Riversland, you alone are worthy of such a gift.

"But as I look upon you now in its light, a second path for you is revealed to me. My Lady, if you allow this disease to claim your body, you will be reborn as daughter to Ahanatar and Chali!"

"To Ahanatar and — ? I — of course, my Lord. I will do as you wish... So they have — ?"

"No, forgive the implication. Ahanatar would never avow his love for another while you live. But the truth is, his heart is captivated, as is hers; together they would produce a daughter fit to be wife to Solon."

"I — I do not understand, Orah. Solon would be half-brother to Ahanatar's daughter by Chali. Such a union is never countenanced in Riversland, though I have heard such is done in the Outer Isles of Shamir. How could it be?"

"The Universe changes, my Lady. Win or lose Martanda, those who survive Valin will require a new leader, a new race to guide them. Solon is elder born to Adrian; both are Lions returned from beyond the gray portals to Martanda. But Hannah is the only living representative of the last Lords of Gurion as they were in their previous flesh; Chali is her only child. Therefore are they the hereditary rulers. Which means that to ensure Solon's place as head of the Endless Dynasty, the first union must be between Chali's daughter and Solon. Thus will Ganym's Solar Race re-begin."

"And you request me to be that person? I, his mother, to marry him when I become his sister?"

"You loved Aland before he was Solon. I do not believe that has been fulfilled or forgotten by you... or by him."

"Yes... yes, Orah, I believe you. I am sure that is why he returned to me without memory. And I suppose I must confess to you alone in the Universe that my love for Ahanatar, though deep and real, has always been diminished by that loss... If I choose to remain in this body, what will happen to my husband?"

"The Gemstone will love and honor you until he dies... Many would pay any price for such loyalty. He will deny his feeling for Chali, explaining it as born of the unrelieved pressure of your dying agony. Chali will eventually take another as a husband and bear him a daughter who will marry Solon and mother the Solar Dynasty. . . And after they have all passed on, you can do as you like. Etan will be yours; you will be as we are."

"Immortal. The odd boon of retaining this flesh. Alone of my generation, one to sit in the company of the gods... I believe that my spirit is deathless anyway, as Oathmaster Matri taught the Horses. So it seems simply a matter of which is better. Can you answer that for me, Lord of Etan? Which will be better for everyone? The amrita tempts my corrupt and dying cells: I hear them crying for its succor; their many voices are as the keening of humanity for the agony of untimely death."

"I am not omniscient, my Lady. Certain things I see on your brow, by benefit of this perfection of Swayam's art. But I do not *know*. You will have to search your heart to discern your truest desire. To be Solon and Adrian's mother and Ahanatar's wife, or Solon-who-was-Aland's wife, Ahanatar and Chali's daughter, and mother to others. But I can at least give you sufficient time to decide." He replaced the brilliant vial in its box and the box in his robe.

"They are not exactly children, you know," she mused softly, with an unfulfilled longing remembering other babies she had known. Soon after their birth, she had been surprised to discover a certain lack of interdependence with her boys, a peculiar distance in attitude that mutually colored their relationships, a wholly unexpected but inevitable separation between her old friends in new infant bodies and herself, failing Elder of her extinct tribe.

She asked, more than half decided, "If I choose death, will I remember this life?"

"If you wish, you may. That option is actually frequently presented. But as you know, few indeed care to remember who or what they were before."

"Adrian did. I wonder why."

"Heramann told me the Lion's last thought at death was of revenge. Adrian said he would have escaped the Redhawks, but the Asur poison in the Gray paralyzed his will. His anger was so undying, he brought along his past to seek vengeance. A questionable motive, perhaps; and it appears he may well lose his chance. Unless there are Asurs abroad and he is old enough to participate. I don't know, he may have had other reasons; but if he remembers them, he has not admitted them to anyone."

Nediva sighed and said, "What if I just ask you to do what you think is best? My mind must be suffering a significant decline from these cancers."

"The fact you ask implies it does not. But even if it were, you alone must choose."

A commotion outside the door erupted suddenly; a moment later, Adrian and Solon burst through, Sevilien and half a dozen Protectors close at their heels.

"Outlander!" cried Adrian in his child's treble. "At last I see you again! These metal oafs tried to keep us out, but we were too much for them. Brother distracted them; here we are! I'd thump you on the back, but I'd not reach much past your tailbone. Life is wonderfully strange, is it not? We are both returned from the grave, it seems."

The Etan picked him up and embraced him. Adrian disliked this enough to drop his dignity and kick like a thirty-four month old child. Solon meanwhile was rather stuffily introducing himself, sounding (except for the high voice) rather like the Maramel equivalent of Kanaan-dora's Doctor of Philosophy.

Orah put Adrian down and picked Solon up. This one seemed less offended by the process, being, after all, something more of a child.

"I must apologize for them, Azure Lord," said Sevilien, "although my heart also swells to see you. I will take them out if you like."

"Princess! I am in joy to see you. It will not be necessary. In fact, I was just meaning to ask you all in. We need help with a decision of some importance to all of you."

"Orah!" cried Nediva, sitting up, horrified. "It isn't necessary! I choose — I choose the natural path." She fell back, panting, as the Protectors began again their palliative ministrations.

"Why, Nediva," said Orah, grinning widely, "I was only going to ask them if we should have supper on your veranda or in the dining hall. I'm famished."

~ ~ ~

Marasad and Hamar joined them for the meal. It was a quiet but joyous dinner in the veranda's sunroom as Nediva looked over them all with her blind eyes and an expression that could only be termed beatific. Her act of choice had cauterized her spirit; the presence of Orah or the amrita (or both) had simultaneously ended her pain. She had been separate from it for many months, as the cancers ravaged her body almost unhindered by the interference of her mind. Once she believed her disease terminal, she had devoted the whole of her energy to the culmination of Oathmastery.

In the rays of the Dying Sun
Commoners drink and sing
Or loudly bewail their fate.
But the Oathmasters
Conserve their waning powers,
Fill their storehouses to overflowing
And actualize their dream.

These lines, attributed to Matri, were often on her lips; she had felt without pride many times she was closer than most of her age to becoming an Oathmaster. But until today, there had persisted a faint but tenacious doubt, flitting through her mind at odd intervals, hinging on the question of whether or not there would be sufficient time... But now, Orah's proffered choice gave her the solace of not one but two viable paths to complete her quest. In the final analysis, did it really matter which route she chose? For if the alternative were presented by such a one from a truth revealed by such a substance as the amrita, how could either be any less than the other?

It will be pleasant to have a healthy body again, she thought dreamily as she stared out over Goldenhome, imagining its appearance at night. *Maramel's capital is such a lovely place. The turquoise water reflects the buildings so flawlessly. It is so clean, so orderly here.*

There had been solace in that as her body sickened. External peace had provided a powerful spiritual anodyne, counterbalancing her individual loss with a perception of the city's collective permanence. She had had the Protectors describe it to her for hours, not just the structure and color of the various buildings, but all the subtle gradations of change that made the city live. And if they stretched the truth on occasion, ignoring some areas that might be slightly less than ideal, they were but participating in a fantasy Nediva willingly created and entered. For in her mind, the city *was* flawless, as impeccable as Para itself, her body the one diseased member in that ideality. *Yes, it will be good to be whole again; to finish the labor of Oathmastery in health, perfection internal growing in perfection external. It will be good... And with my beloved Aland once more...*

~ ~ ~

Adrian was the first to notice that Nediva's faint breath had stilled.

Solon was sitting on several cushions in a large wicker chair beneath a luxurious spiderwort Tradescantia (which we commonly name a Wandering Jew), earnestly debating the Engineer on the equations of the fusion-particle interface. Heramann in his lizard form was pacing back and forth before him, hands clasped behind his back, completely engrossed in the boy's logical flow.

Marasad, Sevilien and Hamar were in a little group around an ivory table, its alabaster legs carved as seaweed vines, its top of silver inlaid with coral formed into ships and exotic fruits. They were earnestly scheming the most effective way to end the Senate's power permanently.

Orah and Adrian were together on an indigo velvet sofa, reminiscing about their first meeting in Gurion, south of the Glaucous. The room was a vision of serenity and quiet joy.

But as he spoke of Cahlil's death, the Lion Elder felt a sudden coldness tighten his chest. He glanced sharply at Nediva, lying propped up facing them and the harbor, and saw that the meager vibration under her robe had ceased.

"Mother," he whispered, for the first time naming her that, then cried in full voice, "Mother!" He was at her side in a moment, in front of Solon by the time it takes a child's heart to beat once.

As they gathered around her, a faint but distinct amber mist flowed from her chest, distended briefly toward each of the twins, then faded and was gone.

"*She has passed,*" Marasad quoted their ancient rite, "*beyond the Girthing Seas, beyond time's power. May the Seven Moons greet her and guide her on her way; may the Sun nourish her with Unending Life.*"

"*May she never be in want for truth and love,*" responded Sevilien and Hamar.

"May she find the happiness of the immortals," added Orah, wondering if she had chosen the better path.

Solon was crying desolately; Adrian tried to comfort him without success. Sevilien took them both in her arms and left the sunroom, Adrian for once not protesting such treatment.

Hamar and Marasad knelt for a moment by the bed, thereby offering their silent gift of a custom reserved for the Royal House. Then they bowed to Orah and also left, followed by all the Protectors except Marel.

"Arama," said Heramann, his cross voice failing to mask his pain, "would you mind explaining why we flew nonstop to and from Etan if you never intended to use that stuff? You've exhausted me for nothing."

"Hmmm? Ah, Airavata, a truly noble death. I do not recall its like for peace or beauty... What did you say?"

"I said — oh, never mind. You used to say the Seven were inscrutable. I would add the commentary that you must be nearing their status."

"Orah," said Marel, "three Protectors arrive from the Founding Lake. They bear the Starlord Ahanatar."

~ ~ ~

The Gemstone received the news quietly, his face nevertheless twisting as conflicting emotions competed for dominance. He knelt over Nediva and gently kissed her brow, not knowing the diverse burdens she had lifted from and transferred to him.

"So," he said at last, "even your powers could not save her. I must confess I suspected it would be so. Thank you for your effort."

"No," answered Orah, "even Etan's ichor could not change her destiny. I ask you to accept this as good."

"My mind blasphemes my heart if I do. Yet I will not betray Zuriel's teachings. I shall not resolve this easily. The children must need me. Or at least Solon. I will go to him."

"To both, Starlord. Adrian has discovered rather late that his body and heart hold rather different beliefs than his un-forgetting spirit. He is as desolate as Solon. More, perhaps, for he has lost both a mother and a friend of two lives. He needs you too, Ahanatar."

"Should I rejoice or grieve the more at this? So the world changes, through birth and growth and death. Changes, and evolves in the process. Although, that is perhaps a judgment. I wonder if the Universe really cares what happens to us. I wonder if we delude ourselves unduly with our own importance... No, don't listen to me. I have felt better... Oh, now I am sorry. I forgot to tell you: Zuriel requests your presence. He stresses it is urgent. I apologize for not telling you at once, as he requested."

"No more could be expected, Gemstone. No time have we lost. Airavata? Ready for another race, or are you still tired?"

"What? Me, tired? You scoundrel! When do we leave, when do we leave!"

The Starlord Ahanatar

23. A Twisted Demon, a Dying Tree

The arc lights of the welding torches working on the fleet looked almost as if the firmament were hiding in the harbor. Orah let the fanciful thought take him for a moment, somewhat surprised his mind still enjoyed such diversions. Had the passing of the Horse Elder, in spite of his knowledge of her future, so deeply affected him? Or was he responding to the others' grief?

~ ~ ~

Soon Goldenhome was far behind; except for the lights of an occasional village, they flew through a darkness that could have rivaled the primeval chaos, before Narain began his dreams of space and time.

"Tell me one more time," said the Etan as they crossed the Coastal Range, "how Barek fell so easily to us. Something about that makes me extremely uneasy."

"It was not all that simple," said Marel, one of the score of Protectors accompanying them. "There were three more attacks from the Fortress after you disappeared. But our superior strategies defeated them. We had broken Valin's back before his warhead attacked us."

"No, there you must make an error. That projectile came from the west. When it was launched, it was not possible to know who was winning."

"Perhaps it wouldn't have exploded if they were victorious," said the Vidyadhara, supremely confident. "But even if we are being baited, it doesn't matter. Most of our force is at the ready; a few million only work on the fleet, as many more labor to repair the Cathedral. Even the tank-cannon are on constant alert: Captains Ramor and Sevilien alternate command of the corps monthly; all the operators rotate similarly. The particle generator is nearly functional: sixty days at the outside. We are strong, Arama, and growing stronger."

"If Valin does by chance hold his major force in reserve," mused the Etan, "it would be logical to wait until we have grown overconfident and our work is nearly completed. Then his stroke could be the more devastating. Marel? What do you think?"

"I think," she answered firmly, "we should be careful to judge Valin's forces as accurately as possible. I myself proposed to the Engineer (a full year ago now) that we should penetrate the Fortress and see —"

"It is a crazy idea!" exploded Heramann. "As I told her at the time. That box is locked more tightly than anybody could hope to open without the force of a particle generator. Even so, we'll be groping in the dark as we search for his power sources, not knowing where we should aim. And if they are double-blinded with interlapping shields, we may never succeed —"

"You're hoping the powerhouses are set into the bedrock underneath the Fortress? Is that it? Not protected by force fields?"

"Or minimally protected. 'Tis logical. If he gets too much heat inside his shields, sooner or later he'll fry his Fortress. The Gray and Slave Rivers can only remove so much thermal activity."

"And if you're wrong? If he's discovered a cold system for powering his shields? Or if he can disperse the heat in other ways?"

"Then we'll have wasted the time it took to build the generator. Valin will be sitting in his fortress, laughing up his sleeve at us, biding his time until he is ready to come out."

"And we don't have much time. Jaya told me no later than the equinox. That is all we have. I want you to speed up the construction. I want you to start melting those mountains within thirty days. Even if we have to get Maralords out there with torches, helping the Protectors."

"It is winter, Arama; the generator is being built very high. I wonder if humans could survive."

"Short shifts. But maybe the Gurions would be more to the point. Among the eastern tribes, there are certainly those accustomed to cold and altitude. We can train them for simple tasks. From what Ahanatar told me, they are more than eager to help."

"It could work. We'll see what can be done... By Almira! This endless night is depressing."

"It certainly is," agreed Marel, sounding more despondent than any machine should. "Tell me one thing, please. Did you learn in Etan what has devoured the stars?"

"That is not quite right, Marel. The firmament is still there. But Martanda has been cut off from it. I would say, doubtless some Rakshasa invention in space — beyond the satellites, yet within the moons' orbits... My sister told me nothing else, save that 'Ishtar has evolved a complex theory how it could be done. Something involving an inter-dimensional transference using the medium of a crystal world. Valin may be pulling Martanda completely out of 3-D space. But even 'Ishtar admits he is guessing. What do you think, Airavata?"

"I think this unrelieved blackness is causing my eyes to play tricks on me. I could swear I see a Rakshasa, not half a league off the port side."

"Marel!" cried the Etan. "Capture that! Heramann, down!"

The Protectors had surprisingly little trouble in forcing the Rakshasa to land. It cowered in the glare of their searchlights, but made no attempt to alter its natural form: it stood about twice as tall as Orah, and was covered with slimy scales, a particularly sickly verdigris. Long and vicious incarnadine fangs protruded at odd angles from its twisted snout; mean looking claws were all it possessed for hands and feet.

"Call off your dogs," it cried, its real or feigned terror transmuting its voice into a fair mimicry of a very old man's dying wheeze, "I am not dangerous."

"That would be the first time one of your race was not," replied the Vidyadhara ungently. "You are always working for evil, serving the Enemy or his ilk. We should slay it now and be done with it, Arama."

"What say you, Rakshasa?" asked Orah. "Why do you follow us?"

"I have lost all stomach for my Lord Valin," it said, trying to force its gritty voice to sound piteous. "What he plans is more than even I can love. I suppose I am a disgrace to my people, but I have reached my limit and will no more serve him. I bring you as testimony to my sincerity complete knowledge of the structure of Valin's Fortress."

"My Lord," said Marel, "this creature's words are as crooked as its tail. It weaves lies to trap us in some infernal scheme."

"That is right," agreed Heramann. "It wanted to be captured so it could pass us false information about its master's Fortress. Doubtless the Asur Emperor sent it for this purpose."

"Why should we believe you?" asked the Etan curiously. What could be more improbable than a conversation with a creature whose kind had served the Enemy always? And yet, something about it made it almost credible: it radiated more of the earthbreath than other Rakshasas he had fought. "Why don't you start by telling us your name?"

"Trentas. That is what I am called. I hoped the Etan Lord might be more just than others. Where else could I go?"

"Anywhere," answered the Vidyadhara. "It is a large world."

"Ah, but Valin owns it. Your small force in the Riversland is the strongest — indeed, almost the only — resistance anywhere. I fear you are Martanda's last hope."

"Why should that matter to you?" demanded the Etan.

"I do not want to see the planet ruined," sobbed Trentas, shaking pathetically. "There is too much of beauty here. Too much of truth."

"Could a normal Rakshasa care about, even say such things, Heramann?"

"So, it is unbalanced besides. A mad Rakshasa could be worse than a typical one, if that's possible. I say, let me tear it to pieces."

Trentas backed up a few paces, its tail twitching in fear.

"No, Airavata. An insane Rakshasa could be as a normal human. I perceive the good in it. It may accompany us. Let's go."

"Very well," grumbled the Vidyadhara. "But if it betrays us, I will be eagerly available to rip out its throat."

~ ~ ~

Vanas was old. How old? Even he could not remember. But he did know he was far more ancient than the two-legged beings who, for the past twenty-seven centuries, had tended him; and who, for the past two hundred years, had tried to arrest the disease rotting him from the inside.

He had known illness before, many times as he had grown to cover the island; yet always before there was a way to turn his life to repair, recover and grow on. But no more. Something was fundamentally wrong, either with the earthbreath itself or with his ability to sap it. He pondered which was the cause during the long winter months of rest, knowing the while it was a futile exercise: there was no difference in terms of the final end.

Vanas, seeking knowledge from all sources, let his memory search backward for his origin. Perhaps his Creator could cure him? He remembered, like a diaphanous dream, the small shrine built around him that long ago had crumbled into dust. How could that possibly have been true? Oh, of course, he was much larger now — it must have been long before he had expanded over the island. Yes, that was certainly right: he must have first grown inside that small marble temple. And before that? Who had built the shrine? Vanas tried to discover the memories, but they were gone, perhaps long ago rotted and irretrievably lost.

He knew the humans who served him must be incapable of healing him, else they would by now have done something to begin a cure. Many attempts had been made, but so far with not the slightest success. The tree had matured to a stable attitude about the whole matter, realizing that all life must sooner or later return to its constituent members, that the cells and fibers composing his trunks and limbs and leaves and roots were at best on loan from the One. Someday, the final payment would come due; that was the way of life.

Finding no advancement to his thought, he returned to his great project. For if he were truly not meant to live forever, at least he could and would leave behind an heir. If only there were sufficient time...

~ ~ ~

"Look, grandfather!" laughed Larilyn. "I was right! The bud grows even in the winter!"

"Yes," said Zuriel, bending close and breathing life and health to it, "you and Chali are correct. The World Tree labors valiantly to create a scion. Vanas must know his time wears thin to work in the frigid air."

It was but slightly past dawn; Larilyn had awakened her grandfather early to traverse the frozen lake. Their fur boots had made the first tracks through the fresh snow to the island. Many others would come later, of course: in all seasons, the Tribe of the Tree followed their one project, pruning dead wood, smearing nutrients and asphalt over the visible places of ill, meditating within his sacred chambers, ministering to Vanas in all ways.

But in spite of the long labors of many generations, they were failing: it was obvious the World Tree was dying. Some theorized Martanda's doom was therein foretold. Others held that healing the tree would save the world; others, conversely, if Martanda could be spared, then the tree would live. For the difference between the world and the World Tree was held to be the same as that of the sun to its light, or man to his soul. The Tribe of the Tree had reverenced him for years beyond remembering and now! now Zuriel was forced to accept that their long charge had passed forever beyond their skill.

He sighed and looked back at their village. The snug cabins tucked into the mountain gave him, as always, the same feeling of life that the tree, even in disease, represented to its fullest. Smoke from the morning fires curled lazily from several of the chimneys, belying the hard winds of the night that had left them this snow. He wondered how the lowland tribes in the valley below were faring, then decided again they did not require his concern in the least — the Gurions were a most resilient and prudent people and were well-prepared and provisioned for this winter.

"Grandfather!" cried Larilyn, looking upward with innocent joy widening her soft brown eyes, "the Engineer returns! And that must be the Etan! They have come! But what is that being with them? It gives me an awful feeling in my heart."

"Another verse completed," murmured Zuriel, as he stared at the entourage descending in slow spirals toward the village. He shared her feeling, but his years of nurturing the powers of the One naturally turned his mind toward analysis. Was this, then, what Ahaman had meant? "It is a Rakshasa, my dear. A lieutenant of Valin. Curious, but not entirely unforeseen. Let us go to them."

~ ~ ~

Chali came from her cabin and beckoned to Orah. Heramann landed neatly a few paces from her. Pointedly ignoring the Rakshasa, she clapped her hands gladly and cried, "How fortunate to see you again so soon, my Lord! It must mean you were successful, the Horse Elder is well?"

"Success is not always apparent in the relative, Lady of the Doves. Nediva is dead." He was impressed by her vibrant health, stunning beauty, and all-around wholesomeness. *The Tribe of the Tree takes good wood and improves it. This one is surely deserving of the highest good.*

"Oh..." she said, blushing as she tried but failed to suppress all of her feelings. "That is most grievous news. Ahanatar — he must be desolate. And his twins! I am saddened for them."

"The Starlord will return within the fortnight. And the boys will certainly accompany him: Adrian would not miss the end of this siege for any price; I doubt Solon can keep from talking technology with our Engineer for very long."

"We will prepare for them; I will console them with my love."

"That is good," replied Orah warmly, pleased to see the foreseen future effortlessly unfolding.

A small group of Tree children had gathered around them, fascinated by the Etan. He looked at the nearest and asked, "Where is Zuriel?"

"He and Larilyn visit the World Tree, my Lord," she answered as her blue eyes expanded with wonder that this wonderful incarnate legend should have spoken to her. "They will be back soon."

"In the meantime," said Chali lightly, "would you join me for breakfast? The Founding Lake food is simple but nourishing."

"I would be honored. Heramann, could you take Trentas —" Orah stopped aghast as he realized the Rakshasa had vanished.

The Vidyadhara was the merest instant longer in discovering the fact. Screaming his war cry, he launched himself into the air, golden wings unfurling in a burst of power. He circled for half a minute, then called, "I see it! A winter fox, almost crossed the lake to the Tree! I told you it could not be trusted!" His last words were swallowed by the distance as he raced after the Rakshasa. Marel and the other Protectors were but moments behind him. But it was plain that the fox would reach the island before any of them could catch it.

Between the island and the transmuted Rakshasa suddenly appeared an older man with white flowing beard and hair, dressed as the others of the Tribe of the Tree in a simple gray woolen robe.

Beside him walked a young red-haired girl of eleven or twelve. "Zuriel and Larilyn!" cried Chali, tasting a bitter inchoate fear.

The Tree Elder, assessing the situation in a glance, thrust his granddaughter behind him and raised his staff. As he did so, he expanded enormously. Reaching down, he picked the fox up and threw it from the island. Trentas had been looking over his shoulder at the pursuit. Now it transformed into an eagle and dove again toward the World Tree. But the delay was just long enough: the Vidyadhara was upon it. In less time than it takes a fowler to behead a bird, the Rakshasa was slain. In death, it resumed its natural form; Heramann brought it and threw it on the snow at Orah's feet.

"You see, Arama. They can never be trusted."

"You should not have killed it, Airavata," answered the Etan, kneeling by the Rakshasa and feeling for pulse.

"The wise do not play with scorpions, my Lord," said Heramann fiercely, his eyes still blazing rage. "It is certainly dead," he added awkwardly as Orah continued to search for signs of life.

The Etan stood, rubbing his hands to remove the slimy oil, and said sadly, "It did not know Valin had programmed it to attack the World Tree. I believe it was sincere in its desire for the good. Its information about the Fortress will be quite valuable —"

"Pah! The Asur Emperor would never have allowed it to speak anything of importance. The whole event is an exercise in treachery."

Zuriel retained his giant form long enough to carry Larilyn across the lake on his shoulder, then set her gently down before Chali. The high ride more than compensated for the terror of the attack; she laughed to see her friend and took her hand, bursting to tell her the news of the World Tree's bud, but waiting in deference to the Etan.

"Greetings, Azure Lord," Zuriel began in his richly melodious voice, but then stopped in astonishment as he had his first thorough look at him. "By Shraddha! I should have foreseen..." His words ended in a tight-lipped silence.

"I am pleased to meet Ahanatar's mentor," said Orah, from grace and confidence ignoring the confusing emotions in Zuriel's fragmented salutation and enigmatic countenance.

"What's wrong, Tree Elder?" asked the Vidyadhara impatiently. "You look terrible." Arama always deserved unqualified respect.

"It's nothing, nothing," replied Zuriel, fighting down his convulsing stomach. "Just for a moment the Outlander reminded me of... of someone I once met. Forgive me, Orah. We do not often entertain visitors in our small valley."

"I was told there was a 'matter of some urgency,' which is why I am here," said the Etan, perplexed, failing to understand Zuriel's conflicting emotions. Perhaps the Rakshasa?

"There is. But... But it can wait 'til after breakfast. I am humbly reputed to be among the best turners of buckwheat cakes among our people. Chali, perhaps your cabin is spacious enough?" Without waiting for a reply, he grasped his granddaughter by the arm and hurriedly entered, leaving the others to exchange quizzical glances.

Chali, shrugging slightly, took Orah by one hand and Heramann by the other and led them into her simple home.

24. Painting and Vision

The main room of Chali's cabin doubled for living and dining; its dominant feature was a large rough-hewn table of red cedar. Eight wicker chairs were arranged neatly around it. Set within the northern wall was a large fieldstone fireplace, cheerfully radiating a welcome and bright warmth. On one side of it was a generous quantity of wood; on the other, a large, well-made tapestry of the World Tree, golden thread woven onto an indigo background.

The western wall had an open door from where the sounds of industrious cooking were already coming. The eastern wall's door, closed, led to Chali's bedroom. The southern wall was broken by the doorway through which they had entered and many small windows. On all the four walls, artfully placed over the rough logs, were many small tapestries, mostly in gold.

Chali directed the Etan and the Vidyadhara to sit in two chairs before the tapestry of the World Tree. She stood beside them and said brightly, "Airavata, Orah, I have something most precious to show you. The Starlord Ahanatar has created a masterpiece of art; I am sure he would be too modest to show it to you. It is just here." She pulled aside the tapestry and stood back, beaming.

"Quite lovely!" exclaimed Heramann with complete sincerity.

But the Etan said with great agitation, "I do not understand, Chali. Why does he depict Jaya destroying Riversland?"

"What? You — he sought to symbolize Ravi's blessing by those golden rays! I — I thought you would love it," she stammered, on the verge of tears.

"Oh, of course. It is perfect, well made. I do see his intent now. Something most marvelous about it. Do forgive me. It has been a week of tiring flights..." His voice trailed off as he stared at it blankly. A few moments later, he stood abruptly, saying, "Ah, excuse me, I think Larilyn needs my help. Marvelous painting. Truly." Orah disappeared into the kitchen, leaving Chali forlornly dividing her gaze between the Vidyadhara and the painting.

"Well," said Heramann, "I think Ahanatar's creation is outstanding, profoundly moving. Very deep. And the mechanical skill! Simply awesome. Best I've ever seen of Arama; Jaya is perfection itself. And I think he must have used a hologram to paint me. It is a living work of art, joyous to behold."

"I wonder what it is that so displeased him," she said softly, mostly to herself. She looked at the painting for a long time, and again found it to be perfect. How could Orah not have seen it? She sat heavily beside Heramann and looked up at Ahanatar's work, wistful, sad, confused.

"Here we are, best hotcakes at the Founding Lake!" exclaimed Zuriel, entering with a heaping platter in each hand. "I'll just — my God!" he cried as breakfast crashed to the floor.

"Is everyone crazy today!" shouted Chali, leaping up to confront him. But the horror disfiguring Zuriel's face ruined her arguments before she uttered them.

"That — that is evil itself," he said with utter repulsion as he stared at the painting.

"Oh, what is the matter with you two?" Chali sobbed desperately. "This is the most wonderful art I have ever seen. It is an exquisite masterpiece; Ravi and Orah are alive —"

"Orah? That is Valin! Killing Evana! Twisting the very essence of Riversland to thrust her to her doom! Do you not see the Emptiness torturing her? The pain in her suffering eyes? By Narain, who could have created such an abomination?"

Orah stood in the doorway with two other full platters, listening intently. When Zuriel glanced at him, he set them down on the long cedar table and began cleaning up the others.

"Here, let me do that," said the Tree Elder gruffly, bending to help. They met eye-to-eye on their hands and knees; Zuriel said in a tight voice, "Why is it?"

The Etan straightened slowly and answered, "It is after all a painting, Zuriel. Certainly it reflects truth, which is why each of us sees what we perceive in our hearts. I do not find Valin there. But I would be curious to know why you do."

"Perhaps," said Chali fiercely as she covered the painting with the tapestry, "we should have breakfast. Hotcakes should be eaten hot, while the butter can still melt on them, and the blackberry honey and maple syrup will not get them too soggy. You can clean up later."

"Grandfather!" cried Larilyn from the kitchen. "I need you in here!"

"Yes, yes of course," he said, rubbing his hands on his apron. "Here — do sit down. We'll have more to replace those in half a moment. Clumsy of me. I'll be right back."

"I really don't understand," said Heramann, "how you two can place such bizarre interpretations on that magnificent work of art."

"It only shows how perfectly it depicts life," answered the Etan abstractly. "No two ever go to the same lake."

"Pass the butter," said Chali emphatically.

~ ~ ~

Breakfast was subsequently a trifle stilted. Heramann, Chali and Larilyn talked about everything from the World Tree's bud to the winter arrangements for the Gurions in the valley below. Zuriel, stonily silent, stole an occasional furtive glance at Orah. The Etan responded by an external silence and an internal analysis: why did the Tree Elder identify him with Valin? Surely it could not be jealousy. Zuriel did not seem a man who could know such an emotion. Certainly his practice of Oathmastery was well-nigh perfect: to manipulate the earthbreath as he had that morning evidenced profound success. Had not Ahanatar said the Tree Elder once fought Valin? So, he had seen him. *Could Valin look like me? It is possible, if my theory about Navril is correct. But for one so acquainted with life, should not his perception cut deeper than the surface? And if it does and the doubt persists, can there be truth in it? I was wrong about the Rakshasa. Could Valin have permitted my escape? Counting the cost of the Tower as negligible when set against the havoc I could wreak if I am twisted? But no, it cannot be! The earthbreath flows in me clearly and purely. That is true and good. I am newly returned to myself, but I am whole and sane.*

~ ~ ~

"Orah," said Chali as they worked on the dishes, "I must apologize for my parents' absence."

He responded simply to give her ample space: "I wondered where they were."

She smiled in appreciation of his humility and continued, "They, particularly Hannah, are too embarrassed about the vote at the Shield Conference."

"Why should that cause shame? It was an emotionally searing time for them. And she did not actually vote at all, she told you that?"

"Yes, all of it. But they no longer hold the least blame for you in Cahlil's death."

"That is good. I am impressed by how calmly you speak of your brother. You have only just learned."

"Grief has changed for me. I lost four years of my youth, not a day of which I remember. For all I know, I may have believed he and all of Gurion were dead. I don't know. But the return of Adrian eases my heart. It should comfort all of us, all the bereaved of Riversland, if only it could be accepted that this happens to everyone, not just those blessed by proximity to the Etanai. It is a boon of incomparable value."

"Most would not believe, dear one. I have heard that there have been cases of complete memory before, in Maramel and Gurion. But still the world finds it easier to accept death as the final ending. Unending life and infinite possibilities terrify mankind."

"Arama," said the Vidyadhara, sticking his head into the kitchen, "Zuriel is ready to talk to you — as soon as you are finished."

"You go ahead," said Chali, "this will take but a minute more."

"I'd help," volunteered Heramann, "but I'd break half of them. And such fine pottery, too. I'm all thumbs."

"Uncommon honesty," murmured Orah as he left them.

"Now tell me," said Chali urgently, "exactly why he and Zuriel interpret Ahanatar's painting so peculiarly. I am most uncomfortable by it."

"It is undeniably confusing," he answered, picking up the towel and scowling at the dishes as if he more than half intended to fulfill his words; "unless they are both projecting their own unrecognized feelings."

"But how can that be? Orah said she was destroying Riversland! He can't believe that, in any way!"

"I believe it could be theoretically possible," Heramann answered in his finest scholarly tone. "In some deeply repressed corner, Orah might feel Jaya is sacrificing Riversland for the sake of humanity as a whole. He has not yet allowed himself to find her, you know. And you must have learned the singularly unpleasant prophecies equating the Azure Lord with the Destroyer of Martanda. Thus Zuriel could view him as Valin; Jaya could be his victim or tool to bring it about. Yes, one could read the future in these ways. Perhaps Zuriel, Arama, you and I have but experienced four different interpretations of the same reality. A sign of an artwork of quality."

"Your words are darker than our night skies," said Chali, viciously scouring the frying pan.

~ ~ ~

The Tree Elder was waiting for Orah on the frozen lake; as soon as the Etan saw him, he began walking toward the island. Orah caught up to him before he was halfway there.

"I must apologize for my behavior earlier, Azure Lord," he said softly as they trudged together through the snow. "I have not been so deluded by the surface of the apparent for many decades. I had an encounter as a young man that almost unmade me; never have I fully recovered. Still, I should have had sufficient foresight to understand."

"That Valin looks like me?"

"So you do know!"

"You have confirmed my theory. It is logical. How else could he still live?"

"Fulfillment for the cherished theories of some... Let me explain our plight, Orah, for the simple truth is: we desperately need your help."

"I do not know what I can do. But I will try, for I share the belief of the Gurions that the Tribe of the Tree represents the epitome of Oathmastery."

"You honor us, Azure Lord. Briefly, as your words imply you know, the World Tree dies. I have bent the earthbreath to his aid as best I could, but have accomplished nothing to halt his decline. I fear he will not awaken again this spring; if so, his seed will not ripen. Even though he spends his time of introspection on it, his resources fail more rapidly daily."

25. Valin's Fortress

Orah, Heramann, Marel, Kumbha and a thousand other Protectors, Marasad and Sevilien for North Maramel, Hamar for Maramel south of the Gray, Zuriel, Elid and Eliora for the Gurions, and Ahanatar, Chali and the twins (simply because they refused to be left behind) stood at dawn before Valin's shield walls where a highway had long ago entered his Fortress. The force fields soared above them for nearly a dozen leagues, gradually planing inward so that the Fortress was entirely enclosed by an opaque sable pyramid.

"Say it again, Marel," said the Etan, refusing to be awed by this monumental creation of Valin's science.

"Valin of the Asurs! This is your last chance. Come out and face us or we will blast your citadel into dust."

Apparently as answer, a portal dilated slowly before them. "It seems he invites us in," said Marasad, "I must confess that, personally, I have no desire to enter his lair. Absolutely none."

"Of all the evils of life, that must contain the worst," agreed Elid, dividing his gaze between Orah and the doorway that revealed only layers of nothingness. "But if you enter, I will follow you. I hesitated once before, and perhaps would have served you better had I been with you."

"No, Sun Lord, Gurion in transition from the Arelai Wars has sorely needed you," answered the Etan warmly, ignoring the fibers of Emptiness stretching through the entryway from the questionable realm beyond. *What must be, will be,* he thought, remembering Joab in Tala. *What hidden connection is there between the master of the third wheel and this place? Mordom of the second and Zared would be more logical thoughts.* He pulled himself back to the present and said, "And, I believe, needs you still. No, I thank you, each of you that would come, but it is better for you all to remain here. I alone must deal with this perversion of my blood."

"Not by yourself!" cried Sevilien, but half a second before the others.

"You would never allow that, would you?" the Etan responded with a smile. "No, I don't think I could stop Airavata unless I chained him, and Marel is useful for analysis and communication. But I will not endanger the rest of you. If we do not return, you have your orders."

He started toward the entryway, but suddenly a voice from the air cried, "Hold, Outlander!" The Arelan Yarin was coming, borne by three Protectors.

"Who is that?" asked the Vidyadhara impatiently.

"Half a moment, old friend. His people have a claim on me. Hail, Yarin of the Syner! I greet you as an ally."

"Well you should," he said, landing before them. "The Arelai have been faithful to your command. We seek the return of our vision."

"What surety do we have you will not resume your evil?" Eliora asked, gently but firmly.

"Staff Elder? Yes, I recognize your voice. We have sworn binding oaths —"

"Oaths have been broken before," said Adrian, without the slightest pretense of gentleness.

"We are a humbled people, my Lord," Yarin said, appealing to the Etan. "We ask but the chance to prove our sincerity."

"Evil growth, long nourished, is not easily checked,'" quoted Zuriel. "Caution is always wise."

"Yarin," said Orah, "Valin's Fortress stands open before us. I am about to enter with the Vidyadhara and the Protector Marel to seek the Enemy. Would you take the fate of the Arelai upon yourself? Would you, assuming their collective destiny, accompany me into this place of incarnate evil?"

Yarin paled but, squaring his shoulders, said, "If it will help the Redhawk nation, I will assume this burden."

"So be it," said the Etan, twisting the lines of Arelai force into him. Yarin's form distorted and shrank under their pressure, transforming within moments into a small sanguine hawk.

"Come along then," said Orah, climbing aboard Heramann.

~ ~ ~

"It was a little trite to change Yarin into a hawk," said the Vidyadhara as they wound their way through the Forbiddings. "But I suppose it makes for quicker travel. You can give him a better form later."

"Why, Airavata!" laughed Orah, "I thought the hawk was your favorite form! You're always roosting on my shoulder like that."

"A hawk! Roosting! You scoundrel! I become a falcon! Not a common, run-of-the-mill hawk! You needn't be insulting."

"Sorry," he answered, grinning, remembering the first time as the shara Mars he had met the Vidyadhara. *The second task that was,* he thought somberly. *And my severest trial occurred in a city very like this Asur Fortress.*

"Where in this black abomination do you think our host awaits us?" he asked, wondering again why Tala kept coming to mind. Could the ambient Emptiness be causing it? Seeping into the cracks of his mind to affect his emotions? Could his will be so easily betrayed? He girded his mind more tightly and attempted to analyze Barek's capital.

They entered through the final portal. The last Forbidding was different from the others: it seemed a wall of perfect Emptiness. They passed it with a shudder of abhorrence, and found they were inside a massive black pyramid, with faces formed of Emptiness. At its apex was an artificial and glaring sun for warmth and harsh light.

A strong breeze blew in their faces as they flew through the winding passageway, but Orah felt certain if the entry were closed, the air would be perfectly still. Inside the final shield, there was absolutely no trace of the earthbreath. A nauseous vertigo gripped him as he was overwhelmed by his memories of the Tower.

The Fortress was unbelievably vast, fashioned to house millions. All the buildings were identical: towering, massive cubicles of sable stone, windowless, doorless, all equally spaced and of the same height — any undulations in the ground had been long since removed.

"Somewhere near the rivers, perhaps?" answered Heramann. "I can find no more choice real estate in this delightful valley."

"Yes, just there where the Slave divides from the Gray. That one cube sits astride them both. I can discover no other distinguishing marks in any of these. Marel?"

"I can't transmit past his shields. Inside, I am receiving no life readings."

"None? Valin should appear."

"I cannot penetrate a few areas. That building you mention is one."

"So. It is doubly marked. To the roof, Heramann."

~ ~ ~

"Well, now what?" demanded the Vidyadhara crossly, trying his claws on the metal of the building, "tear it down piece by piece?"

"I would not think that necessary," said a single gorlem, rising from a hatch just before them. "Gentleman and associates, if you will follow me." He led them into the building.

Inside all was plain white or stainless steel. They passed deserted room after deserted room, gradually dropping lower and lower. "One would die of boredom in here," murmured Heramann.

"Oh, not really," said the gorlem, as if it had awaited the opportunity of conversation for months. Which was quite possibly the case. "Our sameness melts away individuality for more coherent functioning. That is, it did, when there were more of us. Individuality and civilization are diametrically opposed realities."

"It is apparent from this city that your Emperor is very fond of such a definition," said Marel with obvious disdain. "I have never seen a less creative place."

"Oh, we have our inventions and innovations. But the units are modular."

The gorlem ended its flight before a pair of steel doors, three stories high. "The Master awaits you inside," it said, then brushed against a panel. With a quiet whirring, the doors opened inward.

The Etan walked slowly in, the others following closely.

~ ~ ~

For two hours, the leaders of Riversland patiently awaited the Azure Lord's return, staring uncomfortably into the oppressive blackness revealed by the open portal, following their own thoughts, memories and dreams, occasionally commenting on nothing of much importance. Suddenly Sevilien distinguished a gradation in the shadow and cried with agitation, "Someone returns!"

It was Orah, alone; as soon as he emerged, the portal snapped closed behind him.

"A trap!" he shouted wildly. "They are slain! Fire the generator! Destroy this place of evil." His eyes were wide with terror, he was apparently on the verge of collapse.

"It is ready, as you know," said Elid slowly, confused by the Etan's appearance and words. "But before, you said we should study the Fortress —"

Orah turned toward him and cried savagely, "It is too evil! Any who tried would be destroyed. Now is our one chance to slay the Enemy. Fire the weapon! I command you!"

"As you wish," said Marasad, refusing to doubt the Azure Lord. The first explosions began, marked by rising clouds of dust and steam as the particle beams melted bedrock, seeking the underground powerhouses.

"As the Engineer told you," said Solon, understanding a great deal more of logic than life, "if Trentas lied, it may take some time to locate the shields' sources."

"Yes, yes. But hurry! As quickly as possible! We must seal Valin's tomb."

"What transpired, Orah?" asked Chali fearfully. "Where is Airavata? And Yarin?" But her words changed to a scream as a single carmine feathered arrow burst through his chest.

"A fine shot!" exclaimed Adrian, highly pleased with himself. "Dead between the shoulder blades. I may grow into a useful body yet."

"What madness — !" shouted the others, but then stared aghast as the Etan's body transformed into the hideous form of a Rakshasa.

"He said there were still a couple left in there," chuckled the Lion Elder.

"But how did you know?" asked Chali incredulously as the generator ceased firing. One powerhouse must have already been destroyed: the first of the six shields trembled violently and disappeared. Trentas' detailed knowledge about the Fortress' structure was, at least initially, accurate.

"Certain mannerisms. Particularly the wildness in his eyes. He never looked like that, even when, overcome by despair, he saw his companions' transparency in Gurion. It simply could not have been the Outlander."

"But what if you had been wrong?" persisted Ahanatar, only slightly jealous.

"I saw an arrow pierce his heart before. He was fully recovered in twelve hours. I felt the test worth that much time."

"We are fortunate your eyes are so clear," said Zuriel with complete sincerity. "I am humbled."

The others murmured their assent, but the Lion Elder shook his young head firmly and answered, "No, it was a lucky hunch. That's all."

"I pray your hunches remain so accurate," said Solon, then abruptly started walking toward the camp. Perhaps the Protectors were finished making lunch.

"So do I, Aland," whispered Adrian, staring at his brother's back. "By the breath and future of Martanda, so do I."

~ ~ ~

The Asur Emperor Valin faced the three of them from the far end of the long hall revealed by the opening of the double steel doors. He stood slightly above the floor on a featureless silver stage, chosen perhaps to contrast with the complex designs on his sable robe. He was smiling at them, but there was no warmth in it. Rather, it was cold, cruel, mocking.

He waited until Orah was within ten paces of him, noting with grim amusement that the Etan was not surprised to see him. Then he said in Ganym tongue, "Welcome, father. Your new body resembles the old rather closely, does it not?"

They stopped and eyed him as cautiously as if he were a wild beast, cornered and therefore capable of any extreme of violence. Finally Orah said, using his softest voice, testing the waters of Valin, "Navril?"

"Of course. Who else would have been so wise?" His lips curled farther upward, becoming a grin that verged on purest sadism.

"You murdered me. And stole my clones." Simple facts, spoken without inflection, as if he were reciting ancient history.

"I would do so again! You and Swayam were so proud, judging us all unworthy. I remember how all my brothers and sisters grew old and died! And to how many millions before I was born did you refuse immortality? I ended forever your selfish, petty reign. Surely you don't think I regret it?"

"Many of our children returned as my brothers and sisters in Etan, Navril. You could have shared true deathlessness."

"If and when Swayam decided I was ready for it. Thank you, but no thank you."

"Not Swayam. He who created Father."

"That myth again! Your belief in an omnipotent good underlying the Universe was the strangest delusion of all. Power is power. It alone is, and can be used by anyone who dares wield it. Those who build, those who destroy, what difference to energy? Your demiurgic fancies never amused me. To hear them now is pitiful."

"You can still embrace the One, Navril. No one can flee it forever. Eventually comes the reckoning."

"Your metaphysics borders on the absurd! His great ape mother ate some protean fruit on Ganym, or the cosmic radiation mutated her genes, and the hairless Swayam was born. An accident of fate, following the initial example of life itself: in a nearly infinite universe, it is inevitable that somewhere, at sometime, even infinitesimal probabilities will produce something more interesting than poisonous gas and inanimate rock. Where is the glorious order of this?"

"Where is your mother, Navril? What have you done with my Jaya?"

"Never could follow logic, eh, Arama? Amazing how little you've changed. Leor has been supremely useful to me. You Etanai are such marvelous blood factories. I drain her dry; within twenty-four hours, her capillaries are filled again. Think of it, father! Complete transfusions of immortal blood every single day! Not that I have needed so many of late. My cells have begun to learn the art, as I long hoped. Five thousand years! For so long have I retained this body. A magnificent achievement, is it not? I believe now I'll never need the clone bank again."

"You're mad, Valin," stated Heramann flatly, slipping closer to him as his tail did violence to the floor.

"Ah, your lizard. That is something of a surprise. Two hundred thousand years! But then, that icebox was rather well built. I have often wondered if suspended animation could endure forever. At one time, I thought of keeping some of my bodies frozen in space, to cover all possibilities. But I have of course devised far superior systems now —"

"Vampiring Leor's blood, for example," said the Vidyadhara, using the distraction of his tail's motion to continue slipping closer.

"It worked well. But it is no longer necessary, for your master himself has delivered the fulfillment of my desire." He took something from his robe, touched it in a complicated way, then let it fall open in his hand.

"You do have it!" cried Orah, staring with horror at the iridescent vial Valin held aloft and turned slowly so they could see it from all sides. The Asur Emperor's mordant laugh rolled brutally all around them, oddly seeming to come from everywhere — or nowhere.

"Of course, you utter fool! Why do you think I permitted a Lord of Etan to come to Riversland? Or your victories over my primitive, earlier model robots? Or your escape from my Tower? Ah, you Etanai are so pathetically foolish. To think that Swayam's progeny, no less than Arama reborn, has personally delivered the Elixir of Immortality to me!"

Heramann launched himself viciously at Valin. The Vidyadhara's head made a resonant thump as it collided with the wall.

Valin's hideous cachinnation of desecration and death echoed through the empty hall, changing finally into equally vile words, "You thought to end me, Slave of Etan? Know my power to be greater far than your childlike fantasies! I grow in strength from age to age, while you and yours stagnate and decay. Every act of violence feeds me and weakens you! Every word, every thought of anger or hate or lust or greed increases my unending dominion!

"Even your desire to destroy me adds your energies to mine! There can be no hope for you! None! What can Swayam do to me? Etan will crumble before my lesser servants! After Martanda is mine, who then will keep me from the Eternal Throne? If by chance your so-called Grandfather exists, even he shall one day bow before me!"

"Blasted hologram," said Heramann, rubbing his swelling forehead.

"The Grandfather will destroy you!" cried Marel.

Valin defamed the hall again with his laughter and said, "Assuming for the sake of argument he is in fact not solely a singularly unpleasant myth, still his reaction time must be rather too slow, eh? He hasn't paid overmuch attention to this world lately, has he? Maybe he's sleeping! But, since we are partaking of such logically indefensible dreams, I would submit a hundred million years could not equal half a minute to him: such would be the obvious limitation of such a universal sempiternal being's life. By the time he notices me, I will have amassed sufficient energy to conquer him. Any power of creation can be equaled or bettered! The earthbreath is only one expression of absolute energy. I will rule all!"

"Mad as the grease slugs of Ganym," muttered Heramann, walking back to Orah through the hologram of Valin.

"If you drink that, you will surely die!" exclaimed the Etan. "Only one fully in contact with the One can master it."

"I feared something of the kind. So have I waited to talk with you. But now that you plainly tell me so, I am doubly reassured it is wholly innocuous. What a sweet irony. Here comes the great Lord of Etan, bearing such an incomparable boon to Riversland. But instead of sowing life, he brings death after death, simply because he forgot who he was! What a marvelous working of Fate! And you believe in the fundamental order of life!" He opened the vial and stared entranced at its contents.

"It won't work, Navril!" shouted Orah. "We will find you and chain you!"

"Oh, I think not. Your twin Krishanu and brother 'Sravasa are captured now too, by the way. You will enjoy that thought throughout the unending years...

"My creation of the Tower was but an early, stumbling attempt to counter the earthbreath with my own powers. There you needed poisoning and constant physical abuse to keep from discovering its one flaw. For I did not know how to cancel the force which was, after all, responsible for the creation of Martanda. It took me much longer to learn how to perfect this Fortress. But I have! How does the prospect of spending the balance of Eternity inside my pretty little city appeal to you? I wondered for centuries what punishment would be suitable for you, murderer of my family. I don't suppose you'll ever actually die, even after the earthbreath that gives you life is withdrawn from you for a million million years. But you will certainly become largely dysfunctional. I may visit you occasionally to see how you are adjusting to your prison, may even fill this place with Etanai. It is such a good work. It'll make a dandy zoo."

"My generator —" began Heramann, but Valin's coarse laugh shredded the Vidyadhara's argument even before his words,

"Let it fire! Oh, let it fire! The shields will fall; this small fortress will implode upon itself, trapping you forever away from the earthbreath." He laughed again and drank the whole of the amrita. "Hmm. Rather sweet."

"Well," said Orah, "it was worth a try."

"I would have said the same. Not that it would have mattered, you know. Another body would have replaced this one within the hour if it killed me. But I must confess to an attachment for this particular frame."

"A common delusion," said the Etan. "Tell me one thing."

"Perhaps. I have all Eternity to do with as I please."

"Where is Leor?"

"Not that. I relish your anguished curiosity too much."

"Krishanu? And 'Sravasa?"

"Why not? You'll never see either of them again. They are imprisoned in Athalia in Tilvia. They were as gullible as you. And as blind."

"How about how you alone escaped Swayam's destruction?" asked Heramann grumpily.

"I didn't. But fortunately, I had just installed a marvelous invention on the clone bank to allow my disembodied spirit to re-enter it at will."

"Of course!" exclaimed Orah. "I should have guessed. Brilliant."

"Yes, I am... Refreshing to have one of Ganym to talk to, compared to those latter-day children... But, you know, it was rather silly: I made the slightest miscalculation, and could not make the cursed thing work... I floated around that dial for nigh onto two hundred thousand years, trying to nudge it to its correct position... I almost despaired, fearing even the nearly perfect structure of the clone bank might... at last decay... before I could... move the dial..."

"But finally you succeeded," breathed Heramann, fascinated in spite of his abhorrence.

"Yes... Or, to be quite truthful, no... Actually, chance. . . aided me. About ten thousand years ago... A minor... earth... tremor..." He stopped completely, his eyes bald and bulging, as if they betrayed the advent of terminal apoplexy.

"What's the matter with old cachinnation?" said the Vidyadhara sourly, "his transceiver on the blink?"

"By Narain's unending dream!" cried Orah, "Althea was right! It worked!"

"He's dead?" asked Marel, sounding more hopeful than any machine should logically be able to.

"No," said Heramann, "definitely not. And that is our boon, because if he were, we'd have a brand new Valin almost before we missed the old one. Right, Arama?"

"Catatonic. For a decade with luck. Possibly more, probably a little less. It worked! By the Seven! I believe now Zuriel's Tree will finish his seed."

Yarin fluttered madly around Orah's shoulder; the Etan laughed and said in Gurion-tongue, "Sorry, Arelan. I suppose my store of the earthbreath is sufficient to restore your form." He breathed on the hawk, returning the human body.

"Would you please tell me," flustered Yarin as soon as he could speak, "what is going on?"

"Simple enough," said Heramann, kicking through the hologram of the immobilized Valin, just to be sure. "Here stands the Enemy, terror of Martanda, frozen as he kept me (though from a different cause) for the next decade, more or less. All of which is too marvelous to believe, except for the simple fact we are apparently trapped in here... I don't suppose, Arama, he is actually vacationing somewhere in this lovely city, do you?"

"Not very likely. He would have no desire to be trapped in here either. He is rather more of a sadist than a masochist."

"But look here," said Yarin, "we walked (or rather, flew) in here easily enough. Certainly we should be able to leave."

"We can try," answered the Vidyadhara, "but I think this is entirely a remote-controlled operation."

"Orah," said Marel, "forgive a poor machine's ignorance. But does all this mean you intentionally drank from the Lethe? That it was all pre-conceived?"

"Not by my thought. But yes, I suppose Althea planned it, using my amnesia as the final fact to convince Valin I carried the amrita for a vastly different purpose."

"Did she foresee how it could awaken other sleeping memories in you?" asked Heramann.

"I think not. But Leor may have, for she remembered her life as Jaya from birth, and directed my steps to find Sesha. I believe she hoped it would be so."

"But why?" persisted Marel. "Why give him immortality? Even for a ten years' respite?"

"It is useful to have him in a specific, localized form. It is also true that he had immortality anyway, although he didn't realize it. By the equinox. The transfusions succeeded. Only such a massive overdose could short-circuit the process. We are fortunate he swallowed the bait."

"Can the future of Martanda truly lie with such bizarre machinations?" asked Yarin quietly, almost too quietly.

"I would be careful about judging the Etanai," cautioned Marel. "Remember your people."

"Life may appear complex, Areian," explained Orah. "But our actions have been linear, simple and straight. We have proceeded as we have because we knew no alternative."

The Vidyadhara, finding multidimensional metaphysics utterly boring, yawned and asked, "Arama, do you suppose you could direct your occasionally omniscient brain to find us a way out of here? Trapping Valin is wonderful, but of rather limited value if we are ourselves victims of his web."

~ ~ ~

They searched for a thoroughly unpleasant fortnight, but could find no exit. The rivers passed through the Fortress, but were separated from it by the same barrier of Emptiness that surrounded the whole of the city. Whenever the Etan felt for the earthbreath externally, he could find no echo of it at any distance — it was as if the forces enveloping the Fortress were infinite in all directions. The rest of Martanda (the whole of the Universe, for that matter) could have become (or could have always been) non-existent; they could be alone in a cosmos of nothingness, where the memory of any other life was but a delusion born of the madness of eternal loneliness. So perfect was the prison.

The buildings were as identical inside as out. Spotless empty room succeeded spotless empty room endlessly, as if the Fortress had been manufactured by a mad robot who had filled the valley with a single model far beyond the dictates of reason. To a creative spirit, the stripped sameness of pointless repetitions was such material as madness is made of.

After ten days of frustrating search, they found the only exception: on the bottom floor of an outer building was a small gray machine for synthesizing food and water, manipulating Emptiness to manifest substance in much the same way that the Etanai used the earthbreath. Yarin was the only one who required hydrocarbon nourishment to survive, but he perceived the evil nature of the machine's product and willingly declined it. Nor did he need it: Orah manifested abundantly for him from his reserves of the earthbreath. Someday, the Etan knew, he would have to become more sparing in the use of his substance. He might eventually find the merest motion too expensive. But that day was still far off in time; by then Yarin would be long dead. Orah lavished them all with marvelous feasts. For, rightly or wrongly, he blamed himself.

~ ~ ~

"Clever worm," muttered Heramann on the fourteenth day as they finished a floor-by-floor, room-by-room exploration of their forty-eighth building. "Not the smallest loophole anywhere."

"Now, don't turn sour on me," exclaimed Orah emphatically. "Any relative structure must be imperfect, must contain a flaw."

"Well," answered the Vidyadhara, "perhaps this place is the exception that proves the rule. But if anyone would know, it would be that gorlem —"

"That sleazy fellow will do us no good," said Marel disdainfully, "I feel it in my circuits. He is just as trapped as we are."

"We should at least try to catch him," said Yarin with sudden interest. "It could be no more boring than this routine, might even be fun."

~ ~ ~

It took three days of effort, but finally they cornered the machine on a ground floor. "Don't harm me!" it cried. "It's not my fault!"

"Start with your name," answered the Etan with good spirit. Yarin was right: the chase was more than just a break in the monotony, it had actually been enjoyable. Then he shuddered at the implication for his future that such a feeling imperfectly concealed.

"I was never given a name," sniffed the gorlem, "only a code."

"Why don't you tell us the truth," demanded Orah sharply. "You're also imprisoned here. There is no advantage to be gained by lying to us."

"What do you mean? I am a nameless gorlem."

"Heramann, scratch his skin a bit, about half a claw length deep or so. Enough to hurt, but not disable, not yet."

"No! Don't hurt me. Please! You're right. It's true. I'm not a gorlem." The black cube distended and distorted into a small Rakshasa, only one and a half times as tall as Yarin. "How could you possibly know?" it asked in its most pathetic voice. It sounded rather like a dying weasel.

"My friend occasionally has spells of great-mindedness," answered the Vidyadhara, keeping his grip on the captive extremely tight. "Not much escapes him at those times. He perceived this place deserted but for Valin and two Rakshasas."

"Two out of three isn't too bad," murmured Orah.

"Well, it looked as if Valin were here," continued Heramann. "I was deceived at less than three paces, you may recall. But I would like to know where the cell-mate of this abomination of all that is good is hiding."

"Valas left just after you arrived!"

"Just got up and walked out, huh? Try another one," said the Vidyadhara, squeezing the Rakshasa viciously around the midriff.

"Valas did, I tell you!" it squealed in fright. "The portal was open for an hour. Valas assumed the Etan's form to order the shields destroyed."

"There seems some possibility in that, Engineer," said Marel analytically. "It would be a logical act — for Valin. Though the Rakshasa must have failed, else the Enemy's holographic projection wouldn't still come through."

"Why? Why go to such lengths?" exclaimed Yarin incredulously. "If he wanted the Forbiddings down, why not simply turn them off?"

"They're wired to trigger a thermonuclear explosion that will annihilate half of Riversland when they are destroyed," replied the miserable Rakshasa. "My Lord Valin wants to strike a permanent blow here."

"Such a perverse mind," said Marel with what sounded very like a shudder.

"This still does not explain why he could not do it himself," persisted the Arelan. "Or could have, until he discovered catatonia."

"Well, he would have, of course," said the Rakshasa. "But don't you see how delicious it is for them to do it to themselves? My Lord Valin has a most exquisite sense of justice."

"That is the most twisted thing I have ever heard," said Yarin in an odd tone. Orah glanced at him curiously.

"Why are you still here?" asked Heramann, pressing the attack.

"I had no choice. Someone had to lead you to the Council Hall while Valas went through the portal."

"That I do not believe," said the Etan. "We would not have left so soon. Try again. But first your name, descendant of Salash."

"I am Vritrans, Azure Lord. I request your mercy."

"Keep to the point," ordered the Vidyadhara, violently squeezing it to stimulate its memory. "Why are you locked in here with us?"

"I don't see why I should tell you."

"Hrai, Arama. I think it wants me to kill it."

"That could be a favor," remarked the Arelan. "There is nothing worthwhile here, nothing of interest, nothing to do save wander through eternally duplicated and meaningless rooms."

The Etan looked at him again with great interest then said, "Heramann. Marel. Continue this, will you? Yarin, could we talk for a moment?"

"You want it kept alive, Commander?"

"For the moment. Airavata, see if you can loosen its tongue a little."

"Azure Lord, mercy!" squeaked Vritrans in terror.

"Pathetic little beast, isn't it?" said the Etan to Yarin in his best stage whisper.

As soon as they were behind closed doors, the Arelan began eagerly, "Thank you for asking me aside! I only just realized when we captured that creature that I have shamelessly forgotten to thank you for the return of my sight. Vision seemed such a commonplace thing before I was blinded. I missed almost all of the beauty around me everywhere, saw life only in superficial ways, colorless, flat. Now I long to see again the world of my youth: the variegated leaves of autumn, the golds and crimsons of sunsets, the cerulean blue of the winter sky. So much I did not appreciate when I had the chance; now there is nothing but these featureless whites and blacks repeating mindlessly, truest nothingness. This could be the hell earned by my earlier life."

"Is it within your power to transform hell into heaven, Yarin of the Syner?"

"I do not understand you."

"You — your people — aided the Asurs in leading Riversland toward misery and death. Could you reverse that? Could you bestow life, happiness?"

"That is what we live for! The hope that we may make amends."

"What would you do if you were free and your people no longer blind? And Valin and I were both removed from Martanda?"

"We would work with Maramel and the tribes of Gurion to create a better world. A world of harmony and love. And peace." He could no longer endure the Etan's gaze and stared flushing at the ground, feeling his soul an unobstructed vista.

"No, look at me, Yarin. Into my eyes. Tell me what you see."

"I see — a garden, beautiful! And a foreign land — no! A different world... A perfect civilization... But it decays. Corruption... War... Death... Hope... Rebirth..." His voice trailed off as he stared at the visions.

"No, continue. Vocalize."

"Refugees fleeing... Martanda, a new dream... Civilizations rising, decaying, falling, rising... The plague returns... No! Martanda burns!" He screamed and struck at the Etan, his fists flailing. "Murderer! No!"

Orah held him until the madness subsided. When he released him, the Arelan fell panting to the ground.

"I could not pledge the Redhawk nation to aid you in this," he said through tightly clenched teeth.

"Truly, I believe you. I do not doubt you have seen clearly. But you have read but one alternative. You must view the other." Orah flung out his empty hand; before Yarin on the dark pavement blossomed images of a second possible future.

The Arelan watched silently as the power of Valin increased unchecked, expanding and devouring first Martanda then the solar systems of star after star with his poisonous perversions. Fair it seemed for a time, but the civilization of high technology was sick, a pallid thing that secreted a corruption more vile than Yarin's mind could fully grasp. He watched as long as he could, then moaned and covered his eyes. "It is horrible. Horrible. Never have I dreamed such evil could exist. Annihilation is indeed preferable."

"Death can be the doorway to life, Arelan. Look again."

Martanda was burning still, cauterized by the Etanai, but now Yarin saw the Seachime Cathedral, freed from the planet, a starship once again, bearing a precious seed of life. Aboard was a full complement of refugees, racing toward Kanaan-dora and a future free from evil, for Valin was chained to the Martanda he had sought to absorb and corrupt.

Yarin bowed his head and said softly, "I was — we were — wrong, Azure Lord. Your way is hard. Hard, but better."

"If ever we find the exit from this tomb," said Orah, "your people will no longer be blind."

~ ~ ~

"Now, Heramann," argued the Etan, more than slightly frustrated, "Perfection in the created Universe is simply not possible. There must be a flaw somewhere. Does nothing at all penetrate this Fortress?"

"Not the least molecule," answered Marel. "Not even radiation. Nothing goes in or out past his planes of Emptiness."

They were on top of the building where they had captured Vritrans. They had brought the Rakshasa up to see if the somewhat more open air might help loosen its tongue. But so far, it had given no further information. The only significant change was that the

Vidyadhara no longer held it: Orah had ordered it released when it promised not to try to escape. The Rakshasa sat cowering on the low parapet, looking forsaken and utterly miserable.

"And yet," said Yarin thoughtfully, "we see the rivers flowing through here. Even if we cannot actually touch their water. Why?"

"He permitted an exception to tantalize us with impossible hope," said Vritrans, sitting up a little straighter with a rather different light in its eyes.

"So you admit you are a prisoner?" asked Orah, surprised.

"I see little reason to deny it longer. You have treated me honorably. Most of you, that is," it added, eyeing Heramann. "I could never satisfy the Emperor. Finally he locked me in here. A rather cruel end for a noble Rakshasa. I retain no love for him."

"The service of your people to him was always mistaken," said the Etan, taking full advantage of this apparent change of heart. "Unlike the Asurs, you are creatures of the earthbreath. You should not aid him."

"Engineer," said Marel, from disbelief ignoring this novel digression, "I remember that once you said you entered Ganym's civilization from the future. Could that, or something similar, be reproduced here? Transport us into the past? Or future?"

"Doubtful. To do it before, I passed the event horizon of a microscopic super-symmetric plasmic body — a 'black hole,' if you will, for the gravity there is so intense that even rays of light can't escape... And even if we could reproduce that experiment, it might not improve our position in the slightest: I calculated as well as possible the correct initial conditions — it was all completely theoretical, of course, no one had ever done it before — but I failed by a matter of almost three hundred thousand years! It may be truly random. One might come out anywhere in the past (even before the Universe existed) or the future (how about long after the last sun is dead?) or in any place — inside a supernova, or a million parsecs from the nearest galaxy."

"Maybe there is a higher intelligence governing it," theorized Marel, not so easily dissuaded. "You emerged in a neighboring star system, at a time when your presence was extremely useful, even critical, as I understand it. It could happen that way again."

"I wouldn't want to wager the future of humanity on that possibility," answered the Vidyadhara. "But, it hardly matters. Black holes are conspicuously absent in all this blackness."

"Yet some force absorbs all light," offered Yarin excitedly, eager to clutch at any possibility. Quite recently realizing the fate of his people was inexorably linked with his escape, his ardor had increased beyond all previous limits. His breast ached for the blind infants of the Arelai, guilty only by association. The thought that they would spend their entire lives without once knowing the wonder of vision tortured him. "The same thing, I would wager, has swallowed the firmament. It must be related to black holes. Somehow, it must be."

"I think not," said Marel sadly. "The Engineer's 'superplasmic bodies' must be an extension of the life of the earthbreath, a logical limit of certain of its principles. But Valin's Emptiness is of a different order of reality entirely."

"But look here," said Orah, trying out the improbable logic, partially because no possibility should be excluded, partially because he knew what so deeply troubled the Arelan, "Isn't it possible to step out of the present in other ways? I am certain Oathmaster Brihas did something of the sort to us in Maramel. Surely it can be done."

"How?" asked the Rakshasa in an odd tone.

"I don't know. Actually, I must confess I have not the vaguest idea. It would have to involve some interesting manipulations of the earthbreath, certainly. As things stand, I suppose I have nothing but time to work on it."

"Wait a minute!" cried Yarin. "I have another idea! Valin is a most cautious monster, isn't he, Vritrans?"

"Why, I suppose you could call him extremely meticulous," replied the Rakshasa, shifting from claw to claw uncomfortably. Heramann noted this and became a little more alert.

"He must have labored long here, weaving his accursed webs of Emptiness. During that time, I wonder if there were ever a danger he might have been trapped? That something might slip somehow and he would be isolated from the Universe?"

"What are you getting at?" asked the Rakshasa, trying but failing to conceal his agitation.

"What cautious miner would not provide an exit from the shaft? An escape hatch, impossible to seal from without."

"He did, of course, while he was perfecting the Fortress. But after it was done, naturally he removed the means." Vritrans eyed them furtively, seeking compassion or at least understanding in the tight semi-circle of enemies.

"Certainly he would have. But did he have time to finish his construction? Could he have foreseen the Outlander's escape from the Tower of the Corpse? Did he plan to lose the wars in Riversland? Or rather, was he not taken by surprise?"

"Absurd!" laughed Vritrans, suddenly calmed. "This Fortress has been perfected for two centuries." Yarin looked at it with surprise and wondered where his logic had failed.

"No!" exclaimed Orah, suddenly seeing the truth. "It would be far too much to expect Navril to commit two errors. He must have foreseen at least the potential of these losses. The trap he did succumb to was planned by Althea long in advance. We must certainly give him such credit.

"But was not one failure sufficient? I say he certainly intended for the shields to fall, thereby destroying the World Tree and Riversland and permanently imprisoning us here, either through the instrumentality of his Rakshasa impersonator or, if that touch of sadism failed, by his own action. The Rakshasa did not succeed, of course, else Valin's projection would have terminated. And his own hand cannot at the moment move, much to his chagrin, if he could but know. So, an abnormal and temporary situation is continuing.

"I think, Sir Rakshasa, you were here only to ensure our immediate conversation with Valin. It was essential for him to ascertain the harmlessness of the stolen amrita before he locked us away from the Universe. He must have planned his divergent schemes to the minute. And I think further you had every intention of leaving before the Fortress became inaccessible. You did not enter Valin's hall with us; perhaps you actually did leave, then discovered that something had gone awry and returned."

"You're crazy!" cried Vritrans, backing up the parapet. "I am as much a prisoner as any of you."

"Then why did you not tell us before? I say you only just invented the idea! I say you remained here only to make sure we don't find the doorway! Airavata!"

The Vidyadhara dove toward the Rakshasa, but Vritrans was faster. It leaped over the edge and plunged toward the concrete. Heramann raced after it, but was too late — the Rakshasa crashed into the pavement with a rather repulsive squashing sound like an overripe melon would make, meeting a similar end.

"Betrayed his master by its very loyalty," murmured the Etan. "I simply cannot understand what they see in him."

~ ~ ~

Half a month of further searching revealed absolutely nothing new. They surveyed the Emptiness everywhere, on all sides, above, below, yet found nothing that revealed the vaguest of differences. A glimmer of light was more than they hoped for, but some faint feeling of the earthbreath should certainly have touched them from somewhere. But there was nothing, nothing at all.

"Diabolically well hidden," muttered Yarin during their nightly meeting in the hall with the hologram of Valin. "I almost believe the Rakshasa was just another sadistic twist to this whole evil dream."

"How long 'til the equinox, Marel?" asked Orah.

"Five and a half days."

"What difference does that make?" demanded Heramann acrimoniously. "You accomplished your task. Valin stands there, frozen to the world. Althea can think of some way to arouse the Etanai to deal with him now — without telling Swayam a word."

"Perhaps. But Leor may have had other reasons for her urgency. She never fully explained why time was critical. Valin's impending immortality may be concomitant with other losses. Perhaps disastrous ones."

"Look at him standing there," said Yarin. "That place is probably the functional opposite of this. Impossible to enter without his permission. His officers must be going frantic, trying to pry him out of there."

"He may remain inaccessible for long periods. They may not even have missed him yet. He always was a quiet, reclusive boy," mused the Etan.

"Yes, there he stands," said the Vidyadhara, "the would-be ruler of Martanda. At his fingertips are the means to chain us here eternally, to desecrate who knows how much of the world. And somewhere nearby is the control for that cursed hatch, and somewhere —"

"The control for the transceiver!" cried Marel. "How many holes would he require? The answer has been visible all along!"

As one they descended onto the hologram, seeking the source of its transmission. Marel quickly discovered that it was projected from the floor beneath the stage. But the covering was immovable. The floor was made of the same sable metal as everywhere else in the Fortress, but was backed by a shield of Emptiness, as this was the lowest level.

"Well, now what?" said Heramann caustically. "Wander around again until we discover where this relays to?"

"We could search the exterior of this building for a transmission," said Marel doubtfully. "It could broadcast to the hatch."

"Whyever should it!" snapped the Vidyadhara, impatiently. "It could be an infinitesimal light-wire, embedded in the metal anywhere. We've got to open the cover."

"No," said Orah quietly, "I think I can — yes, I do feel it! I can follow its course. The earthbreath flows through it." He closed his eyes and raised his hands, then turned around in a slow circle before heading due north. At the wall he stopped and said, "Marel, exact measurements please. We don't want to waste any time outside." Then he led them from the building.

They traced its unerring line to the exact center of the Fortress. There the Etan felt the impulse beaming downward from the apex of the pyramid. From this spot alone, he could feel the subtle difference: at the heart of the artificial sun was the faintest shimmer of the earthbreath.

"I can pass through that," he said thoughtfully, "and so can Airavata. And possibly we can pull Marel through before the heat melts her. But I am afraid, Yarin, you would not survive."

The Arelan stared at him for a full minute as the meaning of these terrible words sank darkly through his soul. Then, straightening slowly but resolutely, he nodded, turned from them, and began walking blindly away.

Orah waited a long moment, then took four steps after him, clapped him on the shoulder and said warmly, "The Redhawk nation has passed its final test, Yarin. You have purified your race. Let us go."

"The heat —"

"The earthbreath is my life, Arelan. It is the essence of my soul. As long as I am not removed from its connection with the One, whatsoever I will in its presence is done. Let us — all of us — leave this accursed vale."

26. Malinnoir

The Starlord Ahanatar and the Lady Chali of the Doves walked through the wet snow where Orah and the others had disappeared over a month before. It would have been a beautiful night four years earlier, but now the black nothingness above seared into their souls like an eternal anathema. The lights from their small encampment did little to decrease the weight of the abomination overhead; they instinctively drew closer together to share the warmth of their hearts.

"But why tonight, Chali?" persisted Ahanatar. "Why should tonight be any different from last night or last week? The portal remains closed."

"I but intuit it, Gemstone. What more can I tell you? I feel the life quickening in the air and in my blood. Something wonderful lies about us in these winter mountains."

"Riversland is forever burdened by hope in preference to fact," he said, his tone at once gentle and subtly anguished. *How much like Nediva,* he thought, *how very much...* Then he drew her to him and kissed her, enjoying her surprise almost as much as her spirited response.

"I don't suppose that is quite what you meant, Lady of the Doves?" he said with a chuckle that began deep in his healing heart.

"It may have something to do with the coming spring, my Lord," she said, coloring slightly, but nevertheless eagerly staring up into his wise eyes for confirmation.

They walked on silently for a while, breaking snow toward the Forbiddings, then stood fifty paces from the Fortress and stared at its dark shields.

"Mother of Life," Chali suddenly sang in a full-throated and lovely voice, "hear my words!

> *There are among your children*
> *Those who remember the long pledge*

Those who honor thy love
Unfolding the mysteries of Being.
Mother of Life!
Do not forget your little ones
Crying to you from the secret garden
Wandering lost and afraid
Through the dark night."

As if in answer to her praise, a lone star appeared directly over the apex of the Fortress' pyramided Forbiddings. It drifted rapidly down toward them, growing much larger before resolving into its constituent members.

"By the Seven —" breathed Ahanatar, not sure if he were witnessing a miracle. Then he screamed and shouted his joy, over and over again until none of the others who had also patiently waited could hope to be asleep, until the star stopped before them and words became a superfluous redundancy, more than usually inadequate to express feeling: "Orah!"

Only Elid and Eliora, feeling responsibility for the Gurions, had left. As the others gathered around the four liberated ones, thumping their backs, embracing them, crying gladly over them (except for Marel, that is — no one thumped or embraced or cried over her — but then, she didn't mind, at least not so much), Orah discovered the blessed reward of hope. He silenced them finally and said, "My friends! Never can we be defeated. Not while one yet lives and loves as do you. This is the one truth the Enemy will never be able to distort or hide from us.

"Marasad King, is the fleet prepared?"

"It is, my Lord!"

"We sail on the equinox." He cut short their cheering with a hand. "But first, we must evacuate the whole of Riversland east of the Coastal Range. Not one must remain."

"But, Outlander!" cried Adrian, aghast. "The whole of Gurion? Whatever for? Brother says we can bring these Forbiddings down in a matter of hours. We would have done so weeks ago, but since that Rakshasa desired it, we deemed it imperative to wait."

"That was the height of wisdom," said the Vidyadhara, peering down his lizard's nose at the boy. "If these shields are destroyed, the eastern end of Riversland will become nothing other than so much radioactive dust."

"The Tribe of the Tree will not desert Vanas," said Ahanatar, his blue eyes flashing a cold fire. "Their love will hold them. No matter what the danger."

"No," answered the Etan slowly, as much from sadness as pity, "I suppose they are that stiff-necked, even though the World Tree does not need and never has needed their aid in the — no, never mind. It is proper that they do so. But everyone else will proceed to Maramel as quickly as is humanly — or mechanically — possible. Yarin will explain further, but I must continue on, to seek my Leor before our time is lost."

"She was not there," murmured Zuriel as if it were no news to him. Orah looked at him curiously, but made no other comment.

"Outlander!" exclaimed Adrian, his volume attempting to mask his nervousness, "never have you requested my presence. And I have not forgiven myself for failing to enter Valin's Fortress with you. I would accompany you now."

"Your body is that of a boy —" began the Vidyadhara.

"He slew the Rakshasa, Orah," interrupted Sevilien, the controlled calmness in her voice but partially concealing her awe.

"He alone knew it was not you," added Hamar, sharing her feeling.

"I have nothing else to do," pleaded Adrian. "All these others are immersed in their various tasks — or each other," he added, glancing with vague contempt at Ahanatar. "I cannot recall ever being more bored."

"Very well," responded the Etan, never fond of denying any reasonable request. "Marel, one attack sphere, please. Airavata, let's go."

"Where — ?" asked Chali, demonstrating perfect mastery of the earthbreath as an amethyst and silver tiara floated from her forehead to Orah, symbol of Riversland's blessings.

"The transmission comes from the northwest," he answered, surprised and pleased at her skill. He responded to the gift of the diadem by bathing her in a shower of golden light, each ray filled with perfect knowledge. "We will follow it to its source. If we are not back by the equinox, sail. We shall follow you."

"Azure Lord," implored Yarin, reaching toward him, "my people —"

"On the equinox, Arelan. Their sight would have returned no matter what they had become or resolved. I do not believe in eternal execrations. You yourself have grown enough — you can decide whether or not to tell them. Coming, Adrian of the Gurions?"

Together they mounted the Vidyadhara, the Lion Elder seeming very small and inconsequential beside the Etan. Heramann lunged upward, circled once in farewell, then was off, beating his mighty wings as if raging to conquer space and time to return Arama to his Jaya. The attack sphere was already overhead; the lights of its component Protectors bringing the memory of dappled beauty to counterpoise the utter nihility of Valin's night.

So the Lion Elder Adrian is the one who fulfills Zuriel's prophecy, thought Ahanatar, feeling a pang of sorrow.

Chali, experiencing still the sublimity of Oathmastery, from empathy knew his state fully. She squeezed his hand and looked up at him with love blessing her warm hazel eyes. He returned her gaze with thankfulness and accepted the correctness of this way. Thus far had his Vow taken him.

Solon, staring wistfully after his brother, exclaimed, "Yarin! Tell us this tale!"

~ ~ ~

"What is that valley, Marel? I feel strongly drawn to it." It was late afternoon. They had flown steadily and fast over the Majestic Mountains, pausing only twice at relay stations built high on mountain peaks.

"It is Malinnoir, Arama. The Retreat of the Oathmasters." The valley opened wide and pleasant beneath them, a perfect vision of verdancy.

"Why is it not frozen down there?" asked Adrian.

"Hot springs, Lion Elder," answered the Protector. "The valley is covered with them."

"I would like to visit there someday," said Orah dreamily, remembering Vashti and Ganym's Surasa. "It must be a lovely place. But rather lonely now with the Oathmasters barred from Martanda."

"I don't know if it is important, Arama," said the Protector. "But there is in fact one still left, a little old lady —"

"What? How could it be? Why didn't you tell me?"

"You did not ask. The last survey here was last summer." Which fact did not even imperfectly answer the earlier questions, but Marel felt she should say something and nothing else came to mind.

"Order the attack sphere to follow the line of the transmission. We will catch them before they leave Riversland."

"If we are delayed?"

"They should continue on until they meet resistance or find the source of the broadcast. Then they should return and report."

~ ~ ~

The Malinnoir Valley was indeed lovely, its beauty delicately structured around a theme of profound simplicity. Fruit trees planted artistically near the hot springs were flowering already in the first progression of spring, belying the adamant winter cloaking the mountains above. Most of the trees had the look of several missed prunings, but otherwise were vibrantly healthy.

Numerous small rainbow marble buildings dotted the slopes, seemingly randomly placed; their columns and porticoes spoke warm invitations to the travelers. Next to the stream running the length of the valley was a large and brilliant silver spire, similar in shape to those of Maramel, but ornately sculpted over its entire surface.

They stood before it, examining the markings, but none of them had seen such representations before. It was like a strange hieroglyphic, but even Orah with his thousands of remembered lives could not recall the like.

"Most bizarre characters I've ever encountered," mumbled Heramann, translating into his falcon form and alighting on the Etan's shoulder. "I wonder if Swayam —"

"I doubt it very much," creaked an old voice from behind them.

They spun around to see a wizened old, old lady, wearing a faded azure robe and the fairest skin Orah had yet seen in Gurion, not seven paces behind them. A ring set with a single large girasol on the index finger of her right hand flashed iridescent rays at them from the dying sun.

"How did you approach us so quietly?" demanded Adrian, very much on edge. A Gurion never liked such surprises.

She smiled gently but made no reply.

"She did not," supplied Marel, in her most matter-of-fact tone, reserved for moments of gravest uncertainty. "She was not there."

"She is an Oathmaster," concluded Orah. "The earthbreath radiates from her in strength and glory. And yet, how so? The firmament is dead."

"Not dead, my Lord," she responded in her ancient voice, "but Martanda is being torn from it. The Enemy desires a world. For experimentation."

"That does not explain your presence, ma'am," said Adrian, rather tartly.

"The sun yet shines on our world, does it not? I partake of that radiance and remain here."

"Forgive us! We are the guests and behave rudely. I am Orah of Etan; this is Adrian, Starlord, Horse Lord and Lion Elder of Gurion; this is Airavata of the Vidyadharai; this is Marel, a Protector suzerain of Maramel."

She curtsied briefly to each, her lithe movement surprising in so aged a frame. Then she said, a hint of springtime beginning to melt her tone, "I am also remiss. There are so few visitors anymore... I am Roella of Malinnoir, the last Oathmaster of Martanda."

"My Lady, I am honored. Brihas told me rays of the daystar walked our world. I consider myself blessed by our fortunate meeting."

"So, he got a stroke or two in before his light failed, eh? That tale would be worth hearing." She laughed, and it was not a crone's cackle, but seemed an innocent mirth from a different and eternally youthful world. A brief vision of Ganym before its corruption flashed in Orah; Heramann remembered Calantha as it was in his childhood; Adrian re-experienced Gurion before the First Redhawk War; and Marel floated for a short moment in a pleasant memory she had not known she possessed. Then Roella continued, her ever-softening voice drawing a gossamer veil between each of them and their experiences, "It is nearly sunset. Would you care to share my repast, then spend the night here? It might help you, to continue fresh with the dawn."

"I thank you," said the Etan, still tasting the sweetness of his vision, "hospitality in a foreign land is always welcome. But we are bent upon a most urgent quest. Regretfully, I must decline."

"It is your freedom that deludes you now, Arama. I tell you plainly, Lord of Etan, you will never find your Leor if you leave here tonight."

"It seems," said Orah, staring at her, "there is more here than the surface reveals... We accept with all good will your kind offer, Roella of Malinnoir."

"Marvelous!" she cried, clapping her hands and hopping around as if she were a school girl. "My home is just over here." She began walking away.

The Etan started after her, but the Vidyadhara cried, "My Lady! Half a moment! The markings on this spire are unparalleled in our experience. Could you elucidate?"

"Later, perhaps," she said without turning her head or slackening her pace. "Now I want to share my dinner with you."

~ ~ ~

Roella would answer no more questions, but busied herself industriously in her small kitchen, leaving her guests to amuse themselves in the other room. It was sparse by practically any standards. The only object of interest (indeed, the only object at all other than the stone bench generously matted with heather, the stone table and four wooden and hemp chairs) was a small replica of the carved spire on the stream, affixed to the center of the table.

"It seems she is of the belief paucity is inherent in spirituality," opined Marel.

"Goodness," said the Vidyadhara testily, "how our sphere does run on, doesn't she, Arama? Makes me wonder about the state of her lubricants."

"Heramann," said Orah, forestalling the Protector's rebuttal, "this small model is an exact similitude of the original. It is as perfect a reproduction as I can recall ever having encountered."

"Probably laser holographic work," said Marel excitedly, forgetting her riposte.

"Here we are," said Roella, bearing two full platters in each hand with another two precariously balanced on each arm. "If you could help me - thank you, Orah. There... I heard you commenting on my work. Do you like it?"

"It is perfectly done," he said, absolute sincerity covering well his doubt.

~ ~ ~

The meal ran rather too heavily to dried and stewed fruits to suit Adrian well. But his appetite was proportionate to his size; there was a small cheese he claimed as private property. He easily finished first and, promising to return momentarily, went out into the gloaming.

Marel was hovering over the spire, her lights flashing at it. Adrian strolled down to her and asked without much curiosity what she was doing. "Recording it for the files," she answered eagerly. "There was no mention of it in the earlier reports. That I find most peculiar."

"Perhaps it hasn't been here very long?"

"How could it come then? That frail old human could hardly carry it."

"I'm not altogether convinced of that. An Oathmaster has many strange powers." Adrian sighed as he stared at the blank sky. "I wonder why we wait here," he said, not expecting a reply.

"Arama seeks what he has lost. He dare not overlook the least clue, however doubtful the source."

"I know, I know. But Valin has her. Has been stealing her blood."

"Adrian!" cried Heramann from Roella's porch. "The Oathmaster desires your tale."

"Foolish boy, have you not yet realized the Enemy's dominion is as vast as Martanda?" said Marel softly after the Lion Elder.

~ ~ ~

Three large beeswax candles formed a triangle around the replica of the spire on the table. The dishes were gone; the shadows from the model fell trembling in three directions. Oddly, one pointed directly at the Etan and one at the Vidyadhara; the third was reaching toward Adrian's vacant seat. By accident, or careful design?

"Ah, good, sit, sit," crooned Roella. "I would hear the tale of your life. Strangers are a rare boon in this valley, a vintage wine to be enjoyed to the dregs."

"I am to be first, then?" Adrian asked, sitting again in his chair. "Very well, but there is not very much in the telling. Deeds of treachery and valor, yes, but little of import other than my few moments with the Outlander as he passed among us." With vague

"Althea must have told you I was fully conscious from birth. That is why I could not remain in Etan — the daily sight of you there, unknowing of our shared past, would have been unbearable. I suppose I would have learned to adjust, but I weighed the strands of time and saw the faintest possibility of awakening in you what you had forgotten: uncomfortably far in the future, but nevertheless viable. So I convinced Althea to carry me from the Immortal City, swearing her to secrecy. From her good spirit, she built my home Ezera, the hill where first you danced in Riversland.

"I spent happy ages there, enjoying the silence of communion with the Mother. But one day, the thought came to travel northward, that there was a need for me in the unknown lands across the Lethe. I dismissed it as a fanciful distraction for years, but at last decided to journey beyond the Great Ridge and see if there were in fact peoples other than the Etanai in Martanda.

"I entered Gurion long before Ahaman founded his kingdom and found a peaceful but barbaric race. At first, I thought they were simply uneducated; but then I discovered traces of a much higher civilization, decayed and fallen many millennia before. With further analysis, I learned the Gurions of that age were universally affected by a strange moral blight. It reminded me sadly of the corruption of the latter days of Ganym.

"I passed into Maramel before Dalmara and the first Maralords, and discovered our ship. Central was most helpful in explaining what had happened after I died on Ganym, but he was also convinced Swayam had destroyed the Enemy. He felt the current troubles with humanity were part of an inevitable cyclic pattern, nothing more."

"He would," murmured Heramann. Orah silenced him with an icy glance.

"Throughout Riversland," continued Roella without noticing either, "particularly among the happy fair-skinned race along the White River, I heard wild stories, strange rumors and impossible myths about a hidden valley in the Majestic Mountains and a people vastly different from the common humanity of the world, more evolved than even the Etanai.

"Eventually, I discovered Malinnoir, and found the extraordinary tales were, if anything, too conservative: the

Oathmasters understood the entire range of the powers of the One. We of Etan have reaped the highest benefit of that primal force of the earthbreath — the amrita is its purest essence — yet have with only one or two exceptions not as well known it.

"For long millennia I lived here, knowing the One as never on Ganym. A hundred centuries passed as I knew the Good and desired no other life or world.

"Then was I betrayed by my prolonged innocence. I remember still every detail of the high meadow where I sat among the late summer alpine flowers, dreaming of perfection throughout the expanding spheres. Over the copen mountains you came striding to me, my Lord, a lovely song of Ganym psalming on your lips. You laughed with me as you told me you had discovered your past in Etan. I had no doubt of you, how could I have? The One burned in you more brilliantly than I dreamed I would ever see.

"But, of course it was a superb lie; I have lived in slavery ever since, slowly decaying as my reserves of life have been stolen from me.

"After many years, I by chance learned how to project my spirit through my stolen blood. Patiently I filled these mnemonic images with life, though the effort drove me further into the ultimate nihility which has become my certain destiny. I fail now; I can no longer give the faintest energy for these eidetic bodies into my cells; there is nothing left of me but the mournful memory of stolen hope. I am lost and alone, perhaps the only such doleful being anywhere in Narain's created time."

"Roella," said Orah, softly, to match her failing words, "where is Leor? Where is your master form?" He leaned close over her.

She reached up a shaking cerulean hand and gently touched his lips. As it fell weakly back again, she whispered still more softly, "Arama, beloved, must you seek more pain? I tell you, my prison is unflawed. I have tried to break its wall for forty-nine centuries. These projected forms were the only way; I am too weak now to nourish them or create more."

"But don't you see! Leor is *inside.* From outside, we could succeed."

"Don't you think I've tried? He has built it of the same Emptiness he surrounded you with at the Fortress. It is as impenetrable as it is inescapable."

"One - oh - seven point three hours," she answered without the slightest inflection.

"What difference does that make?" asked the Vidyadhara impatiently. "Valin is catatonic. Why this persistent assumption the equinox remains important?"

"It's logical. Consider that Leor is wholly ignorant of what is happening in the world. How she can have kept faith and hope alive at all is a miracle; I suppose Navril may have actually nourished it for his own ends. But only in twisted ways. We cannot assume she has been told anything true since she was first shut away from the world. Although she created four projections in Riversland, I believe she knows nothing of them, not even if they succeeded in gaining independent form and life. I conclude, therefore, she set a limit to her hope; indeed, knowing her, I assume she expended her last energies to create this tetrad of mnemonic bodies only because she had selected a specific date. I feel it is the equinox for many reasons, logical and intuitive; perhaps the most important being that the Enemy would have gained true immortality from her blood by then, thereby accomplishing one of her two great purposes in returning. A definite limit, then the end."

"But what could she do?" asked Adrian. "You people are indestructible."

"To the Etan is gifted an alternative," said the Vidyadhara. "At any time, she may coalesce her life into a single thought and gift it back to the Mother, point to infinity."

"How did you know that, Airavata?" asked Orah, staring at his friend with a new respect.

"How could it be otherwise? An immortal spark can exist at all only if in continual contact with the One. It may be possible to remove all dimensions from that point, so that it loses all ability to act in the world; but the contact itself is severable never. Even Valin at his core has that, else he would not be. His manipulations of Emptiness may succeed in chaining the motions and senses of others; but their existence, never."

"Never without free will," agreed Orah. "The surrender back to the Ascendant Source is the ultimate secret and ability. But not just of the Etanai, Heramann. Of all."

"And so," said Adrian, stretching his mind to grasp the difficult concepts, "you believe Leor will close her life in the created Universe? Return to Para?"

"Yes, you could say it like that. Yes, in the sense you mean it. Although your words implying action might lead to confusion, for 'close' and 'return' imply distance and time. But in fact, there is neither. The spark of individuality is forever established in its Source of universality; it can never be taken from it, regardless how lost or distorted that fact may become. It is a simple reality, a natural law, like gravity. Life *is.* To do or to perceive, Life needs the mechanics of a manipulating medium — the earthbreath, the powers of Evolution. Without them, Life can only *be.* This is how the Enemy imprisons — by cutting off the One from its ability to express through the earthbreath — locking Being away from becoming, as it were. Yet how he manages to do such a thing is inconceivable to me. Logically it seems impossible."

"But, if I follow you correctly, this means Valin himself is a manifestation of the One!"

"Didn't I just say that?" said Heramann. "In his heart is the One. How could it be otherwise? There is hope in this, Adrian of the Lions. If we can open him to that perfection, his illusory outer form will fall."

"He has encrusted his own heart with a prison of Emptiness," said the Etan. "This he aspires to do to all of Creation."

"I do not understand you! Is not evil absolute?"

"It is eternally so. The illusions of the Enemy can never be fully destroyed, for at the core of every existing object is dissolution hiding. Sometimes it is more manifest, sometimes less, but always lurking behind all life. But when Emptiness is contained and controlled, it is not evil; rather, it is the force that opens a pathway for further progress. For the sapling to grow, the seed must be destroyed. This force is the inverse of the earthbreath, its functional opposite."

"The essence of the motion of the Creative is the silence of the Receptive," added the Protector. "Else there could be no expansion of life."

"I have often thought we over-engineered the spheres, Arama," said Heramann, looking at her disapprovingly.

"What are you still doing here?" asked Orah sharply. "I told you to contact Central. Why didn't you go?"

"You didn't tell me what to say," she answered with a sniff.

"Under-engineered, Airavata. Listen, Marel. Relay the hologram to Central. Have him decipher it. Highest priority. Also, I want to know if anywhere in Riversland there is a pocket not reflecting the earthbreath. If he does not know of any — no, even if he does — I want the Protectors to map the entire land to the resolution of one ten-thousandth of a league. Within forty-eight hours. And set up a permanent relay so you don't have to fly off again. Understood?"

"Understood," she said as she shot into the sky.

"Let's get some sleep," said the Etan as he stared after her, a rapidly diminishing star. "Maybe we'll think more clearly in the morning."

"I just don't know where we went wrong with those spheres," said Heramann, lighting one of the candles.

27. A Question of Balance

Marel returned just as they finished their breakfast.

"It is done," she reported. "Sorry for the delay, but I had to travel quite far before I could contact anyone. But now you will have permanent transmission capability to Central within a few more hours."

"Did he recognize the inscriptions?"

"No, he assumes as you that Roella developed a personal code. He expects it deciphered within the day. He thought the suggestion those were star maps highly intriguing and is using that as the keystone of a preliminary hypothesis.

"I also contacted the attack sphere tracing Valin's broadcast. They passed two more relay towers in the mountains, then headed out to sea just before dawn. I told them to leave units periodically to keep a channel open to us."

"Very wise," said Orah warmly. "The Counselors would be envious of your foresight. Did Central have any suggestions where Leor's prison might be?"

"None," she answered as her lights flashed a brief pattern of pleasure because of the compliment. "He was particularly silent about it. But the mapping commences."

"Good... So, where first, Airavata?"

"I haven't the vaguest idea, Arama. Somewhere around here? This is where she met Valin, wasn't it? So he probably had his trap set nearby."

"Possibly. He wouldn't have wanted to arouse anyone's interest by his work. It would have to be in a fairly secluded area. These mountains could hide any number of secret little valleys."

"I wonder," said Adrian thoughtfully, "if Ahanatar might have intuited a profound truth. His painting placed Evana on the Cliff of the Foundling."

"That is a thought — yes! I am powerfully drawn there. I suppose we might as well search there as anywhere."

"That is a long flight," said Heramann, "nearly twenty-four hours. If there is nothing there —"

"We would still have three days to come back if the Protectors find anything here. But I don't think they will. I feel nothing in these mountains now."

~ ~ ~

Orah, with Heramann as falcon on his left shoulder and Marel floating near his right, stood with Adrian on the Cliff of the Foundling and stared over the world, coloring in the light of early dawn. The abutment was exactly as Ahanatar had drawn it: a brutal expression of granite falling in sheer planes on three sides. The fourth side was the termination of the Great Ridge north of the Lethe. To the west lay the ocean, brume-covered in the awakening day; to the north lay the rolling plains of Southern Maramel, late winter field and forest disappearing into hazy brown and turquoise distance. The Cathedral was just visible; the Etan was reminded of his first sight of Maramel with Brihas, Ahanatar, Nediva and Hamar.

The land was beautiful; it wrenched his heart to think it might be lost. He looked away from it to study the large obelisk of silvery basalt on the very point of the promontory.

"It commemorates Ahaman, First Lion King of Gurion," explained Adrian. "He was found as a babe on this spot. Ahaman created Gurion, uniting the warring tribes of the day into one socially integrated unit. Science, medicine and the arts achieved their first flowering during his reign. He never claimed it, but he was of your race: his skin was cerulean."

"No, that is impossible. None of Etan have journeyed to the north, save only Leor and myself. That history must have distorted with time."

"Why would anyone have invented so improbable a tale? Before Evana came among us, the only knowledge of the azure race was in Ahaman's Prophecy of your coming."

"I don't know if I should interrupt you, but you might be interested to know that this monument is a counterfeit," said Marel, flashing an indigo light at it.

"What do you mean? My grandfather's great-grandfather erected it —" began Adrian, but then realized that could not be true, for there was not the least sign of weathering of the stone. It looked as if it had been quarried yesterday. "Why in Martanda would anyone steal Ahaman's obelisk?"

"It is not stone at all," said Marel, meticulous as always. "Textured steel alloy... I could nudge a corner of it with my laser..."

"If you don't mind," said Adrian, edging away, "perhaps you could wait until we move back a few hundred paces." Suddenly it was uncomfortably reminding him of Roella's spire in the Malinnoir Valley.

"I do not think that will be necessary," said a feminine voice from the monument. A polychromatic but tenuous vapor flowed from it, coalescing gradually to form a translucent human shape.

"Ravi, I presume," said Orah with his deepest bow.

"Her shade, Arama," she answered, floating before them. "A projection of one of Leor's projections, if you will. Roella alone you actually met in the flesh."

"You each created a storage place for your power? Roella's in the spire, yours here in the obelisk, Evana's somewhere near her tomb, Jessie's on the ridge where I met her?"

"Exactly so. It was necessary to focus the energy as it gathered: the ability to manipulate the earthbreath came slowly through the blood; it needed to be complete for independent life to begin. After the flesh was slain — Jessie by the lion; Evana by Jyot; myself by the Asurs of the Tower — our projected minds returned to their place of gathering, awaiting Leor's freeing to be able to reunite with her."

"Each of the focal points retains not only the residual energy, but also the memories of your experiences in Riversland? That was their second purpose?" asked the Vidyadhara didactically, trying to overcome his extreme discomfort at this peculiar business of the living dead. How had such a beautifully simple thing as existence become so thoroughly complex? Did the eternal conflict with the Enemy of Being necessitate such bizarre convolutions? Twisting life and love into strange inhuman parodies of themselves? If there was no other reason for condemning Valin, this partially vivified memory of Jaya would be a more than sufficient cause. For the first time since they escaped the Fortress, Heramann felt the sanguine anger welling up. He hopped from the Etan's shoulder and resumed his lizard form, the more easily to pace his frustration into the rock of the cliff.

"Yes," answered Ravi, looking at the Vidyadhara with compassion, understanding his dark mood, "three of us still believe reunion may occur, although there is certainly no apparent reason. Roella alone despaired and sought to modify you."

"To forget your four-fold existence?" asked Orah, too busy trying to understand to notice Heramann's fey mood.

"No, only to convince you Leor was already dead. We others disagreed — Jessie the most strongly — but felt if it were not meant to be, she would surely fail and you would continue the search. Yet I must confess to surprise you came here! This is why it took me some time to gather my residual potencies enough to be able to come out."

"Why? Where would I go?"

"Why, to speak again to Evana or Jessie. You know where to contact their shades. We all assumed you would go to one or the other of them. Coming here was an extremely low probability. I'll wager they're both disappointed."

"I assumed you were all more interconnected: if one of you died, all must lose your power. I did not understand how fully independent each of the four of you was."

"Five of us, actually. Though the first did not manifest as intended at all. I didn't know enough of the mechanics, and put too much potency into my first attempt. She developed without memory of who she was; the effort so drained Leor that it took several millennia to build up the will to try again. It was a rather melancholy time of hopeless dejection."

"Who?" choked Adrian, a half-crazed expression in his eyes.

"Who was the first projection? Is that your question? You were right, Lion Elder, Ahaman was of Etan. He was Leor's forgetful first."

Heramann stopped pacing long enough to stare at her; Adrian was divided between the desire to fall at her feet and run away as quickly as possible down the ridge. With a supreme effort, he dedicated himself to stability in the storm and did neither. He said, his voice sounding strangled from inconsonant emotions, "So. The royalty of Gurion is the offspring of amnesia."

Ravi smiled tenderly at him, doing what she could to ameliorate his distress, "Even though forgetful of himself, Ahaman read the threads of time correctly and knew the future. Were it not for his work, Valin would not stand paralyzed today. There is no infamy for your race in this." How could simple knowledge cause pain? She had not expected such a response. Were the Enemy's roots truly so deep?

Orah, realizing at last that two of his companions were most uncomfortable by this conversation with Ravi's shade, decided to attempt immediate resolution. "A brief respite. Pathetically short at best if we fail. Ravi, where is your master form? Where is my Jaya?"

She looked at him with perfect love and answered the long question of his complex search with utter simplicity (as always, the mark of unalloyed truth), "Where first you danced in Riversland, brother. She whom you seek lies imprisoned within the hill named Ezera."

~ ~ ~

Silence sang like the murmur of versicolored waters over the Cliff of the Foundling. The dawning wind had died; even the morning birds were stilled, as if to honor the wonder of Orah staring dumfounded at Leor's projection's shade. Then the Azure Lord of Etan threw back his head and whooped his unbounded joy, for he believed now, believed to the furthest range of his being, that he would free her.

"Of course," said the Vidyadhara, no longer the least upset, "of all places, she would have been the most comfortable there, the least suspicious of Valin. It must have been all too easy for him."

"Time!" cried Orah.

"Seventy-one and a half hours," said Marel.

"Ravi, do you talk to the others?"

"Yes, except Roella, now that her spire is destroyed."

"Can you unite into one?"

"It might help? Yes, I suppose we could. We'd have to be together — in space, I mean. We are limited to a short radius of our focal points."

"Very well. Central, are you listening?"

"Raptly," he answered through Marel. "Most interesting system. What will you humans come up with next?"

"Listen. I want every available man, woman and child of Maramel and Gurion taken to Ezera immediately. We're going to have as much life-force there as we can manage within forty-eight hours. And I want this obelisk brought there, and Evana's power source, and Jessie's.

"I only wish Roella could be added to you others."

"Possibly she can," said Ravi. "When she died, where did her energy go? Did you see it?"

"It is here," said Adrian, taking the damaged model from his tunic. As with Heramann, the prospect of action eclipsed all other concerns.

"We can begin now, then. Here, place her so that she touches my obelisk."

Adrian leaned the model against the monument; an ethereal mist passed from it into Ravi. "It worked," she said, becoming distinctly less transparent. "I am increased. She of me who was Roella apologies for attempting to alter your intention. I was overcome by despair at the loss of the Oathmasters. I saw no hope."

~ ~ ~

The conglomerate of the energies of Jessie-Evana-Ravi-Roella stood, substantial as ever in life, on the top of Ezera with Orah. The surface of the hill sparkled in brilliant silver and gold eddies in response to their presence. "Ready when you are, beloved," she said.

Together they thrust their uniting energy through the dancing life of Ezera at the inner layer of Emptiness that surrounded the living quarters turned prison. Thrust it and were repulsed as the hill responded in wild geysers of sanguine and ebony; threw it again more forcefully and were the more violently turned back. For an hour they strained at that unyielding wall; Ezera answered as if it were madly dancing the end of the world. But they made not the slightest progress.

"We need more energy," Orah said finally. "Let us wait until all have gathered. All the good of Riversland shall share in this mighty assault of Valin's evil. It must fall."

"I wonder what will happen to me if it does not," mused the united energies of the four projections. "I suppose that even she in me who was Roella never wholly gave up hope. We all kept our mnemonic units perfectly intact, desiring reunion... Not that we didn't always feel we were truly Leor," she continued dreamily, as

Ezera echoed her feelings with a slowing syncopation of turquoise and emerald, "even though we knew we were most certainly not, were in fact nothing but the smallest fraction of her spirit.

"If she returns to the Source tomorrow dawn (as I assume she will if we cannot break Valin's curse), I suppose I will be drawn in with her. That would be all right, returning to Narain. But I would miss the life here with you."

Orah put an arm around her and said, "We won't think of defeat. We will only assume the prison can be unmade. We'll try again tonight and continue until it falls. I only wish we could let her know we are trying to break it. Maybe if she pushed from the inside at the same time —"

"No, there is so little left of me there, I doubt I could do a thing... She must be preparing now for the final in-pouring of her spirit."

"The way you change pronouns is bewildering. I sometimes have trouble remembering where you are."

"It is understandable, isn't it? Oh, I need some beauty! Look with my eyes. The world dances again in the garb of spring. Let us walk together through Riversland and remember other seasons of beginning." Ezera reflected her thought with a wonderful display of delicate vernal blossoms of extremely rich yet perfectly harmonious tints.

"Why not? There is nothing more to do here until tonight. I share your need and desire. Have you seen Airavata lately?"

"No. But can't we be alone today? If it is possible to find room among these millions you gather here."

"That's why I'm looking for him. Fly us out of here for a while."

"I'm not sure of my range. Well, no, I guess I could go pretty far. I feel better than we did in quadruplicate."

"Here comes Marel. I'll have her carry us up the ridge, near where you made me climb as Jessie. What a night that was."

"You reintegrated beautifully. I was so proud of you."

"Arama," said the Protector. "The attack sphere reports heavy gorlem resistance over the North Mereds. They are returning at full speed."

~ ~ ~

They wandered down the ridge in silent communion for long hours that seemed all too fleeting, as the land's reawakening life heightened their rapt enjoyment of their reunited presence. After the sun had well turned toward its setting, they sat where they had four years before and looked over Gurion, remembering improbable experiences, sharing impossible dreams.

Finally, knowing they must return to their labor below, he began softly, "Such a beautiful land, Leor. I wonder — why, what's wrong?"

"I — I blush to hear you call me that. I am naught but her projected energy. I am not an independent being. By tomorrow dawn, I will be reabsorbed into her — or die. It is not proper."

"I suppose not," he said heavily. "But sitting with you here is exactly as if I sat with you here. With all of you, I mean, not just a reflected image."

"I know," she said, squeezing his arm and leaning closer into him. "And I love Riversland too, Arama, as much as I am capable. It is everything we lost on Ganym. The Gurions are strong and true; the sensitive Maralords, exquisite artists. I wonder if we shall find other such examples of beauty on the other continents? If not, these two races alone seem a more than sufficient seed to found a new world."

"If you add the Etanai, it is truly more than sufficient."

"You don't really think they would come, do you?" The ache in her voice was as much from frustration as sorrow. Would it always be necessary to stand alone before the Darkness?

"No. No, you're right of course. I don't. They would not see the need or share the desire. If Martanda falls, Swayam will sail Etan out of this system altogether. Yet my heart grieves at this and declares that a few might pursue an independent path, might join us in our long pledge to serve these children. Althea, perhaps, for she not only knows them, but empathizes with all her spirit. And where she goes, Bhishaj will surely follow. And 'Sravasa and Krishanu must have discovered the mortal races during their north-westward journey. I hope they have learned to love them as we do. Others might come as well, if they could be made to look away from Etan for a time. 'Ishtar, perhaps. And Malinda, Mirabeth and Mirabel. And 'Vanya. And even Lemuel-Tamara. If not, perhaps we

will be able to recall the Oathmasters. There is much to hope for."
He did not know how much he believed what he said, but it offered
at least a marginal solace.

"Arama," she said, the regret in her tone become almost a solid
substance, "it is late. We'd best go." She stared over the world she
was about to lose for the balance of Eternity, trying to press it into
the deepest recess of her memory. For she knew she would be
drawn back from Narain if the impression was engraved deeply
enough.

"I suppose so, Jaya," he agreed, the futility of his attempt to
offer mere words on the altar of bereavement tasting like the
bitterest of galls. Yet even as the melancholy threatened to engulf
him, he again attempted to affect with language what action alone
could hope to alter, "I said we should not think of it, but I suppose
I must be pragmatic and admit the possibility: if you are gone
tomorrow, I want you to know I love you. Though Infinity and
Eternity stand between us again, I will find you again. Somehow I
will learn how to regain your soul from that withdrawn, to wrest it
one more time from the Grandfather."

"Hush," she said, putting her fingers to his lips. "Such thoughts
are not right. Or necessary."

He stared at her for a long moment, then, throwing his arms
around her, embraced her fiercely. "Jaya, I — I —"

"No, Arama, no. I know. I know. I love you too."

~ ~ ~

They began at sunset, Orah and Leor standing on the summit of
a bronzed Ezera; the Protectors filling the skies over them; the
peoples of Riversland a living sea at their feet. Even the Tribe of the
Tree had come, bearing the ultimate gift of a petal of the World
Tree's only flower. Among all those who had known and loved the
Azure Lords in Riversland, Heramann alone was missing. For some
reason, the Vidyadhara was simply gone.

"We'll have to begin without him," said the Etan sadly.

"He'll be along soon, I'm sure," said Leor softly. "Let it begin."

Throughout the night, as Ezera burned more and more
brilliantly golden, Orah stood motionlessly, staring at the
Emptiness blinding the firmament, gathering the scattered
impulses of the earthbreath to him. If the power he used to dance

the destruction of the Asur army at the Ridge of Man was as a mountain of force, this was more like a continent of concentrated energy. Mercilessly, he sapped the power of the One from the Gurions and the Maralords, from the whole of animate and inanimate creation in Riversland and as far as his uniting energy could reach through Martanda. Adding precious drop to precious drop, he molded a force greater than any used since Creation began.

And then, finally, it was done. Nothing more could be borrowed from the Grandfather's creatures, save the energy of the sun itself. Patiently, the Azure Lord of Etan waited for the first rays of the dawn. He was supremely confident: he knew beyond question that it would be enough.

The sun kissed his face with its early brilliance; the final moment was come. Raising the amassed power as if it were a gargantuan sledge, the Dancer of Etan brought it down in one final blow to avert the prisoner's doom.

For a heartbeat that seemed to last throughout an entire cycle of Creation, the Universe was utterly stilled, halted before the expectation that it just... might... work...

The Etan felt the Emptiness distend... quiver... begin to slowly break, like a slow-motion dream...

But then he learned that it was not just the Emptiness of the prison but the fabric of Creation itself that was breaking! Even as he forced the energy of the One at Valin's wall, refusing to let it recoil in the slightest, Orah learned with infinite horror that he must *not* succeed: to violate the dominion of Emptiness would negate not just Leor's prison, but the entirety of the Cosmos! For if the earthbreath could forcibly destroy its functional opposite, the duality that made the Universe would be set at naught: all of Creation would in an instant be transformed back into the amorphic water of the Universal Ocean, the Grandfather's modeling clay.

With limitless sorrow, Orah loosed his hold on the earthbreath.

The borrowed energies of the earthbreath struck the Emptiness; Valin's wall trembled but held, breaking the attacking force back into its constituent parts. The surface of Ezera exploded in millions of beams of coruscating opalescence, the loaned energies returning to their sources, flooding back in a moment what had been drained over long hours. Conscious minds shielded themselves the only way they could: within seconds, Leor stood alone, looking over Riversland. Alone, for because of them all, the Etan had thought her energy too limited and believed it unnecessary to tap it. She knelt by him and took his hands, waiting for shocked breath to return. The Protectors recovered the most quickly and descended to shower the fallen humans with their healing light.

~ ~ ~

Inside her prison, the shadow that once had been Leor felt the wavering of the Emptiness. She paused for a long moment, waiting without hope. When the distention of the Emptiness abruptly ended, she confirmed her belief the wall could never break. Drawing the final measure of her desecrated life into the point that was the essence of all she was, she gave it joyfully back to the Mother, pausing only to wish health and peace to everyone still bound to created time.

As the Lady of Etan's life passed back into the primal beginning, her body disintegrated into a fine powder, like the last memory of a thoroughly consumed fire.

~ ~ ~

Above, on the surface of Ezera, a little shiver ran through the projected Leor. Orah's eyes popped open; he jumped up, knowing he had failed. "I am sorry, Jaya," he said, misreading the tears in her eyes.

"You did your best, my Lord. The whole of the energy of the earthbreath in Martanda would not have sufficed. It is not in the nature of the fundamental forces to clash in their pure forms."

A joyous whooping and screaming suddenly erupted among some of those below. "Why are they cheering?" he asked in anguish.

"It is the Arelai. Your curse is ended; they rejoice in their vision."

"But now it spreads to everyone. Why?"

"They see me standing here. They don't understand: they think you succeeded. How will we ever be able to tell them?"

Adrian came stumping up Ezera on his short three year old legs and said, "Well, Outlander, now what? There must a nutcracker somewhere we can use on this hickory."

Marel drifted up and said, "They seem to be all right. A few suffering from strain and exposure. Nothing much. What do we do now? Head to the fleet?"

"When is the equinox?" asked Orah, knowing perfectly well the answer.

"About ten minutes ago, Lord of Etan," said Zuriel, climbing up the east side of the hill. "It was but moments after the dawn this year. I wonder what you are going to do now? We are anxious to return to the Founding Lake. If you no longer need us."

Kumbha floated up and said in Sevilien's voice, "Commander, we are eager to act. Please instruct us."

Central said through Marel, "Arama, the attack sphere wonders where it should meet the fleet. When do you sail?"

Orah looked over Riversland and saw a score of others climbing toward them, including Haman and Hamar, Elid and Eliora, Marasad, Solon, and Ahanatar with Chali. "Jaya," he said desperately, "what am I supposed to do?"

"Well," she said thoughtfully, staring toward the south, "to begin with, you can tell me who that Etan is riding your private dragon."

~ ~ ~

Heramann had not had to travel all the way to the antarctic; he had met Althea hurrying northward, riding the Saraman Swiftfoot, quite far from the pole. She had exhorted the Vidyadhara to his greatest speed, terrified of arriving after the equinox. For her prescience was wonderfully clear, but not yet perfect.

She leaped from Airavata's back; he transmuted down and flew as falcon to his favorite perch. "I feared to come too late!" she cried. "If your blow had succeeded —"

"Then I would have unmade the world. This I realized at the last instant, sister, and stayed my hand, hoping the while I might be wrong. But it is true, isn't it? The two aboriginal forces must not directly collide."

"I saw this doom impending and hurried north to dissuade you. Valin must not win so easily."

"Why should he want to destroy the Universe?" asked Leor, confused. "I thought he desired to rule all."

"He desires to end all. Someday, he will succeed. But only when we are ready and permit it. His scheme was so secretly buried I did not intuit it until the tetrad of your projections came together. That strengthened my perception enough to know what you were about. The only thing I haven't been able to understand, even though Airavata has tried to explain —"

"Perhaps because I tried to explain," said Heramann ruefully. "She would have been here far earlier but for my stubbornness. I was adamant about bringing Swayam back with me. It took her an hour to convince me."

"What can you possibly need to know from us?" asked Orah, frustration and confusion competing for control of his spirit.

"Why, what you were doing it for, of course," she answered, smiling gently at him. "Why in the name of the Seven Thoughts of Narain did you want to throw so much pure energy at my poor little usurped hill?"

"Why! Because Leor is inside here, of course!" he exclaimed, utterly astonished. "Or was, as the equinox is now quite definitely passed."

"I must be growing old, brother. You say our sister Leor is (or was until a few minutes ago) inside this Emptiness-shrouded hill? Is that it?"

"Yes, that is the truth, isn't it?"

"Orah, you've lived too long in Etan, I can see that. Who is that standing next to you, holding your hand?"

"What!" he cried, dropping the hand. "Why, you know it is Leor's coalesced projections! She passed her spirit into the lifeblood Valin was stealing —" He stopped and stared at Leor in wonder. "You can't mean to imply — ?"

"That hollow memory of a woman was not Leor, had not been for years. Yes, that is what I mean. Arama, behold Jaya. Leor, behold Orah. I hope this settles the introductions."

"But Althea!" cried Leor. "My projections! All five of them! They all died. This body is but the projections' projection! It has not the spirit or the breath of immortality of a true Etan."

"Leor, Leor! Of the spirit, the memory below in Ezera has rejoined the Mother. Yet you are still here. That means the Point Spirit of man is but illusion only. The soul as a limited entity is, dear forgetful girl, only a way of looking at (or understanding) omnipresence. You always were Leor, in every meaningful sense.

"As to the 'immortal breath,' as you name it, I don't suppose brother has misplaced his second vial of the amrita?"

Orah stopped staring at Leor long enough to remove the silver box from his robe, finger it in a peculiar complicated pattern, and take out the brilliant multi-hued vial. He handed it to Althea, saying, "You are the Healer. You deserve the honor."

"Somehow I knew you would still have it," she said, chuckling; "though I did chance to bring along more, just in case.

"Leor who was Jaya before, take the ichor of Swayam into your blood, immortal breath to life-breath, Eternity to spirit. In the name of the Sacred Powers of the Mother, Narain and the Grandfather, rejoin the twice-born."

As Leor tasted a single fulgent droplet of the amrita, Althea said, "I welcome you again to our fellowship, sister. The second time in one lifetime! Now there is an event for 'Ishtar's Recorder!'

"Well, Orah," added the Healer of Etan with a joyful laugh, "what do we do now?"

End of ORAH, THE DEATHLESS DANCER
in which is described one half of Gana's sixth task

Leor

EPILOGUE

Orah stood with Leor on the prow of Dalmara's Pride and watched the rushing emerald water breaking past the ship. They had sailed exactly forty-eight hours after the equinox. Which, after all, was not bad, considering the distance everyone had to travel.

Overhead, five hundred spherical silver clouds paced their passing, each composed of eight thousand Protectors. Behind, the ships of the fleet — thanks to Heramann and Solon, the mightiest armada in the history of Martanda — kept time to their surging rhythm.

"Tell me, my Lady, one thing that puzzles me," Orah said, hardly yet believing she stood there beside him again at last.

"Of course, beloved. Anything. Anything at all." She looked up at him with her perfect azure eyes forever laughing and dancing their supernal joy.

"What happened to the energy of your first projection after Ahaman died? Did it disperse throughout Riversland, or return to the Grandfather?"

"Neither, Arama. Forgetful of his source, he has taken on form after form. And he will continue to do so until he remembers his heritage. Then will he re-merge into me."

"So he wanders Martanda still? Who is he? Can you tell?'

"I can recognize myself, yes. In fact, you know him quite well, my Lord. Can't you guess?"

The Etan thought of the many he had loved in Riversland. Adrian was strong enough in spirit, but too imperfect. Nediva was an obvious choice, as was Solon; but both somehow seemed unlikely, from their deep attachment to each other if for no other reason. Ahanatar and Chali were exceptional beginners, but not yet perfected. Hamar, Marasad, Sevilien, and Ramor had obvious deficiencies. In fact, Orah could think of no single individual that was perfect enough to hide Jaya's power. Except perhaps Zuriel, or

Elid, or Eliora? But intuitively he weighed them and their attitude toward him and found he had to discard them all.

"Arama," said Marel, flying up to them, "the attack sphere has returned. They sustained no losses during their retreat from the Mereds."

"Very good, Marel. Thank you. Ah, tell me one thing. Who do you think is the most perfect being native to Riversland?"

"No fair!" exclaimed Leor. "This is our game."

"She is my most trusted adviser! She never gives way to emotion, but always has the wisest and most well considered counsel. Why can I not ask her?"

"Why are you so certain it must be a human?"

And then, with the final clue, he knew, had known all along, but had subconsciously refused to believe it, denying the possibility in a most prejudiced and unenlightened manner.

"Should I speak, Commander?" asked the Protector, patiently floating an arm's length away.

"No, Marel," he answered, staring at her with wide eyes. "No, it is not necessary after all. Tell me rather why of all the millions of Protectors of Maramel, you alone are never away from my side."

"Why? Why, I don't really know. Someone needs to relay your commands to our mechanical forces; I suppose for simplicity it is easier to continue with one Protector. I helped you when you first came; I guess it was just chance I was there at the right time, helped repair the Pride of the Sea. Then it became a habit, easier to continue than change. . . Have I displeased you? Would you prefer another? A Counselor, perhaps, would be more ideally suited, Miran for example, or —"

"No, Marel! No, certainly not. I wouldn't trade you for the entire Universe. In fact, I order you to stay by me always. Priority Swayam."

"As you wish, Arama," she answered, her wildly flashing lights indicating immense pleasure.

"Me too, Orah," said Leor, squeezing him.

"Truly, this world is passing strange," said the Etan, staring into the west, misty turquoise in the new day.

The historical record of the seven tasks of Gana continues in
SHAMARA, THE DAUGHTER OF THE GODS
THE FALL OF ETAN, VOLUME II
THIRD THUNDER, BOOK II

APPENDIX:
THE SIXTEEN SHIELDS OF GURION
THE TEN OATHS AND THEIR
PERFECTIONS

SHIELD	OATH	PERFECTION	OATHMASTER
Dove	Nonviolence	Invincibility	Brihas
Cow	"	"	"
Kaystarbha or Seven Stars	Non-stealing	All wealth presents itself	Jamad
Sun	Truthfulness	All words are fulfilled	Satya
Lightning	"	"	"
Fire	"	"	"
Serpent	Celibacy	Adamantine strength	Vasuki
Hawk	Non-grasping	Knowledge of past and future	Ila
Staff	Purity	Intuition	Matri
Horse	"	"	"
Lion	Contentment	Supreme happiness	Santosh
Mountain	Austerity	Perfection of body & senses	Viswam
Eagle	"	"	"
Scroll	Study of the One	Understanding The cries of all creatures	Kali
Moon	"	"	"
Tree	Unalterable Surrender To the Grandfather	Permanent Awareness of the One	Shraddha

Brihas pledged that sixteen Oathmasters would journey to Gurion; six advanced practices would be given, following the ten oaths. The rise of the Asurs blocked the Oathmasters' intent to create full knowledge of Ascension in Gurion.

Additional books by MSI:

ASCENSION! An Analysis of the Art of Ascension as Taught by the Ishayas

This book clearly explains the ancient teachings of the Ishayas, an ancient order of monks who were entrusted by the Apostle John to preserve the original teachings of Christ until the third millennium. The Ishayas hold that the original teachings of Jesus were not a belief system at all, rather a mechanical series of techniques to transform human life into a constant perception of the perfection within the human heart. Real expansion of consciousness occurs only through direct, personal experience. Ascension! is an invitation to awaken to the innermost Reality of your wonderful, exalted soul. This text also includes a description of the Ishayas' 27 Ascension Attitudes. $11.95.

ENLIGHTENMENT! The Yoga Sutras of Patanjali
A New Translation and Commentary

The Yoga Sutras of Maharishi Patanjali are the most concise formulation in history of the mechanics of the growth of consciousness. They are a systematic and complete understanding of the psychological, emotional and physical transformations that occur as an individual develops full enlightenment. His text of yoga was designed to help *anyone* rise to this state of human perfection, and this process of development is called Ascension, or rising beyond the boundaries of ignorance. $15.95.